John W. Hart

Karl Barth
vs.
Emil Brunner

The Formation and Dissolution
of a Theological Alliance,
1916–1936

PETER LANG
New York • Washington, D.C./Baltimore • Bern
Frankfurt am Main • Berlin • Brussels • Vienna • Oxford

BX
4827
.B3
H29
2001

Library of Congress Cataloging-in-Publication Data

Hart, John W.
Karl Barth vs. Emil Brunner: the formation and dissolution
of a theological alliance, 1916–1936 / by John W. Hart.
p. cm. — (Issues in systematic theology; vol. 6)
Thesis (Ph.D.)—University of Oxford, 1993.
Includes bibliographical references and index.
1. Barth, Karl, 1886–1968. 2. Brunner, Emil, 1889–1966.
I. Title. II. Title: Karl Barth versus Emil Brunner. III. Series.
BX4827.B3H29   230′.044′0922—dc21   99-19449
ISBN 0-8204-4505-3
ISSN 1081-9479

Die Deutsche Bibliothek-CIP-Einheitsaufnahme

Hart, John W.:
Karl Barth vs. Emil Brunner: the formation and dissolution
of a theological alliance, 1916–1936 / John W. Hart.
–New York; Washington, D.C./Baltimore; Bern;
Frankfurt am Main; Berlin; Brussels; Vienna; Oxford: Lang.
(Issues in systematic theology; Vol. 6)
ISBN 0-8204-4505-3

The paper in this book meets the guidelines for permanence and durability
of the Committee on Production Guidelines for Book Longevity
of the Council of Library Resources.

Printed in the United States of America

Karl Barth
vs.
Emil Brunner

Issues in Systematic Theology

Paul D. Molnar
General Editor

Vol. 6

PETER LANG
New York • Washington, D.C./Baltimore • Bern
Frankfurt am Main • Berlin • Brussels • Vienna • Oxford

ACKNOWLEDGMENTS

It is a privilege to be able to thank several people who were of special help in the preparation of this book.

First, thanks are due to T.J. Gorringe, my dissertation supervisor at Oxford University. Rather than becoming more weary, he became more and more excited about this project as it developed. One of the marks of an outstanding supervisor is his ability to keep his students moving forward in fruitful directions. For his helpful comments and guidance at pivotal moments, I am quite thankful.

I am grateful for the encouragement of Dr. George Hunsinger, Director of the Center for Barth Studies in Princeton, and for his help in guiding this work to publication.

My warmest appreciation goes to the Karl Barth-Archiv in Basel. The Barth Nachlaßkommission was extremely generous in granting me access to the fascinating Barth–Brunner correspondence. In addition, Dr. Hinrich Stoevesandt, former director of the Barth-Archiv, treated me to an unforgettable time of research assistance and hospitality.

I gratefully acknowledge permission to cite extensively from © the German original version *Karl Barth/Emil Brunner, Briefwechsel 1916–1966*, by Theologischer Verlag Zurich (2000), edited by the Karl Barth–Forschungsstelle at Göttingen University under the direction of Eberhard Busch.

Thanks are due as well to the Emil Brunner-Stiftung in Zurich. The director, Dr. Werner Kramer, was quite responsive to all my inquiries. I gratefully acknowledge the Stiftung's permission to cite from one of Brunner's unpublished manuscripts, "Was ist und was will die sogenannte Oxford–Gruppenbewegung", which was essential to Chapter Six. Most gracious was Frau Lilo Brunner-Gutekunst, who not only welcomed me into her home, but openly shared with me many helpful insights about her father-in-law.

Dr. Paul Molnar, the editor of Issues in Systematic Theology, and Bernadette Alfaro, Production Assistant at Peter Lang, offered valuable advice during the final preparations of this book.

Finally, my deepest appreciation and love go to my wonderful and supportive family—Becky, Brian, Carolyn and Emily—who enabled this project to be an adventure full of joy.

TABLE OF CONTENTS

ABBREVIATIONS

Barth–Brunner	*Barth–Brunner, Briefwechsel 1916–1966*
Barth–Bultmann	*Barth–Bultmann: Letters 1922–1966*
Barth–Thurneysen I,II	*Barth–Thurneysen Briefwechsel* (TVZ edition)
CD	*Church Dogmatics*
EvTh	*Evangelische Theologie*
KfrS	*Kirchenblatt für die reformierte Schweiz*
MRA	Moral Re-Armament
OGM	The Oxford Group Movement
Rev.Theology	*Revolutionary Theology in the Making* (Barth–Thurneysen letters, English translation)
Romans I, II	*The Epistle to the Romans*, 1st and 2nd edns
SJT	*The Scottish Journal of Theology*
ThExh	*Theologische Existenz heute*
Th&Ch	*Theology and Church*
TVZ	Theologischer Verlag Zurich
WGWM	*The Word of God and the Word of Man*
ZThK	*Zeitschrift für Theologie und Kirche*
ZZ	*Zwischen den Zeiten*

INTRODUCTION

People in the future...will not be completely wrong to always shake their heads a bit regarding our opposition—you in good company, I probably more of a kind of theological crab, with whom it is impossible to deal, one who had once justified such lovely hopes. And...they will rack their brains how things were at that time with the unity and disunity of "dialectical theology".

(Barth to Brunner, October 1930)

The 1934 natural theology debate between Karl Barth and Emil Brunner has become a classic text in theological study, as well as one of the easy hooks upon which to hang a description of Barth's theological intentions. The premise of this book is that what happened between Barth and Brunner in 1934 was the culmination of several long-running theological arguments between them. Not only is this background essential in order to understand what the 1934 debate meant for both theologians, but a look into the previous eighteen years of their theological alliance also sheds light on the development and fundamental intentions of both men.

This book is an historical-theological exploration into the beginnings, development, and break-down of Barth and Brunner's theological alliance. It is common knowledge that Barth and Brunner appeared together on the scene in the early 1920s as partners in "dialectical theology", as it is well-known that their partnership broke up over the issue of natural theology in 1934. Nonetheless, it is remarkable that, beyond the 1934 debate (and its lead-up from 1929), no extensive research has been devoted to these broader questions: How and why did these two men become theological allies? What, precisely, were there points of agreement? How did their theological relationship develop over time? What were their continuing points of disagreement, and how did these affect the 1934 debate?

It is the purpose of this book to answer these questions, through a kind of "narrative theology". The method of investigation involves a close reading of Barth and Brunner's writings from 1919 to 1936, supplemented significantly by the insights provided by their newly published correspondence.[1] The limits of this book prevent an exhaustive investigation of the theological development of both Barth and Brunner over this twenty year period. Rather, this book will examine how both theologians developed their theological programs in relation to each other. As such, this book complements similar investigations of Barth's relationship with his other dialectical colleagues.[2]

The Barth–Brunner relationship sheds helpful light upon the interpretation of Barth. It does not require special insight to understand what led Barth to take his leave of Bultmann and Gogarten. But the break-up of the Barth–Brunner alliance was, and to some extent still is, puzzling. If Barth felt it necessary to angrily cut himself off from Brunner, a theologian so close to his own position when viewed in the context of theological history, it must point to certain positions held by Barth which he would not compromise. This thesis will argue that such is the case. Barth's rejection of "theological fellowship" with Brunner shows how completely radically he understood and worked out his fundamental insight from 1916—"*God* is God and God is *God*", and thinking about this God can only be "a theology which, like a spinning top, supports itself on only one point".[3]

In addition to exploring the Barth–Brunner alliance in depth, this book makes two important contributions to Barth studies. First, a study of the Barth–Brunner relationship clearly supports the thesis of "continuity" over the thesis of "stages" in understanding Barth's early theological development.[4] The issues which divided Barth and Brunner remained constant throughout their twenty year relationship. Though Barth's own theological development clarified for him the severity of these disagreements, the shape of the Barth–Brunner debate remained essentially the same from *The Epistle to the Romans* through *Church Dogmatics*. In particular, an examination of the Barth–Brunner relationship emphasizes the radicalizing effect of Overbeck upon Barth in 1920, and, correspondingly, de-emphasizes a turning-point with *Anselm: Fides Quaerens Intellectum*.[5] The recent publication of Barth's first dogmatics lectures at Göttingen helps to establish the over-riding continuity in Barth's thinking from 1921 to 1932.[6]

Second, the Barth–Brunner relationship also clearly shows that Barth's rejection of natural theology was grounded in theological, not political, reasons. The issues raised by Marquardt have led to an intensive re-evaluation of the influence of Barth's politics on his theology.[7] In particular, Winzeler follows Marquardt's lead by connecting Barth's opposition to natural theology to his political resistance to Nazism.[8] While the Barth–Brunner relationship indicates how the political and church struggles of the early 1930s increased the intensity of the Barth–Brunner debate, Barth's outright and uncompromising opposition to Brunner's experiments with natural theology was clearly voiced as early as 1929, with still earlier protests registered in his Göttingen dogmatics lectures.

This book follows the Barth–Brunner relationship through six periods.

Chapter One explores the coming together of these two Swiss pastors as theological allies (1916–1919) through their common bonds in Religious Socialism and the Blumhardts, and the common friendship of Eduard Thurneysen. Their earliest correspondence reveals that, right from the start, Brunner disliked Barth's theological "one-sidedness", while Barth was suspicious of Brunner's attempt to bring Idealist philosophy and Reformation theology "under one arch". Barth's first edition of *Romans* and Brunner's review of it are the central texts.

Chapter Two examines the critical period when Barth and Brunner's theological alliance solidified (1920–1924). For Barth, a new radicalism emerged through the impact of Overbeck and Kierkegaard. God's sovereignty became understood dialectically, and the task of theology was viewed as an "impossible possibility". For Brunner, both Barth's second edition of *Romans* and Ferdinand Ebner's *The Word and Spiritual Realities* led him to reject the previous influence of Neo-Kantianism on his thought and forced him to re-think his theological position. The correspondence reveals a pivotal meeting in August 1920, when Brunner was confronted with Barth's new Overbeckian radicalism. The major texts studied are Barth's second edition of *Romans* and Brunner's *Experience, Knowledge and Faith* (1921), "The Limits of Humanity" (1922), and *Mysticism and the Word* (1924), as well as Barth's review of the latter.

In Chapter Three, it is seen how Barth and Brunner, now filling academic posts, developed their theologies in different directions (1924–1928). Learning from the Reformers and the Protestant scholastics, Barth developed his program positively through his dogmatics lectures at Göttingen, later revised in Münster and published as *Christian Dogmatics* (1927). In these works, Barth reconstituted his dialectical thinking in Trinitarian terms. Brunner, on the other hand, moved towards philosophical theology. In three important lectures, as well as in his two 1927 books (*The Philosophy of Religion from the Standpoint of Protestant Theology* and *The Mediator*), Brunner sought to make contact with philosophy, affirming positive lines of thinking and combating ideas contradicted by the Gospel. Again, a pivotal face to face encounter in 1924, recounted in the correspondence, reveals the depth of Barth and Brunner's differences.

Chapter Four covers the fraying of the Barth–Brunner alliance (1929–1932). This is ground that has been well covered by scholarship—Brunner's "The Other Task of Theology", "The Question of the 'Point-of-Contact' as a Problem of Theology", and *The Divine Imperative*; Barth's Anselm book and *Church Dogmatics* I/1. This book also explores other decisive but overlooked works, particularly Barth's first pointed (though veiled) criticism of his dialectical colleagues ("Theology and Modern Man", 1930) and Brunner's *God and Man* (1930). Also, the correspondence records two significant meetings (in 1929 and 1930) and a "parting of the ways", declared by Barth in January 1933. It is shown that during this period, Brunner finally sloughed off the radical Barthian dialectic which he had marginally included within his theological system from 1922 to 1928. The exchanges between Barth and Brunner in this period are decisive, indicating, in Barth's words, "material opposition occurring right down the line".

Chapter Five examines the climax of the Barth–Brunner debate—the 1934 articles on natural theology. The study of this well-covered engagement is enriched through the insights provided by the correspondence, which records, among other things, an attempt at reconciliation in the summer of 1935.

In Chapter Six, this book makes a unique contribution to the understanding of Brunner's theology, as well as establishing a new factor in the Barth–Brunner debate—the Oxford Group Movement. This hitherto entirely overlooked factor decisively influenced Brunner from 1932 on, and was clearly linked in Barth's mind as forming one piece with Brunner's affirmation of natural theology. Due to Brunner's changing ecclesiology and pneumatology under the impact of the Group Movement, the Barth–Brunner debate spills over from the first article of the Creed into the whole scope of the third article. The correspondence is particularly illuminating here—Brunner's ill-conceived invitation for Barth to join in a meeting of his Oxford Group fellows in Autumn 1933, their aborted 1935 debate over the Movement for a Swiss magazine, and their heated final debate in front of friends and colleagues at Schlößchen Auenstein in 1936.

Finally, Chapter Seven analyzes the reasons for the break-up of Barth and Brunner's theological alliance, focusing upon personal characteristics, material commitments, and especially theological method. Six methodological contrasts are summarized: the use of dialectic, dogmatics *vs.* philosophy, the task of theology, theology *vs.* anthropology, the use of the Reformers, and the appropriation of Kierkegaard.

In the end, the story of the Barth–Brunner alliance shows the gulf which separates Barth from all modern theologians, not only from his obvious adversaries (e.g., Schleiermacher and Bultmann) but also from his nearest colleagues, like Brunner. Barth is ruthlessly and consistently concerned with doing theology which profoundly respects the ontological and noetic distance between the self-revealing God and his sinful and elected Church—a theology which is radically "dialectical".

NOTES

1. *Karl Barth–Emil Brunner Briefwechsel, 1916–1966*, ed. by Eberhard Busch (Zurich: Theologischer Verlag, 2000).
2. For Barth and Rudolf Bultmann, see James D. Smart, *The Divided Mind of Modern Theology* (Philadelphia: Westminster, 1967). For Barth and Friedrich Gogarten, see Peter Lange, *Konkrete Theologie?* (TVZ, 1972).
3. Barth to Brunner, October 24, 1930. Hereafter cited as *Barth–Brunner*, KB: October 24, 1930 (#81), p. 209.
4. Thus, this study argues against the conventional understanding of Barth's development first suggested by Hans Urs von Balthasar, *The Theology of Karl Barth*, trans. by John Drury (New York: Holt, Rinehart and Winston, 1971). Von Balthasar's argument has become the standard explanation of Barth's theological development, repeated by many, e.g.: Eberhard Jüngel, "Barth's Life and Work", and "Barth's Theological Beginnings", in *Karl Barth*, trans. by Garrett E. Paul (Philadelphia: Westminster, 1986), pp. 22–52, 53–104; Henri Bouillard, *Karl Barth* (Aubier: Éditions Montaigne, 1957); and Thomas F. Torrance, *Karl Barth* (London: SCM, 1962).
5. This book will show that the "point of no return" in the Barth–Brunner relationship was reached between the publication of Brunner's "The Other Task of Theology" in 1929 and Barth's visit to Marburg in January 1930, well before Barth's preparation for his 1930 Bonn seminar on Anselm which led to his 1931 book.
6. *The Göttingen Dogmatics*, trans. by Geoffrey W. Bromiley, 2 vols (Grand Rapids: Eerdmans, 1991–). Other scholars who have had access to this new publication also see continuity as a more helpful model for Barth's development; see especially Michael Beintker, *Die Dialektik in der "dialektischen Theologie" Karl Barths* (Munich: Chr. Kaiser, 1987); Bruce L. McCormack, *Karl Barth's Critically Realistic Dialectical Theology* (Oxford: Clarendon Press, 1995).
7. Friedrich-Wilhelm Marquardt, *Theologie und Sozialismus* (Munich: Chr. Kaiser, 1972).
8. Peter Winzeler, *Widerstehende Theologie* (Stuttgart: Alektor Verlag, 1982).

CHAPTER ONE

Coming Together (1913–1919)
Thurneysen, Kutter and the Blumhardts

You are, in fact, dangerously one-sided.

(Brunner to Barth, January 1918)

Nevertheless, our common front and main tendency remains the same.

(Brunner to Barth, November 1918)

Background to the Barth–Brunner Relationship

Karl Barth was born May 10, 1886 in Basel, Switzerland. He began a theological degree at the University of Bern in 1904. As was the custom, he also spent some terms in Germany—under Harnack at Berlin, under Schlatter at Tübingen, and under Herrmann at Marburg. Barth was ordained in 1908 and worked in Marburg for a year as Martin Rade's editorial assistant at the leading theological liberal journal, *The Christian World*. After serving for two years as the assistant pastor for the German Reformed congregation in Geneva, in 1911 Barth accepted a call to serve as pastor for the Reformed church in Safenwil, an agricultural and industrial town in Canton Aargau half-way between Basel and Zurich.[1]

Emil Brunner was born December 23, 1889, outside of Zurich. He began his theological studies at the University of Zurich in 1908. After finishing his first degree, Brunner remained at Zurich to pursue doctoral studies, being awarded the Th.D. in 1912 for his dissertation, *The Symbolic in Religious Knowledge*—a work on religious epistemology which, relying heavily upon Kant, Schleiermacher and Bergson, rejected both the "scholasticism" of orthodox Protestantism and Hegel's "speculativism".[3] Brunner then served as interim pastor for the church in the village of Leutwil (Canton Aargau) from September 1912 to Easter 1913.[4] After a year teaching

French in a secondary school in England, and another year serving on active duty in the Swiss army, Brunner served for six months as the assistant pastor to Hermann Kutter at the Neumünster in Zurich. In 1916, Brunner was called to be pastor for the village of Obstalden (Canton Glarus).

By the beginning of 1919, Barth and Brunner found themselves standing side by side as theological allies. In understanding their coming together, it is helpful to highlight three of their common influences.[5]

First, the central figure in the establishment and maintenance of the Barth–Brunner relationship was Eduard Thurneysen.[6] While serving in Zurich as assistant secretary of the YMCA in 1912, Thurneysen began to move in Brunner's circle when he became involved in the Religious Socialism movement. Brunner and Thurneysen formally met at the 1913 Aarau Student Conference.[7] Their friendship was cemented when Thurneysen was called to serve as pastor in Leutwil in June 1913, following Brunner's stint there as interim pastor.

Thurneysen and Barth met as theological students in Switzerland, and then again as visiting students together in Marburg.[8] When Thurneysen became pastor in Leutwil, he renewed his acquaintance with the pastor in nearby Safenwil. Barth and Thurneysen soon struck up a deep personal and theological relationship which was to endure throughout their lives.[9]

Thurneysen was crucial in maintaining Barth and Brunner's theological and personal relationship throughout the period investigated in this study. He introduced them to each other in the 1910s, brought Brunner on board *Zwischen den Zeiten* in the 1920s, and mediated in their final split over the Oxford Group Movement in 1936. As the Barth–Brunner and Barth–Thurneysen correspondence clearly reveal, Thurneysen was the indispensable middleman in the Barth–Brunner relationship.

A second factor influencing both Barth and Brunner was the thought of Johann Blumhardt and his son, Christoph, of Bad Boll, Germany. Johann Blumhardt was a pastor serving in Möttlingen in the 1840s when an experience of healing radically changed his thinking: no longer was his ministry focused on the pietistic "Jesus and the unconverted heart", but rather "Jesus and the real power of darkness".[10] "Jesus is victor" became Blumhardt's watchword, and his theology became oriented on the coming of God's Kingdom, stressing eschatology, promise, and hope. Blumhardt laid particular stress upon God's sovereign freedom and humanity's constant need to receive (not possess) God's ever new revelation through the Holy Spirit.[11] Christoph Blumhardt took over his father's message and related it more expressly to socio-political movements.[12]

Brunner had been influenced by the Blumhardts from birth—his father was a close friend of Frederic Zündel, who was Johann Blumhardt's biographer and Brunner's godfather.[13] Through Zündel, Brunner's father came to know Christoph Blumhardt personally. Barth first heard Christoph Blum-hardt during a visit to Bad Boll during his student days in Germany, "though with no basic understanding".[14] It was Thurneysen who re-intro-duced Barth to Blumhardt during their early years as pastors. Barth was struck by the way in which Blumhardt "raised a whole series of questions once again that had to break through...the limitations of both liberal and pietistic theology".[15] From Blumhardt, Barth learned to stop thinking from humanity to God, but rather from God to humanity, "to begin with God".[16]

> I still thought and preached along the old lines...But beyond the problems of theo-logical liberalism and religious socialism, the concept of the kingdom of God in the real, transcendent sense of the Bible became increasingly more insistent, and the textual basis of my sermons, the Bible, which hitherto I had taken for granted, be-come more and more of a problem.[17]

Finally, Barth and Brunner were both influenced by the Blumhardts' most ardent disciples in Switzerland: Hermann Kutter and Leonhard Ragaz. Kutter was pastor of Neumünster in Zurich, Ragaz the professor of theol-ogy at the University of Zurich.[18] These two men combined Johann Blum-hardt's emphasis on the victorious Christ's coming in his Kingdom with Christoph Blumhardt's social emphasis. More specifically, they understood the political movement of Socialism to be a sign of the kingdom of God.[19] Under Kutter and Ragaz's leadership, "Religious Socialism" became a vital factor in the politics and church life of Switzerland in the first decades of the century.

Brunner's family became involved with Religious Socialism and attend-ed Kutter's Neumünster church.[20] Brunner was catechized by Kutter, did his doctoral studies under Ragaz, served as Kutter's vicar for six months in 1912, and later married one of Kutter's nieces.[21] Again, Barth was intro-duced to Kutter by Thurneysen.[22] From Kutter, Barth learned "to speak the great word 'God' seriously, responsibly and with a sense of its importance"; Kutter "represented the insight that the sphere of God's power really is greater than the sphere of the church".[23]

World War I broke out during Barth's tenure in Safenwil. If the tumb-ling of the alliances into war surprised him, of greater shock was the sup-port given to Germany by his former theological teachers, who signed a manifesto supporting the Kaiser's war policy.[24] Immediately after its publi-cation, Barth wrote to Thurneysen: "Marburg and German civilization have lost something in my eyes by this breakdown, and indeed forever".[25] Barth's disillusionment extended back behind Herrmann and Harnack, reaching all the way to the font of nineteenth century Neo-Protestantism: Friedrich Schleiermacher.[26]

In addition to this theological questioning, the behavior of the Socialists towards the war was equally disappointing and sobering for Barth. Despite Socialism's fundamental commitment to non-militarism, Barth watched in disbelief as national party after national party rallied patriotically around their respective flags and supported their homelands in the war.[27] The Great War was also a turning point for Brunner: "With this event my faith in progress was shattered and my Religious Socialism began to look suspiciously like a beautiful illusion. But my Christian faith itself was not thereby shaken".[28] Brunner responded by renewing his study of the Bible and the Reformers.[29]

The "hopeless compromises" of both liberal theology and socialism brought Barth to a point of crisis: where could he turn to understand God and the world?[30] Jüngel writes:

> He returned to intensive theological labors. Then came not only the break with "liberal theology" but also his rejection of the identification of the Kingdom of God with social action, which he had previously adopted from Kutter...Meanwhile, the realistic hope in the Kingdom of God, as espoused by both Blumhardts, had become decisive for Barth, and it remained so. The "urgent need for preaching" both required and led to a new theological foundation.[31]

What was the essence of Barth's insight at this time?[32] It was a breakthrough to the fundamental insight of Blumhardt and Kutter: the "Godness of God", that "*God* is God" and "God is *God*".[33] This included the realization that "God means the crisis of humanity, [which] led Barth to the conclusion that theology is no human possibility, that human beings *cannot* speak of God".[34]

> Barth was discovering in the Bible...something which liberal theology had tended to obscure, namely, the fundamental discontinuity between God and man. The righteousness of God is opposed to human righteousness; God's word and ways are not the word and ways of man.[35]

This new thinking began to evidence itself in the beginning of 1916, especially in sermons where Barth spoke of the necessity to "begin joyfully with the beginning" and to "recognize that God is God".[36] Barth's new approach was cemented during a brief holiday with Thurneysen in Leutwil at the beginning of June 1916, when they committed themselves "very naively ...to go back to academic theology to clarify the situation".[37] Fifty years later, Barth recalled that momentous time:

> It was Thurneysen who once whispered the key phrase to me, half aloud, when we were alone together: what we need for preaching, instruction, and pastoral care was a "wholly other" theological foundation. It seemed impossible to proceed any further on the basis of Schleiermacher...We made a fresh attempt to learn our

theological ABCs all over again. More reflectively than ever before, we began reading and expounding the writings of the Old and New Testaments. And behold, they began to speak to us...The morning after Thurneysen had whispered to me our commonly held conviction, I sat down under an apple tree and began, with all the tools at my disposal, to apply myself to the Epistle to the Romans.[38]

The common influences of the Blumhardts and Religious Socialism were significant "points-of-contact" for Barth and Brunner. Brunner was raised on this theological perspective; exposure to it through Thurneysen led Barth to a fundamental theological breakthrough. It is important to recognize that it is upon the ground of Religious Socialism, rather than "dialectical theology", that the Barth–Brunner alliance was originally formed.

The Beginning of Barth and Brunner's Theological Alliance (1916–1919)

The Barth–Brunner Correspondence Begins

There is no record of Barth and Brunner's first meetings.[39] Most likely, Thurneysen made the introductions and encouraged the development of the relationship. In any case, by 1916 Barth and Brunner had begun a correspondence.

Barth and Brunner's first exchange focuses on personal issues of faith and Christian living. In April 1916, Brunner writes Barth to thank him for a recent sermon.[40] Brunner begins: "I can simply say a loud Yes to it".[41] However, he has one reservation with the sermon's content. Barth's point had been the necessity of "deciding today" for or against God, to which Brunner asks:

Do you believe this "decide-for-oneself" is such an instantaneous matter? Is not the misery precisely that we have already often decided, but we lack the *power* which follows from this decision?...Many have *honest* wills, but few have serious, i.e., powerful wills...That's how I would have gone home from your sermon: "He's right, and I've known what he said for a long time—but!"

Brunner encloses an advance copy of his critique of an article by Paul Wernle which had been published in the Swiss Reformed Church journal, *Kirchenblatt für die reformierte Schweiz*.[42]

Barth thanks Brunner for the article, though he thinks "it is completely useless to fight with [Wernle] and his gang at the *Kirchenblatt*. We have more joyful things to do".[43] However, Barth's comments to Thurneysen about Brunner's article are much blunter:

I found it to be too indirect and academic. One must deal with Wernle either by doing absolutely nothing or with a 42-cm cannon, preferably the first. But *this* kind of discussion with *these* "opponents" seems to me to be unprofitable, for, quite simply, nothing comes of it.[44]

Barth and Brunner saw each other the following month at the Swiss Religious Socialism Conference in Brugg, where they discussed Barth's "The Righteousness of God".[45] Brunner writes Barth to follow-up on their conversation. His main point is, again, that the faith-response Barth calls for is not clear. Yes, we must "once again recognize God as God". But Brunner feels that Barth fails to distinguish this action (faith) from the "'usual' activity", and that Barth describes the Christian's response too passively: "We must in some way direct our energy, our innermost will, to a different goal, and in this sense, of course, to 'do' something, even if it is merely 'repenting'". Brunner ends by enclosing one of his published sermons, which he believes shows "how far we intend the same thing".[46]

In July, Brunner writes Barth in response to Barth's sermon, "The One Thing Necessary": "I cannot argue with you about it—it has simply delighted me, grasped me, and also tormented me." Brunner's torment concerns his own Christian life.[47] He confesses:

> As you know, I have been a student of Kutter for a long time (longer than either you or Thurneysen). But as often as I have attempted "to let God matter, to let Him speak", it has not helped me forwards. Naturally, I am to blame for this, and I know that Kutter and you are nevertheless right...I probably preach the same way as you did at Aarau—but often only with a half-clear conscience.

Brunner finds Kutter and Barth's style of faith to be too abstract: "I soon find that all I have in my hands is an empty word with four letters,[48]...an abstract thought, with which I can neither understand nor master my life". But when Brunner gets frustrated with this empty faith, he finds himself swinging to the "other extreme": "'the Good should matter'..., a system of ethics which, up to a point, shines through one's life, but naturally (as little as 'the law' in Paul) has no power":

> I've always had the feeling—and my moral experiences confirm it—that I have still not made headway towards God, that my faith has produced nothing.[49]

This leaves Brunner experiencing the Christian life as a "vicious circle":

> In order to have this perpetual faith, one must become a completely different person. Again and again I find myself to be lazy and unfaithful; my faith is so weak that it often does not make headway over-against the robust old Adam. Therefore, I need first to be a different person in order to have faith; but I have to have faith to become a different person!

Brunner confesses all this to Barth because he hopes to receive more con-crete guidance on this issue than he has from Kutter. Poignantly, Brunner ends with the salutation: "With kind regards, your still somewhat-fallen-short companion on the way".

Barth responds immediately and with great pastoral care:[50]

> I understand you very well. It is exactly the same for me as for you, in every point…You really don't mean, with this utter lack, that you are in some sense a special case? I *really* experience the same things—you are in no way a "fallen-short companion on the way". This you must *believe*.

Barth goes on to repeat the point of his sermon and the insight of his theological turn:

> It really becomes clearer and clearer to me that this religious labyrinth has no exit …It is a question of God, and why do we marvel if he is not found in the psychological labyrinth of our religious experience? "Why do you seek the living among the dead?" (Luke 24:5)…We are not Pietists; we can know and really *know* that faith in no way consists…in taking this whole psychological reality as serious and important. Rather, with our eyes closed as it were, we hold on to God.

For Barth, the key to Christian living (as well as Christian thinking) is to turn one's focus from human subjectivity to divine objectivity:

> Does not the entire misery of our situation simply exist in that, again and again, we turn back to ourselves, instead of stretching out to the Objective? Don't we fail—due to some kind of *hubris* whose inner power causes us to neglect the "God in us" (of which you wrote so beautifully and correctly in the *Gemeindeblatt*[51])— to give our obedience and trust to God as *God*, God above all in his objectivity?

Barth seconds Kutter's response to Brunner's questions: "He understands the problem only too well, but he does not *want* to understand it, i.e., to let this sequence of thoughts into his mind". Barth's specific counsel to Brunner is to do what Barth does:

> I *cut off* these thoughts the moment I notice the trap being laid…[and] wait until joyfulness, faith, 'enqousiazein, etc. return (sometimes they don't return for a long time). And this objective hold on God as God is always more important to me compared to the previous…unavoidable variations of the inner life. I believe that here unfolds the constant which I (as well as you) have sought in vain in my subjective faithfulness.

Barth concludes his letter suggesting that they, as "companions on the way", should henceforth say "*Du* instead of *Sie*", and ends with a phrase that would remain characteristic of Barth throughout his life: "For my part,

I do *not* believe in your unbelief".

Barth and Brunner were next brought together when Thurneysen invited several of his colleagues, who were also part of this movement of theological re-orientation, to a study week in Leutwil in February, 1917.[52] Thurneysen asked Brunner to speak on "The New World in the Bible", but this theme did not appeal to Brunner.[53] So Thurneysen suggested Brunner speak on "something like 'God's Word in the Bible'", addressing the issue of a spiritual *vs.* historical understanding of the Scriptures, thus being "closer to his other question concerning religious knowledge". Thurneysen then asked Barth to pick up the theme on which Brunner had passed. Barth agreed, producing his now famous lecture, "The Strange New World of the Bible".[54] This lecture attempts to answer the question, "What is the one truth that these [Biblical] voices [and stories] evidently all desire to announce, each in its own tone, each in its own way?" (32). After considering incorrect answers to this question,[55] Barth suggests the correct answer is: "The word of God is within the Bible" (43). Barth argues that when we approach the Bible, "we find God" (44), that is, the triune God, who purposes, begins, and brings to life "a new *world*" (48–50). Barth concludes:

> In all men, whoever and wherever and whatever and however they may be, there is a longing for exactly this which is here within the Bible. We all know that. (50)

This lecture shows that Barth has completed his theological breakthrough: he has moved away from the anthropocentric theology of Neo-Protestantism—a theology of culture, history, morality and religion—to a theocentric, Word-centered theology of revelation. Barth has re-discovered the Bible as the Word of God, and has learned to read it "*with* the authors of scripture as well as *about* them".[56]

The Leutwil conference was a success for the small "movement". However, Thurneysen felt that Brunner had done a poor job.[57] Barth, for his part, was becoming tired of Brunner's increasing demands on his time:

> The good and trusting Brunner would be quickly disappointed if he knew how quickly I am at my wits' end with him at times. You well know my numerous exhausting opportunities, and you must quietly explain it to him.[58]

Barth's First Edition of *Romans* and Brunner's Review
In June 1916, one month after committing themselves to re-learning their 'theological ABCs', Barth writes to Thurneysen that "a copy-book with 'comments' is coming into being in which I summarize everything in my own language".[59] By November, Barth decides to direct these efforts toward the publication of a commentary on *Romans*, in order to "snatch it from our opponents".[60]

The Epistle to the Romans (which appeared in January 1919) is a frontal attack on the contemporary state of New Testament studies. Although the "historical-critical method of Biblical investigation has its rightful place", Barth's

> whole energy of interpreting has been expended in an endeavor to see through and beyond history into the spirit of the Bible, which is the Eternal Spirit...If we rightly understand ourselves, our problems are the problems of Paul; and if we are to be enlightened by the brightness of his answers, those answers must be ours.[61]

Barth's commentary revolves around the concept of the "Godness of God", and it reclaims the theme of eschatology,

> the irreversible movement from a doomed temporal order to a new living order ruled by God, the total restoration...of the original, ideal creation of God. This movement of a doomed world, which still knows its true origin but cannot get back to it on its own, is due solely to God, who shows his mercy in Christ. In Christ he implants life in the dead cosmos. In Christ he implants a seed which will sprout and spread overpoweringly until everything is transformed back into its original splendor. All this will not take place in plain view but will work itself out eschatologically.[62]

One can see in *Romans* the beginnings of positions which Barth would develop in the ensuing years: ethics built upon justification, which eliminates "ethics" except as an activity of God (234, 459, 526–527); and an actualist view of the Holy Spirit (understanding the Spirit wholly as a divine *gift* and never as a religious-moral *possession*)(266). The weakness of the commentary is that Barth fails to penetrate more deeply into the biblical thought-world of the Apostle Paul: many found in its "heavy linguistic freight" the determining influences of Platonism, Neo-Kantianism, Religious Socialism, Romanticism, and Idealism.[63] Nonetheless, Barth's new insights shone provocatively through the book.[64]

As Barth reviewed the proofs of *Romans* in November 1918, Brunner writes to ask if he could look at them, "for I am also completely occupied with Paul".[65] Barth takes up Brunner's "friendly offer with great thanks ...[since] you certainly know Paul better than I do; I only really know *Romans*".[66] One week later, Brunner responds with extensive comments.

Brunner begins by giving *Romans* high praise; he places it "next to Kutter's *Das Unmittelbare* as my favorite".[67] Brunner admires both the style of the book ("In your work, Paul is *right*...[It] simply and unperturbedly...expounds the matter as it is") and its content ("It signifies nothing less than a revolution of 'theological' thinking; it is a return from the modern empirical-psychological-historical individualism to the transcendentalism of the

Bible"). Brunner sees Barth taking Kutter's "raw material" and forming it into a "complete 'theological'...achievement".

While maintaining that "I follow you very much in your main point", Brunner brings up for the second time what will become a long running criticism of Barth: Barth's "one-sidedness". This controversy first appeared in a letter to Barth on January 30, 1918.[68] Brunner had taken issue with a common theme running throughout Barth and Thurneysen's book of sermons:[69]

> You are, in fact, dangerously one-sided. Legitimate "humanism" is treated as unfairly as Luther treated Erasmus. As the final word about the matter, it would naturally be false to view humanity merely as God's chess-pieces, to so overlook all human responsibility and activity as do the sermons on the forgiveness of sins and "The Other Side". Ultimately you remind me of the Reformation's objectivity of God, which so diminishes all subjective opinions ...or perhaps completely overwhelms them. But this should absolutely not be the final thing; one should emphasize that which our ancestors forgot, and thus one should understand them (Kutter also) with a grain of salt. When I *preach*, I cannot do anything differently than you. But I still need something different for myself. In sermons, I must think *only* about laying the foundation, but for myself, I must also think about building-up. For myself, I cannot get along with the Reformers alone—I also need my "humanists" Fichte and Kierkegaard (I also find much of value in Kutter).

Brunner believes Barth's one-sidedness makes itself felt in *Romans* even more severely than before. The point of contention is Barth's *sole* acceptance of the Reformers, whereas Brunner seeks to follow a line incorporating the Reformation *and* Idealism (Eckhardt and Fichte "saw as much truth as the Reformers"). Brunner sees Barth's one-sidedness working itself out detrimentally in two places. First, predestination:

> It seems to me that you—like me—consider predestination to be a fundamentally godless thought; but, on the other hand, you still want to thrash the Idealists with their "freedom", to annoy them with formulations which, despite all your protests, deny human beings as such and make them marionettes.[70]

Second, Brunner has problems with the fact that Barth makes all human morality relative: "Certainly it is a major gain if you clear away the cult of morality...But to tear open a chasm [between 'God' and 'Good'] contradicts the spirit of the Bible".[71] Brunner goes on to make a remarkable statement which casts doubt on whether, in fact, he understands Barth's theological breakthrough:

> [Your book] is a renunciation in principle of the Idealist understanding of history ...I cannot agree with you here; I look at the Bible with much more Platonic eyes. In pure loyalty, in moral seriousness...I see [in the world] a spark of that imme-

diacy, a seed of that believing objectivity, a little spark of that love of Christ and trust in God. I see no essential difference between the Idealism of Fichte and the faith of Luther...except that perhaps Fichte knew more clearly than Luther did what disinterested devotion to God is...

I do not overlook how deep this opposition is. In any case, it's good for us Idealists to see the matter with your eyes. We must, indeed, come out from Idealism, and it is a good thing when you make us out to be so bad, so that we come through where we should come through.

Brunner concludes:

Nevertheless, our common front and main tendency remain the same...And so I must only conclude by saying that you see the truth completely differently ...I really feel like I am your confirmation student taking instruction about faith in God. Nevertheless I know that you will never teach away that which I have brought up here against you.

Two days later, Brunner follows up with another long letter, where the issue of Idealism *vs.* the Reformers is replaced with that of Pietism *vs.* "objectivity".[72]

Ever since I was Kutter's confirmation student (1905), the problem of faith and Pietism has been a big practical issue for me, and Kutter's "transcendentalism" has frequently...impeded me...Your *Romans* also has this aspect. "Objectivity" so easily becomes a comfortable intellectualism (as history proves).

Brunner offers a Pauline "monologue", which tries to do justice to the complete giftedness and objectivity of justification, while still incorporating the moral-religious seriousness of spiritual growth in sanctification. The gist of this "monologue" is that, while one must seek God with all of one's heart, this seeking is only directed towards being justified by God. Thus, one cannot be side-tracked by evaluating one's spiritual "progress"—only God's summons to "proceed further" is relevant. Thus, one must

act like the most scrupulous Pietist...but *never stop* there. Never stay at the A, but press on to the B which comes out of the A...Kierkegaard is completely right: if you take God with only a little seriousness and honesty, then all inner and outer comfortableness comes to an end...Let your Idealists stimulate and direct you; but let them carry you and direct you to *God*.

Brunner adds a long postscript, trying again to express his opinion of *Romans*:

The main accomplishment is the constant speaking, so to speak, from God's standpoint, and the steadfast holding on to this, which is precisely not a "stand-

point", through all the entanglements of the older and newer questions …What I
have against you coincides with what I've already written concerning Kutter and
Fichte. I will make it my task to show that Paul represents the perfection and fulfillment also of that "series" (Eckhardt-Fichte), and that his views can be expressed just as well in their language as in Luther's.

After reading Brunner's two letters, Barth writes to Thurneysen, expressing his confusion.[73] He is particularly confused about Brunner's passion
for Idealism: "I'm surprised that, in fact, hitherto I have not wanted to begin anything positive with his two main idols, Eckhardt and Fichte…I am
not really sympathetic to Brunner's effort to have everything brought under
one arch". Barth concludes: "Explain him to me a little bit, so that, if it
should be, I can enter into serious communication with him". But instead of
waiting for Thurneysen's reply, the next day Barth answers Brunner.[74]
Barth offers *"provisional* thanks", indicating that Brunner's final decision
regarding Barth's treatment of Pauline ethics will have to wait until Brun-ner
has read the proofs of Romans 12–14. As for Idealism, Barth replies:

> Eckhardt and Fichte have, up to now, said appallingly little to me. I must take
> these two with a new seriousness. But regarding whether you're close to Paul if
> you want to put him under *their* wing: where do they have the characteristically
> rolling, motion-like, dramatic-historical sense which is so characteristic of Pauline
> thought? Would it not be better to put them alongside *John*?

The following week, Thurneysen weighs in with his reactions to Brunner's letters of November 28 and 30:[75]

> My first and last impression is a certain sorrow; I had truly expected a somewhat
> different reaction to your *Romans*. Has he really listened? Instead of this, he
> comes immediately with his boxes and tests to see if your "shot" (as he calls it)
> fits inside one or the other.

Thurneysen is distressed by Brunner's outright rejection of predestination
and his disproportionate concern for moral progress in the Christian life:

> He is probably a mystic in secret, and obviously an out-and-out individualist. He
> even attempts, in his frenzied monologue, to take over in a new way the entire
> Pietistic asceticism and analysis of the soul.

Thurneysen is not optimistic about Barth engaging in serious discussion
with Brunner:

> It seems that his thinking prevents making a serious material discussion with him
> possible. *Romans* has simply disturbed him in an important way, and he attempts
> to respond to this disturbance. All you can do is to say to him kindly and firmly

that Paul himself has already considered his objections re: Humanism! Ethics! Freedom! Development!—and it is for that reason (and others) that he has written *Romans*. I think that one should reject Brunner's considerations *in globo*, rather than considering them point by point.

However, Thurneysen advises Barth to be cautious in replying to Brunner:

> He is one of our brightest friends, and there could develop between you and him a running "naval engagement" over a wide distance. Therefore, it would be important to negotiate:…he rejects predestination—therefore he must answer our question how he conceives of the reality of a sovereignly acting God. Invite him to have a conversation about religion!

But before Barth can incorporate Thurneysen's advice into a longer response to Brunner, Brunner writes Barth again. Having read the proofs of Romans 12–13 ("it is *entirely* successful"), Brunner encloses a draft of a proposed review of *Romans*:

> I would appreciate it if you would write to me a short anti-critique if you are not completely in agreement with my expressions. All the work I put into this review —if one can call it work—has given me great joy and profit. Moreover, I have truly observed how great our commonality and how trivial our division is.[76]

Brunner asks that Barth return his review with his comments "*as soon as possible*. Wirz wants to publish it [in the *Kirchenblatt für die reformierte Schweiz*] first thing in the new year". Brunner adds that he still sees the need for them to talk personally about the ethical issues Brunner raised in his "monologue"—"what counts in practical life, pastoral office, pastoral care, etc."

Barth replies by return mail.[77] He warmly welcomes Brunner's review:

> You have done fundamental and illuminating work. I have no need of an anti-critique…You have *put* yourself as an ambassador (in this case as a clarifying theologian) between the theological brotherhood and my Paul, and you perform your office *masterfully, better than I could ever do it*…I fondly thank you for the friendly, full-of-understanding reception which you offer to this confederate on the theological stage.

However, Barth has one major reservation with the *style* of Brunner's review. Barth would have preferred that Brunner, instead of taking the position of a neutral interpreter of Barth's position, would have thrown himself into the fray as Barth's "confederate":

> [This] would have had the advantage that the "direct action" would have been continued, instead of giving the bourgeoisie time to recover. Naturally, you want that

as little as I do. All I mean is that what we must fear like the plague is the possibility that the bourgeoisie will immediately calm themselves again with the impression that "our understanding" is only a question of the newest, most-refined "ism"—one that is admirable, but also debatable within the scholarly guild...I repeat, I do not say this as a criticism of your work...It is only this: I think that we must take our small insight into Biblical truth and immediately begin to publicize it through direct Biblical thinking and speaking.

Barth concludes "in the hope of the continuation of [our] common research! We should soon speak to one another personally".[78]

Brunner's review of *The Epistle to the Romans* takes up the entire February 22, 1919 issue of the *Kirchenblatt*.[79] Subtitled "An Up-to-Date, Unmodern Paraphrase", Brunner opens his review by calling Barth's work "astonishingly objective and...naïve". Its objectivity is that it puts forth Paul's thoughts directly, its naïveté that it enters into no scholarly discussion (63).[80] Brunner's review highlights four ways that Barth's commentary sets theology and biblical-interpretation in a new direction. First, its method goes against the historicist presuppositions of the times, because Barth sides with the Fathers and Reformers' conviction about the "absolute division between the 'Word of God' as absolute truth and the 'word of man'"(64). For Barth, the task of biblical studies is to uncover the "essential things".

Second, Brunner praises Barth for emphasizing the "dualism" of biblical eschatology (65–66). This dualism maintains that since the world is "out of joint" due to the Fall, it is necessary that the "living, active God, as totally 'other'...break into the world of our experiences". This dualism flies in the face of "the optimistic concept of evolution which rules almost undisputed over our religious, moral, and scientific thought".

Third, Brunner sees in *Romans* the replacement of moral idealism with theological actualism:

> For Paul it is not a question of reading something of God into the natural and historical world, but of becoming witnesses of a real intervention of real, new, creative factors into the natural course of history. (67)

Looking past the historical to the "other-worldly" reality, Barth develops his actualism not on the basis of "an uninspired dogma of inspiration" but rather "with a steady, unexpressed appeal to that divine reservoir in us and under understood through the basic knowledge of the living God in Christ" (68).

Fourth, Barth replaces subjective piety and psychology with objective faith, thus standing against everyone since Schleiermacher ("the patron saint of modern theology") (68-70). Barth emphasizes the "absolute" nature of faith—it is a question of God acting and of humanity being apprehended rather than *vice versa.*

Brunner suspects that there will be criticism of Barth's book on many different grounds, but he concludes:

> The decisive factor, however, is that someone has finally noticed again that there is a third dimension, and indeed someone who is equipped to tell us what it is to be seen there. He has assumed the responsibility for finally leaving aside all the various matters of modern investigation and making the central thought of the Bible really the central point that influences everything else. This is the knowledge of the supra-worldly movement of the Kingdom of God, which in Jesus came from hiding into clear sight and which reveals in him its goal: Immanuel. (71)

Despite the storminess of their future relationship, Brunner would never give Barth anything but praise for what *Romans* achieved for modern theology, seeing it as "a breakthrough to a completely new return to a theology oriented on the Word of God".[81] However, Robinson is astute in observing that Brunner's enthusiasm for *Romans* indicated an already existing division between the two pastors:

> It is not without importance that this Brunnerite reading of the first edition, possible though it was in terms of what Barth had written, focused rather well upon precisely those things that Barth sought to overcome in the second. The "steady, unexpressed appeal to that divine reservoir in us" may have been what made the first edition of Barth's *Epistle to the Romans* intelligible and acceptable to the very first Barthians who joined the movement before the second edition was published. But it was precisely that which was eliminated in the second. In the preface to the second edition Barth says the positive reviews of the first edition so "dismayed" him that he awoke to "self-criticism." For this we are indebted, among others, to Brunner.[82]

Summary

The beginning years of the Barth–Brunner relationship reveal two young pastors—both deeply influenced by the "Let God be God" perspective of the Blumhardts and Hermann Kutter, and sharing the friendship of Eduard Thurneysen—moving towards a theological alliance based on a shared commitment to Religious Socialism. From the beginning, there was a distance in their friendship, and the relationship was cultivated mostly through letters and meetings either at conferences or in the presence of Thurneysen.[83] In addition, as their correspondence and Brunner's review of Barth's first edition of *The Epistle to the Romans* indicate, inklings of serious differences were present from the start.[84] Though sharing the common influences of the Blumhardts and Kutter, Barth was more taken by their emphasis on

God's objectivity, Brunner with the new spiritual vitality their teaching brought into the life of the Church.[85] When World War I shook their Religious Socialist optimism, they both found themselves returning to the Bible and the Reformers for guidance. But, again, they heard different things. Brunner understood their disagreement as Barth's "one-sided" stress on God alone (predestination) *vs.* his own concern for the growth of the Christian life ("humanism" and moral-religious effort). Barth understood their dif-ferences as his prophetic use of "direct Biblical thinking and speaking" *vs.* Brunner's "bringing everything (i.e., the Reformation and Idealism) under one arch". In the long run, these differences would not disappear. Indeed, they would become more pronounced.

NOTES

1. For information on Barth's life, see: Barth, "Autobiographical Sketches of Karl Barth from the faculty albums...at Münster and Bonn", in *Karl Barth–Rudolf Bultmann: Letters, 1922–1966*, trans. by Geoffrey W. Bromiley (Grand Rapids, MI: Eerdmans, 1981), pp. 151–158; Eberhard Busch, *Karl Barth*, trans. by John Bowden from the 2nd rev edn (London: SCM, 1976); Jüngel, "Barth's Life and Work".

2. For information on Brunner's life, see: Brunner, "A Spiritual Autobiography", *Japan Christian Quarterly*, 21 (1955), 238–244, and "Intellectual Autobiography of Emil Brunner", trans. by Keith Chamberlain, in *The Theology of Emil Brunner*, ed. by Charles W. Kegley (New York: Macmillan, 1962), pp. 3–20; Hans Heinrich Brunner, *Mein Vater und Sein Ältester*, (TVZ, 1986); J. Edward Humphrey, *Emil Brunner* (Waco, TX: Word, 1976), pp. 15–16.

3. *Das Symbolische in der religiösen Erkenntnis* (Tübingen: JCB Mohr, 1914). See Wendell G. Johnson, "Soteriology as a function of epistemology in the thought of Emil Brunner" (unpublished doctoral thesis, Rice University, 1989), pp. 13–14. Johnson's dissertation is the only extensive study of Brunner's early years. He clearly establishes Brunner's early commitment to Idealism. See also Dietmar Lütz, *Homo Viator* (TVZ, 1988), p. 266.

4. Letter from Frau Lilo Brunner-Gutekunst to J.W. Hart, January 10, 1993. Although Leutwil is close to Safenwil, there is no direct evidence that Barth and Brunner met during this year.

5. Beyond both being Swiss Reformed pastors.

6. For information on Thurneysen's life, see Busch and Rudolf Bohren, *Prophetie und Seelsorge: Eduard Thurneysen* (Vluyn: Neukirchener Verlag, 1982), pp. 156–168.

7. *Barth–Brunner*, EB: July 3, 1916 (#4), p. 8, note 6.

8. Busch, pp. 37, 50.

9. Thurneysen describes their relationship during the Safenwil–Leutwil years in "Intro-

duction", in *Revolutionary Theology in the Making*, trans. by James D. Smart (Richmond: John Knox, 1964), pp. 11–25 (p. 11).

10. Barth, "Blumhardt", in *Protestant Theology in the Nineteenth Century* , trans. by Brian Cozens and John Bowden (London: SCM Press, 1972), pp. 643–653 (pp. 644–645).

11. See H. Martin Rumscheidt, *Revelation and Theology* (Cambridge: Cambridge University Press, 1972), pp. 9, 11.

12. Torrance, *Karl Barth*, pp. 36–37; John D. Godsey, "Barth's Life Until 1928", in *Karl Barth: How I Changed My Mind* (Richmond: John Knox, 1966), pp. 17–33 (p. 21); Jüngel, "Barth's Life and Work", p. 31.

13. "It was from [Zündel] that my parents received something of spiritual reality which became an element in the climate in which I grew up" ("Spiritual Autobiography", p. 239).

14. "Autobiographical Sketches", p. 153.

15. "Blumhardt", p. 652. See Barth, *The Christian Life*, trans. by Geoffrey W. Bromiley (Grand Rapids: Eerdmans, 1981), pp. 256–260. See also Busch, p. 84.

16. Smart, p. 60.

17. "Autobiographical Sketches", p. 154. Lütz (pp. 202–204) argues that Blumhardt gave Barth a prophetic understanding of theology—theology is a "preparer of the way" for the *living* God in his freedom.

18. Bohren, pp. 51–52.

19. "Intellectual Autobiography", p. 5.

20. Ibid., p. 4.

21. H.H. Brunner, pp. 61–62, 121, 389; Stefan Scheld, *Die Christologie Emil Brunners* (Wiesbaden: Franz Steiner, 1981), p. 100, note 71. See also "Spiritual Autobiography", p. 239; Bohren, p. 157.

22. Barth, "Concluding Unscientific Postscript on Schleiermacher" in *The Theology of Schleiermacher*, ed. by Dietrich Ritschl, trans. by Geoffrey W. Bromiley (Grand Rapids: Eerdmans, 1982), pp. 261–279 (263). See also Barth, "Introduction" in *Revolutionary Theology in the Making*, pp. 65–73 (p. 72). Also see Busch, p. 76.

23. Quoted in Busch, p. 76.

24. Barth, "Evangelical Theology in the 19th Century", trans. by Thomas Wieser, in *The Humanity of God* (Atlanta: John Knox, 1960), pp. 11–33 (p. 14).

25. Barth to Thurneysen, September 4, 1914, in *Revolutionary Theology in the Making*, p. 26 [*Karl Barth–Eduard Thurneysen Briefwechsel*, ed. by Eduard Thurneysen, 2 vols (TVZ, 1973, 1974), I, p. 10]. Hereafter cited as *Rev.Theology*, KB: September 4, 1914, p. 26. Since *Revolutionary Theology* translates only portions of the correspondence, letters available just in German will be cited as *Barth–Thurneysen I*, KB: September 4, 1914, p. 10.

26. "Concluding Unscientific Postscript", p. 264.

27. Busch, pp. 82–83; "Autobiographical Sketches", p. 154; *Rev.Theology*, KB: February 5, 1915, p. 28.

28. "Intellectual Autobiography", p. 7.
29. Bouillard, p. 176.
30. "Autobiographical Sketches", p. 154.
31. "Barth's Life and Work", p. 25.
32. For the meaning and significance of Barth's "first turn", see: Busch, pp. 72–92; Torrance, *Karl Barth*, pp. 33–47; Smart, pp. 57–82; Bouillard, pp. 85–95; Jüngel, "Barth's Life and Work", pp. 31–33; Werner M. Ruschke, *Entstehung und Ausführung der Diastasentheologie in Karl Barths zweiten Römerbrief* (Neukirchen–Vluyn: Neukirchener Verlag, 1987), pp. 13–24.
33. H.H. Brunner, p. 123.
34. Ruschke, p. 23.
35. Godsey, p. 23. See also F.-W. Marquardt ("Vom gepredigten Jesus zum gelehrten Christus", *EvTh*, 46 (1986), 315–325), who maintains that Barth's turn was learning the difference between having a *concept* of God ("God in Christ") *vs.* the *reality* of "God in his revelation itself" (p. 316).
36. See especially "The Righteousness of God" in *The Word of God and the Word of Man*, trans. by Douglas Horton (London: Hodder and Stoughton, 1928), pp. 9–27 and "Das Eine Notwendige", *Die XX. Christliche Studenten–Konferenz (Aarau, 1916)* (Bern: Franke, 1916), pp. 5–15, quoted in Jüngel, "Barth's Life and Work", p. 31 and Busch, p. 89.
37. "Autobiographical Sketches", p. 155; *Rev.Theology*, KB: June 26, 1916, pp. 37–38.
38. "Concluding Unscientific Postscript", p. 264.
39. They may have met at the Aarau Student Conferences in the early 1910s (Busch, pp. 78–79), and it is possible that they met during Brunner's interim pastorate in Leutwil from 1912–1913.
40. "Der Pfarrer, der es den Leuten recht macht", *Christliche Welt*, 30 (1916), 262–267.
41. *Barth–Brunner*, EB: April 1, 1916 (#1), pp. 3f.
42. "Grundsätzliches zum Kapitel 'Die Jungen Theologen'", *Kirchenblatt für die reformierte Schweiz*, 31 (1916), 57–59. Paul Wernle was a theology professor at Basel belonging to the "history of religions" school, and the "revered teacher" of Thurneysen (Busch, pp. 73, 75).
43. *Barth–Brunner*, KB: April 12, 1916 (#2), pp. 4f.
44. *Barth–Thurneysen I*, KB: April 24, 1916, p. 130.
45. *Barth–Brunner*, EB: June 9, 1916 (#3), pp. 5–7.
46. "Geist", *Gemeindeblatt für die reformierten Kirchgemeinden des Kantons Glarus*, 3:6 (1916).
47. *Barth–Brunner*, EB: July 3, 1916 (#4), pp. 7–10.
48. "G-o-t-t", that is "G-o-d".
49. Brunner's daughter-in-law remarks that Brunner always questioned the vitality of his Christian life: "'My prayers are not long enough, I don't live out love. I am not faithful enough. I am not humble enough. I do not live enough what I preach'. There was always, *always* this self-questioning" (Interview with Lilo Brunner–Gutekunst,

January 13, 1992).

50. *Barth–Brunner*, KB: July 9, 1916 (#5), pp. 11–14.

51. "Geist", see above note 46.

52. Busch, p. 101.

53. *Barth–Thurneysen* I, ET: January 17, 1917, p. 170.

54. In *WGWM*, pp. 28–50.

55. "History" (pp. 34–37), "morality" (pp. 37–41), and "religion" (pp. 41–44).

56. Geoffrey W. Bromiley, "The Abiding Significance of Karl Barth", in *Theology Beyond Christendom*, ed. by John Thompson (Allison Park, PA: Pickwick, 1986), pp. 331–350 (p. 333).

57. *Barth–Thurneysen I*, ET: February 20, 1917, p. 175. See also Thurneysen's negative report on a visit from Brunner (ibid., ET: July 26, 1917, p. 218). On the other hand, Thurneysen reacted favorably to Brunner's article "Konservativ oder Radical?", *Neue Wege*, 12:2 (1918) (ibid. ET: March 1, 1918, p. 266). Also, Thurneysen was favorably disposed to Brunner's suggestion that Brunner review Barth and Thurneysen's collection of sermons (*Suchet Gott, so werdet ihr leben!* (Bern: G.A. Bäschlin, 1917)) in *Neue Wege* (ibid., ET: February 2, 1918, p. 262). The review was written but never published (*Barth–Brunner*, EB: November 18, 1918 (#9), pp. 21f.; KB: November 20, 1918 (#10), pp. 22f.).

58. *Barth–Thurneysen I*, KB: February 21, 1917, p. 178.

59. *Rev.Theology*, KB: July 27, 1916, p. 38.

60. Quoted in Busch, p. 98.

61. "Preface to the First Edition", in *The Epistle to the Romans*, trans. by Edwyn C. Hoskyns, 6th edn (London: Oxford University Press, 1933), pp. 1–2 (p. 1). References to the 1st edn of *Romans* are from *Der Römerbrief*, ed. by Hermann Schmidt, 1st edn (TVZ, 1985)].

62. Von Balthasar, p. 48. See also Ruschke, p. 180.

63. E.g., Godsey, p. 24; Philip J. Rosato, *The Spirit as Lord* (Edinburgh: T&T Clark, 1981), p. 26; von Balthasar, pp. 48–49; Ruschke, p. 101.

64. Ruschke, p. 189; Katherine Sonderegger, "On Style in Karl Barth", *SJT*, 45 (1992), 65–83 (p. 77).

65. *Barth–Brunner,* EB: November 18, 1918 (#9), pp. 21f.

66. Ibid., KB: November 20, 1918 (#10), pp. 22f.

67. Ibid., EB: November 28, 1918 (#11), pp. 23–28; Berlin, 1902.

68. Ibid., EB: January 30, 1918 (#8), pp. 17–21.

69. *Suchet Gott, so werdet ihr leben*

70. See *Romans I*, pp. 370–387.

71. Brunner continues: "It is interesting how much you speak of faith and how little of love as the highest thing...Between you and Kutter 'a great chasm has been fixed' (Luke 16:26). Thus the entire moral area does not have a positive connection to the kingdom of God...and everything which we cannot understand other than as first steps [toward the Kingdom] is purely 'world' for you".

72. *Barth–Brunner*, EB: November 30, 1918 (#12), pp. 28–33.

73. *Barth–Thurneysen I*, KB: December 1, 1918, pp. 304–305.

74. *Barth–Brunner*, KB: December 2, 1918 (#13), pp. 34f.

75. *Barth–Thurneysen I*, ET: December 8, 1918, pp. 306f.

76. *Barth–Brunner*, EB: December 16, 1918 (#15), pp. 36f.

77. Ibid., KB: December 17, 1918 (#16), pp. 37–40.

78. However, Barth cannot pass up continuing their argument of the past month: "I am reading Eckhardt now, but he continues to be very problematic for me. Take care before you bring *him* together with *Paul*."

79. "The Epistle to the Romans by Karl Barth", in *The Beginnings of Dialectical Theology*, ed. by James M. Robinson, trans. by Keith Crim and others (Richmond, VA: John Knox, 1968), pp. 63–71.

80. Throughout this book, page numbers of works examined in depth will be cited in parentheses within the text.

81. H.H. Brunner, p. 124. For Brunner's comments on the first edition of *Romans*, see: "Toward a Missionary Theology (How I Changed My Mind)", *Christian Century*, 66 (1949), 816–818 (p. 816); "Spiritual Autobiography" p. 240; "Intellectual Autobiography", p. 8. See also Robert H.E. Mielke, "The doctrine of the Imago Dei in the theology of Emil Brunner" (unpublished doctoral thesis, Drew University, 1951), p. 4.

82. James M. Robinson, "Introduction", in Robinson, *Beginnings of Dialectical Theology*, pp. 9–30 (p. 20). Robinson's argument is buttressed by Barth's November 17, 1920 letter to Thurneysen (*Barth–Thurneysen I*, p. 442).

83. Brunner would write many years later, "I have been acquainted with Karl Barth—though only slightly—since 1917. I have never been in close relationship with Barth (as is often said)" (quoted in Edgar L. Allen, *Creation and Grace* (New York: The Philosophical Library, 1951), p. 6).

84. Brunner speaks of their "parallel", rather than interdependent, theological development ("Missionary Theology", p. 816).

85. "Spiritual Autobiography", p. 240.

CHAPTER TWO

Common Front (1919–1924)
Rejection of the Schleiermacherian Tradition

> *Must another's "clock" always point to exactly the same hour as yours in order to reveal "an excellent way of thinking"?*
>
> (Brunner to Barth, May 1921)

> *I certainly do not want to treat [Brunner] badly, and I very much value his cleverness. But why does he have such little clarity with his intelligence?*
>
> (Barth to Thurneysen, December 1924)

A Movement Emerges (1919–1921)

Barth's Breakthrough Radicalized: The Second Edition of *Romans*
1919 saw the publication of *Christianity and Culture*, a collection of the writings of Franz Overbeck (1837–1905).[1] In the critical Overbeck, Barth saw "the *negative* side of the point which has now to be dealt with *positively*".[2] Barth was so impressed and challenged by Overbeck that he published a review of the book.[3] Barth's review focuses on Overbeck's eschatological critique of modern theology, which has "been living until now in a house built on sand" (57). Since Christianity means Christ and faith (which are non-historical and other-worldly), Overbeck argued that when the Church loses its eschatological orientation and looks for "progress", it becomes this-worldly, Christianity, "religion" (60–64). Barth seconds Overbeck's contention that "modern" Christianity had so accommodated itself to the times, losing its eschatological nature, that it had become something entirely different (64–68). Finally, Overbeck argued for the "Christian-ness" of theology (68–71). Barth concludes his review by emphasizing the value of Overbeck's "mighty STOP!":

The matters dealt with in this audacious undertaking are too large for the theo-

logian to be able to pass all the way through the narrow door of Overbeck's nega-
tion—even if we think we know something of Blumhardt's *Yes*, which is the other
side of Overbeck's *No*...The next work for all of us...is to remain standing before
that narrow door in fear and reverence, and without clamouring for positive pro-
posals; to understand what is at stake and to realize that only the impossible can
save us from the impossible. (73)

In particular, Barth was struck by Overbeck's statement that "theology
can no longer be re-established except with audacity".[4] Barth's appropriation of this phrase was an intentional "grotesque misunderstanding"—rather
than following Overbeck's logic (which would lead to the end of all theology), Barth understood it as pointing out the bankruptcy of liberal theology
and the need for theology to "begin again at the beginning".[5] Taking over his
radical critique of religion, Barth used Overbeck to "to radicalize what he
had learned from the theology of the two Blumhardts".[6]

Another decisive influence on Barth at this time was Søren Kierkegaard.
Barth summed up the decisive thing he learned from Kierkegaard in the
preface to the second edition of *Romans*:

If I have a system, it is limited to a recognition of what Kierkegaard called the "in-
inite qualitative distinction" between time and eternity, and to my regarding this as
possessing negative as well as positive significance: "God is in heaven, and thou
art on earth."[7]

Barth employed Kierkegaard's "infinite distinction" against the optimistic
thinking of Neo-Protestantism, with its assumption of a basic continuity between God and humanity. The impact of Kierkegaard on Barth's thought
was primarily critical: theology cannot think from humanity to God; humanity stands under judgment and crisis; theological language can only be
paradoxical; God is both revealed and hidden in Christ; religion is the most
dangerous enemy of God; human ethics stand in radical need of God's justification.[8] Although Barth's appropriation of the negative significance of
Kierkegaard's polemic threatened to overshadow its positive significance, he
always presupposed that underlying God's No was God's Yes—Christianity has to do with a God of revelation, who bridges the infinite qualitative
distinction between God and humanity in grace and redemption.[9] However,
Barth maintained that it is only from a clear understanding of God's No that
God's Yes can be clearly spoken about.[10]

The result of Overbeck and Kierkegaard's influence on Barth was to
radicalize the insight of his theological re-orientation of 1916. As early as
1920, one could hear the impact of these new influences on his thinking.
"The first evidence of this change is the address on 'Biblical Questions, Insights and Vistas' given at the Aargau Conference of 1920".[11] It is in this

lecture that Barth first employs the distinctive phrases which would characterize *Romans II*: God is "wholly other"; the knowledge of God is "the wisdom of death"; God's Yes is hidden in the form of His No; God brings a
crisis upon humanity; as well as the polemic against religion.[12]

The impact of Overbeck and Kierkegaard (as well as contact with the
young German pastor Friedrich Gogarten[13]) stimulated Barth to publish his
new thinking. When Barth's publisher requested another edition of *Romans*,
Barth supplied him with a completely revised commentary, "reformed root
and branch".[14]

For the purposes of this book, a few key emphases in *Romans II* must
be highlighted. The over-riding theme of the commentary is the consistent
thinking-through of the concept of *diastasis* ("distance")—the Kierkegaardian "infinite qualitative distinction" between time and eternity, Creator and
creature, God and humanity. For Barth, this is both an *ontological distance*
("God is in heaven, and thou art on earth", (10)) and a *epistemological distance*: God is only known by his sovereign self-revelation through His gift
of faith, and even in His revelation He remains the hidden God.[15] "Distance" works itself out in many ways in the commentary, primarily in
Barth's doctrine of God.[16]

Such a doctrine of God means that theology can only speak dialectically.
The ontological and epistemological distance between God and humanity
means that theology, since it deals with the "impossible possibility of God",
is a "position which cannot be a position" (530).[17] Positively, dialectic
means "a theology of pointing".[18] Since theology means pointing to the
living God and not theorizing about theological truths, doing theology can
be compared to painting "a bird in flight".[19] Barth's dialectical method also
has a negative implication: *Romans II* issues a consistent and loud "No!",
because the encounter between *this* God and *this kind* of humanity is crisis
and confrontation.[20] In particular, Barth's "No" is directed at "religion" and
the "religious man".[21] For Barth, religion is the clearest evidence of human
sin (229–270). But it is not only "religion" in a general sense which opposes
God; Barth argues that it is specifically the Church which stands against
God (332–333). Nonetheless, this negative dialectic in *Romans II* is built
upon the fundamental Yes which God speaks to humanity in Jesus Christ
(31).[22]

One also sees in *Romans II* an increased emphasis upon what has been
termed Barth's "actualism".[23] This term points to Barth's stress upon God
as a *living* and *acting* "person" (*vs.* a static being) who is entirely free and
sovereign, even (especially) in his self-revelation.[24] "Actualism" also refers
to Barth's understanding of humanity's relationship to God: everything from
God is given as a gift, and cannot be held as a possession.[25]

Finally, *Romans II* is the last writing where Barth relies so explicitly on philosophical concepts and terminology.[26] Barth himself singles out the decisive influence of Plato, Kant and Kierkegaard on the second edition (4).[27] Barth will later refer to his use of "a strange incrustation of Kantian-Platonic conceptions" in *Romans II*.[28]

Barth maintains that in his revision of *Romans I*, "the original position has been completely reformed and consolidated" (2).[29] However, the changes in the second edition of *Romans* should be understood more as radicalizing what Barth had learned in 1916. *Romans II* was not a step in a new direction, but a leap further along the same line as before.[30] Robinson interprets Barth's citing of Galatians 1.7 at the beginning of the preface ("I did not go up to Jerusalem...but went away into Arabia", (2)) as suggesting that the second edition, "under the influence of such radicals as Overbeck, Kierkegaard, and Dostoyevsky (all absent from the first edition), [moved] out into a more isolated, desert position than that of the first edition".[31]

Brunner: Staying the Course

In 1919, Brunner received a scholarship for a study year abroad, which he spent at Union Theological Seminary in New York. When he returned, he was struck by how much Overbeck had impacted Barth and Thurneysen. Soon after arriving back in Obstalden, Brunner received a Sunday visit from Barth and Thurneysen, who were vacationing nearby in their friend Rudolf Pestalozzi's summer home, the Bergli.[32] It was not a pleasant visit, at least for Brunner.[33] Barth and Thurneysen offered a blunt critique of Brunner's morning sermon, saying that Brunner preached "cheaply, psychologically, boringly, churchly, without distance, etc." This "crushing blow" prompted Brunner to read Barth's review of Overbeck's *Christianity and Culture*. In a letter following up on their visit, Brunner takes issue with Barth and Thurneysen's new radicalism, distinguishing between their Hegelian, dialectical No and his own Kantian, critical No:

> For Kant, the No is critical, like the watch-dog who barks at everything except the person who lives in the house. But the dialectical watch-dog barks at everything in principle.

He argues that the Bible, too, employs a critical rather than a dialectical No: "it reserves an area where the rush of the dialectical No should stop: the sphere of the resurrection and its anticipatory event—faith". Brunner grants the proper place for a No, but feels that Barth's over-emphasis on "distance" is the wrong approach:

> Your placing of the accent on fear and distance (correlated to divine fear...but in the end simply and absolutely fear) sounds *very* much like a gate of entry to God from Sinai...The maintaining of the distance is a dynamic and thus an un-

limited principle—there is no stopping it, as little as with the Law. The dialectical watch-dog will tear apart anyone who dares to approach God.

In contrast, Brunner argues that "the Gospel ultimately means something positive":

> The question is not *whether* something positive appears (the dialectical No), but *where* it appears (the critical No): Christ appears *in* time, the kingdom of God grows *in* time together with the weeds, we *have* this treasure in earthen vessels, faith *justifies* proleptically-forensically.

For Brunner, Overbeck's rejection of the historicity of Christianity is a specific example of the dialectical No sweeping away everything, rather than making critical distinctions. He also argues that it has always been the institutional Church which has opposed the message of God's nearness and simplicity by offering distance and "complicated dialectical tricks". Brunner warns Barth: "You have strayed into a very dubious neighborhood". He suggests that Barth and Thurneysen would have more success stressing Blumhardt's Yes (which places the emphasis on the content of faith) rather than Overbeck's No (which stresses the dynamic principle of guarding the distance). Brunner concludes:

> For me, this entire development is an excellent proof that I am correct when I maintain that content *and* dynamic, knowledge and experience, the objective-material and the subjective-personal…form an insurmountable polarity.

In this letter, one can see Brunner's great suspicion of Barth's developing dialectical theology as well as his fundamental adherence to Kantian critical philosophy. In understanding the Barth–Brunner relationship, it is necessary to gain some insight into Brunner's philosophical influences.

The impact of Kierkegaard upon Barth was welcomed by Brunner, since he had been studying Kierkegaard seriously from the time he began his pastorate in Obstalden.[34] But Brunner was influenced by the thinking of the Danish philosopher in a different way than Barth. While Kierkegaard most influenced Barth's doctrine of God and his polemic against Christendom/religion, Brunner's thinking was shaped more by Kierkegaard's teaching about "truth as subjectivity" and his doctrine of "existence". Another key difference in the way Barth and Brunner appropriated Kierkegaard concerns his three stages of aesthetic, ethical and religious life—these were ignored by Barth, but were taken up *in toto* by Brunner.[35] In all his writings from 1920 on, Brunner worked within the schema of Kierkegaard's stages: the sense of non-seriousness at the end of the aesthetic stage; the sense of pride which leads to despair, which leads to a recognition of sin and alienation in the ethical stage; and the need to move from spectator to self-commitment, which is understood as the leap of faith into the religious stage.[36] Brunner, much more than Barth, drew upon Kierkegaard's *anthropological-experiential* terminology (existence, existential, encounter, anxiety, decision).[37] Thus, Barth and Brunner learned different things from the Dane: Barth heard the *critical* Kierkegaard whereas Brunner heard the *existential* Kierkegaard.

A second decisive philosophical influence on Brunner was the critical philosophy of Immanuel Kant. One does not have to read far in any of Brunner's books or articles to find a positive reference to Kant.[38] The significance of Kant for his theology is seen particularly in the fields of epistemology and ethics. Brunner incorporated Kant's distinction between "things in themselves" and "things as known" into his understanding of revelation and reason. In addition, Brunner took over from Kant's ethics the concepts that religion and morality are closely bound, and that personal responsibility is central.[39] Brunner went so far as to write (in 1921) that dialectical theology is, in part, "the return to the truly critical scientific concept of transcendental Idealism".[40]

Brunner's Kantianism was reinforced and colored by Neo-Kantianism.[41] Brunner was influenced by Paul Natorp, the leader of Neo-Kantianism at Marburg, and regularly quoted him in his works of this period (1919–1924).[42] Natorp sought to find an independent place for religion alongside, not within, human culture. He emphasized that there was a border or limit between the temporal and the transcendent; God is beyond objectivity and thus not an object of human knowledge.[43] Natorp also drew upon Kantian ethics in understanding the Law: it is the reflection of the Good which is the goal of humanity, and God graciously gives humanity the power to fulfill the demands of the Law.[44] In particular, Brunner took over Natorp's Idealist understanding of God as "origin" and of humanity as "spirit":

> The philosophy of origin…is the philosophy of freedom, act and responsibility, because it alone gives an entry to that fundamental paradox of "autonomy", the I, which at the same time is infinitely more than "I, that authority under which all life of the spirit stands".[45]

Brunner also appreciated Natorp's staunch opposition to the rising influence of materialism, historicism and determinism.

One may be tempted to read into Brunner's articles from the early 1920s a "dialectical" critique of modern theology. In fact, Brunner's protest against Neo-Protestantism is less radical than Barth's—his attack is still largely that of an Idealist against a theology which is governed by an opposing world-view (i.e., naturalism).[46]

Brunner's major work from this period—*Experience, Knowledge and*

Faith—is a study in religious epistemology.[47] The book is dedicated to Kutter, and Brunner also acknowledges the impact of Barth and Gogarten on his thinking.[48] The book takes a form which will become typical in most of Brunner's future writings: it constitutes an analysis of and attack on some "provisional half-truths" ("experience" and "knowledge") followed by a presentation of the resolution of these inadequate positions as found in the Gospel ("faith").

Brunner charges into the attack from page one: theology has come under the sway of modern forms of thought—historicism and psychologism— "which we can call in one word the *subjective-anthropological...*theme: humanity is the measure of all things" (1). Before moving on to a new basis for theology, it is necessary to reveal the erroneous presuppositions and consequences of modern thinking (3). Brunner attempts to give an objective presentation of "religion as experience" (from mysticism through St. Francis and Pietism to Schleiermacher and Romanticism)(6–20) and its opposite, "religion as knowledge" (from Gnosticism through the reaction against Schleiermacher to religion as science)(21–31). He then offers "an impartial but not neutral criticism" of these half-truths by examining their "ultimate presuppositions" (31). "Psychologism" (represented by Schleiermacher and Ritschl) presupposes "monism and empiricism": "they know no original opposition between givenness and freedom, between nature and Spirit" (58). This presupposition of the basic continuity of all reality is what Elijah, Paul and Luther struggled against: theirs was "the struggle for the other-sidedness of faith" (59). Brunner then takes on the opposite error, "Intellectualism", as represented by Bergson and Hegel. The problem here is an arrogant system-building, whereas "genuine philosophy ends not with a system, but with *pointing*" (80).[49] Brunner relies heavily on Natorp to argue that only a critical philosophy of origin can effectively resist "Intellectualism", because: it alone respects the border between the finite and the infinite (82– 83); it is a philosophy of freedom and responsibility (83–84); and it overcomes the illegitimate opposition of practical and theoretical reason (85–86).

In Part III, Brunner turns from his negative task to his positive one: the answer to the question of religious knowledge is faith, which he calls "pure objectivity":[50]

> Either faith is understood solely as relation to God, i.e., that one absolutely presupposes God, or there is no faith...Faith is knowledge of God. The only proof of God is faith, the pointing to God itself...It is, simply said, nothing other than *being judged by God alone*. (90)

Brunner employs Kierkegaard to argue that faith means freedom, personeity, decision, the recognition of guilt and the need for forgiveness, and, most fundamentally, the response to God's "reality, power, personality" in His Word (124–125).[51]

Brunner concludes his book in a manner characteristic of his thought throughout his career: he puts forward both a rejection and an affirmation. He rejects a knowledge of God in which "God is pulled down into the sphere of the human; humanity throws across a bridge which leads to eternity; humanity secures a part of the work of redemption"; this is "idolatry" (129). However, Brunner immediately qualifies this rejection with the affirmation that such an

> attempt...would not be possible without God. Even in the ugliest and most satanic forms of religion there is something of God. The religious masking of godlessness is never without a reminder of the true God...Therefore it can only be a question of showing that whatever truth they have comes under judgment, where they must finally be shattered...Their witness, then, is what they are *not*. (130)

Thus, Brunner ends his work with what will become a typically "both-and" conclusion:

> Human experience and knowledge...are thereby placed under the judgment of God, under the universal judgment under which everything which is world is put ...There stands open no other possibility than an ultimate denial of oneself and affirmation of God, a final disregarding of *human* possibilities and seeing...which is only possible on the other shore of God, precisely—faith.
> But in this disregarding is understood the fulfillment...Faith anticipatorily understands that for which "the creation waits with eager longing"; that everything natural and historical "points to"—without knowing it—the Beyond, which all human seeking and asking always means (despite itself)...the Word-itself, the Origin, the reality behind mere appearance, Being-in-itself. (131–132)

Experience, Knowledge and Faith reveals how deeply enmeshed Brunner's thinking is in critical philosophy and Neo-Kantianism.[52] While Brunner has joined a "common front" with Barth against Neo-Protestantism, he is waging the battle with the weapon of critical philosophy rather than with "crisis theology". It is important to Brunner to establish both the promise and the limit of philosophy—human knowledge points to the reality of the Origin but only arrives at the crisis-point of the border region between God and humanity.[53]

> Thus, philosophy is to guard...the border, [like] Moses at the border of the promised land, summoned to lead them to it, but without the possibility of himself crossing over into it. It is "Moses", it is the "Law", that comes this far. Yet we understand correctly what "this far" means. A border is a border, not a bridge. (120)

Experience, Knowledge and Faith is a Neo-Kantian and Kantian critique of the epistemology of Neo-Protestantism. It would take a serious reading of *Romans II* for Brunner to appreciate and appropriate Barth's radical dialectic of the ontological and epistemological distance between God and humanity.[54]

The Barth–Brunner correspondence in 1921 illustrates an on-going dynamic which kept Barth and Brunner's personal relationship from ever becoming close—Barth's bluntness and Brunner's sensitivity. On May 13, 1921, Brunner writes to let Barth know that *Experience, Knowledge and Faith*—which he had presented to the theology faculty of the University of Zurich as his inaugural dissertation—has been accepted.[55] Therefore, Brunner is beginning preparations for a lecture course on "Idealism and Religion":

> I have selected this theme because it consumes me—since Aarau, for the first time correctly.[56] But I still haven't turned the corner: If Plato already had everything essential—as Natorp's people maintain—then why does one need *Jesus Christ*? the *event* of Good Friday-Easter?

Barth replies that Brunner is "a bit of a dangerous customer for such lectures".[57] Barth suggests that beyond "giving excellent arguments [against Idealism], you must also offer a more excellent way of thinking". More pointedly, Barth exclaims:

> Oh, stop being constantly entertained by *this* problem-setting of positives and moderns! How does that concern *us*? And why do you always grumble about the Natorp people!

Brunner is clearly upset by Barth's note:

> Surely you don't want me to believe that *you* don't consider it to be valuable to reflect on the problem which drove Kierkegaard during his life: Socrates-Plato *vs.* Christ, or the idea of God *vs.* the historical revelation of God? What else is your grasp of Overbeck's "super-history" than an answer to this question, and what else is meant by my (apparently more clumsy) expression than an explanation of this idea as well?[58]

Brunner is annoyed with Barth's inability to hear their commonality amidst their different forms of expression: "Must another person's 'clock' always point to exactly the same hour as yours in order to reveal 'an excellent way of thinking?" Brunner concludes tartly: "I would ask you...to write your fellow seeker of the truth a little less papally". Barth writes back in exasperation:[59]

From the east and the west comes the echo of your complaints about me.[60] Do I have to write a commentary to every postcard?...Dear friend: take everything in the humor and innocence in which it was meant. And above all: don't take me— and yourself—so bloody seriously...*Therefore, let there not be quarreling between you and me.*

"Dialectical Theology"

The enormous response to *Romans II* revealed that Barth's new theological orientation had touched a chord among younger theologians, and that he "had been allowed to take a step which many people had been waiting for and to do things for which many people were prepared".[61] The movement which began to center around the leadership of Barth became known as "Dialectical Theology" or the "Theology of Crisis".[62] Dialectical theology took shape most clearly with the launching of its mouthpiece, the journal *Zwischen den Zeiten* ("Between the Times"), in January of 1923.[63] The contributing editors of the journal were Barth, Thurneysen, and Friedrich Gogarten,[64] who worked under the supervision of Georg Merz, the managing director of the German publishing firm Christian Kaiser Verlag.[65]

After the first number of *Zwischen den Zeiten* appeared, Thurneysen wrote to Barth, tentatively suggesting that Brunner be invited to contribute articles periodically:

> With all my misgivings I would like to do it, for I find that our common presuppositions are broad enough, and it would also be a bit of special instruction which we could not, in fairness, say would be detrimental to the whole thing.[66]

Barth responded less than enthusiastically: "I agree with a prudent use of Brunner".[67] For his part, Brunner was always quite conscious of the fact that he never pierced the "inner circle" of the Barthian movement.[68] Nonetheless, with his extensive literary output, Brunner quickly became recognized as a major force in the new movement. As early as 1924 one observer could remark that Brunner "is probably the ablest of the Swiss Group, including Kutter, Barth, and Gogarten".[69]

"Dialectical theology", "Theology of Crisis", or "Theology of the Word" —the theological movement that sprang up in the early 1920s behind the leadership of Barth, Brunner, Gogarten and Bultmann would fundamentally change the face of theology. Thirty-five years after the founding of *Zwischen den Zeiten*, Barth described the meaning of dialectical theology:

> What began forcibly to press itself upon us...was not so much the humanity of God as His *deity*—a God absolutely unique in His relation to man and the world, overpoweringly lofty and distant, strange, yes even wholly other. Such was the God with whom man has to do when he takes the name of God upon his lips... We then concluded (from approximately the middle of the second decade of our

century on) that we could not side with [the prevailing theology] any longer. Why?...[Perhaps it was] the discovery that the theme of the Bible, contrary to the critical and orthodox exegesis which we inherited, certainly could not be man's religion and religious morality and certainly not his own secret divinity...The stone wall we first ran up against was that the theme of the Bible is the deity of *God*, more exactly God's *deity*...Only with this perspective did we feel we could henceforth be theologians, and in particular, preachers—ministers of the divine Word.

Were we right or wrong? We were certainly right!...The ship was threatening to run aground; the moment was at hand to turn the rudder an angle of exactly 180 degrees.[70]

However, unaddressed ambiguities in the movement would lead to its fractious break-up within a decade: Was its real theme "Word" or "existence"? Was the original ground and development of "dialectic" found in God, in humanity, or in the relation between them? What was the place and function of anthropology in theology?[71] Specifically regarding Barth and Brunner, ambiguities existed from the start. Except for the common critique of nineteenth century theology, Barth's radically dialectical *Romans II* formed quite a contrast to Brunner's Neo-Kantian *Experience, Knowledge and Faith*.

From Pastors to Professors (1922–1924)

Barth at Göttingen: Back to the Reformation

In early 1921, Barth received an invitation to fill a newly created post of *extraordinarius* professor for Reformed Theology at the University of Göttingen. This was a "decisive event" for Barth:

It was no longer a question of attacking all kinds of errors and abuses...Suddenly, we had been given an opportunity to say what we really thought in theology, and to show the church our real intention.[72]

Barth's first task was to plunge into a study of the Reformers.[73] Through this work—especially his preparation for a lecture course on Calvin—Barth looked back on *Romans II* as being "somehow at the corner between nominalism, Augustinianism, mysticism, and Wycliffe, etc., which was not itself the Reformation but out of which nevertheless the Reformation afterwards issued".[74]

Only now were my eyes properly open to the Reformers and their message of justification and sanctification of the sinner, of faith, of repentance and works, of the nature and the limits of the church, and so on. I had a great many things to learn from them. [At that time] I "swung into line with the Reformation", as they used to say.[75]

Barth's writings during these first years in Göttingen reveal a continuation of the dialectical theology of *Romans II*, with increasing signs of the impact of his Reformation studies. In "The Need and Promise of Christian Preaching", Barth gives "an introduction into an understanding of my theology" (97).[76] He describes his theology as "a kind of *marginal note*, a gloss", "a *corrective*, as the 'pinch of spice' in the food" (98) which arose from the question of preaching: "not How *does* one do it? but How *can* one do it?" (103). Barth pointedly asks contemporary Protestantism: "Is our own [theology] basically a *theologia crucis*", that is, a theology of "the divine judgment and divine justification" (130, 133)? In "The Problem of Ethics Today", Barth defends his dialectical method against his critics:

> We are tempted in Fichtean insolence to grasp for ourselves what does not belong to us. But we must once again and with special urgency be reminded... [that there] is no way from us to God—not even a *via negativa*—not even a *via dialectica* nor *paradoxa*. The god who stood at the end of some human way—even of this way —would not be God.[77] (177)

This is because the "two central conceptions of the dialectic of Paul and the Reformers"—faith and revelation—·

> expressly deny that there is any way from man to God and to God's grace, love, and life. Both words indicate that the only way between God and man is that which leads *from* God *to* man. Between these words—and this is the inner kernel of the theology of Paul and the Reformation—there are two other words: *Jesus Christ*. (179–180)

Brunner at Zurich: A "Dialectical-Dialogical Turn"

The year 1922 was an important one in Brunner's theological development. Two books—Barth's *Romans II* and Ferdinand Ebner's *The Word and Spiritual Realities*—caused him to reconsider fundamentally the shape and structure of his theology.

Brunner started receiving drafts of Barth's revision of *Romans* as early as May 1921.[78] However, it was not until he had read the published version that he writes Barth with his comments.[79] He is effusive in his praise:

> It is the most important theological book to appear in years. It is impossible that theology will pass by it without taking direction from it...With each chapter I am newly amazed at the completely unparalleled tenacity with which you...persevere through the swamps and jungles of the older, deeply-rooted, customary ways of

thinking.

Brunner praises its all-out polemic on modern theology:

> I do not know of *any* book (except, perhaps, Kierkegaard's *Sickness unto Death*[80]) in which the well-tended garden of theology is so fundamentally uprooted, such that it is, finally, once again possible and necessary to begin completely from the beginning. All the tidy little hedges and little beds have disappeared. This time it is not the exquisitely precise work of the skillful gardener; rather, the settlers' steam-plow has gone through it and brought to the surface —in a huge clod—what has, for a long time, lay intact under the finely-sieved humus of the topsoil.

With an astonishing humility, Brunner confesses that Barth has won him over to the "dialectical No":

> I was glad that I was not completely unprepared to be assailed by this colossal thought. This scandal was already powerfully indicated to me for the first time on that always memorable (for me) Sunday in Obstalden in August 1920. For more than half a year I kicked against the pricks without breaking through. Then your first proofs arrived (chapters 2–5)...Understand me when I say that after studying these proofs, the entire letter to the Romans has brought liberation for me. Instead of offering me scandals, it offers me *the* scandal. Now I see for the first time the logic of the scandal, its entirety, its encompassing significance for *everything*.

This letter is crucial evidence concerning a "dialectical" phase in Brunner's theology. In the autumn of 1920, Brunner neither understood nor accepted Barth's new radicalism (prompted by Barth's study of Kierkegaard —whom Brunner had known longer and read differently—and Overbeck). But in May 1921, when he first saw the drafts of Barth's revision, he began to read Romans with new eyes. Finally, after reading through Barth's revised commentary over Christmas 1921, Brunner claimed he finally understood "the logic of *the* scandal...in its encompassing significance for *everything*"—that is, the "distance" and its accompanying radical and comprehensive judgment on humanity in all its expressions, including religion and ethics. In coming to an understanding of Barth's "dialectical watch-dog", Brunner would be able to break away from the influences of Neo-Kantianism and speculative Idealism.

Brunner's adoption of Barth's Overbeckian insight provided him with a negative criterion with which to re-think his theology. However, it was Ferdinand Ebner's *The Word and Spiritual Realities* which gave Brunner a positive way to re-formulate his theology.[81]

Ferdinand Ebner was the founder of the so-called "I–Thou" philosophy.[82] Ebner's influences included Kierkegaard, the language philosophies of J.G. Hamann, J. Grimm, and W. von Humboldt, and the prologue to the

Gospel of John.[83] The negative component of Ebner's philosophy was his attack on speculative Idealism, in particular the way Idealism isolates the self.[84] The positive component centered on two concepts that would decisively influence Brunner in his theological re-thinking: "I–Thou" and the "Word".

Ebner's philosophy, as expressed in *The Word and Spiritual Realities* was built on three presuppositions.[85] First, human existence is spiritual existence. Humanity's spirituality signifies that human being is "directed fundamentally to a relationship with something spiritual *outside* of it, *through* which and *in* which it exists" (81). Thus, the human spirit is not monistic but dualistic, or, more precisely, *dialogical*. Second, the spiritual entity outside humanity is named the "Thou", and the spiritual entity inside humanity —the "I"—has its existence only in relationship to this Thou (81, 84–85, 187).[86] Third, the ground, bearer and "vehicle" of the I–Thou relationship is the spoken *Word* (153). Most importantly, the "word" does not convey some*thing*, but a person. Ebner grounds his "Logosophy" in the phenomenon of the human capacity for language (located in the human reason); this is the "Archimedean point" of philosophy (154–161).

Ebner suggested that his philosophy made three important contributions. First, it overcame the Kantian division between "things in themselves" and "things as they are known" by bridging the ontological-epistemological divide with the concept of the word, which entails both being and knowing.[87] Second, it distinguished between two kinds of knowledge: the impersonal-obective knowledge of things in the world, and the personal-existential knowledge of spiritual beings.[88] Ebner's third contribution was the fruitfulness of his philosophy for theology. His "word ontology-epistemology" and "I–Thou" schema offered a productive way to understand the relationship between a transcendent God and finite humanity.[89]

Brunner was immediately conscious of the importance of Ebner's "I–Thou/Word" schema for his thinking: "My eyes were opened by Ferdinand Ebner".[90] Brunner's reliance upon Ebner grew steadily over the next decade, until, in *Truth as Encounter* (1938), Brunner explicitly proclaimed the I–Thou philosophy to be the comprehensive basis of his theological program.[91] Ebner's first contribution to Brunner's thinking was his critique of Idealism.[92] The combination of Barth's "No" and Ebner's "Word" enabled Brunner to move to the point where he could criticize Idealism with the same force with which he also attacked naturalism. Second, Brunner was able to build Ebner's thinking onto his fundamental commitment to Kierkegaard, since Ebner himself was deeply influenced by the Dane.[93] Ebner's distinctions between "personal-Thou" and "impersonal-it" truth developed Kierkegaard's distinction between subjectivity and objectivity; Kierkegaard's "faith as decision" was filled out by Ebner's "Word", which summoned one personally to decision.[94] Third, and most importantly, the call-response dynamic of Ebner's understanding of the Word would (as early as 1924) become fundamental to Brunner's anthropology: humanity is essentially responsive/responsible (*verantwortlich*), and its essential nature is its ability to speak (*Wortmächtigkeit*) and to be addressed (*Ansprechbarkeit*).

It is crucial to observe how Brunner's embrace of Ebner's "I–Thou"/ "divine summons-human response" schema blunted his adoption of Barth's "dialectical No".[95] Underlying Ebner's philosophy was a strong sense of correlation—dialogue is not the same as dialectic, and relation moves in a different direction than distance. Barth and Ebner led Brunner to abandon his Neo-Kantianism. However, it is not clear whether Ebner's concept of "Word" *overcame* or merely *replaced* Brunner's previous Idealist concern for divine-human relatedness. Rather than sharpening the ontological and epistemological discontinuity between God and humanity, Ebner's influence moved Brunner back to searching for divine-human continuities.[96]

On the strength of *Experience, Knowledge and Faith*, Brunner was granted the status of lecturer at the University of Zurich.[97] This enabled him to begin work in academic theology at the same time that Barth began his professorship in Göttingen (1921–1922 winter semester). Brunner's inaugural lecture as lecturer—"The Limits of Humanity"—discusses the relationship of religion and culture.[98] "Limits" is very much a transition work, as all of Brunner's theological and philosophical influences (old and new) show their impact. In the lecture, Brunner attempts to demonstrate that—contrary to Natorp—religion can exist outside the limits of human possibilities (76–77). He argues historically that "religion which recognizes the decrees of culture as unappealable has always been domesticated religion, ster-ile and uninteresting" (78). Rather, a "living religion" always relates itself to the "other side" beyond culture (79): "Religion does not exercise only this or that kind of critique of culture, but it puts humanism itself into ques-tion, because it puts humanity into question". He argues that every philoso-phical attempt to place religion within culture (from Kant to Schleiermach-er to Hegel to Feuerbach) has proved to be unsatisfactory (79–81). In con-trast,

evangelical and Reformation faith is not oriented to experience, nor to humanity, but to God. Not progressively-realized freedom, but guilt and redemption; not the immanent process of thought, but the most abrupt dualism between God and humanity; not the rising line of development, but the broken line of the cross—these are the offensive (to humanistic ears) themes of religion…It is in this threatened break of its relationship with culture that religion begins again to remember its transcendental contents. (81)

Brunner next takes up the question "What is humanity?" He answers: "To be human is to be, essentially, a questioner. 'To question' means to seek meaning and relationship. Humanity strives for home" (81–82). However, the failure of both human thought and will to find the way "home" indicates that "tragedy" is not accidental, but "the specific characteristic of life" (82–84):

> It is precisely human beings, who grasp at the fires of heaven with titanic passion and power, who must most deeply encounter the curse of mere humanity. Thus, the same limits of humanism—the law of truth and of the Good—which give our thinking and willing their humanity and worth, create for us at the same time the great predicament out of which they provide no escape, the predicament of... being born of the earth. (84)

This predicament is the crisis of judgment, understood as our guilt (85–86). The knowledge of this crisis as judgment and guilt brings to light the essence of human being:

> It is only here, where one takes responsibility for one's situation, that the crisis reaches its complete sharpness and depth. And only here, where one knows oneself to be guilty, is one able to know the Other before whom one is guilty, which religion has given the name: God. For from him alone, the ground and judge of our spirituality, comes the predicate which we much too rashly confer upon ourselves —the predicate of personality. (86)

This is where, "with astonishing clarity, the distance comes to the fore":

> Here, where the hyphen between God and humanity is erased and in its place a slash appears; here, where the religious claim to having God and experiencing God yields to the knowledge of a wholly Other...here, where one is shaken through this knowledge to the core of one's being, where nothing remains for one other than questions...here and here alone is God known...Only in this predicament does the view open to the wholly Other in whom our redemption is insured. We gain the standing-place on the far side of the limits of humanism precisely where we recognize—in unconditional awe and with absolute pathos—the distance. (86–87)

Therefore, one must not do away with the limits of humanism: "Just the opposite: one must see them sharply and clearly, and continually recognize them. For only as one sees them does one see the Other" (88).

> Therefore, at this point critical philosophy and the fear of God join hands. Their common Ultimate is the indication of that which is on the other side of us, our Origin which is at the same time the origin and goal of all being. Therefore religion (understood as that which bases itself on its proper ground and not on human ex-

periences) will not oppose critical philosophy as an opponent, but, on the contrary, will welcome as its best ally a philosophy which sees its office as standing guard at the limits of humanity. For it indicates both the place where humanity ends and where that which is greater than humanity becomes visible. (88–89)

Brunner appends to his lecture "A postscript for theologians". He bemoans the fact that, since Schleiermacher, theology has come under the fatal domination of "psychologism" (89). As opposed to Schleiermacher's confining of religion to the realm of "feeling" and religious experience, theology must "pull out the root of this disease: the confusion of divine grace with religious experience" (93). After tracing modern theology's subjectivism back to a twofold root in Schleiermacher—his apologetic interest and his "legitimate fear of intellectualism",[99] Brunner argues that theology's sickness can only be cured through the rejection of "psychologism…in its entire dangerousness" (95–96).

It must be seen again that that which is given in religion is not that which exists objectively between God and humanity; that no analysis of religious consciousness or experiences leads to God; that only the venture of putting God first as the presupposition of all statements—the venture of faith—will put religion in its proper place. (96–97)

Like *Experience, Knowledge and Faith* (and most of his works over the next ten years), "Limits" reveals Brunner as a polemicist pointing out the inadequate half-truths of modern philosophical presuppositions.[100] More importantly, in this lecture one can see the juxtaposition of the many influences in Brunner's thought.[101] As a Kantian, he seeks to establish solid grounds for the legitimacy and necessity of critical philosophy in guarding the limits of human capabilities. As a Kierkegaardian, he illuminates the *via negativa* from despair to God. As a dialectical theologian, he wages all-out war on the subjectivism of modern theology and Schleiermacher. Finally, as a newly-enlightened Barthian, he is able to stress the radical meaning of the "distance"—religion itself stands under judgment, and faith is not a "having", but a "hoping". Thus, with "Limits", Brunner can be correctly viewed as a "dialectical theologian". However, his "Barthian turn" after reading *Romans II* would soon be counter-balanced by the dialogical theology offered through the "I–Thou" philosophy of Ebner.

Schleiermacher (1924)

Mysticism and the Word

In a letter to Barth in June 1923, Brunner reveals that Barth will soon see a new book: "my offensive against Schleiermacher".[102] Barth replies that seeing Brunner's manuscript would help him prepare for his upcoming lecture course on Schleiermacher.[103] At the end of August, Brunner sends Barth a copy of his proofs, following up in September with another batch.[104]

Brunner's book, *Mysticism and the Word*, is a sustained attack upon Schleiermacher, and by implication, upon his Neo-Protestant successors.[105] The book constantly contrasts what Brunner believes to be two fundamentally opposed understandings of God and religion: "mysticism in its many hues, and the Christian faith" (2). Brunner asserts that nineteenth century theology has sold out to the former: "Modern theology is a secret yearning after an irresponsible orientation towards mysticism, a compromise between mysticism and faith" (4). Opposed to mysticism is the theology of the Word:

> Where there is Word, there is clarity as clear as day...Mysticism seeks dusk and silence. Faith finds the day in the Word...Here is the center of the storm. *Either mysticism or the Word.*[106] (5)

Brunner singles out Schleiermacher for attack in his book because

> he is the most significant of those...who tried to work out the contents of Christian faith in mysticism, and he is certainly one of the greatest factors in this intellectual development. (6)

Brunner's negative thesis is that Schleiermacher's program—binding together a "philosophy of immanence" with Christianity—is "a colossal self-deception" which thoroughly distorts the Christian faith (11). Underlying this is Brunner's positive thesis—"Biblical-Reformation" theology takes the Word of God as the principle of theology (12).

The book is divided into four parts. In Part One, ("The Modern Understanding of Religion"), Brunner presents Schleiermacher's legacy to Protestant theology: in seeking to give religion independence from philosophy (chapter one), Schleiermacher constructed a view of religion which was neither intellectual ("Religion is not knowing"—chapter three) nor moralistic ("Religion is not doing"—chapter four) but mystical ("Religion is feeling"—chapter five). In Part Two, Brunner attempts to demonstrate how Schleiermacher's legacy has led to a misunderstanding of Christian essentials: modern theology misunderstands what Reformation theology meant by the Word (chapter six), ethics (chapter seven), and the "Other" (chapter) eight). Part Three examines how Schleiermacher and his followers have distorted the fundamental Christian doctrines of christology (chapter nine), sin (chapter ten), redemption (chapter eleven), eschatology (chapter twelve) and history (chapter thirteen). Finally, Part Four examines the "ultimate presuppositions" of these two opposing understandings of religion.

Brunner's basic criticism of Schleiermacher is that he understands religion as "the unification of the consciousness of God and self-consciousness ...—identity, mysticism" (76). Brunner designates this union with the phrase "an identity philosophy of immanence"—in short, a philosophy which stands at the opposite pole of the Kierkegaardian-Barthian-dialectical "infinite qualitative distinction" between God and humanity. The philosophical form of Schleiermacher's theology is identity and immanence; its religious form is mysticism (77–78). Both, Brunner maintains, indicate Schleiermacher's misunderstanding of Christianity:

> In the Bible as for the Reformers, revelation is precisely that which Schleiermacher rejects: the communication of a miraculous, supernatural knowledge of God and divine things, and faith is nothing other than the holding-as-true of this divine communication in opposition to human experience and understanding.[107] (82)

Not surprisingly, Brunner finds that the development of Schleiermacher's religious mysticism and philosophical "identity-immanence" wreaks havoc on the fundamental doctrines of the Christian faith.

In the final part of the book, Brunner takes on Schleiermacher with the weapons of Kantian philosophy and dialectical theology. He argues that the fundamental problem of Schleiermacher's theology is that he presupposes that the divine-human relationship is one of continuity rather than that of contradiction.[108] While Schleiermacher correctly saw the danger of speculative Idealism, the correct way to address this threat is not Schleiermacher's return to naturalism and immanentism with his concept of "feeling". Rather:

> Perhaps nothing can help us here as much as the sober reflection which we call critical thought...Through the idea of Truth and the idea of the Good one first becomes...truly related to the Spirit, to God, in the double sense: one is intimately bound with God and one is held in infinite distance from God. (376)

Brunner concludes that, despite occasional breakthroughs, Schleiermacher's theology is subsumed under mysticism:

> Therefore, in a word, the Schleiermacherian theology, despite its Christian-sounding formulas, has much less to do with the evangelical faith than with pagan mysticism. It is, as is all Christian mysticism, *theologia gloriae*, not *theologia crucis*... The cross means: paradox, opposition to *all* experience...Faith is precisely know-

ing that this Word is entirely not ours, not given, not able to be experienced or proven, but that we stand in absolute contradiction to it, yet it is called ours...in that we (as Luther said) are put in the place where Christ stands; faith is nothing other than letting God speak. (388–389)

In a postscript, Brunner maintains that it has not been his intention to "dispose" of Schleiermacher (390). Rather, what he has "definitively rejected" is continuing to build theology on Schleiermacher's foundations. This is because "Schleiermacher's entire thinking (and that of all his theological descendants) is determined by one word: '*and*'", whereas "Biblical-Reformation faith stands or falls with the word '*solus*'" (390–391).[109] Thus, Brunner concludes, "the result of our scholarly study is a clear distinction: *either* the Christian faith *or* the modern understanding of religion".

In *Mysticism and the Word*, one sees Brunner at his most dialectical. The book also represents Brunner's sharpest attack on Idealism: although he pointedly rejects Schleiermacher's "naturalism", he grants Schleiermacher's justified reaction against the extreme rationalism of orthodoxy and the Enlightenment.[110] Noticeable, too, is Brunner's first attempt to sketch an anthropology based on Ebner's "I–Thou" philosophy—this would become fundamentally important in his later debate with Barth.[111] Some have remarked that Brunner's attack on Schleiermacher is based on a "gross misunderstanding".[112] It is more helpful to understand *Mysticism* as Brunner's (and dialectical theology's) declaration of war on Schleiermacher as the source of all that has gone wrong with modern theology.

Barth on Brunner on Schleiermacher

When Barth writes to Thurneysen in mid-October 1923, he says of the manuscript of *Mysticism*: "It seems to me to be entirely good, and I think it is very serviceable".[113] Barth writes to Brunner at the end of October with his comments on the manuscript, after having read about one-third of it.[114] His overall verdict:

> Generally, I have the highest admiration for you as you slaughter the man (a certainly much-deserved act), which will not only make an impression but mark an epoch.

However, Barth is somewhat uncomfortable with *Mysticism*:

> You know, I *cannot* drag an individual historical person and his work over the coals like this, because I cannot get rid of the feeling—although such an extermination has the highest justification—that "in some way" injustice is done. But perhaps it is only my unhelpfulness and short-sightedness and ignorance which cause me to "wait" (despite all the disgust with which Schleiermacher fills me) and see whether or not something might be there.

Barth states that the goal of his upcoming Schleiermacher lectures does not include Brunner's "battle plan", but only, "so to speak, statistical aims".[115] Nonetheless, "in the first hour I will give my students appropriate notice of your book as the *real* slaying of the dragon".

When Brunner sends Barth his last batch of proofs, Barth writes promptly with his reactions.[116] Besides suggesting that Schleiermacher's sermons are a valuable resource in understanding him, Barth writes that he would have preferred

> that the positive elaboration of the Bible, Reformation, etc., had been in the shortest, enigmatic form—at best only in the form of a marginal gloss—to allow more room for a more comprehensive presentation of Schleiermacher himself.

He adds:

> Too often the book is like a trial, an admirable pamphleteering intention taking place under the guise of a serious-scholarly investigation. But these are only formal thoughts.

Hence, Barth has "nothing to object to as regards the contents".

However, Barth becomes increasingly dissatisfied with Brunner's case against Schleiermacher. In January 1924, Barth writes to Thurneysen:

> Brunner's book will work "worm powder"...What a swinging of the battle axes! ...In any case, everything is a little more complicated than Emil Brunner thinks with his "Word".[117]

In a circular letter in February 1924, Barth writes of his own struggles over his Schleiermacher lectures:

> For four hours I have been at his *Christian Faith*. Whew, what a cuttlefish! First I institute all kinds of special inquiries (Brunner seems to me to be a bit lacking in these, but at the *essential* point he is *right*) concerning the relation of the different parts to each other...The stuff is really brittle wherever one touches it, just one gigantic swindle, one is frequently inclined to cry out in wrath. However, the insight that the way taken by this undoubtedly very wise and honest religious man is a *blind alley* makes the situation quite clear, but the question: How then? is only the more alarming. It is not really sufficient just to refer to "Reformation". Brunner is much too cheerful for me at that point. Where actually is the divine *Providence* at work in the history of theology as we now have to see it? Three centuries of rubbish? That in itself is really a problem! And to what extent was the Reformation in some measure jointly responsible for this rubbish?[118]

Barth's reservations with Brunner's *Mysticism* grew with his own study of Schleiermacher. When one compares Barth's lectures on Schleiermacher to *Mysticism*, one sees an immediate contrast: whereas Brunner's book is a thoroughly polemical attempt to overthrow the fundamental insights which govern Schleiermacher and all modern theology, Barth's lectures are a straightforward historical description of Schleiermacher with minimal interpretation or analysis.[119]

Barth begins his lectures with a prolonged study of Schleiermacher's sermons, maintaining that they are the best way into "the characteristic lines of Schleiermacher's thinking and utterance" in their "inner coherence" (3, 10). When he comes to Schleiermacher's academic theology, Barth argues that "the true theme of his theology" was "the *debate* between Christianity and modern culture" (138). This focus led Schleiermacher to subordinate theology to philosophy:

> To determine the nature of Christianity, one does not go to Christianity itself but to a court which stands over against both it and similar structures, and which quite apart from Christianity knows what is what in matters of religion and the church …I need hardly say that we have here the methodological source of the modern study of religion. (149)

In his survey of *The Christian Faith*, Barth draws attention the fundamental significance of the title:

> "The Christian Faith"—not, then, dogmatics? No, deliberately not…"Christian Faith" denotes programmatically the change in contents that we have already noted…Revelation is not reflected in dogma nor is it in this refraction the subject matter of dogmatics. But *Christian faith*, a specific form of religious self-consciousness…is the subject matter…This is the great Copernican revolution [of] Schleiermacher. (187)

Barth fundamentally questions Schleiermacher's apologetic intention in the Introduction. Foreshadowing a later more vehement "No!", Barth states:

> Is the real point of Part I anything other than…to anchor Christianity, not in its Christian determination, but in the necessary presupposition of this, namely, in the universally valid theses of ethics and the philosophy of religion? To be sure, Part I of *The Christian Faith* is not a natural theology…[But] the Introduction is at least a substitute for a natural theology…and Part I is to be viewed as in fact a two-way bridge between this substitute natural theology and the dogmatics proper.[120] (201)

In the end, Barth joins Brunner's fundamental rejection of Schleiermacher. Regarding Schleiermacher's understanding of the Word of God, Barth remarks:

Nothing remained of the belief that the Word or statement is as such the bearer, bringer, and proclaimer of truth, that there might be such a thing as the Word of God...As I see it, what we have in this doctrine...is Schleiermacher's mystical agnosticism. (210)

He cites Brunner approvingly,[121] and concludes in a similar vein:

For me the results of this study are fairly shattering...I was not prepared to find that the *distortion* of Protestant theology...was as deep, extensive, and palpable as it has shown itself to be...If we...cannot find in Schleiermacher a legitimate heir or successor of the reformers, if we cannot see in the indubitable domination of his thinking the gracious guidance of God but the very opposite, a wrathful judgment on Protestantism which invites us to repentance and conversion instead of continuation, then the only possibility that remains—and I do not see how one can avoid this—is obviously that of a *theological revolution*, a basic No to the whole of Schleiermacher's doctrine of religion and Christianity, and an attempted reconstruction at the *very* point which he have constantly seen him hurry past with astonishing stubbornness, skill, and audacity...There is no occasion for triumphant superiority at this tomb, but there is occasion for fear and trembling at the seriousness of the moment and in face of our own inadequacy. (259–260)

In his circular letter of February 5, 1924, Barth informed Georg Merz that he would review *Mysticism and the Word* for *Zwischen den Zeiten*.[122] It is not clear why Barth picked up this task. On the one hand, a review would draw attention to Brunner's book with the seal of approval of the journal of dialectical theology. On the other hand, given Barth's growing misgivings, his review could open up a division within dialectical theology at the fundamental point where it was supposedly united—its rejection of Neo-Protestantism.

Barth's article begins by sketching Brunner's argument, emphasizing that *Mysticism* is not intended to present Schleiermacher's views, but to refute them (52).[123] Barth then ticks off the strengths of the book: behind the polemic is "solid objective work"; Brunner's criticism of Schleiermacher's academic works is appreciated (although he regrets that Brunner ignores the sermons, pp. 52–53); and Brunner has successfully led the charge of dialectical theology at this fundamental point:

Brunner's clearly formulated thesis fundamentally stands, and awaits a *material answer*...Undoubtedly, Brunner, in this book, says that which also Gogarten and I have in our own hearts against the theology on which we grew up, and Brunner says it much more clearly, more strikingly, and more obviously that we do...Others cannot get the better of "us" until one (fundamentally) proves (not only asserts) that Brunner has done the matter injustice. (53–54)

Barth then offers four "misgivings" he has about *Mysticism*. First and formally:

> How dangerous, I think, that Brunner's presentation, almost from the first page, takes on the character of a…clever, all-knowing and all-determined *prosecutor*, assigning "poor Schleiermacher"…the position of the defendant, and thus has turned it into a trial. (54)

This style can easily give one the impression that, "'in some way', violence and injustice has happened" (55).

Barth then offers three material criticisms. First, he argues that the term "mysticism" is much too restrictive to do justice to such a complex thinker as Schleiermacher (not to mention all of the nineteenth century theology which Brunner also attacks) (56–58).[124] Barth's second material criticism concerns Brunner's oft-repeated phrase "Biblical-Reformation thinking" (58–61). It is Barth's contention that Brunner "has not developed and grounded his *own historical position*" (58). It is fine for Brunner to cite Plato, Paul, Luther, Calvin, Kant and Kierkegaard, but one cannot simply assert that behind these names, under the term "Biblical-Reformation thinking", there exists a fixed theological unity. Barth agrees with Brunner that, in fact, Schleiermacher does not develop a "Biblical-Reformation" theology. But—"*so long as we still have a doctrine of the Church*"—one cannot simply write off Schleiermacher from "*theological fellowship*" without doing so "directly in the form of the *exposition of scripture*" (60).

Barth saves his weightiest criticism for the end:

> I confess that I cannot get past a sentence in a book which, in other respects, I like as little as Brunner does—that is the concluding word of the well-known book on Schleiermacher by Heinrich Stolz.[125] It goes: "Schleiermacher does not succeed everywhere; but the achievement as a whole is so great *that its stability can be threatened only through a corresponding opposing achievement, not through a single pointed criticism*". (61)

This need for a "corresponding opposing achievement" is not only daunting —it implies a fearful judgment on the Reformation:

> I ask myself if Brunner—and here my misgivings with his book are the most dense —…has brought to his readers' awareness just how *fearful* the historical situation is? If one accepts his judgment of Schleiermacher, is one aware of the unheard of (nearly "eschatological") historical *gap* before which one stands, and the unheard of historical *task* one faces as a Protestant theologian…? Isn't Brunner, in his occupation with Schleiermacher, wrong in his lack of faith in the historical *power* of Reformation truth and, even more, in a lack of faith in the rule of divine *providence* and leading of the Christian Church—if it stands thus with Schleiermacher, cannot Reformation truth only be understood as *judged in wrath* also? Brunner is much too certain, much too plucky, much too racy with his slogan "Word *contra*

Mysticism!" (62)

One cannot simply "dispose of" Schleiermacher, Barth argues:

> The Schleiermacherian heresy is no accidental single appearance, but it is the gi-
> gantic representative of a false development which began not that far from the
> Reformation itself. Is it not then clear that an "equivalent", an energetic, serious
> Yes must exist in order to carry a real "disposing" No over-against Schleiermacher
> —that is, a theological *revolution* which in its depth and energy is not less than
> the Reformation itself? (63)

Barth concludes that what must happen today is for theologians to be rightly
"alarmed" by the "*hubris* of three centuries", with the realization that this
necessarily entails being alarmed with themselves too.

> And only in this state of being alarmed should then, perhaps, the attack against
> the false gods of our age be launched, so that the attack would really come "from
> the side of eschatology" and not from somewhere else...Brunner's intelligent and
> knowledgeable, *apropos* and commendable book is to me in this sense too "un-
> alarmed". I know and reflect upon the fact that, in other respects, I myself have
> also already failed, in the same way, of being "unalarmed". (64)

It is not possible within the limits of this book to investigate Barth's on-
going theological dialogue with Schleiermacher.[126] However, one can say
that, despite the obvious softening of his polemic and his growth in appreciation of Schleiermacher, Barth's fundamental material opposition to Schleiermacher remained identical to that of Brunner's in *Mysticism*: in the place
of "distance" is continuity, in the place of faith is feeling, and there is no
secure place (formally or materially) for the Word of God. Throughout his
life, Barth consistently expressed his fundamental disagreement with Schleiermacher's achievement.[127]

It is true that Barth also repeated his criticisms of Brunner's *Mysticism*
throughout his life: the inadequacy of the term "mysticism",[128] the inappro-
priately triumphant "disposing" of Schleiermacher,[129] and the vague citing
of "Biblical-Reformation" thinking.[130] However, Barth's continuing criticism of *Mysticism* in no way signified a "turning-point" in the Barth–Brunner relationship.[131] Along with his criticism of *Mysticism*, Barth also continued to praise Brunner's book.[132] The ambiguity of Barth's appraisal of
Brunner's work on Schleiermacher is clearly revealed in a 1960 interview
with Barth.[133]

> Finally, I [Tice] showed him my summary of his Schleiermacher critique.[134] After
> he read it over carefully...I asked, "Is it a fair treatment?" He replied, "Not com-
> pletely. It is correct, but I don't like the impression it leaves. It makes me look

like a lawyer accusing him, doesn't show that I love him as my neighbor...Never
have I done such a thing as Brunner. After his book, I said to him we should get
together and study the matter. He said he couldn't [and deep, flushed emotion
crept into Barth's face, halfway between tears of sorrow and rage], that he had
burned his papers! He was done with him! [A sweep of the arm, a look of extreme
disgust.] Imagine! For me, Schleiermacher is present, within the church, my comrade, the finest of them all!"[135]

Several months before "Brunners Schleiermacherbuch" appeared in
Zwischen den Zeiten, Brunner received the proofs from Thurneysen, read
them "with a little anxiety", and responded to Barth.[136] He readily concedes
Barth's formal objection:

> I never had a good conscience while I wrote the book; the "feeling, that injustice
> has happened" never left me, no matter how often I tried to justify it to myself...
>   Thus I was not surprised by your criticism from this side, and I must grant it...
> I feel that I was much too outspoken, acting too certain and confident of victory.

However, Brunner does not accept Barth's material criticisms. First, he argues that Barth has fixated on the term "mysticism" to the exclusion of the
other terms Brunner used to describe Schleiermacher (e.g., cultural-Protes-
tantism). Second, Brunner rejects Barth's suggestion that the book should
have been a more objective presentation of Schleiermacher's theology:

> For me, Schleiermacher is not the first thing which is important in the entire mat-
> ter. Therefore the objective presentation which you desire...was not a goal which
> I considered. I doubt whether something so general as that could be understood in
> the current intellectual situation.

Third, while Brunner grants that his undeveloped citation of the Reformers
"was a very questionable action", he argues that "for me it was a question
here less of argument than of elucidation. Without the contrast I did not
trust myself to make anything clear". Finally, Brunner rejects out of hand
Barth's suggestion that he should have drawn from Schleiermacher's sermons: "You know well enough that one can read almost anything that one
wants to out of the sermons".
      After agreeing again with Barth's charge of "triumphalism", Brunner
shares how he sees their respective roles in their theological alliance:

> Indeed, I must almost say this: in general, I may only venture my work because
> you always stand in reserve. It is as if *the* responsibility which I must bear myself
> as a pastor (as well as a lecturer), as a theological writer I unconsciously may or
> must roll off onto you. Do you find this separation of powers incorrect? It seems
> to me that there are many things which *you* should not write but that absolutely
> must be written. Historical analogies come to mind: not for all the world would I

like to play the role of "Melancthon" in our movement; but by all means say "Calvin" (distinguished from Luther only according to formal matters) and you have formulated a necessary thing, which is only as good as long as it is deniable... I will always carry out this denial quietly; but I lack the power or (what is the same thing) the authority to make this denial publicly. You will have to be eco- nomical with your power in making this denial. In this sense I would like to say: this is the ultimate task of "Barth"—he, unfortunately, must constantly cast off "Brunner" publicly, even though "Brunner" constantly gets up and comes back for more...But this doesn't cause me difficulty...—the engine can run fine at hot temperatures as long as the radiator works.

The final word on *Mysticism* and "Brunners Schleiermacherbuch" comes from Barth in a letter to Thurneysen on December 8, 1924.[137] Barth en- closes a letter from Brunner to Georg Merz concerning Barth's review, which Merz had passed on to Barth. Barth comments:

My review has made [Brunner] a little colicky, since he devoured the booklet like John of Patmos (Rev. 10:9–10); this is thoroughly in order...I certainly do not want to treat him badly, and I very much value his cleverness. But why does he have such little clarity with his intelligence?

Summary

This chapter has indicated the complexity and ambiguity of the Barth–Brun- ner relationship in the years 1919–1924. Without a doubt, they saw each other as theological allies, fighting on the common front against Neo- Protestantism while trying to bring the Blumhardt/Kutter God-centered theology to the fore. However, what Barth and Brunner held materially in common began, in this period, to be over-shadowed by what they did not share: Barth's Overbeck-inspired dialectical theology of distance *vs.* Brun- ner's deep philosophical affinity first for Neo-Kantianism, then for Ebner's I–Thou philosophy. This difference is exemplified by their common but different appropriation of Kierkegaard—Barth responded to Kierkegaard's doctrine of God (as wholly Other, *incognito*, known in paradox), while Brunner took over his doctrine of faith and anthropology (the leap, the mo- ment, despair, participant *vs.* spectator).

The Barth–Brunner correspondence is especially helpful in revealing this underlying lack of unity, particularly Brunner's letter of September 2, 1920 concerning Overbeck. This letter sums up the contrasts between Barth and Brunner at the end of 1920: Barth was more radical-dialectical, Brunner was more reforming-critical; for Barth, the enemy to be attacked was reli- gion/Christianity, while for Brunner, the enemy is improperly grounded philosophy. As the correspondence further shows, it was not until Brunner began receiving Barth's proofs of *Romans II* in May 1921—five months after *Experience, Knowledge and Faith* was written and presented to the University of Zurich—that the meaning of Barth's radical dialectic began to affect him. Consequently, Brunner's writings through 1921 "had no great part in the spiritual birth of dialectical theology itself"; they were an "accompanying phenomenon".[138] Contrary to the opinion of the majority of Brunner scholars,[139] Brunner's "dialectical" period cannot be considered to have begun until 1922, with "The Limits of Humanity". However, although "Limits" reveals Brunner at his most dialectical, it is a mistake to cite this as evidence that Brunner had made a "dialectical turn". Rather, "Limits"—written fresh from the impact of *Romans II*—is where one sees the strongest impact of Barth's radical dialectic on Brunner's thinking.[140]

Barth's dialectical distance ruptured Brunner's confidence in Neo-Kantian philosophy into a crisis at the beginning of 1922. However, following immediately on its heels, the appearance of Ebner's "I–Thou" philosophy allowed Brunner to reconstruct the Idealistic theme of relation while respecting the Barthian distance. Although Ebner's thought struck at the heart of Brunner's Neo-Kantian philosophy, "Ebner's influence changed nothing" of Brunner's "fundamental view that there exists a dialectical relationship of completion between 'critical philosophy' and revelation".[141] Brunner's quick embrace of Ebner opens him up to the charge that he did not really understand the radical nature of Barth's No to all bridge-building. Did Brunner simply exchange Neo-Kantianism for Ebnerianism?[142]

The Barth–Thurneysen correspondence documents Brunner's ambiguous standing within "dialectical theology": Barth can both write "I feel like I am at cross-purposes with him...without being able to say precisely what the issue really is",[143] and, at other times, include Brunner within "the circle of our friends and 'fellow-seekers of the truth'".[144] The Barth–Brunner correspondence of May 1921 also reveals the difficulty Barth and Brunner had in establishing a close *personal* relationship. Brunner wrote about his first lectures at Zurich with evident excitement, certainly in part because it meant that he was not being left behind by Barth's move to the academic world. But Barth squashed Brunner's enthusiasm, hitting again on a sore point of controversy—Brunner's affinity for Idealism, and philosophy in general. One can only assume that Barth intended his May 14, 1921 postcard to be a note of congratulations; nonetheless, it included a few barbs. The sensitive Brunner was upset by this response, and turned to Thurneysen for his intervention, as well as accusing Barth of a unnecessary narrowmindedness ("all clocks must point the same way"). By this point, Barth was fed up with all of Brunner's touchiness, and in a less than conciliatory way ("Don't take me—and yourself—so bloody seriously!") terminated the discussion. This personal difficulty—Barth's tactlessness, Brunner's sensitivity—will characterize their correspondence throughout the period covered in this book.

In 1919–1924, Barth and Brunner were not developing in concert. For Barth there were two decisive developments. First, his exposure to Kierkegaard and Overbeck led him to bring the ontological and epistemological distance between God and humanity to the front of his theology. Second, with his move to the academic world in Göttingen, he began to develop a sense for the contributions of historical theology—both the Reformers *and even Schleiermacher*—for his "corrective theology". For Brunner, on the other hand, this period was more a time of "staying the course". His focus remained on the philosophical issues underlying theology, and the existential-anthropological issues of coming to faith. This remained in the forefront of his writings from *Experience, Knowledge and Faith* to "The Limits of Humanity" to *Mysticism and the Word*. However, during this period he received two sharp nudges: a powerful (but ultimately temporary) push by Barth towards a radical dialectic, and a persuasive appeal from Ebner, which Brunner seemed to appropriate as a way to have his cake (Barthian dialectic) and eat it too (remaining true to the *relation* posited in Idealism).

Barth and Brunner were united as theological allies in the period 1919–1924 because they shared a common front: they left Neo-Protestant theology behind, and were forging a renewal of evangelical theology based on revelation and an emphasis on God's transcendence. This alliance would remain firm until 1930. However, serious cracks would begin emerging from 1924–1928—in this next period, they stood "back to back".

NOTES

1. *Christentum und Kultur*, ed. by Carl Albrecht Bernoulli (Basel: Benno Schwabe, 1919). Overbeck was professor of church history at Jena (1864–1870) and of critical theology at Basel (1870–1897).
2. Quoted in Busch, p. 115. See also *Barth–Thurneysen I*, KB: January 5, 1920, p. 364: "Our Melchizedek has appeared—Overbeck".
3. "Unsettled Questions for Theology Today", in *Theology and Church*, trans. by Louis Pettibone Smith (London: SCM, 1962), pp. 55–73 (p. 58).
4. *Christentum und Kultur*, p. 16.
5. Jüngel, "Barth's Theological Beginnings", p. 56. See also Barth, *Romans II*, pp. 3–4 .
6. Jüngel, "Barth's Theological Beginnings", p. 65.
7. *Romans II*, p. 10.
8. See: Torsten Bohlin, "Luther, Kierkegaard und die dialektische Theologie", *ZThK*, N.F. 7 (1926), 163–198, 268–279; Graham White, "Karl Barth's Theological Real-

ism", *Neue Zeitschrift für systematische Theologie und Philosophie*, 26 (1984), 54–70
(p. 58); Robert L. Reymond, *Brunner's Dialectical Encounter* (Philadelphia: Presbyterian and Reformed, 1967), p. 7; Torrance, *Karl Barth*, pp. 44–45. W. Lowe notes
that Barth drops the adjective "infinite" from Kierkegaard's formula in the body of
Romans II, since "infinite" implies a difference in quantity, not in kind ("Barth as
Critic of Dualism", *SJT*, 41 (1988), 377–395 (pp. 382–383)).

9. McCormack, p. 239.
10. See *Rev.Theology*, KB: May 31, 1920, p. 51. See also *Romans II*, pp. 38, 229.
11. "Autobiographical Sketches", p. 155. In *WGWM*, pp. 51–96.
12. See also *Romans II*, pp. 42, 57, 69, 169–170, 229–270.
13. See *Rev.Theology*, KB: October 27, 1920, p. 53.
14. Ibid.
15. Pp. 29, 38–39, 98, 369, 422–423. See Beintker, pp. 32–34. See also James C. Living-
    ston, *Modern Christian Thought* (New York: Macmillan, 1971), p. 328, and Ernst-
    Wilhelm Wendebourg, *Die Christusgemeinde und ihr Herr* (Berlin: Lutherisches Ver-
    laghaus, 1967), p. 226.
16. See pp. 43, 330–332.
17. "The word 'dialectic' was used, not in the Hegelian sense of a thesis and an antithe-
    sis united in a higher synthesis, but in the Kierkegaardian sense of an absolute para-
    dox" (Arthur C. Cochrane, *The Church's Confession under Hitler* (Philadelphia:
    Westminster, 1962), p. 64).
18. Ruschke, pp. 108–109.
19. "The Christian's Place in Society", in *WGWM*, pp. 272–327 (p. 282).
20. See Paul L. Lehmann, "The Changing Course of a Corrective Theology", *Theology
    Today*, 13 (1956), 332–357 (p. 341). See also Hermann Volk, "Die Christologie bei
    Karl Barth und Emil Brunner", in *Das Konzil von Chalkedon*, ed. by Aloys Grillmei-
    er and Hermann Bacht, 3 vols (Würzburg: Echter-Verlag, 1954), III, 613–673, p. 614;
    Winzeler, p. 155.
21. See Robert W. Jenson, "Karl Barth", in *The Modern Theologians*, ed. by David F.
    Ford, 2 vols (Oxford: Blackwell, 1989), I, pp. 23–49 (p. 28).
22. See also p. 229. Barth's "No" was "an attempt to let God himself in all his justify-
    ing grace call the bluff of civilized European man, in order to induce him to think so-
    berly" (Torrance, "Introduction", in *Theology and Church*, pp. 7–54 (p. 22)).
    Ruschke, pp. 179, 192; George Hunsinger, *How to Read Karl Barth* (Oxford: Oxford
    University Press, 1991), pp. 30–32; Jerome Hamer, *Karl Barth*, trans. by Dominic
    M. Maruca (Westminster, MD: Newman, 1962).
24. G.C. Berkouwer, *The Triumph of Grace in the Theology of Karl Barth*, trans. by
    Harry R. Boer (Grand Rapids: Eerdmans, 1954), p. 191.
25. Ruschke, p. 17. See Barth's treatment of faith and the "new man" (pp. 149–164 and
    the Church (pp. 340–361, especially pp. 360–361).
26. Hans Frei, "Niebuhr's Theological Background", in *Faith and Ethics*, ed. by Paul
    Ramsey (New York: Harper and Row, 1957), pp. 9–64 (pp. 40–41). See also Ralph

Common Front (1919–1924)   57

P. Crimmann, *Karl Barths frühe Publikationen und ihre Rezeption* (Bern: Peter Lang, 1981), p. 145; and Ruschke, pp. 113–118.

27. Smart correctly observes that although Kierkegaard's influence is more obvious because of the generous use of his terminology in *Romans II*, it is Overbeck who was the more decisive and long-lasting influence on Barth (p. 104).

28. *Credo*, no translator given (New York: Scribners, 1962), p. 185.

29. See Busch (pp. 119–120) for a summary of the key changes in the second edition.

30. Ruschke, p. 179.

31. Robinson, "Introduction", p. 23.

32. For information on the Bergli (located above Oberrieden on Lake Zurich, seven miles south of Zurich), see Busch, p. 145.

33. *Barth–Brunner*, EB: September 2, 1920 (#19), pp. 42–53.

34. Brunner, "Spiritual Autobiography", p. 241.

35. For a description of Kierkegaard's stages, see Frederick Copleston, *A History of Philosophy*, 9 vols (London: Burns, Oates & Washbourne, 1946–1975), VII, pp. 342–344.

36. Noland P. Murray, "Personalism in the Ethical Theory of Emil Brunner" (unpublished doctoral thesis, Duke University, 1963), p. 26; Mary Warnock, *Existentialism* (Oxford: Oxford University Press, 1970), pp. 344, 347; R. Roessler, *Person und Glaube* (Munich: Chr. Kaiser, 1965), p. 26.

37. Reymond, p. 9. See also Hermann Volk, *Emil Brunners Lehre von der ursprünglichen Gottebenbildlichkeit des Menschen* (Emsdetten: Verlagsanstalt Heinr. & J. Lechte, 1939), p. 9.

38. "I began at an early age to search for a scientifically satisfying formulation of my faith…The epistemological works of Kant…kindled real enthusiasm in me…I have generally held to the critical standards of Kant up to this day" ("Intellectual Autobiography", p. 5).

39. Johanna Konrad, "Zum Problem der philosophischen Grundlegung bei Emil Brunner", *ZThK*, N.F. 12 (1931), 192–216 (pp. 194, 214). See also Paul K. Jewett, "Ebnerian Personalism and its influence on Emil Brunner's Theology", *Westminster Theological Journal*, 14 (1951–1952), 113–147 (p. 128, note 56).

40. Brunner, "Ist die sogenannte kritische Theologie wirklich kritische?" *KfrS*, 36 (1921), 101–102, 105–106 (p. 106).

41. See: Copleston, VII, pp. 361–362; Mariano Campo, "Natorp", trans. by Robert M. Connolly, and Lewis White Beck, "Neo-Kantianism", in *The Encyclopedia of Philosophy*, ed. by Paul Edwards, 8 vols (London: Collier-Macmillan, 1967), V, pp. 445–448, 468–473; Simon Fisher, *Revelatory Positivism?* (Oxford: Oxford University Press, 1988).

42. "Sogenannte kritische Theologie", p. 105. See also comments on Brunner's *Experience, Knowledge and Faith*, above pp. 32ff.

43. Natorp's book on religion, published in 1894, is entitled—with a clear allusion to Kant—*Religion innerhalb der Grenzen der Humanität* (*Religion Within the Limits of*

Humanity).

44. Johnson, pp. 78–80. Fisher (pp. 12, 341) maintains that though Barth also read Herrmann Cohen and Natorp while at Marburg, Neo-Kantianism was mediated to him through Wilhelm Herrmann. See also Crimmann, p. 15; Eberhard Busch, "Dialectical Theology", trans. by H. Martin Rumscheidt, *Canadian Journal of Theology*, 16 (1970), 165–74 (p. 167); Dietrich Bonhoeffer, "Die Geschichte der systematischen Theologie des 20. Jahrhunderts", in *Gesammelte Schriften*, ed. by Eberhard Bethge, 6 vols (Munich: Chr. Kaiser, 1958–1974), V, pp. 181–227, (pp. 221–222).

45. *Erlebnis, Erkenntnis und Glaube* (Tübingen: JCB Mohr, 1921), pp. 83–84. See also Christof Gestrich, *Neuzeitliches Denken and die Spaltung der dialektischen Theologie* (Tübingen: JCB Mohr, 1977), pp. 28–30.

46. In "The Poverty of Theology" ("Das Elend der Theologie", *KfrS*, 35 (1920), 197–199, 201–203), Brunner attacks the poverty of Neo-Protestant "critical-historical theology". The article explores four forms of modern theology's fundamentally naturalistic axiom: causalism (198), empiricism, historicism (201), and psychologism (202). Brunner's thesis is straightforward: "This axiom (i.e. world-view) is false and contradicts the idea of God in the Bible" (198). Brunner puts himself on the attack against modern theology again in "Sogenannte kritische Theologie". His main point is that "critical theology" is *not* critical, because, through its empiricism and psychologism, it is completely bound within the categories of causal-science (105). Brunner argues that the historical-critical method stops with a supposed "objectivity, and never moves on to the question of *meaning*" (105–106). He ends with a Kantian call to "return to the truly critical scientific concept of transcendental Idealism" (106).

47. *Erlebnis, Erkenntnis und Glaube.* Citations are from the 2nd rev. edn (Tübingen: JCB Mohr, 1923). The prefaces of both Brunner's *Experience, Knowledge and Faith* and Barth's *Romans II* are dated September 1921.

48. "I have made a light revision based on the important knowledge and insight which I gained from Karl Barth's second *Der Römerbrief* and Gogarten's *Die religiöse Entscheidung* [Jena: Eugen Diederichs, 1921]. I can only hope that this book is able to say (in its imperfect expressions) what it intends in agreement with them" (iv).

49. Brunner singles out Plato, Kant and Kierkegaard as examples of philosophers who adhered to this "fundamental principle of Idealism" (pp. 79–80).

50. Faith is treated in four chapters: "Pure Objectivity" (*vs.* subjectivity), "The Fissure" (*vs.* psychologism), "The Original" (*vs.* historicism) and "The Irrational" (*vs.* intellectualism).

51. In this section, Brunner also expresses his doubts about Overbeck's radical critique of Christianity (see note 1, p. 107).

52. Volk, *Gottebenbildlichkeit*, pp. 11–12.

53. Ibid., p. 9.

54. Nonetheless, Barth was pleased with *Experience, Knowledge and Faith* (*Barth–Brunner*, KB: November 30, 1921 (#30), pp. 65–67). Barth particularly appreciated how Brunner clarified Barth's position for the public: "You have performed for me

and others the very important service of once again clarifying for me my Whence? and Whither?" See also Barth's praise of Brunner's book in *Barth–Thurneysen II*, KB: December 11, 1921, p. 21.

55. *Barth–Brunner*, EB: May 12, 1921 (#24), pp. 58f.
56. Natorp had given a lecture at the Aarau Student Conference in March 1921 (*Barth–Brunner*, KB: March 14, 1921 (#20), p. 53, note 1).
57. *Barth–Brunner*, KB: May 14, 1921 (#25), pp. 59f.
58. Ibid., EB: May 15, 1921 (#26), pp. 60f.
59. Ibid., KB: May 26, 1921 (#27), pp. 61f.
60. Brunner sent Barth's May 14 postcard to Thurneysen, "with the request to use your influence with our friend so that he will restrain himself for the love of God" *Barth–Brunner*, KB: May 26, 1921 (#27), p. 61, note 1.
61. Quoted in Busch, p. 120. See *Barth–Brunner*, EB: January 5, 1922 (#32), p. 71: "You cannot escape creating a school, despite your best efforts to be so critically opposed to this inevitability. Besides, why should you not be heard, and why should not many people notice that here, once again, *theo*-logy is pursued?"
62. Barth's 1922 address, "The Word of God and the Task of the Ministry" is the classic text on Barth's dialectical method (in *WGWM*, pp. 183–217). The argument is clearly set forth in its three thesis statements: "*We ought to speak of God*" (p. 186); "*We are human, however, and so cannot speak of God*" (p. 198); "*We ought therefore to recognize both* that we should speak of God and yet cannot, *and by that very recognition give God the glory*" (p. 212).
63. For summaries of the positive program of dialectical theology, see: Wilhelm Pauck, "The Church-Historical Setting of Brunner's Theology", in Kegley, pp. 25–38 (pp. 35–37); Volk, *Gottebenbildlichkeit*, pp. 3–5; Eberhard Jüngel, "Von der Dialektik zur Analogie", in *Barth-Studien*, pp. 127–179 (pp. 140–141); Lorenz Volken, *Der Glaube bei Emil Brunner* (Freiburg: Paulusverlag, 1947), pp. 3–4; Ernst Neubauer, "Die Theologie der 'Krisis' und des 'Wortes'", *ZThK*, N.F. 7 (1926), 1–36; Paul Tillich, "What is wrong with the 'Dialectic Theology'?", in *Paul Tillich*, ed. by Mark Kline Taylor (London: Collins, 1987), pp. 104–115.
64. Gogarten was a Lutheran pastor from north Germany. It was the study of Luther that profoundly re-directed Gogarten's thought onto lines similar to Barth's. He reacted positively to Barth's *Romans I*, and met Barth for the first time at the 1919 Tambach Conference. Gogarten's own fame came the following year, through the article "Die Krisis unserer Kultur", *Christliche Welt*, 34 (1920), 770–777, 786–791. Barth viewed Gogarten as "a dread-nought on our side against our opponents", "a first-class cruiser of the best Dutch kind, doubtless the man…who will give the call to battle in Germany" (quoted in Busch, p. 117). However, from the beginning, the alliance of Barth and Gogarten was never a comfortable one. Barth frequently expressed to Thurneysen his doubts about the direction in which Gogarten's theology was developing: see *Rev.Theology*, KB: February 26, 1922, pp. 88–89; October 7, 1922, pp. 110; February 18, 1923, pp. 121–122; July 21, 1924, pp. 188; July 31,

1924, pp. 189–190. For information on Gogarten, see Lange, as well as John McConnachie, "The Barthian School: 3. Friedrich Gogarten", *Expository Times*, 43 (1932), pp. 391–395, 461–466.

65. Busch, pp. 113, 147. Although neither an editor nor founder of *Zwischen den Zeiten*, Rudolf Bultmann was also considered to be one of the five pillars of dialectical theology (along with Barth, Thurneysen, Gogarten and Brunner). Barth and Bultmann's "common theme was originally the Word of God and human existence, certainly with different emphases, but both were originally in view" (Hans Grass, "Karl Barth und Marburg", in *Aus Theologie und Kirche* (Marburg: N.G. Elwert, 1988), pp. 212–221 (p. 220)).

66. *Barth–Thurneysen II*, ET: February 12, 1923, p. 141.

67. Ibid., KB: February 16, 1923, p. 145.

68. In "Intellectual Autobiography" (p. 9), Brunner points to his year in the United States (1919–1920) as the reason that he never became an "intimate member of the circle" around Barth.

69. H.R. MacKintosh, "The Swiss Group", *Expository Times*, 36 (1924), 73–75 (p. 73).

70. Barth, "The Humanity of God", trans. by John Newton Thomas, in *The Humanity of God* (Atlanta: John Knox, 1960), pp. 37–65 (pp. 37, 40–41).

71. Jüngel, "Von Dialektik zur Analogie", pp. 141–142; Volk, *Gottebenbildlichkeit*, pp. 6–7; Jüngel, "Barth's Life and Work", pp. 41–42.

72. Quoted in Busch, p. 126. For Barth's feelings of being overwhelmed in his new post, see: *Rev.Theology*, KB: November 18, 1921, p. 76; KB: December 11, 1921, pp. 79–80; and "Autobiographical Sketches", p. 156.

73. See *Rev.Theology*, KB: January 22, 1922, pp. 81–82. For a reconstruction of Barth's teaching schedule, covering his entire academic career in Göttingen, Münster, Bonn and Basel, see David Allen Fraser, "Foundations for Christian Social Ethics" (unpublished doctoral thesis, Vanderbuilt University, 1986), pp. 447–450.

74. *Rev.Theology*, KB: January 22, 1922, p. 82; see also ibid., KB: June 8, 1922, p. 101.

75. Quoted in Busch, p. 143.

76. In *WGWM*, pp. 97–135.

77. In *WGWM*, pp. 136–182.

78. *Barth–Brunner*, EB: May 12, 1921 (#24), p. 58.

79. Ibid., EB: January 5, 1922 (#32), pp. 68–72.

80. In *Fear and Trembling and Sickness unto Death*, trans. by Walter Lowrie, 2nd edn (Princeton: Princeton University Press, 1954), pp. 141–262.

81. *Das Wort und die geistigen Realitäten*, in *Schriften*, ed. by Franz Seyr, 3 vols (Munich: Kösel, 1963–1965), I, pp. 75–342.

82. Martin Buber published *Ich und Du* a year after Ebner's book appeared (in *I and Thou*, 2nd edn, trans. by Roland Gregor Smith (New York: Collier-Macmillan, 1958). Brunner's thinking was impacted by Ebner, not Buber—he did not read *Ich und Du* until 1927 ("Comments by Brunner", in I. John Hesselink, "Encounter in Japan", *Reformed Review*, 9 (1956), 12–33 (pp. 32–33)).

83. Volken, p. 17; Wilhelm Stolz, *Theologisch-dialektischer Personalismus und kirchliche Einheit* (Freiburg: Universitätsverlag, 1953), p. 7, note 2. For Kierkegaard's specific contribution, see Johnson, pp. 74–75.

84. Yrjö Salakka, *Person und Offenbarung in der Theologie Emil Brunners* (Helsinki, 1960), pp. 90–91; E.P. Heideman, *The Relation of Revelation and Reason in E. Brunner and H. Bavinck* (Assen, Netherlands: Koninklijke Van Gorcum, 1959), p. 2; Alistair E. McGrath, *The Making of Modern German Christology* (Oxford: Basil Blackwell, 1986), pp. 94–126 (p. 101).

85. For this summary, see Volken, p. 14.

86. "The I and the Thou are the spiritual realities of life. To develop the consequences and the knowledge that the I exists in its relation to the Thou and not outside it, that ...gives a new task to [philosophy]" (p. 85).

87. Volken, p. 16; Murray, p. 31.

88. Volken, pp. 16–17.

89. Roessler, p. 24; Salakka, p. 92.

90. "Comments", p. 33. In March 1922, Brunner thanked Ebner for *Das Wort*, commenting on "our deep spiritual community" (in Ebner, *Schriften*, III, p. 456). See also a February 1923 letter from Brunner to Ebner (ibid., p. 501), where Brunner remarks on the "profound commonality of our findings". Commenting about Ebner's insights at the end of this life, Brunner maintains that the "I–Thou philosophy is not philosophy at all, but the center of Biblical revelation, made evident as such and formulated theologically: the name of God" ("Reply to Interpretation and Criticism", trans. by Marle Hoyle Schroeder, in Kegly, pp. 325–352 (p. 341)).

91. Cited here from *Truth as Encounter: A New Edition*, trans. by Amandus W. Loos and David Cairns (London: SCM, 1964), pp. 114–118. "A certain inner disposition to dialogical thinking can be presupposed for Brunner, since in the early phase of his theology he was, like Ferdinand Ebner, a follower of the Bergsonian philosophy of life" (Scheld, p. 205). Brunner was supported in developing the implications of Ebnerian philosophy by Friedrich Gogarten, who stressed the social, inter-human implications of the "I–Thou" schema for ethics. See Gogarten's *Glaube und Wirklichkeit* (Jena: Eugen Diederichs, 1928), pp. 6, 9, 99; Mielke, pp. 26–27.

92. Murray, p. 29; Salakka, pp. 90–91; Horst Stephan, "Der Neue Kampf um Schleiermacher", *ZThK*, N.F. VI (1925), 159–215 (pp. 166–167).

93. This is Jewett's main argument, "Ebnerian Personalism" (see pp. 119–121, 125–126).

94. Brunner's ability to combine Ebner with Kierkegaard further confirms that the main thing Brunner heard from Kierkegaard was *not* the "infinite qualitative distinction" (*contra* Jewett, "Ebnerian Personalism", p. 119).

95. Barth expressed his suspicions about Ebner's philosophy as early as October 1922 in reference to Gogarten's I–Thou Christology (see *Rev.Theology*, October 7, 1922, p. 110).

96. For the earliest evidence of Ebner's influence on Brunner, see *Experience, Knowledge*

and Faith, pp. v, 119; *Mysticism and the Word*, pp. 89–94, p. 395, note 1 (see above, p. 46); and "The Fundamental Problem of Philosophy according to Kant and Kierkegaard" (see below, p. 71).

97. *Experience, Knowledge and Faith*, p. iv. See also *Barth–Brunner*, EB: May 12, 1921 (#24), pp. 58f.; August 23, 1921 (#28), pp. 62f. Brunner remained as pastor at the Obstalden church until 1924.

98. *Die Grenzen der Humanität* (Tübingen: JCB Mohr, 1922). Here cited from *Ein offenes Wort*, ed. by Rudolf Wehrli, 2 vols (TVZ, 1981), I, pp. 76–97. The title is a deliberate reference to Natorp's *Religion innerhalb der Grenzen der Humanität*.

99. Brunner writes that Schleiermacher sees apologetics as "the necessity of debating with culture..., the search for a proof of God in some form, the anchoring of religious things in the necessities of reason. In the last century, the pressure from this side was so strong that faith could not resist the temptation. It *was* falsified in that the question of God became a question of "and" and "also"...The co-ordination is unavoidable. God is robbed of His own uniqueness" (94).

100. This style is remarkably similar to the "apologetic interest" he criticizes in Schleiermacher.

101. Except for Ebner.

102. *Barth–Brunner*, EB: June 9, 1923 (#33), pp. 72f.

103. Ibid., KB: June 12, 1923 (#34), pp. 73f.

104. Ibid., EB: August 27, 1923 (#35), p. 75; EB: Without date (the editors place it after Brunner's letter of August 27 and before Barth's reply of October 4) (#37), pp. 75f.; KB: October 4, 1923 (#37), pp. 78–80.

105. *Die Mystik und das Wort* (Tübingen: JCB Mohr, 1924). The subtitle of the book is "The opposition between the modern understanding of religion and Christian faith as represented in the theology of Schleiermacher". For an in-depth treatment of Brunner's view of Schleiermacher, from his doctoral dissertation (1912) through *Myticism and the Word*, see James K. Graby, "The Significance of Friedrich Schleiermacher in the Development of the Theology of Emil Brunner" (unpublished doctoral thesis, Drew University, 1966), pp. 21–166.

106. Brunner defines Schleiermacher's mysticism on pp. 55–56.

107. After this point is made, Brunner lays out an anthropology influenced by his reading of Ebner: "The word is the fundamental fact of the spirit, even if we take 'word' first in its general sense...That humanity has the word is the origin of its rationality, its not-destroyed image of God, and the sum of the Gospel of redemption" (p. 90). The concept of word is also fundamental to a correct explanation of ethics: "It is the address, the imperative,...which establishes morality. Ideas do not call out to me. They are timeless and objective. But the moral address grasps me personally and makes me a person for the first time. I am—in the sense of being human—first through this, that I receive the address as being a *responsible* [*ver*-antwort*liche*] subject over-against it. Conversation has begun. Address means answer [*Antwort*]" (p. 94). Brunner concludes that this Ebnerian anthropology faithfully expresses the bib-

lical-Reformation doctrine of humanity (pp. 97–98).

108. "Continuity is constitutive of Schleiermacher's method" (345). Also see pp. 352, 357–358.
109. "With this "God alone" is said everything that they intended. Their life work is nothing but a commentary on this one word" (p. 391).
110. Bernard E. Meland, "The Thought of Emil Brunner", *Journal of Bible and Religion*, 16 (1948), 165–168 (p. 167).
111. See pp. 89-94; Bouillard, p. 179.
112. Gestrich, *Neuzeitliches Denken*, p. 352.
113. *Barth–Thurneysen II*, KB: October 13, 1923, p. 193.
114. *Barth–Brunner*, KB: October 27, 1923 (#39), pp. 83–85.
115. Barth's doubts about Brunner's all-out attack are also expressed in *Barth–Thurneysen II*, KB: October 31, 1923, p. 196.
116. *Barth–Brunner*, KB: January 18, 1924 (#40), pp. 85–87.
117. *Barth–Thurneysen II,* ET: January 30, 1924, p. 217.
118. *Rev.Theology*, KB: February 5, 1924, pp. 167–168. Barth repeats similar concerns in ibid., KB: March 4, 1924, p. 175.
119. *The Theology of Schleiermacher*. For a study of Barth's lectures, see John H. Thiel, "Barth's Early Interpretation of Schleiermacher", in *Barth and Schleiermacher*, ed. by James O. Duke and Robert F. Streetman (Philadelphia: Fortress, 1988), pp. 11–22.
120. See also p. 204.
121. Pp. 217, 219–220.
122. *Barth–Thurneysen II*, KB: February 5, 1924, p. 225.
123. "Brunners Schleiermacherbuch", *ZZ*, VIII (1924), 49–64.
124. Specifically, Barth maintains that to be faithful "to the nature of the dark *riddle* of Schleiermacher" (p. 58), one must also point to the decisive importance of Schleiermacher's concern for apologetics, ethics, and cultural-religion.
125. *Christentum und Wissenschaft in Schleiermachers Glaubenslehre*, 2nd edn (Leipzig, 1911), p. 121.
126. For Barth's later works on Schleiermacher, see: "Schleiermacher's Celebration of Christmas" (136–158) and "Schleiermacher" (159–199) in *Theology and Church*; "Schleiermacher" in *Protestant Theology*, pp. 425–473; and "Concluding Unscientific Postscript". For analysis, see: James E. Davison, "Can God Speak a Word to Man?", *SJT*, 37 (1984), 189–211; Alice Collins, "Barth's relationship to Schleiermacher", *Studies in Religion*, 17 (1988), 213–224; Alasdair I.C. Heron, "Barth, Schleiermacher and the Task of Dogmatics", in Thompson, pp. 267–283; Duke & Streetman; Lütz.
127. See *Protestant Theology*, pp. 472–473; "Concluding Unscientific Postscript", p. 272.
128. *Protestant Theology*, p. 436; "Concluding Unscientific Postscript", p. 266.
129. "Concluding Unscientific Postscript", p. 266.

130. *Protestant Theology*, pp. 428–429. In his review, Barth also voiced suspicions about Brunner's reliance on Ebner's I–Thou philosophy: "Whether the branch onto which he throws himself (occasionally fairly far)—the Ebnerian theory of the 'Word'—is really capable of bearing this weight, I cannot judge" (p. 58, note 1). See also "Concluding Unscientific Postscript", p. 266.
131. *Contra* Gestrich, *Neuzeitliches Denken*, p. 345.
132. "Autobiographical Sketches", p. 155; *Protestant Theology*, p. 426; *The Theology of Schleiermacher*, pp. xvi–xvii.
133. Terrence N. Tice, "Interviews with Karl Barth and Reflections on His Interpretations of Schleiermacher", in Duke & Streetman, pp. 43–62. The interview cited is from July 28, 1960.
134. Tice's summary included the following sentence: "Like Brunner, Barth recognizes a strong mystical element in Schleiermacher's ideal for the religious life (and in fact there is scarcely a single negative element in Barth's critique which was not already clearly enunciated in Brunner's book), but he believes, against Brunner, that it is essentially subordinated to and determined by the task of conducting one's life in the world, above all in the world of culture" (p. 54).
135. Tice, p. 50. See also Lütz's insight (p. 169) that, after reading *Mysticism and the Word*, Barth realized that Brunner was not up to the challenge of attacking "the false gods of our age".
136. *Barth–Brunner*, EB: July 31, 1924 (#43), pp. 96–101.
137. *Barth–Thurneysen II*, p. 297.
138. Gestrich, *Neuzeitliches Denken*, pp. 27–28.
139. Scheld, p. 94; McGrath, p. 100; Mielke, pp. 24, 37; Johnson, pp. 83–90. Salakka (p. 62) and Volken (p. 8) also see *Experience, Knowledge and Faith* as the emergence of Brunner's dialectical period. However both Salakka (p. 105) and Volken (p. 9) note that Brunner is still carrying some previous philosophical baggage. Although they would not support this thesis as strongly as it is put here, both Volk (*Gottebenbildlichkeit*, pp. 9–12) and Neubauer (p. 15) also fail to see this work by Brunner as "dialectical".
140. Equally dialectical is Brunner's "Die Krisis der Religion", *KfrS*, 37 (1922), 65–66. Here Brunner appeals to Gogarten's *Die religiöse Entscheidung* rather than to Barth's *Romans II*.
141. Gestrich, *Neuzeitliches Denken*, p. 33.
142. Anders Nygren, "Emil Brunner's Doctrine of God", trans. by Gero Bauer, in Kegley, pp. 177–186 (pp. 181, 183, 185).
143. *Barth–Thurneysen I*, KB: May 11, 1919, p. 326. See also ibid., ET: May 20, 1921, p. 491.
144. Ibid., KB: May 30, 1921, p. 492.

CHAPTER THREE

Back-to-Back (1924–1928)
Dogmatic vs. Philosophical Theology

*You must take account of the fact that in my work there remains an "X" of which
you have not laid hold.*

(Barth to Brunner, March 1925)

*There are other tasks which also must be done, which you, rightfully, don't do at
present, but which I have taken up.*

(Brunner to Barth, December 1927)

Barth's First Dogmatics (1924–1925)

In becoming a professor of theology, Barth faced the task of developing a
constructive way of thinking theologically which could support his new
theological insights.[1] If *Romans II* was the "alarm" for theology to wake up
from its Neo-Protestant sleep, and if "The Need and Promise of Christian
Preaching" spoke of theology as a "marginal gloss" and a "pinch of spice",
the Professor of Reformed Theology now faced the challenge of developing
a dogmatic theology faithful to the reality of the "wholly other" God.[2]

> None of [what we learned from 1916 through 1920] involved as yet a Dogmatics
> with consideration of concept and method, but rather on the contrary how we
> would at that time have laughed at such possibilities. But the trouble has been that
> we have never been *silent* and now we are in for it: The confounded "Barth-
> movement"…wants to know where it goes from here and craves to hear from us
> the B and C that come after A. The foolish world marvels at my rise "from
> peddler to big businessman", but at times I…feel much more like declaring a
> liquidation…and relinquishing it to Emil Brunner, who, as a result of our clearance
> sale, would open up his own enterprising grocery store.[3]

Barth's first extended reflection about this task was prompted by a letter from Brunner.[4] In October of 1923, Brunner was nominated to fill the chair of *ordinarius* Professor of Systematic and Practical Theology at Zurich;[5] thus, he, too, was facing the task of preparing lectures in dogmatics for the 1924 summer semester.[6] In his letter, Brunner sets out the four major ways in which dogmatics has been done throughout church history: 1) based on a confessional text; 2) as biblical theology; 3) as history and sociology of religion; and 4) as speculative theology. Brunner states a preference for the confessional approach (since it makes it clear that a theologian works out of a specific faith commitment), and indicates that he's thinking about writing his dogmatics in explicit connection to Calvin's *Institutes*. Brunner asks for Barth's thoughts on the matter.

Barth responds quickly, welcoming this dialogue with Brunner:

> eventually it would be worth consideration and desirable if we could together aim for at least similar plans (and thus a similar matrix) for the upcoming *disciplined* Reformed teaching.[7]

Barth offers a larger "table of possibilities" than Brunner:

> 1. "Loci" in connection with *Romans* (Melancthon!)
> 2. Biblical Theology à la Beck
> 3. Speculative à la Biedermann
> 4. Scholastic (in place of Peter Lombard: Calvin's *Institutes*...or the Genevan Catechism of 1545)
> 5. "Prophetic", i.e. to be Calvin himself, to pound on the table, and, under constant control—1) through the Bible, 2) through the Early Church + Reformation —to go one's own chosen way
> 6. Confessional: the stuff of dogmatics is the "dogma"; if the degenerated modern-Reformed Church gives us nothing of this kind, then we clearly stand again at the *beginning* of the Reformed reformation. We have to ask which dogma was *there before* the confessions, and would come thus to the Apostles Creed. Confessional writings to be used *heuristically*. The authority of Scripture as the origin of all this stuff, obviously.
> 7. The clear mischief: Schleiermacher and everything which creeps and flies after him.

Barth's choice of dogmatic approaches is similar to Brunner's:

> #1 would be tempting, but I want to take the bull by the horns. For a long time, #4 appeared to me to be the only possibility. For the moment, I am inclined to a combination of #5 and 6...Thus it will be a question of finding a well thought-out ranking from above (revelation) to below (prophecy as the true meaning of the divine Word), into which, then, dogmatics fits into its (determined!) place. But how?[8]

Barth began his dogmatic lectures in the 1924 summer semester.[9] The first five paragraphs of *The Göttingen Dogmatics* are particularly relevant for this book. Barth defines dogmatics as the "scientific reflection on the Word of God which is spoken by God in revelation, which is recorded in the holy scripture...and which now both is and should be proclaimed and heard in Christian preaching" (summary statement, 3). Barth asserts that a prolegomena to dogmatics is not necessary in itself, but only because of the current theological situation:

> A science needs prolegomena when it is no longer sure of its presuppositions,... when it does not any longer...understand the self-evident things with which any science commences. (18)

Barth apologizes that "instead of drawing straight *from* the subject we must first speak *about* the subject, reaching an understanding with those to whom we speak...about the point from which we are doing dogmatics" (20). In §2, Barth argues that dogmatics is the task required by the Church as it receives the Word of God in preaching and asks the critical question "To what extent is it the *Word of God*?" (24).

The first chapter, entitled "The Word of God as Revelation" begins with paragraph §3—"*Deus dixit*" ("God speaks"). The Church's venture and obedient response of preaching is based only on the prior fact of God's speaking. After unpacking the meaning of God's speaking in §3.3,[10] Barth concludes the paragraph with a section on the situation of preacher (§3.4). Barth's point here is that it is not the world which challenges the church's preaching; rather it is the indirectness and hiddenness of "the *Deus dixit* that puts us in that exposed position" (64).

From the situation of the preacher, Barth next turns to "Man and his Question" (§4). As the Word of God is directed to humanity, so is preaching. But "what is man?" (§4.2). This is not a general question to be answered through an appeal to philosophy, because it asks "about the man who is presupposed by...revelation" (72). *This* person is a being "who is separated from God but should not be so"; he is a "pilgrim", one who is "not at home", whose being is "in contradiction" (72–73).[11]

After further exploring the nature of humanity's contradiction (§4.3), Barth confesses to the circular reasoning of this paragraph's summary statement.[12] Barth, however, defends *this* kind of circular argument (80–83). First, theology is necessarily "the begging of the question par excellence"—it must presuppose the actuality that God addresses humanity in revelation (this is theology's self-grounded axiom). Second, circular reasoning is acceptable for theology if it constantly moves in the proper direction: *from* God *to* humanity *back to* God (*vs.* modern theology, whose circular thought moves in the opposite direction). Thus, Christian preaching "must start with the presupposition that man knows, understands, and accepts God's Word", *not* with the contradiction—preaching is less telling new information and more a "reminding both him and myself that God is on the stage" (85).

Barth turns next to the content of God's Word by treating the Trinity (§5). Barth argues that Christian theologians have universally missed the crucial point that the failure to place the Trinity at the very beginning of dogmatics is to work with a general concept of God rather than to reflect upon the God who reveals himself in revelation (97–98). What, then, does the Trinity tell us about the God of revelation? In a statement indicating the fundamental continuity of Barth's thinking from *Romans II* to the *Church Dogmatics*, he states:

> The problem of the doctrine of the Trinity is the recognition of the inexhaustible vitality or the indestructible subjectivity of God in his revelation.[13] (98)

For Barth, the doctrine of the Trinity is the *dogmatic formulation* of his actualist thought form—God is the sovereign subject and personal content of his revelation.

Several observations should be made about *The Göttingen Dogmatics*. First, these lectures show Barth taking a non-systematic, *loci* approach to dogmatics—he attempts to write a dogmatics that is a consistent "thinking-after" the event of God's self-revelation.[14] Second, *The Göttingen Dogmatics* reveals that Barth has firmly anchored his dialectical theology in the doctrine of the Trinity. Barth's letters to Thurneysen from this period clearly reveal this:

> In regard to the incarnation it is best at any rate to proceed cautiously that one may not run his head into the exclusive "Jesus Christ"-pit of the Lutherans. Everything indeed depends on *this* denominator, but this denominator "somehow" under everything. A Trinity of *being*, not just an economic Trinity! At all costs the doctrine of the Trinity! If I could get the right key in my hand there, then everything would come out right.[15]

"God is God" had been the theme of Barth's theology since his breakthrough in 1916, and it is also the central theme of *The Göttingen Dogmatics*. What is new is that Barth grounds this not in a dialectically "wholly Other" but in the Trinity. In the concept of God's absolute, threefold subjectivity in his revelation, Barth is able to establish God's *freedom* over-against creation, the Reformed *soli Deo gloria*, and a theological actualism.[16] Third, there is a noticeable toning down of Barth's dialectic in *The Göttingen Dogmatics* from *Romans II*. However, this is better understood as a change in *rhetoric*—it is precisely through Barth's Trinitarian understanding of God's "inalienable subjectivity" that he gives the ontological and epistemological distance a deeper biblical and dogmatic grounding.[17]

Interestingly, *The Göttingen Dogmatics* stresses the importance of the personal human crisis for revelation. Barth devotes an entire paragraph to the role of anthropology in the act of revelation.[18] Revelation "is the answer to our question how we can overcome the contradiction in our existence" (§4 summary statement, 69). Therefore preaching, as pure doctrine, must arise "in the narrow defile between the Bible with its witness to revelation and the people of the present with their question" (275–276). Barth here shows the continuing influence of Kierkegaard's more subjectivist emphases.[19] Although it appears that Barth wants to shut off all human possibilities towards the knowledge of God, his inclusion of anthropology *within* the doctrine of revelation (as well as some ambiguous expressions) indicate that he has not yet reached a clear way of dogmatically formulating the ontic-noetic distance.[20]

The Göttingen Dogmatics also points to future disagreements between Barth and Brunner. Barth treats natural theology only briefly in §15 of *The Göttingen Dogmatics* ("The Knowability of God"). He clearly states his disappointment with the older dogmaticians' use of natural theology.[21] At points he explicitly rejects natural theology:

> Either God speaks, or he does not. But he does not speak more or less, or partially, or in pieces, here a bit and there a bit...If God *speaks*, then *God* speaks, and we have to do with the one Logos that the prophets and apostles received, the one revelation in the incarnation which the people of the Bible know and attest as either promised or manifested...If God does not speak, then it is not God that we hear in those supposed voices of God but a voice from this world, from this unredeemed world, from the contradiction of our existence... Either God or man, either revelation or not; between these millstones the grain of what is called natural revelation must be ground. It has no independent existence.[22] (92–93)

However, Barth retains the ambiguity of his expressions about "man and his question", leaving open a *via negativa* to God.[23]

In addition, Barth begins to formulate in *The Göttingen Dogmatics* his position on what would become a pressing issue with Brunner (as well as with Gogarten and Bultmann) in another five years—does theology have to justify itself to philosophy? Barth's answer here is No, an answer he will continue to give ever more strongly until he finds his final formulation in his book on Anselm:

> Dogmatics is not an attempt to defend or establish Christian theses before the forum of other sciences, whether it be that of philosophy or of the exact sciences. It measures them by its own measure...We must first work out the principles of

> Christian proclamation according to their own criterion…Apologetics is a later
> concern.[24] (319)

This is because theology must proceed without guarantees, being based on
no other foundation than a revelation which is self-grounded:

> We have not made a possibility out of the venture of talking about God. We have
> not built a bridge over the abyss. We have simply described…the one Word of
> God which might give us cause to make this venture.[25] (271)

Barth's first lectures in dogmatics are extremely helpful in establishing
the profound continuity in Barth's thinking from *Romans II* through *Christian Dogmatics* to *Church Dogmatics*.[26] The *Göttingen Dogmatics* shows
Barth struggling to bring to properly-grounded expression his theological
axiom that "God is God". Human knowledge of God, because of the ontic-
noetic distance, was an "impossible possibility" in *Romans II*. In *The Göttingen Dogmatics*, humanity's ability to know God is now given in God's
Trinitarian self-knowledge; it is not a general human possibility, but a "possible reality" grounded, limited, and controlled in the self-knowing reality of
God as God speaks in his revelation.[27] Thus, one can observe the Anselmian *credo ut intelligam* already *in nuce* in *The Göttingen Dogmatics*—
the reality of the possibility of the knowledge of God is presupposed in
revelation.[28]

Brunner: Philosophy, Revelation, and Law (1924–1925)

"The Fundamental Problem of Philosophy according to Kant and Kierkegaard"

At the end of 1923, Brunner was invited to give a lecture to the Kant Society in Utrecht and to the Philosophical Society in Amsterdam.[29] Entitled
"The Fundamental Problem of Philosophy according to Kant and Kierkegaard", it became his first contribution published in *Zwischen den Zeiten*.[30]

The lecture is divided into three parts: a critique of Neo-Kantianism, followed by an appraisal of the value of Kant and Kierkegaard's contributions
to philosophy. Brunner rejects Neo-Kantianism because it fails to take its
own slogan seriously—"Back to Kant!" should mean a "return to that fear-
lessness of an absolute asking of questions, which has become completely
foreign to our specialist, culture-positivist age" (32). Brunner admires
Kant's seriousness, his "fear of God, his unerring sense for that which
Kierkegaard called the qualitative difference between God and humanity":

> To see this border, to guard this border—that is the characteristic content of his

critical philosophy...Thus, genuinely critical philosophy means the end of all the vanity of science...It has—as does Old Testament piety—the absolute pathos of distance. Indeed, it is—precisely as it is *critical*—nothing other than making this separation, this crisis, this dualism, count in the form of critical reflection. (33–34)

Kant's value for contemporary philosophy is that he recognized the limits of human knowledge and the existence of the divine-human distance (35–37). Even more importantly, Kant correctly pressed on beyond the issues of "pure reason" to those of "practical reason", for

> only where the hypothetical imperative of the rule of thinking becomes the cate- gorical imperative of the rule of living does [philosophy] become serious. For only here is it no longer a question about things, but about myself. (38–39)

At this point, Brunner reveals for the first time his incorporation of Eb- ner's "I–Thou" thought into his Kantian framework to develop an anthro- pology which would remain consistent (though continually developed) throughout his career:

> It is only through this categorical imperative that I first know that I am an "I", a responsible subject. I am *response-able* [*ver-antwortlich*] only in that my *re- sponse* [*Antwort*] is demanded...My personeity is called in being through the "Thou shalt!" This appeal is the ontic and noetic ground of my freedom...Free- dom, said [Kant], is known in no other way than through the Should. It is not an experience...but it is rooted only in that claim and it is also only known in it. It is the knowledge of the divine claim, of the divine summons, of my being addressed by God, that brings to my consciousness my human worth. Freedom and respon- sibility are one and the same thing. (39)

The law not only grounds human worth in calling forth freedom and re- sponsibility; it also points to the fundamental contradiction within human existence, "the unfathomable, shocking knowledge of radical evil" (40). Thus, Kantianism's ruthlessly critical mode of reflection pushes human thinking to a paradoxical limit—human thought is put in "'crisis', which can no longer be translated other than by the word judgment" (41).

However, Kant does not "speak the final word" about this crisis. This is where Brunner introduces Kierkegaard. Kierkegaard's great contribution is taking Kant's argument one step further: from Idealism's "aesthetic" think- ing to Kant's "ethical" thinking, Kierkegaard moves on to "existential thinking"—guilt is the essential characteristic of human existence (44). Fol- lowing Paul and Luther, Kierkegaard understands humanity to be in a "situ- ation of despair in light of the divine demand". If a solution is possible, it must come from the other side of all human reflection, not as a possibility of human thought, but as "the absolute paradox" (45).[31] Here, the limits of philosophy have been reached; "if philosophy understands its own meaning, it must become silent".

Brunner concludes his lecture arguing that while the purpose of philosophy is to point out the crisis of human limits, this crisis is also the limit of philosophy itself: "Whether there is an Other-side of [philosophy's] limit is not for us to know, but it is *revealed* to us,…philosophy cannot know nor want to know this" (46). Rather, what is encountered at the limits of philosophy is faith. Thus, critical philosophy and faith walk hand in hand: "faith …is the fulfillment of the law, the fulfillment of critical thought".

"The Fundamental Problem of Philosophy according to Kant and Kierkegaard" provides considerable insight into Brunner's theological orientation at the end of 1923. In this lecture Brunner definitively announces his break with Neo-Kantianism, thus confirming his move, after reading *Romans II*, towards a radical dialectical critique.[32] More importantly, this lecture reveals the fundamental philosophical and theological commitments that Brunner will continue to hold and develop throughout his career as a theologian. We see here Brunner's clear commitment to Kantian philosophy, which maintains that all that humanity can discover on its own about the meaning of life is that it faces both an epistemological and moral limit.[33] Also apparent is Brunner's appropriation of Barth's dialectical thinking: Brunner builds on Kant's gulf-crisis by making it absolute and theological. Kierkegaard, as always, remains influential, because his existential philosophy is thoroughly practical and not speculative, and because he places the crisis at the center of the meaning of human existence, and, thus, of faith. Finally, one can see Brunner's first employment of Ebner: the entire structure of Brunner's "*response*-able" anthropology, which appears for the first time in this lecture, would remain constant throughout his life.

This lecture not only reveals Brunner's fundamental material commitments, but also his major concerns as a theologian. As this book will demonstrate, the matrix of issues surrounding law/responsibility/ethics is always at the center of Brunner's thinking.[34] Here Brunner reveals his life-long interest in the philosophical side of theology—for him, philosophy is essential for theology, but only in its "practical", ethical expression. Although it is only hinted at in this lecture, we will see an increasing interest on Brunner's part in conducting theology as an attack on the misunderstandings of contemporary thought.[35]

The 1924 Pany Meeting: Law and Gospel

In August 1924, Brunner paid a visit to Barth, who was vacationing with Thurneysen in Pany, Switzerland. Apparently they had a very animated discussion which centered on the nature of revelation and law in dogmatic prolegomena. Brunner continues the discussion with Barth by letter.[36] Their disagreement at Pany had taken the following shape: Brunner argued that Barth's use of "God speaks" emphasized too much *that* God speaks, rather than *what* God says; conversely, Barth accused Brunner of building his prolegomena on "the dialectic of the Law and Gospel in such a Lutheran way" that he "had made revelation entirely dependent upon justification". Brunner acknowledges Reformed theology's concern about such a "narrowing", but he does not see this as a legitimate threat.

> On the contrary, I cannot see how the Gospel can be delimited other than through its (dialectical) opposition to the Law as a necessarily contingent, authoritative and paradoxical communication, as the *Deus dixit* in the strongest sense of the autonomous, *semper et ubique*-occurring knowledge of God through ideas.

Following their discussion, Brunner "plowed through" again Calvin's *Institutes* (II, ix–xi) and the corresponding sections of Luther's *Commentary on Paul's Epistle to the Galatians*. But this has only confirmed Brunner in his opinion: the Reformers taught that the criterion of revelation is justification and that there is a natural knowledge of God through the law:

> How can we understand the *Deus dixit*...as only a believed paradox if we miss the point where the break with the law—thus with the *ratio*—carries itself out: in the justice χωρις του νομου?...How can we distinguish the arrogant *Deus dixit* of a *quilibet* from the true *Deus dixit*? Can we distinguish it other than materially: Christ and "what Christianity practices"?

Brunner concludes:

> Thus, it seems to me, I have no reasons to construct my prolegomena differently. The dialectical opposition of Law and Gospel is not specifically Lutheran, but is clearly found in Calvin and the New Testament. If we seek criterion elsewhere— perhaps [as you do] in the relation of the *Deus absconditus* and *revelatus*—then we run the danger of placing the cosmological opposition— finite and infinite, absolute and relative—over the ethical opposition, which... would, at best, lead to a religion of an amazingly contemplative miracle-worship, but not to faith in God's justification.[37]

Barth reveals his reaction to the Pany discussion in a letter several months later to Thurneysen:

> If only one could persuade Emil to be somewhat more narrow-minded [learning from the Scholastics] instead of listening to everything so recklessly...I have a vague feeling that Emil, with his "Law and Gospel", is rushing headlong to destruction—into the arms of Althaus and Holl. He should pay attention.[38]

The Pany meeting addressed an issue that would remain central in the

Barth–Brunner debate. Since his 1916 insight, Barth wanted to stress the pure miracle of revelation, that God is "inalienably subject" in his revelation, and that faith has no reasons other than the miraculous work of the Holy Spirit. It is true that in *Romans II*, *The Göttingen Dogmatics*, and later in *Christian Dogmatics*, he granted the importance of humanity's self-awareness of its personal crisis in the contradiction of human existence. But (as is already seen in *The Göttingen Dogmatics*) Barth's bow in this direction was secondary to his principle attempt to offer a doctrine of revelation with no "guarantees". Brunner, on the contrary, never swerved from understanding humanity's knowledge of its crisis as being a necessary preparation for the breakthrough to the Absolute. For Brunner, this was simply putting in Kantian terms the Reformation understanding of the knowledge of sin through the Law which prepares for the reception of the Gospel. Thus, in their earliest dogmatics, Barth and Brunner significantly disagreed over the issue of the knowledge of revelation.[39]

"Revelation as the Ground and Subject Matter of Theology"
On January 17, 1925, Brunner delivered his inaugural lectures as *ordinarius* Professor of Systematic and Practical Theology. Entitled "Philosophy and Revelation", the two lectures continue his thinking as seen in "The Fundamental Problem of Philosophy" and *Mysticism and the Word*. Examined here is the first and longer lecture, "Revelation as the Ground and Subject Matter of Theology".[40]

Brunner begins by defining the task of philosophy: its role is to question "the presuppositions of every other science, of knowing itself, of the possibility of knowledge itself" (98–99). This task puts philosophy and theology into "the closest connection", a relationship which inevitably involves "the conflict between two ultimate...points of view which both cannot be the ultimate" (99). Brunner argues that this conflict is settled not according to which science gives the best answer, but rather which one asks "the question of all questions...more deeply,...more thoroughly, more stubbornly" (99–100). Philosophy fails to question at a decisive point—the point of human reason—because the laws of reason "are the ultimate, universal presupposition" of philosophy itself. Thus, theology can profitably use only that philosophy which is serious in its question-asking. Not surprisingly, for Brunner, the only philosophy which "goes a good stretch of the way together" with theology is "critical philosophy".

Brunner continues by arguing that theology values critical philosophy for its "sobriety": both in the realm of thinking and action, critical philosophy brings us before the possibility of limit (101–102). Repeating the argument of "Fundamental Problem of Philosophy", Brunner presents the schema of being claimed/addressed/commanded/ responsible, with the resulting knowledge of radical evil and that our lives remain "continually and fundamentally in question" (103–104).

Brunner then develops a theological understanding of truth—truth as event, revelation, Jesus Christ:

> The special nature of Christianity stands or falls with this faith, that in Christ God himself acts with humanity and speaks to it, and indeed, it is He himself. This is what the Christian means—this miracle—when he speaks of revelation. (108)

Brunner recognizes that this statement raises two questions, and that responding to these questions "describes the entire circle of theology's tasks": 1) giving "a precise definition of the concept of revelation" (what does "God was in Christ" mean?), and 2) providing an account of this faith "from the point of view of general reflection" (what are the grounds of this faith in view of natural reason's disagreement with it?) (108–109). Brunner maintains that the biblical view of truth as revelation is that revelation is an event, unique, contingent, and personal (112). Therefore, *if* revelation happens, it is "the tearing of continuity, the breaking-in of the wholly Other, in a word: a miracle" (113). Revelation is *divine* movement and divine *movement*—it is an act of discontinuity from the other side (114), "the forgiveness of guilt" (115). Therefore, the presupposition of Christian revelation is human guilt and sin.[41] Brunner then defends this understanding of revelation against the claims of reason. He argues that revelation is not *ir*rational but *anti*-rational, while at the same time being the fulfillment of rationality: "That is the dialectical double-relationship in which the Christian faith and reason stand". This is familiar Brunnerian ground: thought which follows the necessity of theoretical principles approaches the border which limits both human thought and action; this limit confronts us as Law which we cannot fulfill; to conclude that behind this Law is a Law-giver "is precisely the step from…philosophical knowledge to faith" (119–120). Brunner then hints at a direction he will pursue in the following years concerning the task of theology:

> Perhaps theology is a further thinking-through of faith, especially from the side where faith is threatened by the general consciousness of the times…, which also explains the essentially polemical character of all vital theology. Theology is an attack on intellectuality perverted by sin, it is the obedience of faith spreading out into the realm of thought, and thus it is the shaking of all apparently certain positions of knowledge, a questioning of all supposed solutions, the act of leading thought to the point where one no longer knows anything by oneself. (120–121)

Brunner concludes by arguing that the theologian is the scientist who knows that no human being has the answer to the question of existence, but that it can only be given (121).[42]

"Law and Revelation"

On January 23, 1925, Brunner traveled to Marburg to give an address entitled "The Question of Humanity in Humanism and Protestantism". Afterwards, the Marburg faculty was given the opportunity to engage Brunner in discussion. It was a disaster. Brunner describes it to Barth in a letter written the following week:[43]

> I was so exhausted [from my travels] that I had to forego engaging with the somewhat plebeian jostling of Heidegger and the sharp polemic of Tillich. So I was silent, and thus I lost the battle. I was not entirely guiltless about this result—because I wanted to pack too much into my lecture, my formulations came out much too unprotected.[44]

In passing this news on to Thurneysen in March, Barth adds:

> In Marburg, Brunner did not cover himself with fame: it seems he appeared to be quite shallow...He fails to recognize the situation if he thinks it is still sufficient to bugle as he saw fit to after the ordeal in Pany.[45]

Brunner writes Barth next on March 10.[46] After sharing his progress in dogmatics, he brings up his Marburg lecture again.

> You know that I made a leap to Marburg and came home with burned fingers. I leapt too carelessly, and provoked the opponents too much, and was not fresh enough to parry their almost enraged counter-attack. And so the matter ended somewhat lamentably, namely, with my loss of speech. I have now attempted to make up for the omission in an essay that is just now appearing in *Theologische Blätter*...I would be very grateful...if you would send me a postcard stating... whether I have succeeded in more clearly defining the relationship of philosophy and theology, and implicitly that of faith and culture, than it has been done hitherto. For as far as I am concerned, this is the greatest danger which now threatens us. I felt it clearly in Marburg. The Marburgers considered my rough Kantianism simply as something from a hayseed, because, since Natorp, phenomenology and the truth of metaphysics has come to the fore. We must beware both.

Brunner's re-worked lecture appeared under the title of "Law and Revelation: A Theological Foundation".[47] The essay is another attempt to explain the relationship of philosophy and theology in terms of the concept of border. What is unique here is Brunner's emphasis on the Law as the key operative concept at the border.

Brunner begins by stating that there are two ways to understand the relation between God and humanity: 1) the way from humanity to God (which means human thought and action, thus philosophy), or 2) the way from God to humanity (which means the miracle of revelation) (53). Between these two possibilities exists no middle ground. However,

> there is a border where both touch each other, thus where they…touch like two army spearheads *over-against* each other. This *common* point, which is precisely the point where there is a collision, is the Law.

Since "*the Law is the border-region of philosophy and theology*", it is appropriate for both the theologian (who "wants to make it clear how revelation encounters the natural person") and the philosopher to focus on the concept of the Law.

Brunner asks three questions in the essay. The first is, "What is the Law?" Again, the arguments are familiar. Human thinking reaches its highest point in conceiving of a moral law, but falls short since philosophy knows nothing of a "*Law-giver*", of radical evil, of a fall of sin, or of humanity's "breaking loose from its original being-in-God" (54–55). Thus, from the perspective of philosophy, "the Law stands between us and God" (56).

Brunner then asks, "What is revelation?" He argues that "revelation is where…*God becomes immediate to us*, where *God himself* speaks to us", and that it is God's grace which bridges the gap which separates God and humanity. The Reformation slogans (*sola fide, soli Deo gloria,* justification by faith) mean that revelation is philosophy's polar opposite, not only in the direction of its movement, but also in its form: it is an event, most specifically the contingent fact of history of Jesus Christ (*vs.* philosophy's preference for timeless ideas). Brunner announces: "To create this clear insight—that and why revelation is folly and a scandal for reason—is the task of theology" (57).

Brunner's final question is, "In view of revelation, what is the new understanding of the Law?" Whereas the Law sets humanity on its own way, revelation shows us our original relation to God. Here, Brunner develops a concept which will become increasingly important for him: the image of God. Humanity is created in an "*original similarity*" to God which is "grounded in their *original dissimilarity*". But humanity wants to grasp this gift as its own act, as emancipation from God. In this desire, humanity "*has changed God's gracious will into his law*"—"The *law is the punitive self-assertion of God* over-against the false self-assertion of humanity". Therefore, in typical Brunnerian balance, the Law is "both a *remembrance of God* and a *remembrance of the Fall*".

Brunner concludes his essay by pointing to the double significance of the

Law. In the positive sense, the Law is the way in which God encounters humanity as humanity proceeds on its own way to God. Negatively, the Law, as that which indicates humanity's sin, separates God and humanity. The Law is

> the stage prior to the "face of God"…It is God and yet not God, God as he wants to be *for* us but as he maintains himself *against* us, therefore: the wrathful, judging and rejecting God.

As human beings, all that we do occurs within the sphere of the Law; a change in affairs can only come from God (58). Therefore, the Law brings a crisis: it brings knowledge of sin and judgment, which points to the need for the revelation of grace. At this point, Brunner backs off a bit from his earlier statements against a natural knowledge of God.[48] He states that revelation alone makes possible the "full" knowledge of sin, but that philosophy would not be true if it did not know "something of the Law". Thus, theology, in holding to this double aspect of the Law, "remains at the same time both near and far from philosophy".

Barth writes to Brunner soon after "Law and Revelation" appears.[49] He is not entirely content with what he has read:

> Now that I see more clearly where you're headed, I have nothing to say *against* you. Except that a demon (whose voice I still cannot translate into a scientific formula) prevents me from *following* you: 1) in your *undertaking as such*, which seems to me (as you usually conduct your undertakings) to be "somehow" too grandly designed (I still don't know clearly enough what theology is, so I can hardly venture to think about its relationship to philosophy …); and 2) in the *execution* of your undertaking, which appears to me to be "somehow" too simple, too unambiguous (it's the same here as with your other works…I see you giving answers where I am really first stirred up at discovering questions).

As for Brunner's undertaking, Barth has "fundamentally *no desire whatever*" to have his theology so closely-bound to a particular philosophy:

> how strange it makes me feel to look at you with your "foundation"[50]—where one must first be converted from being an Aristotelian into a Kantian, and then from a Kantian into a Christian, and also that as a Christian one *must* necessarily be a Kantian (which I will concede is the most desirable and helpful position).

Regarding the execution of Brunner's argument, Barth has three main objections. First, Brunner's opposition between Law and Gospel is too harshly Kantian: "Is not the Law *also* revelation, not only punishment and opposition? Or does the praise of the Law in Psalm 119 count only as a 'limit of humanism'?" Second, while philosophy *as such* can "sense" something of the "Law" in the theological sense, it can *say* nothing, and that is a matter of importance. For then one must consider whether philosophy can "sense" the "Gospel" just as much as the "Law".

Why does Brunner call it a "theological foundation" if he builds upon an understanding of the Law which is common to Kantian philosophy? Third, Brunner's argument is quite simply "too thin and uncertain as a theological *foundation*". Barth concludes:

> While I am grateful that by the means of your clearer formulations many people better understand my "abracadabras", you must certainly take account of the fact that in my work there remains an "X" of which you have not laid hold.

Brunner replies with four observations.[51] First, he thanks Barth, as he did during the correspondence concerning *Mysticism and the Word*,[52] for reprimanding him about his "certainty":

> It was not my intention…to lay a theological foundation—but the devil provoked me to write that in order to irritate the Marburgers, to show them that I would not capitulate on account of their blasts. Now, I think, it sits there, condemned: "foundation"—and nothing was intended other than a preliminary attempt to define the borders of philosophy and theology.

But Brunner's second point is less conciliatory: "We cannot avoid this task" of attacking philosophically weak theology. It is not a question of arguing philosophy, but a question of pointing out poor theological conclusions (like those of Tillich) which are due to the appropriation of bad philosophy. Third, Brunner argues that his understanding of Law-Gospel is truly Pauline and Calvinist—the Law is the tutor for the Gospel ("this point-of-connection (*Beziehungspunkt*) [cannot be] surrendered") and only subsequent to faith does one correctly see the Gospel in the Law. Finally, Brunner defends his program of distinguishing reason and revelation.

> I am not capable of speaking of revelation in the Christian sense without marking out the border of revelation against that which is not revelation, i.e., reason. Perhaps this comes in my genes, being the son of a teacher; but clarity as such appears to you to be somewhat pedantic and dangerously certain. But how do you answer your students when they ask about your doctrine of revelation: "Yes, revelation is necessary—one does not know Christ through reason. But doesn't the person who knows nothing of Christ know the Law just as well as the person who does?"

Brunner argues that Barth cannot escape the question of revelation and reason in the long run:

It is more important that we clarify the relationship of reason and revelation—which is identical to saying that we must clarify the concept of revelation—than that we be instructed in all the subtleties of the doctrine of the Trinity.[53]

Brunner's three lectures from late 1923 to early 1925 show how central the issue of theology's relationship to philosophy is for him. They reveal his determinative commitment to Kantian philosophy, and they clearly indicate how he was beginning to define theology's task as pointing out the errors and unfulfilled truths in philosophy—what he would name "eristics" in 1929.[54] His meeting with Barth at Pany clarified how differently he and Barth were approaching the task of constructing dialectical theology. An indication of the growing distance between Barth and Brunner is given by Thurneysen several months later. Georg Merz had heard Brunner deliver a lecture on "Reformation and Romanticism" at a Luther conference, and wrote Thurneysen that, based on what was said, Brunner should be completely brought back "into the family".[55] Thurneysen's reaction is more reserved: "I propose that we recognize him as a 'cousin'".

Interlude: Correspondence (1925–1927)

From the middle of 1925 to the middle of 1927, the Barth–Brunner relationship remained "on hold". Their correspondence during this period is not focused on on-going theological discussions, although there are still occasions for Barth and Brunner to continue to define their differences. In early 1926, Brunner appealed to Barth to restrain his movement towards a more pronounced *Reformed* position, while Barth maintained that "'Luther' means [the] transition from dialectical to *direct* communication".[56] A visit at the Bergli in August 1926 revealed "a non-bridgeable chasm between our thinking" on the issue of eschatology—while Brunner emphasized the continuity between creation and redemption (exemplified in understanding salvation as *restoration*), Barth stressed the radical newness of redemption (salvation as *new creation*).[57] When Brunner alerted Barth to an up-coming article in *Zwischen den Zeiten*[58], Barth replied:

> If you see in me a certain skepticism toward your position [it is because] I cannot agree with the sounds of victory which I…think I hear ringing out from Zurich, because I really have never thought that it's possible in only a couple of years for the walls of Jericho to fall down in the face of our trumpet-blowing…My occasional (and certainly unsightly) displeasure with you can be compared somewhat dramatically to a ship's fireman, who knows that the ship has sprung a leak and has to be safely guided out of the depths—when people should be running to man the pumps, everyone in the first class section is still dancing the fox trot.[59]

At the end of 1927 Barth received an invitation to teach at the University of Bern.[60] Brunner confessed to a general discomfort with the proposed move: "We would sit somewhat densely on top of one another: you in Bern, me in Zurich, and Eduard in Basel is almost too much".[61] Although he was open to Barth's return to Switzerland, Brunner revealed how threatened he feels by Barth:

> But I must urgently ask you to keep this entirely to yourself. For what kind of laughter would ensue if it gets out that Brunner wrote Barth that he should not come, that he is irreplaceable over there! Please, spare me that! All the more since I really do not risk to say: do not come. [If you do come, the] good for Switzerland is certain—but precisely in that you will also harm us, the Zurich faculty. For you will damage it thoroughly, the students will listen to you instead of me; I really cannot complain about that, since, in all honesty and seriousness, I consider you to be a better theologian than myself (while I can give myself a certain pedagogic priority).[62]

Major New Works (1927)

The year 1927 was an important one in the Barth–Brunner relationship, as both men published major books which clearly indicated that they were heading in different directions.

The Philosophy of Religion from the Standpoint of Protestant Theology is Brunner's attempt both to attack Neo-Protestantism's "philosophy of religion" methodology while re-establishing such concerns on the grounds of revelation.[63] Divided into two parts, the book proposes to analyze "The Problem" currently facing the philosophy of religion and how a proper understanding of "The Meaning of Revelation" provides the solution.

In the first chapter, Brunner begins with a very "Barthian" definition of theology:

> [The] miracle of divine revelation…is the presupposition of Christian theology. Christian faith…would cease to be faith…if it wanted to ground the truth of this affirmation on a universal truth. Either revelation supplies its own grounds or else it is not revelation. The only man who can look for some other foundation beside the *Deus dixit* is the man who withholds belief from the *Deus dixit* and wants secretly to replace revelation by symbol. (16)

Brunner then defines the accompanying task of the philosophy of religion as the

> part of Christian theology [which] carries on the discussion with the common consciousness of truth, i.e. with philosophy; it is that chapter of Christian theology

whose business is to start from definitely Christian presuppositions, and give a well-founded description of the relations between revelation and rational knowledge on the one hand, and between revelation and religion on the other. (17)

This task is particularly urgent at present, Brunner argues, due to "the need of the times, which demands very special attention to this problem; and the need of the times always has determined and always should determine the perspective of theology" (18).

Correlating his understandings of revelation and philosophy of religion, Brunner writes of a "point-of-contact" for revelation in humanity:[64]

Revelation fits and meets human consciousness. It is not a matter of indifference that this consciousness should be defined as human...The locus in which revelation and the spirit of man meet each other cannot be assigned positively but only negatively: it consists in receptivity...The negative point of contact [*Berührungspunkt*] is a consciousness of vital need which is at the same time a consciousness of guilt. Therefore...any account of the faith evoked by revelation should be preceded by another account giving the results of man's investigation of universal characteristics, which investigation would lead up to the aforementioned point of contact [*Punkte*]...It is necessary to start from revelation as known to faith; in doing so we have only to bear in mind that revelation is always the answer to a question on man's part...Faith is certain that revelation alone enables us rightly to apprehend that need, that vital incapacity, which is the presupposition of faith; and that thereby revelation itself begets its own presupposition in the crucial sense. (19–21).

In chapter two, Brunner examines four major "'one-sided' half-truths" (31), each of which collapses the paradox between revelation and its particular emphasis: orthodoxy (Scripture), rationalism (reason), pietistic and Romantic subjectivism (religious experience), and historicism (history). Then, in Part Two, Brunner carries on the search for the positive meaning in each of these four "half-truths": rationalism correctly sees reason as the place where revelation encounters humanity; subjectivism respects the human longing for God; historicism correctly understands the historical nature of faith and the Church; and orthodoxy rightly holds the Bible to be the Word of God. In the chapter on Rationalism, four points stand out: 1) Brunner repeats his familiar Kantian critique of speculative Idealism; 2) he again brings in his argument about the Law's crucial role; 3) for the first time he coins a phrase which will remain determinative for him:

The emancipation of reason, as most clearly expressed in the principle of autonomy, is thus, as Hamann puts it, really a "misunderstanding between reason and itself"; it is reason's [*Vernunfts*] refusal to perceive [*vernehmen*]. (91)

Fourth, Brunner employs the infamous term "point-of-contact" [*Anknüp-*

fungspunkt] for the first time:

> [Man] manifests, at one and the same time, the Creator's glory and its perversion. And owing to the perversion he cannot himself be aware of it: for he can only know it at the point and in the degree in which the original truth is restored to him.
>
> The whole man, as so described,...is the "point of attachment" [*die sogennante "Anknüpfungspunkt"*] for revelation. The "capacity" which manifestly suffices the divine Creator as a point of attachment [*anzuknüpfen*] is no special sense, but our consciousness of ourselves as human, and this again is only the inner division as it is reflected in consciousness. (97–98)

At the end of his book, Brunner again defends an aggressive, polemical "philosophy of religion" as the primary task of theology:

> It is the "isms" that are the enemies of faith. Behind every "ism" there stands a faith [which] makes...an absolute out of a relative..."Isms" are thus idols. It follows that the controversy of faith with the "isms", which is the task of theology, is conflict with idolatry.
>
> Hence, an objective, neutral, or "purely scientific" theology is a monstrosity. For genuine theology...is always born of the passion of faith...It is part of the task of the church, i.e. a part of the conflict of the *ecclesia militans*. (183–184)

The Philosophy of Religion is an important work in understanding Brunner's development and his relationship with Barth, for this book is a prime example of what Brunner will officially announce in 1929 as his program of "eristics".

Appearing just a few months later, Brunner's *The Mediator* is dialectical theology's first christology.[65] It is divided into three parts: "Preliminary Considerations", "The Person of the Mediator", and "The Work of the Mediator". For the purpose of this book, the last two doctrinal portions are of secondary interest.[66] What is fundamentally important for the ensuing Barth–Brunner debate is Part One, which clearly shows Brunner's different theological approach.

"Preliminary Considerations" is the culmination of the critique of modern theology and philosophy which Brunner had been developing since *Experience, Knowledge and Faith*. The section attempts to trace back the theological and philosophical errors of Neo-Protestantism, contrasting its position with that of genuine Christianity. Brunner begins with a chapter on "The Antithesis: General and Special Revelation". While Christianity understands revelation as being based on a single, unique, once-for-all event in history (24–25), nevertheless it recognizes a general revelation as an "indirect form" and presupposition of special revelation (31–33).[67] Brunner resolves the relationship between special and general revelation in his typical "both/and, neither/nor" manner:[68]

> What the "natural man" knows apart from Christ is not half the truth but dis-
> torted truth. No religion in the world, not even the most primitive, is without
> some elements of truth. No religion is without profound error, an error which is of
> its very essence. (33)

Brunner, aware that this argument has been criticized by Barth, carries
on a footnote discussion with him. He acknowledges that to speak of "revelation" in this general sense runs the risk of treating it as an impersonal concept.

> This danger can be avoided, of course, by renouncing this work of comparison al-
> together. Until now this has been Barth's attitude—and with good reason—
> whereas I see that this cannot be done if we wish to avoid the danger of gradually
> falling a prey to a kind of spiritual conservatism which may lead to obscurantism.
> Discussion with the thought of the day, with philosophy and religion is—it is
> true—certainly not the primary and most important task of theology; but we have
> no right, on that account, to neglect this duty altogether or to leave it to the next
> generation.[69] (note 1, 24)

After examining how modern theology has brought about the effacement
of the distinction between general and special revelation (as seen in Schleiermacher and Ritschl (chapter two) and in christology (chapter three)),
Brunner reaches the heart of his "preliminary" argument in chapter four. He
reiterates his thesis from *Mysticism and the Word*: the "deepest reason" that
modern thought has obliterated the distinction between general and historical revelation is because of an underlying "identity philosophy"—the
"assertion of the continuity of human existence with the divine or with the
Absolute" (119). The goal of reason is to unite all truths into an inclusive
system, divine truth being the principle of this synthesis. But this attempt is
challenged by revelation: divine truth is a transcendent gift (rather than immanent achievement) which *happens* in a single event. Mysticism, moral
effort and philosophies of historical development—which all attempt to
construct a fundamental continuity between humanity and God—have
clearly failed to convince the modern person (120). One of the main reasons
for this is that the principle of continuity prevents one from taking seriously
what is obvious to everyone: "No one doubts for a moment that the world,
life, and culture are full of contradiction, for the fact is blatant enough".[70]

This leads Brunner, in chapter five, to his final point: modern theology
and philosophy fail to take sin seriously.

> It is round [the fact of evil] that the battle must be fought out, whether the as-
> sertion of continuity, the self-assurance of the modern mind is true, or rather, why

it is not true. Here lies the key to the understanding of the Christian faith and its opposition to the modern mind. (121)

Here Brunner brings his Kierkegaardian- and dialectically-supplemented Kantianism to clear expression:

> If Kant had maintained his doctrine of radical evil, he would have been obliged to admit...that the will which has been infected with evil cannot possibly cleanse itself from evil in its own strength. He would have been obliged to admit that the gulf between man and the Divine Will is one which man cannot bridge. [Guilt] would have remained standing, and with it the "gaping world of human existence" (Kierkegaard). (130)

Brunner then develops a Christian doctrine of sin which explains the nature and meaning of the God-human discontinuity and challenges the "continuity principle" of modern philosophy and theology.

"Preliminary Considerations" clearly points out the direction in which Brunner is heading, and it offers the clearest prefiguring of his later natural theology debate with Barth:[71]

> Only when a man finds all ways of escape blocked does he believe. Knowledge of sin, in this universal sense, is the presupposition of faith. This is the first point. The second point, however, is this: this presupposition is never produced by anyone save by faith, the divine revelation, the faith in the Mediator[72]...[The Word of God] is addressed to one who, although he no longer possesses the word, when the word is once more given to him is able to recognize it as the original word, the word of his state as a being created by God. Hence also his present sinful condition is not without God, nor without a revelation of God; but this revelation of God is the opposite of what some call revelation, and it has two aspects. It is God, and yet it is not God, in His Essence, who is here revealed. "The wrath of God has been revealed from heaven"...Reason is not without a knowledge of God, but it is not the living God which it knows, and...it is a confused and uncertain knowledge of God, a kind of twilight knowledge. (151)

At the beginning of the 1925–1926 academic year, Barth moved from Göttingen to the University of Münster.[73] During his first year there, he completed his lectures on dogmatics. The following year, Barth offered his dogmatics lectures again, in a thoroughly revised form. He was amazed that, after his experience with the two different editions of *Romans*, "here too hardly one stone remains on another"; he felt that "some demon or other is now forcing me to write out everything twice".[74]

Throughout 1927, Thurneysen urged Barth to publish his dogmatics.[75] Barth finally agreed to publish his prolegomena as the first volume in a series under the title *Christian Dogmatics in Outline*.[76] What is immediately apparent in Barth's move from *The Göttingen Dogmatics* to *Christian Dog-*

matics is that, while many structural equations can be made, he completely re-worked and greatly expanded the beginning parts of his prolegomena.[77] For the purposes of this book, two points should be highlighted.

First, one can see the beginnings of Barth's use of Anselm to reach a final grounding of his dogmatics.[78] The four references to Anselm in the first two sections of *The Göttingen Dogmatics* (Prolegomena, Doctrine of God) have almost doubled in *Christian Dogmatics'* Prolegomena alone. Of particular importance is Barth's use of Anselm in §7.3, "The Actuality of the Word of God", where Barth argues for the sovereign subjectivity of God (131–136).[79] Since God is not object, how can we know him? Barth follows Anselm's method in the *Proslogion*: the prayer of faith precedes the attempt to know God, because God is only knowable from faith. Barth latches onto the Anselmian phrase that would prove so helpful in three years' time: "*credo ut intelligam*". The way of theological knowledge is the human activity which "thinks after" the prior act of God's revelation. Knowledge (*Erkenntnis*) is acknowledgment (*Anerkenntnis*).[80] The possibility of knowing God's revelation is grounded in the prior actuality of God's revelation.[81] While Barth does not give this Anselmian insight a priority in *Christian Dogmatics*,[82] it is clear that he is moving to the place where he can finally ground revelation in itself rather than on human possibilities, which is the dogmatic expression of the ontological and epistemological distance of *Romans II*.[83]

Second, Barth's inability to push Anselm's insight to its final consequences is due to the fact that Barth still makes an essential connection between revelation and humanity's existential situation. This is seen explicitly in six of Barth's paragraph summary-statements, where "the contradiction of humanity" is intimately incorporated into the doctrine of Trinity, as well as into the objective and subjective possibility of revelation.[84] Most important are paragraphs §§5–6—the Word of God and the human person as preacher and hearer. In the first subsection of §5, Barth introduces a change in his "method of reflection", from "phenomenological" to "existential" thinking (69–70)[85]:

> We would have to understand everything we have done up to now concretely as an action in which we ourselves are involved. For we can only really insert a person if we, at all points, insert ourselves. (70–71)

Barth expands on this change of method in §6. The fact that a person hears God speaking to him presupposes "some kind of distance between God and himself"—"he is not at home with God" (93–94). Therefore, the speech of God which addresses humanity existentially is the uncovering of our contradiction (96–97)—our human existence itself becomes questioned (97–100).

The possibility of hearing God's Word is not a human one but God's (102), because "God's Word is the answer to humanity's question", and because "the question is grounded in the answer (namely in God's Word)" (103).

> He has built no bridge to God, but God has built one to him. He can only ask. He is only a question. But precisely thus he points to the fact that God has addressed him. Because this is so, the sermon has to proclaim God's law, God's wrath, God's justice and thereby the questionable standing of humanity, but all of this is grounded in the peace, the majesty, in the mercy of God, as the proclamation of reconciliation, of the knowledge of God's Yes, not from an ultimately unknowing human No. (105–106)

Barth emphasizes that he is not arguing for a negative human possibility for revelation, i.e., a natural knowledge of sin through "existential despair". Nonetheless, the shape of his argument connects humanity's possibility (in its being-questioned and being-in-contradiction) to God's actuality in revelation in such a way that it undercuts Barth's attempt in *Christian Dogmatics* to free God's revelation from human presuppositions.

While *Christian Dogmatics* shows a great expansion and deepening of the Trinitarian thinking begun in Barth's first dogmatic lectures of 1924, it nonetheless proceeds along the basic lines of *The Göttingen Dogmatics*—a desire to base dogmatics on the Word of God alone, which does justice to the sovereign subjectivity of God over humanity and human reflection about God.[86] The use of Anselm's *"credo ut intelligam"* moves Barth a step closer to his ultimate achievement of placing the actuality of revelation decisively before the possibility of its being revealed to the mind of humanity. However, Barth's step forward in *Christian Dogmatics* struck his theological opponents—and many of his dialectical friends—as a step backward into the world of scholasticism.

"The Beginning of the Hardening of the Arteries" (1928)

Brunner writes Barth immediately after the appearance of *Christian Dogmatics*.[87] He is not entirely taken with Barth's borrowing of the form of scholastic dogmatics:

> I had some anxiety that your speech would lose a bit of its immediate power... But since I see that David remains David even in the armor of Saul, it is not so difficult for him to strike just as certainly with Saul's spear as it was before with his sling-shot (I Samuel 17:38–39).

Brunner admires the positive theological strictness in Barth's thinking, although Barth's "narrow-mindedness" does not discredit Brunner's broader interests:

> There are tasks which also must be done, which you, rightfully, don't do at present, but which I have taken up both in my *Philosophy of Religion* as well as in *The Mediator*, because they force themselves upon me out of my work as a professor —from conversations with contemporaries who make sincere efforts to understand us.

Again, Brunner understands their alliance as fighting at different places along a common front:

> Perhaps you will also occasionally write a few words to me. For I receive no other judgment as so important than that from you..., because we are already —I think now more than ever—allies, even if you lead a great army, with which my modest little banner cannot compete. I find this allocation thoroughly appropriate both materially and personally. But we are allies for this reason; allies with a more genuine sense of fellowship of thought compared, perhaps, to Gogarten or Bultmann.

Brunner receives no reply from Barth. Their correspondence pauses for an entire year, until Brunner writes Barth anxiously in December 1928.[88] He asks Barth for clarification and assurance after receiving a letter from a common student of theirs, which relayed some negative comments by Barth about *The Mediator*:

> I am certain that it is not an *Adiaphoron* to you if I am doing my thing correctly or not. And I want to do it correctly—if necessary, at the cost of a completely new construction of my theology.

Apparently the student had reported Barth's criticism of Brunner's strict antithesis between non-Christian philosophy and Christian theology in Part One of *The Mediator*—Barth maintained (dialectically) that *both* Christian and non-Christian thought stand under God's judgment and grace. Brunner says he agrees that this distinction is provisional, but he repeats that only the Christian can stand outside the Idealist-Realist philosophical debate and see them both as relative. Barth responds a month later, assuring Brunner that their disagreement is "an accomplished fact only in the head of this... young man".[89] Barth then takes up the real matter with a degree of vagueness:

> Now, concerning the apparent and real differences in our points of view. I must confess that at the moment I don't have a very clear picture of them, and I don't feel as if I have the least competence to challenge or endorse...whether you are "doing your thing correctly". I have enough to do taking care of myself, and I have always believed in a type of predestination in theology, in which reciprocal debate appears to be perhaps a useful, but not indispensable, and finally hardly very sig-

nificant, activity.

Barth also takes the opportunity to state clearly his dissatisfaction with both Gogarten and Bultmann's "anthropological" approach:

> I know that I have never gotten on board this thing they call anthropology; but I cannot take it seriously when I read old texts which are generally mixed with philosophy, etc. Perhaps this is to my shame...[But] isn't it better to err on one's own way than to let oneself be tempted onto a strange track—and isn't this what Gogarten means above all? Is this the sign of the beginning of the hardening of the arteries, and must it be so?[90]

By the end of 1928, the differences within the dialectical theology movement were becoming difficult to paper over.[91] One can point to at least three areas where the cracks first appeared. First, the members of the group became aware, over time, that the confessional differences among them—Barth, Brunner and Thurneysen were Swiss Calvinists, Bultmann and Gogarten were German Lutherans—were not insignificant.[92] Second, there was an increasing divergence over the focus of dialectical theology: was its main contribution an understanding of the philosophical prolegomena to theology (Brunner, Gogarten, Bultmann), or to the material dogmatic concepts themselves (Barth)? Finally, differences appeared as soon as dialectical theology moved beyond the doctrines of God and revelation to treat other dogmatic topics, specifically: anthropology, ethics, creation, and Christian living.[93]

The most decisive source of the pressures being felt within the circle of dialectical theology was Barth himself. This pressure was applied first by Barth's favorable turn towards seventeenth century orthodoxy. But it was the appearance of Barth's *Christian Dogmatics* in 1927 which put the theology of crisis group into its own crisis.[94]

Despite these evident cracks, dialectical theology still appeared to be a united front in the view of most of its opponents and more neutral observers.[95] Paul Schempp's observation is typical:

> Are not Brunner, Gogarten, and Bultmann representatives of the same "direction", Barth's comrades in arms?...Yes, there is a front of dialecticians.[96]

Summary

The years 1924–1928 laid the foundation for the Barth–Brunner break-up in 1934. Beginning in 1924, while apparently being allies on the "dialectical front", Barth and Brunner, in fact, stood "back to back". What held them together was their rejection of Neo-Protestantism and their conviction that the way forward in theology was a recovery and re-statement of the Reformers' insight—a theology centered on revelation and faith. From this common perspective, both theologians began to develop their constructive programs. From their first steps, however, they set off in different directions. For Barth, the step forward began as a step backward, taking on board (critically) seventeenth century Protestant scholasticism: he plunged into a dialogue with the *theological past*. The great benefit of the publication of *The Göttingen Dogmatics* during the past ten years is that it shows how quickly Barth moved onto the path of "dogmatic thinking": *Christian Dogmatics* and *Church Dogmatics* no longer require a theory of pronounced "turns". *The Göttingen Dogmatics* clearly reveals the fundamental continuity of Barth's thinking from *Romans II* to *Christian Dogmatics*—the radically dialectical "God is God" of *Romans* is re-stated in *The Göttingen Dogmatics* in Trinitarian terms as "the inalienable subjectivity of God in his revelation".[97] As Barth's whole argument in *The Göttingen Dogmatics* shows, he was struggling toward a way to build dogmatics on God's sovereign revelation alone—the attempt to ground theology's possibility on the actuality of God's self-revelation.[98] In retrospect, what confused Barth during this period was his continued use of Kierkegaard, specifically incorporating humanity's predicament of contradiction into the center of his doctrine of revelation.[99] While Barth retained "humanity as hearer" within his dogmatic scheme, it is clear he was doing all he could to emphasize that this implied no *via negativa*—humanity's knowledge of its contradiction was no more to a true knowledge of God than "a corpse is to resurrection".[100]

Brunner's first constructive steps were in a wholly different direction. Brunner finally adopted Barth's radical "distance" in early 1922, and used it especially in his argument in *Mysticism and the Word* against all "continuity philosophy". This marked his definitive turn away from Neo-Kantian Idealism. But by the time of his 1925 inaugural lectures, Brunner was already weakening the force of the Barthian distance by harmonizing it with his philosophical commitments to Kant and Ebner. Seen in the perspective of the Barth–Brunner dispute of 1929–1934, it is startling how many fundamental Brunnerian arguments made their first appearance in late 1923 to early 1925: an increasingly explicit definition of theology's task as directly challenging the false assumptions of contemporary philosophies; a negative point-of-contact for the knowledge of God in the knowledge of the law, in the limits of reason, and in a personal existential crisis; an "I–Thou" anthropology, employing such terms as *imago Dei*, "humanity's capacity for words", responsibility, freedom, and *humanum*; a not-precisely defined concept of "Law"; and all these elements being supported by a commitment to the Kantian categorical imperative.[101] Brunner frequently employed the term "dialectical" for his theology, but its meaning was closer to "both/and"—a Hegelian kind of synthesis (revelation) beyond thesis (naturalism) and antithesis (Idealism). Thus, this chapter demonstrates the predominance of continuity, rather than "stages", in Brunner's theological development as well. Brunner was continually interested in the philosophical presuppositions of theology, the question of "revelation and reason".[102] As Brunner took his first steps in developing his theology, he stepped *philosophically into the present*. During these years, as Barth embarked on *dogmatic* theology, Brunner engaged in developing a *philosophical* theology.[103]

1927 is a crystallization point for the separate developments in Barth and Brunner. Brunner produced, appropriately, a *Philosophy of Religion*,[104] along with a christology which was both polemically titled (*The Mediator*, in opposition to the non-mediated faith of "continuity-philosophy") and whose entire first section is a prolegomena of philosophical theology.[105] Barth, on the other hand, published his evolving dogmatics for the first time. It was a prolegomena which attempted to completely by-pass philosophical questions in order to "think after" the actuality of revelation. His first use of the Anselmian *"credo ut intelligam"* showed how differently he was developing compared to Brunner's attempt to clear away philosophical hurdles so that "modern man" could believe.

The years 1924–1928 are crucial years in understanding the Barth–Brunner debate. They reveal, first, that the fundamental theological convictions which form the core of their future argument were clearly set *at least* by the end of 1927, if not by the beginning of 1925. These years marked the first and decisive *formulation* of material commitments made in 1920 (Barth) and 1922 (Brunner)—Barth does theology with a "dialectical watchdog" while Brunner works with a "critical watch-dog". However—second —their writings and correspondence (as well as the Barth–Thurneysen correspondence) make it perfectly clear that throughout this period, both men consider the other to be an ally, "at one in the main things".[106] The following two chapters will show how this perception of unity changes: 1) it was not a change in fundamental theological commitments, but rather a breakthrough on Barth's part to a clearer understanding of how to express dogmatically what he had been trying to say materially since *Romans II* (Chapter Four); and 2) it was a result of a changing ecclesiastical-political situation, such that what both men had been saying for eight years suddenly took on new meaning (Chapter Five). It was these new events which provoked Barth's "No!". But it was the theological development in separate directions between 1924–1928 which made future reconciliation impossible.

NOTES

1. Jüngel, "Von Dialektik zur Analogie", p. 128.
2. See Torrance, *Karl Barth*, pp. 53–54. For the role-change implied in the move from Safenwil to Göttingen, see Busch, p. 126; Barth, "Autobiographical Sketches", p. 312.
3. *Rev.Theology*, KB: February 2, 1924, p. 167 (Smart's translation ends before the last "...").
4. *Barth–Brunner*, EB: January 23, 1924 (#41), pp. 87–93.
5. Brunner would hold this position until his retirement in the 1950s.
6. *Barth–Brunner*, EB: Autumn 1923 (#36), pp. 75f. Barth had already twice voiced his concern about an eventual dogmatics course to Brunner (see *Barth–Brunner*, KB: June 12, 1923 (#34), pp. 73f; October 4, 1923 (#37), pp. 78–80).
7. *Barth–Brunner*, KB: January 26, 1924 (#42), pp. 94–96. Barth states: "We are thoroughly companions in suffering". He also congratulates Brunner on his impending academic election: "You have really deserved it...and thus there can and will break out a spiritual Spring in Zurich" (p. 94).
8. Crucial help in Barth's preparation for his dogmatics lectures also came from a most unexpected source: *Die Dogmatik der evangelisch-reformierten Kirche* (1861) by Heinrich Heppe (see Barth's 1935 "Foreword", in *Reformed Dogmatics*, trans. by G.T. Thomson (Grand Rapids: Baker, 1978), pp. v–vii. Heppe influenced Barth to become a specifically *Reformed* theologian (see *Rev.Theology*, ET: November 22, 1923, p. 154). For Barth's definition of Reformed theology, see *The Göttingen Dogmatics*, p. 294 . In addition, Barth's study of Protestant Scholasticism led him to research even further back into the theological tradition—to the medieval scholastics and the Fathers (Smart, p. 147; Daniel L. Migliore, "Karl Barth's First Lectures in Dogmatics" in *The Göttingen Dogmatics*, pp. xv–lxii (xix)).
9. *The Göttingen Dogmatics*, trans. by Geoffrey W. Bromiley (Grand Rapids: Eerdmans, 1991). For key secondary sources on this newly published work, see: Beintker; Ingrid Spieckermann, *Gotteserkenntnis* (Munich: Chr. Kaiser, 1985); McCormack; and Migliore.
10. Interestingly, Barth also picks up Ebner's "I–Thou" terminology here (p. 58).
11. Significantly, at this point Barth acknowledges that *this* human being is "not unknown in philosophical reflection or deeper human self-reflection in general". See also p. 75.
12. "God's revelation...is the answer to our question how we can overcome the contradiction in our existence...But we know ourselves in this regard only as God makes

himself known to us. We would not ask about God had not God already answered us" (p. 69).

13. For Barth's first use of this phrase see below, note 17.

14. S.W. Sykes, "Barth on the Centre of Theology", in *Karl Barth: Studies in His Theological Method*, ed. by S.W. Sykes (Oxford: Clarendon, 1979), pp. 17–54 (pp. 25, 33–35); Migliore, p. xxiii.

15. *Rev.Theology*, KB; April 20, 1924, p. 176.

16. Migliore, p. xxvi; Spieckermann, p. 149; Rosato, p. 35. McCormack's detailed chapter on *The Göttingen Dogmatics* (pp. 327–374) supports the thesis of this book: the Barth–Brunner differences were long-running and fundamental, occasioned neither by a "turn" in Barth or Brunner in 1929–1931, but by long-standing differences that became more and more apparent and unacceptable to Barth as he attempted to clarify his original insight that "God is God".

17. "I understand the Trinity as *the problem of the inalienable subjectivity of God in his revelation*" (*Rev.Theology*, KB: May 28, 1924, pp. 185). See especially McCormack, (pp. 327–328); see also 309–312 and Migliore, p. xxxi. But *contra* Beintker (pp. 137–139, 144–145, 178–179) who argues that theology as "corrective" ("Need and Promise") became theology as "doctrine" in *The Göttingen Dogmatics*—Barth only maintains here a *noetic* dialectic.

18. §4, "Man and His Question"—retained in *Christian Dogmatics* (§6, "The Word of God and Man as Hearer") and pointedly excised in *Church Dogmatics* I/1/§5.1:125–131. For publication details of *Church Dogmatics*, see the bibliography.

19. See p. 77.

20. For statements indicating humanity's possibilities, see pp. 73–74, 340–342; for those stressing the divine actuality, see pp. 79, 84 and 174.

21. See pp. 345–346.

22. See also p. 348.

23. See pp. 348–349.

24. See also pp. 299–300.

25. See pp. 107–108.

26. Migliore (p. lxi), Spieckermann (p. 141) and McCormack argue that the publication of *The Göttingen Dogmatics* definitively sets aside von Balthasar's classic "stage" thesis of understanding Barth (pre-dialectical [through 1919], dialectical [1920–1927], and analogy [1930 on]).

27. Spieckermann, p. 150.

28. See p. 348. See also Migliore, pp. xliv–lxv; Spieckermann, p. 164.

29. *Barth–Brunner*, EB: October 1923 (#38), p. 83.

30. "Das Grundproblem der Philosophie bei Kant und Kierkegaard", ZZ, VI (1924), 31–46.

31. Here, Brunner brings in Ebner again: "[This paradox] must *address* us—so that our freedom is at the same time 'affected', respected and raised up. The subjective expression of this paradox...can only be *believed*. The word, the Logos as paradox;

'practical' knowledge as faith" (45).

32. *Contra* Paul King Jewett, *Emil Brunner's Concept of Revelation* (London: James Clarke, 1954), p. 90, note 14.

33. For sources on Kant's epistemology and ethics, see: Diogenes Allen, *Philosophy for Understanding Theology* (Atlanta: John Knox, 1985), pp. 203–220; J.C. Weber, "Feuerbach, Barth and Theological Method", *Journal of Religion*, 46 (1966), 24–36 (pp. 24–25); Copleston, IV, pp. 54–60. Given that Brunner's fundamental commitment to Kantian ethics clearly contributed to his later conflict with Barth, this study disputes George S. Hendry's thesis in "The Transcendental Method in the Theology of Karl Barth", *SJT*, 37 (1984), 213–227.

34. W.H. Neuser (*Karl Barth in Münster* (TVZ, 1985), pp. 48–49) and Meland (p. 167) point out Brunner's decisive Kantian commitment. However, Salakka (pp. 86–87) is correct is seeing Brunner's Kantianism as a philosophic base upon which he built not uncritically.

35. For Barth and Thurneysen's positive but lukewarm reaction to Brunner's lecture, see *Rev.Theology*, ET: February 1, 1924, p. 165 and ibid., ET: February 1, 1924, p. 165. See also *Barth–Thurneysen II*, KB: February 5, 1924, p. 226; ibid., ET: June 6, 1923, p. 175).

36. *Barth–Brunner*, EB: probably August, 1924 (#44), pp. 101–105.

37. Although Barth responded to Brunner, the letter is lost. However, Brunner responded to this lost letter with a "monologue-like essay" on the "dogmatic Scripture-principle" that he sends to Thurneysen (*Barth–Brunner*, EB: September 16, 1924 (#175), pp. 397-404). After repeating and extending his arguments over this point, Brunner concludes "we are at one in the main things" (p. 404).

38. *Barth–Thurneysen II*, KB: November 26, 1924, p. 293. Gestrich (*Neuzeitliches Denken*, pp. 51–52) argues that although Barth would not explicitly state the oneness (and inverse order) of the Gospel and Law until 1935, he held this view from *Romans II* on ("Gospel and Law", in *God, Grace and Gospel*, trans. by James Strathearn McNab (Edinburgh: Oliver and Boyd, 1959), pp. 3–27.

39. McCormack (pp. 397–399) clearly sees the importance of the Pany meeting but over-emphasizes it, neglecting the significance of the ensuing years for Barth and Brunner to reach clarity and certainty in their positions.

40. "Die Offenbarung as Grund und Gegenstand der Theologie", cited here from *Ein offenes Wort*, I, pp. 98–122.

41. "Without this presupposition the Christian understanding of revelation becomes meaningless. For the act of revelation is always the act of atonement. However, the knowledge of this state of affairs in its entirety...is only possible through revelation" (116).

42. In Brunner's second inaugural lecture, "Gnosis and Faith" ("Gnosis und Glaube", in *Philosophie und Offenbarung* (Tübingen: JCB Mohr, 1925), pp. 29–48) he sees faith's most genuine characteristic as being "humility" (especially when confronted by the limits of human thinking and willing) (36–37, 39, 47). When he contrasts this

with the "pride" of "gnosis", he states his understanding of the difference between theology and philosophy (37–44). Interestingly, Brunner states that faith must say a "decisive No" to apologetics (45), because apologetics can only play with concepts, which are shattered by God's speech and self-communication: "We live by faith and not by sight —that *remains* the rule of Christian knowledge for all time" (46).

43. *Barth–Brunner*, EB: January 28, 1925 (#45), pp. 105–107.
44. Four days earlier, Bultmann had written Barth, confirming Brunner's account and adding that he, too, found the lecture to be "very weak, downright humiliating" (letter from Bultmann to Barth, January 24, 1925, in *Barth–Bultmann*, p. 16 (this trans=lation by author).
45. *Barth–Thurneysen II*, KB: March 4, 1925, p. 320.
46. *Barth–Brunner*, EB: March 10, 1925 (#46), pp. 107–113.
47. "Gesetz und Offenbarung: Eine theologische Grundlegung", *Theologische Blätter*, 4 (1925), 53–58.
48. In a note, Brunner comes out against natural theology: "The bond between [the law of nature and the moral law] is God the Creator, who is at the same time the Lawgiver. But the Creator cannot be known, but can only be believed" (p. 54, note 3). See also p. 55: "Thus, despite all the knowledge aiming at the Absolute, there is no knowledge of the Absolute, no knowledge of God". Brunner says that any human concept of the Absolute is "merely an empty idea of the Absolute" (ibid.). See also p. 56, note 8.
49. *Barth–Brunner*, KB: March 13, 1925 (#47), pp. 114–118.
50. The subtitle of "Law and Revelation" is "A Theological Foundation".
51. *Barth–Brunner*, EB: no date, 1925 (#48), pp. 118–122.
52. See above, pp. 46, 50, and 52.
53. In a handwritten marginal note, Brunner writes: "It is not for nothing that Reformed theology begins with the chapter: *De theologia naturale et revelata*. What is left without right, what is revelation without its opposite: reason?" In the next issue of *Zwischen den Zeiten*, Barth takes a glancing shot at Brunner. In "Menschenwort und Gotteswort in der christlichen Predigt" (*ZZ*, 3 (1925), 119–140), Barth argues that the statement "the Bible is the Word of God because it *is*" does not "mean the proclamation of a *credo, quia* absurdum but rather of a credo, *ut intelligam*, of the irreversibility of this sequence. No *intelligere* can precede the *credo*, not even an ethical *intelligere*. The *credo* is primary or it is not *credo* at all" (p. 124). That this sentence is aimed at Brunner is confirmed by Thurneysen (*Rev.Theology*, ET: April 9, 1925, p. 219).
54. See below, pp. 103ff.
55. *Barth–Thurneysen II*, ET: July 21, 1925, p. 357; Brunner, *Reformation und Romantik* (Munich: Chr. Kaiser, 1925).
56. *Barth–Brunner*, EB: January 7, 1926 (#53), pp. 129–131.; KB: January 10, 1926 (#54), pp. 131–135.
57. Ibid., EB: June 24, 1926 (#55), pp. 135–138; EB: probably July 7, 1926 (#57), pp.

141–145; KB: July 23, 1926 (#59), pp. 147f.. For Thurneysen's comments on this interchange, see *Barth–Thurneysen II*, ET: July 9, 1926, p. 426.

58. Ibid., EB: January 27, 1927 (#61), pp. 149–151; "Der Zorn Gottes und die Versöhnung durch Christus", *ZZ*, 5 (1927), 93–115, in which Brunner surprisingly claims: "Whoever understands the so-called dialectical theology [knows] that it is a question of attempting to think about Christian truths such that the idea…of the hidden God and divine wrath comes into its own again" (p. 95). While Brunner claimed that preparation for the article enabled him to understand "for the first time what you mean and intend with your teaching of the identity of the hidden and revealed God", his article rather reveals his serious misunderstanding of Barth: "*The key to understanding Luther's theology…is the knowledge that one must distinguish between God and God*" (p. 97); on p. 102 Brunner calls this "*the fundamental contradiction of God and God*".

59. *Barth–Brunner*, KB: January 29, 1927 (#62), pp. 151–156.

60. Ibid., KB: October 30, 1927 (#65), pp. 159f.; see Busch, p. 175.

61. Ibid., EB: November 1, 1927 (#66), pp. 160–163.

62. Barth turned down Bern's invitation (Busch, pp. 175–176).

63. Trans. by A.J.D. Farrer and Bertram Lee Woolf (New York: Scribners, 1937).

64. This is the second time Brunner has used this term (*Berührungspunkt*); see above, p. 79.

65. Trans. by Olive Wyon from the 2nd (unaltered) edn (London: Lutterworth, 1934).

66. At this time, Barth and Brunner have no essential Christological differences, other than the Virgin Birth. See *Mediator*, pp. 322–327, 361; Barth, *Church Dogmatics* I/2/§15.3, pp. 183–184, 189–190. Thomas A. Smail ("The Doctrine of the Holy Spirit", in Thompson, pp. 87–110) draws the connection in Barth's mind between the denial of the Virgin Birth and the possibility of a natural theology, based on a human capacity for responsiveness (p. 95).

67. "It is impossible to believe in a Christian way in the unique revelation, in the Mediator, without believing also in a universal revelation of God in creation, in history, and especially in the human conscience" (p. 32). However, Brunner explicitly rejects the view (which he sees in Tillich and Roman Catholicism) of a "two-story" or "graded" relationship between general and special revelation (pp. 32–33).

68. In Brunner's terminology, this is dialectic: "Neither an absolute denial nor an absolute affirmation, but both at the same time, the Christian conception of a general revelation is in principle 'dialectic'" (p. 33).

69. A few pages later, Brunner adds: "It is a striking fact, how many opponents of the so-called 'Dialectical Theology' have facilitated their criticisms by insinuating that we reject every form of general revelation in natural history and in the spirit of man …The question is not *whether* there is any general revelation or not, but *in what sense*, whether it is direct or indirect, thus whether the Christian revelation constitutes the highest point in this general revelation or whether it is something quite different—namely—*the* actual revelation itself" (note 2, 31).

70. It is important to note how this chapter is Brunner's on-going engagement with "modern man": see pp. 102–103, 108 (note 1), 111, 119.

71. Nonetheless, Barth was generally pleased with *The Mediator* (see *Barth–Thurneysen II*, KB: December 30, 1927, p. 555).

72. Brunner reiterates that he is not arguing here for a "negative point of contact" (p. 204; see also pp. 299–300).

73. See Busch, p. 164.

74. *Barth–Thurneysen II*, KB: November 8, 1926, p. 441; KB: December 1, 1925, p. 390.

75. Ibid., ET: February 22, 1927, pp. 463–464; June 7, 1927, pp. 503–504.

76. *Erster Band. Die Lehre vom Worte Gottes: Prolegomena zur christlichen Dogmatik*, ed. by Gerhard Sauter (TVZ, 1982).

77. Because of the importance of *Christian Dogmatics* as the chronological and theological mid-point between *Romans II* and *Church Dogmatics* (in addition to the fact that *The Göttingen Dogmatics* remained unpublished until 1985), there exists a plethora of analyses of this work. See: Torrance, *Karl Barth*, pp. 105–131; Bouillard, pp. 120–133; von Balthasar, pp. 73–79; Smart, pp. 164–173; Beintker, pp. 157–179.

78. Barth led a seminar on Anselm's *Cur Deus Homo?* at Münster in the summer semester of 1926.

79. For the significance of this passage, see Smart, pp. 166–167.

80. See also §25.3 "The Relative Force of the Material Principle of Dogmatics", where Barth asserts that theology is necessarily dialectical, a "thinking after", a new question following every new answer, since God is ontologically and noetically distant from us: "We are *human beings*. That is the simple and decisive reason for the exclusive possibility of dialectical theology" (p. 583).

81. See Barth's similar argument on pp. 304–308 in connection with the actuality of the Incarnation.

82. See the titles of §§14, 17, where Barth still expresses himself in terms of revelation's "possibility" as opposed to its "reality" (*vs. CD* I/2/§§13,16).

83. The importance of Anselm's influence on *Christian Dogmatics* was picked up critically by Hans Michael Müller in his review: "*Credo, ut intelligam*", *Theologische Blätter*, 7 (1928), 167–176.

84. See summary statements to §§10–14, 17.

85. Barth also suggests "ethical" as a synonym for this new method of thinking (p. 71). Whereas Barth intended to relate the speaking God and the hearing person in revelation, some misunderstood his move here as an attempt to base a theology of revelation on the underpinning of existentialist philosophy (*CD* I/1/§5.1:125–126).

86. McCormack, p. 375.

87. *Barth–Brunner*, EB: December 19, 1927 (#67), pp. 163–165.

88. Ibid., EB: December 12, 1928 (#69), pp. 166–169.

89. Ibid., KB: January 14, 1929 (#70), pp. 169–174.

90. In Autumn 1928, Brunner made a lecture tour to the United States, and published

the lectures the following year under the title *The Theology of Crisis* (New York: Scribners, 1929). In these lectures, Brunner follows the pattern of argument he has employed since 1925, most recently in *Philosophy of Religion* and *The Mediator*: he presents a modern misunderstanding, shows why the philosophy behind it is in error and the consequences of this error, and then contrasts it with the biblical understanding. The content of the lectures are familiar as well. In the chapter on "The Quest for Truth: Revelation", Brunner again attempts to do justice to both "revelation alone" and a Kantian-Kierkegaardian-Ebnerian anthropology. In chapter three ("The Quest for Truth: Salvation") Brunner repeats his argument that both naturalism and idealism fail to take seriously the contradiction within human existence, of which all people are instinctively aware (pp. 46–47), while Christianity alone understands this contradiction, and sees its solution in God's act of overcoming the contradiction in Jesus Christ (pp. 59–62). Thus, it is not clear that what Brunner took to America under the name "The Theology of Crisis" was dialectical theology as Barth understood it.

91. In addition, they had begun some modest public criticism of each other, most notably Gogarten's review of *Christian Dogmatics*: "Karl Barths Dogmatik", *Theologische Rundschau*, N.F. 1 (1929), 60–80.

92. "In some way the old controversies between the Lutherans and the Reformed, which were never settled, do cause us difficulties on both sides and will perhaps come to a head in a great explosion *within* [*Zwischen den Zeiten*]" (*Barth–Bultmann*, KB: April 28, 1927, p. 32). See also Bultmann: April 21, 1927, p. 32.

93. Volken, pp. 6–7. For Bultmann and Gogarten's positions in 1928, see Smart, pp. 152–177, and McConnachie.

94. For the clearest expression of this "crisis", see *Barth–Bultmann*, RB: June 8, 1928, pp. 38–39, and KB: June 12, 1928, pp. 40–42. In addition, Barth was not pleased with Brunner's second edition of *Mysticism and the Word* (Tübingen, JCB Mohr, 1928). In the foreword, Brunner rejects Barth's cautioning against placing an "either/or" before Schleiermacher (vi). Barth wrote to Thurneysen that he reserved "a small special anger" concerning Brunner's "malicious stubbornness" (*Barth–Thurneysen*, KB: January 26, 1930, p. 703).

95. Theophil Steinmann's two-part survey of the views of Gogarten, Brunner and Barth recognizes different nuances, but sees them presenting a united front. "Zur Auseinandersetzung mit Gogarten, Brunner und Barth", in ZThK, N.F. 10 (1929), 220–237, 452–70.

96. "Marginal Glosses on Barthianism", in Robinson, *Beginnings of Dialectical Theology*, pp. 191–199 (p. 196).

97. *Contra* Beintker (p. 177), who sees Barth's dialectic being softened as he turns from the "resurrection perspective" (time *vs.* eternity) in *Romans II* to an "incarnation perspective" (union-diversity, divine-human in Christ) in *Christian Dogmatics*.

98. See *Barth–Brunner*, KB: June 12, 1923 (#34), p. 74: "Sometime, probably next summer, I have to begin to climb up to dogmatics. I already contemplate some kind of

scholastic arrangement, wherein all philosophy of religion and the lot are entirely abolished, and it is bolted precisely to the matter: 'On the knowledge of God and ourselves', or still more concisely: 'On God', revelation and (if possible) dogma *presupposed!*"

99. Torrance, "Introduction", pp. 22–23.
100. *The Göttingen Dogmatics*, §15.4:340.
101. Heinrich Leipold, *Missionarische Theologie* (Göttingen: Vandenhoeck & Ruprecht, 1974), pp. 92, 102.
102. Volken, p. 8; Volk, *Gottebenbildlichkeit*, p. 9. Gestrich (*Neuzeitliches Denken*, p. 44) argues that even though Barth borrowed philosophical terms and concepts, nonetheless this was "*no* theological conversation with philosophy".
103. However, Leipold maintains that everything Brunner *says* philosophically he *learns and knows* theologically: "it is a question of the *knowledge of God*, i.e. of a knowledge arising from the revelation of God" (p. 99). Brunner would continually make the same point against Barth from 1929–1935.
104. Volk (*Gottebenbildlichkeit*, p. 14), argues that Brunner never really progresses beyond his upbringing in German Idealism, remarking dryly: "A philosophy of religion must be a difficult undertaking for a dialectical theologian".
105. Nonetheless, Brunner's decision to publish a christology in 1927 probably helped to maintain his bond with Barth. It is important to recognize that *The Mediator* is Brunner's *only* book until 1946 (*Dogmatics* I) which deals with a theological article which is neither concerned with theology's philosophical underpinning (*Experience, Knowledge and Faith, Mysticism and the Word, Philosophy of Religion*, "Nature and Grace", *Truth as Encounter, Revelation and Reason*) nor is inextricably tied to anthropology (*The Divine Imperative, Man in Revolt*).
106. *Contra* Neuser, p. 49. Neuser's observation that "the debate between Barth and Brunner about the 'point of contact' could have obviously broken out since 1925" misses the point: *Why* did it not break out until mid-1929, and then finally in 1934? On the other hand, the Barth–Brunner correspondence shows that Volken (p. 10) is mistaken to understand Brunner's direction during this time as "hidden".

CHAPTER FOUR

Coming Apart (1929–1932)
Eristics, Ethics, and Anselm

We have reached a critical point.

(Brunner to Barth, June 1929)

I can understand as a theological friend only one in whom I have trust that he will not make a pact with the ancient serpent, neither with respect to nature nor with respect to grace. I no longer have this trust in you...[N]othing now remains but for us to renounce the fictitious picture that there is a special solidarity in our work.

(Barth to Brunner, January 1933)

Task and Method in Theology (1929–1930)

Theology, Philosophy and "Eristics"

It has been seen that the relationship between theology and philosophy was a long-running point of contention between Barth and Brunner. In February 1929, Barth delivered a lecture which attempted to give systematic thought to the relationship between philosophy and theology, as well as giving a partial answer to the questions raised by Brunner (as well as by Bultmann and Gogarten).[1]

Barth begins by claiming that his lecture title—"Fate and Idea in Theology"—expresses the "basic problem of *philosophy*": human thought constantly vacillates between two poles, which Barth calls "Realism" (emphasizing the given object itself) and "Idealism" (emphasizing the thought about the given object) (25). This leads directly to the basic problem of theology: since it is also a human science, it must use the same conceptual tools as philosophy, and, thus, it is also caught up in philosophy's polar limits (26–28). But Barth claims that even within the "framework of philosophy", the theologian can witness to something "completely dissimilar", because of "the miracle of God"—grace is the "great limit of the theologian's activity"

$(28-29).^2$

Thus understood, theology faces the constant temptation of wanting to become philosophy (29). Out of a sense of defensiveness about theology's "bound" thinking, theology is tempted to betray its commission by making statements grounded elsewhere than in the Word of God. Theology can resist this temptation only by acknowledging its own weakness *vis-à-vis* philosophy:

> Theology will appreciate how unprotected its work really is, how much all guarantees must be renounced in pursuing it, how much it must simply be ventured in obedience. Thinking and speaking humanly, all too humanly, yet nevertheless letting God's Word be said—that is the task of theology. (31–32)

Thus, the "critical question [for theology is] whether we are doing theology or philosophy".

Barth then explores the problems encountered when one does theology at either pole of human thought. While Realism takes seriously God's objectivity, it falsely presupposes "an inherent human capacity" to know God (39). On the contrary, God's Word always says something radically new to human experience, most concretely that God forgives our sins. Nor is God's Word simply a given object, for "God has sole control" over the event of revelation (40). Since Realism's god is simply "there"—a *being*—as opposed to the God who comes in *act*,

> wouldn't it perhaps be better for this god to be called simply nature? And might it not be better for the theology of this particular god to be called demonology rather than theology? (42)

Idealism's contribution to theological reflection includes: its differentiation between the given and non-given enables theology "to understand revelation as *God's* revelation"; it "aspires to do justice to God's hiddenness even in the midst of his revelation"; and by "stressing God's non-objectivity it reminds us that all human thinking and speaking about God is inadequate" (45–47). However, Idealism's "peculiar pride" must also be questioned by theology: the knowledge of *faith* recognizes that divine truth is purely given, not the product of "divine and human collaboration" (49). Whereas Realism errs towards demonology, Idealism errs towards ideology (47).

In light of these observations, Barth then explores the way of theology *vs.* that of philosophy. Whereas philosophy combines the two poles of human thought through the process of synthesis, theology must proceed dialectically (52–54).

> Why is that? Because theology is in no sense to be anthropology. Because instead

of reflecting on the reality and truth of human existence, it reflects on the reality and truth of God's Word as spoken to human existence...Theology must therefore set out from the point at which philosophy thinks it can arrive ...Moreover, theology claims that this very point can only be given in advance, that reflection on God can only proceed in the form of a thinking *from* rather than a thinking *toward*.[3] (54)

Two criteria are offered by Barth to safeguard theology on its way: election and predestination. These *theological* criteria recognize the priority of God over our knowledge of Him, and that theology always exists in grace (59–60). Thus, for Barth, although theology must use philosophy because it is a human science, it must do so in a dialectical manner in order to stay open to the justifying Word of God.

"Fate and Idea" draws a sharp contrast between Barth and Brunner on the role of philosophy for theology. Gestrich aptly suggests biblical metaphors to illuminate their differing understandings: for Brunner, philosophy is John the Baptist preparing the way for theology, whereas for Barth, the relationship between theology and philosophy is like Moses' indecisive contest with Pharaoh's magicians—theology is always "without guarantees" over-against philosophy.[4] This article marks another major step in Barth's progress towards formulating a theology based on revelation alone.[5]

As we have seen, Brunner's works since 1925, and particularly since *Philosophy of Religion* in 1927, have followed a consistent pattern of argument: "modern thought" (typically "Idealism" and "Naturalism") is described and shown to be lacking, its negative impact upon modern theology is demonstrated (with Schleiermacher and Ritschl as the prime examples), and the correct "Biblical" understanding is explained and applied to the problem at hand. In 1929, Brunner explicitly explains and justifies this theological approach in his article, "The Other Task of Theology".[6]

Brunner begins the article by maintaining that theology's "first and essential task" is "*reflective interpretation*" on the Word of God, that is, biblical and systematic theology (255). However, this task of interpretation is genuine only when it is done "existentially". Brunner then argues that this first task of theology is not separable from a second, polemical task. This second task is necessary because

> this reflection does not occur in a vacuum, but in an historically filled-out situation. The Word of God encounters humanity which has already..., in its own manner, made sense of its existence in one way or the other.

In addition, since the Word of God calls humanity to repentance,

> its coming is an attack, its achievement occurs in struggle. The gospel is polemical

to such an extent that its realization is called a killing, and its reception a death.
Therefore theology, since it can take place only in participation in this coming of
the Word, can be none other than polemical. (255–256)

Theology's polemic attacks false thinking, specifically the "axiom of reason"—humanity's independent reason which arrogantly judges all things,
including God, by its own limited standards (256). In the fight against the
axiom of reason, theology not only overthrows reason's illusions, but also
fulfills its deepest intentions:

> The Word of God...is an "overcoming" and not a rape, an inner conquest, a libera-
> tion. Otherwise...we would have what is known as the *sacrificium intellectus*,
> blind faith, rather than seeing, clear, free faith, which is true faith. (257)

Brunner emphasizes that this second task of theology is not apologetics (a
defensive attempt to justify God). Rather, "the archetype of theology" is *polemic*, because the preaching of the Word of God itself is essentially polemical (258–259).[7] While polemical preaching is, in itself, powerless to bring
anyone to faith, Brunner maintains that it is *this* kind of speech (both in
preaching and theology) which the Holy Spirit uses to bring people to a
saving knowledge of Jesus Christ, because it is *this* kind of speech that appeals to human reason, where existential decisions are made.

Brunner coins a new term for this second task of theology. Since "apologetics" is too defensive, and "polemics" too aggressive, Brunner offers
"eristics", from the Greek 'ερι ζειν, "to debate" (260). Thus

> the task of eristic theology to point out how, through the Word of God, human
> reason is exposed partly as the source of a life-threatening error, and partly as the
> source of an incomplete human quest.[8]

In the remainder of the article, Brunner demonstrates how eristic theology fights on two fronts: *outside the Church* against Idealism and Naturalism, and *within the Church* against an objectivistic dogmatics. What unites
both fights is that eristics is an "existential" task which combats these "theoretical" errors. In order to remain "existential", eristic theology is above all
concerned with anthropology:

> Anthropology, the self-understanding of humanity, is the common ground of faith
> and unbelief. It is the most essential task of eristic theology to point out to
> humanity that it can only rightly understand itself in faith, that only through the
> Word of God does it receive what it seeks, that what it seeks in a distorted manner
> is known only in Christian faith...This sharpening of the anthropological
> question...is the right question, and when the answer is "theocentrically" cor-
> rected, it is the single possible way to force unbelief into existential thinking, to

lure it out of its theoretical attitude...[Theology] cannot demonstrate that humanity is...in contradiction with itself...without emerging out of "objective theoretical reasoning" into the region of the existential. In this manner, Pascal erected his whole "Apology"...out of the thought of the *misère de l'homme*, just as Kierkegaard did from the thought of his own self-contradiction or despair. (260–261)

Brunner claims that this human question about God and human existence is the "point-of-contact" [*Anknüpfungspunkt*] for the Word of God in humanity (262). Here Brunner draws together his previous thinking and takes another decisive step:

It is not a false Pelagian theology that seeks a point-of-contact for the divine Word in humanity...Rather, the fundamental evil of Pelagianism lies in the fact that it seeks a positive rather than a negative point-of-contact. The Gospel does not address itself to a person who knows nothing of God. That contradicts the unanimous witness of experience, the Bible, and all classical Christian theology. From the Gospel it is apparent that there is a human knowing of God which is at the same time a not-knowing, or at least a not-correctly-knowing, not a saving knowledge. Therefore, *theologia naturalis* cannot serve as a foundation for Christian theology. But it is apparent from the Gospel that the entire life and thought and self-understanding of humanity is immersed and submerged in this questionable knowledge of God. Therefore, life, in all of its manifestations, is essentially a question about God, a conflicting *grandeur et misère de l'homme*. This ability to question is the point-of-contact. If humanity *could* not ask about God, it could not be given redemption, because the Word of God would be inaccessible to it...If it did not *have* to ask about God, it would not need redemption, for it would have the Word in itself.

In his discussion about eristic theology's fight against Naturalism and Idealism *outside* the Church, Brunner bases his argument (both these philosophies are half-true as well as half-false) on a doctrine which now assumes central importance for Brunner: the image of God.[9]

It is only because we are in God and know about God that we can ask about Him. It is only because we are related to God—constitutively, not necessarily consciously—that we are human. This is the *imago Dei*, which has not simply been eradicated by sin...Humanity is not a *truncus et lapis*, but human, and that means a being which knows something about God. Humanity's knowledge of God is its humanity—however distorted and questionable this knowledge may be...The greatness of humanity (the *grandeur de l'homme*) is not annihilated through its *"misère"*, but they together form the riddle of the contradiction of humanity. Sin does not make humanity inhuman, but precisely sinful *humanity*. It is no doubt a darkened, distorted, corrupted image of God, but it is not its eradication. (263–264)

Brunner is attempting here to restate the Reformation understanding of nature and grace without falling into the problems of the Catholic approach.[10] He reclaims the grace of Creation by drawing on the Ebnerian concept that humanity is "addressable".[11]

> All people are [addressable], because they are all human beings. This is the contact…"Addressable" does not even mean that they can hear. It merely means that it is not impossible that the Word can obtain a hearing in them… This is the critical difference between Catholic and Protestant theology. Hearing, faith, saying Yes —these are completely the work of God alone; whereas saying No is the work of humanity. That humanity has the ability to say No [does not imply] that it can also say Yes. The removal of this apparently obvious logical deduction is the Reformation, Pauline, Christian doctrine of grace. (268).

Turning to eristics' task *inside* the Church, Brunner argues that eristic theology fights against a "theoretical" understanding of theology. Eristic theology's "existential" flavor is necessary seasoning for the Church's theology, because dogmatic theology is also subject to the temptation of the "axiom of reason"—to present a "non-existential concept of truth" (271). Brunner casts a barb at Barth in light of *Christian Dogmatics*:

> I wonder if Barth, in his transition from the eristics of *Romans* to a more "descriptive" style of dogmatics, has, without meaning to, rendered assistance to the "theoretical misunderstanding", or at least has not strongly counteracted it as thoroughly as it is possible to do through a correct estimation of the eristic task.

In keeping dogmatics existentially grounded, eristics keeps the Church responsible to its actual life-setting in the modern world. Modern people are existentially, not theoretically oriented; the Church must recognize this and respond appropriately in its theology.

> It is not justifiable…to make it difficult for modern people "to believe in anything" by depriving them (in a false enthusiasm for God's honor) of the bridge which God has provided for sinful humanity towards faith. (273)

Brunner concludes his article with a direct appeal to Barth to leave his previously-necessary "one-sidedness" and to embrace the *whole* teaching of the Gospel for the sake of reaching unbelievers with the Good News (274–275).[12] Despite the real danger of falling into "continuity thinking", dialectical theology must seize this bridge:

> It is high time that we…take up (with great care) the problem of the *revelatio generalis* in all its manifestations. To reject a *theologia naturalis* from the start and in every sense is faithful neither to Paul nor to the Reformation. (274, note 7)

As has been seen from the examination of Brunner's writings in Chapter Three, there is little that is new in "The Other Task of Theology". It is wholly incorrect to call this article a "development" or "turn" in Brunner's theology. Rather, it is a comprehensive statement of what he had been doing for at least four years, and what he would continue to do.[13] In the context of this book, "The Other Task of Theology" is best seen as Brunner's response to Barth's *Christian Dogmatics*. Brunner saw Barth's prolegomena as a significant step in the wrong direction, back towards theoretical, objectivistic, scholastic theology. In Brunner's view, Barth's work since 1927 had turned away from the promise of *Romans II*.[14]

Barth spent the 1929 summer semester on sabbatical at the Bergli.[15] In June, Brunner came up from Zurich to meet with him, and there ensued an extremely heated argument over "The Other Task of Theology".[16] Brunner was clearly upset by the discussion, which revealed the depth of Barth's rejection of his program of eristics: "We have reached a critical point". Brunner writes Barth shortly after their encounter, responding point by point to Barth's concerns. Brunner maintains the Barth is unjustified in referring to the "arrogance of eristics", specifically its attempt to "uncover the illusions" of modern people. Brunner responds that, if this is arrogance, what does one call a dogmatics which dares to explain the inner workings of the Trinity? Brunner next attempts to assuage Barth's fear by claiming that eristics is in no way intended to become a prerequisite for dogmatics. He then goes on to disagree with Barth's insistence that theology has but one form—dogmatics:

> The theology of the early Church as well as that of the Reformation in the beginning was not dogmatic in this sense, but was polemical or "eristic". That is, they developed their faith in controversial discussions with the spirit of the times in its principal and most dangerous forms…It was strongly dogmatic at the point of orientation, that is, materially, but it was eristic in form and method. You once called Luther a theological journalist. In this sense, most of the great theological work is journalistic. It…gives a theological explication "of the day", and really works *au jour pour le jour*.[17]

Brunner then defends anthropology as the decisive point for theology today:

> This is where the true opposition exists today (Gogarten is absolutely correct here) just as in 1517 it existed in ecclesiology. Therefore, today anthropology must take center stage, as the doctrine of the Church did in Calvin's time… Here also belongs a *theologia naturalis*. That there is such a theology, no one …can dispute. The only question concerns its value. Thus it is important to lay hold of the question of the *theologia naturalis* in a strongly theologically-grounded manner… The chapter on *de homine* is not in itself the most important one, but it is the chapter where the roots of modern thinking, and thus the opposition to the Gos-

pel, lie…The question of the point-of-contact is a strongly theological one in the attack on the central question. Thus we need a theocentric anthropology.[18]

Brunner's final rebuttal accuses Barth of falling for the "orthodox temptation" of a "timeless" dogmatics. Eristics, by its very nature, does not fall for this temptation: "Precisely because eristics considers timeliness to be a great *bene*, it will put ['theological journalism'] ahead of dogmatics". Brunner concludes by repeating that the only thing which "The Other Task of Theology" has against Barth is Barth's refusal to grant a place to any kind of theological thinking other than dogmatics.

Barth does not reply to Brunner's letter. However, his rejection of "eristics" is clear from his correspondence with Thurneysen. Thurneysen writes Barth after the meeting with Brunner, suggesting that someone should answer Brunner in *Zwischen den Zeiten* "to put a clear question mark after his 'other task of theology'".[19] Barth agrees that someone should write a response to Brunner's essay, preferably a third person.[20]

In the meantime, Brunner asks for another meeting with Barth, and Barth agrees.[21] There is no account of this July meeting; given Brunner's pattern of replying quickly and at length to meetings with substantial disagreement, one can assume that the meeting smoothed over some of the difficulties which arose at their June meeting. Nonetheless, Barth began the winter semester with serious concerns about the developments in Brunner's thinking. In commenting upon Barth's September lecture in Elberfeld on "The Holy Spirit and the Christian Life", Thurneysen touches upon their concerns with Brunner:[22]

> It was theologically important to me, the impressive way you strengthened a concern that must certainly be central in today's position on the matter, and that already sounded in my ears in your Elberfeld lecture like the theme of a fugue, a triple-fugue: the *actuality* of the Word, a sovereign actuality, which has absolutely nothing to do with the "creativity" of artists. Further, I appreciated your clear statement that the battle stands *here*, that it is a question of the *one thing* that must be fought for now—against all tendencies to set up somehow a place to bivouac *below* the summit itself. Emil, for example, clearly wants to go no further here. Your Elberfeld lecture will further indicate a visible signal of the break-up.[23]

Thus, the summer of 1929 marked a turning point in the Barth–Brunner relationship. The provoking incident was Brunner's "The Other Task of Theology". But it has been clearly demonstrated that this article was just another step along the line Brunner had been pursuing since 1925. Thus, Barth's immediate and complete rejection of "The Other Task" shows both that he had not been paying close attention to Brunner's development over the previous four years, and (more importantly) that his own attempt to formulate a "revelation alone" theology had made significant progress—most notably on the relation of theology to philosophy ("Fate and Idea") and the fundamental place of actualism ("The Holy Spirit and the Christian Life"). It was Barth's new clarity, rather than any significant change in Brunner, which led Barth to more and more openly question Brunner's reliability as a comrade in his own theological development.

The Beginning of the End of "Dialectical Theology"

Any remaining sense of fellowship with his dialectical colleagues was broken when Barth visited Marburg at the end of January 1930. Following this visit, Barth lays out a shopping list of grievances and concerns about his "colleagues" in a long letter to Thurneysen. What set Barth off was the combination of conversations with Bultmann and a lecture he had heard a week earlier in Münster "about a new apologetics—not unlike...our friend Emil's". Barth writes:

> Dear Eduard, the whole line is entirely not a good thing; under no circumstances do I want to be associated with it. Is it not the case that all of us, who apparently stand close to each other, have gradually come to want exactly what we...did not want and struggled against from the beginning—to stand in the nearest relationship to...a grounding not in actuality, but to lay the *possibility* of faith and revelation on the table?...What is all this...if it is not the renewal of *the* relationship between theology and philosophy, just like Kant, Hegel, Schleiermacher, De Wette, etc.—only that now, for a change, philosophy has become something negative, existential, etc...Is it just a question of a harmless difference, while the rest of our theologies are "fundamentally" at one? I don't know...but I simply oppose with all the hairs on my head the entire state of affairs...and I don't know whether I should bunch together one great article of resistance and bid farewell to Emil, Paul, Friedrich, Rudolf *e tutti quanti*.[24]

Thurneysen replies that Barth's instincts are correct, and that he should "for once send forth your flash of lightning".[25] However, he singles out Brunner for mercy:

> I would ask for only one consideration: Deal gently with the lad—Emil (cf. II Samuel 18.5!). He certainly deserves as much thrashing as the others, but he may not be abandoned, for somehow he himself hears, even if he does not appear to hear. And therefore for him, it will not be in vain![26]

In 1930 Brunner published *God and Man*, a collection of lectures from a 1929 trip to Holland.[27] The book is a concrete example of Brunner's "eristics".[28] Most significant for this book is a four-page section in chapter three ("Church and Revelation"), where Brunner argues that: humanity exists not only *through* the Word of God but *in* the Word; humanity is called into existence as *human* being through the address of God's Word, which makes us responsible beings; the *imago Dei* is perverted but not destroyed through sin, for we *remain* personal beings; and revelation brings a *restoration* of the purpose of Creation (114–117). In an extended footnote to this passage, Brunner responds to Barth's attack on the *imago Dei* doctrine in "The Holy Spirit and the Christian Life":

> It seems to have escaped Barth's notice that neither Luther nor Calvin has denied the existence of a *revelatio generalis*...Barth is thoroughly justified in his concern not to let the *imago Dei* become a possession of man, but rather to let it be recognized as an act of God's grace. But he overlooks [the fact that only] because man has some kind of knowledge about God can he be a sinner. That man is a sinner, that he can sin, is itself the proof that the *imago Dei* is not effaced. But if this is the case, then one must distinguish the two revelations...It is this distinction alone which makes possible a fruitful discussion with the general history of religion on the one hand, and with philosophy on the other. (116, note 1)

God and Man prompted Barth to send Brunner a copy of a lecture he had recently given entitled "Humanity, the Image of God".[29] The lecture is a direct refutation of Brunner's *imago Dei* argument in *God and Man*:

> That we are created through the Word of God for the Word of God is one thing.
>   That we exist in the Word of God is another thing.
> The hearing of created hearts or ears is one thing, our hearing is another thing.
> *Humanitas* and *personalitas* is one thing, *imago Dei* is another thing.

Brunner's position implies that, since

> our existence is not a non-being in the Word of God; therefore it is not an absolute being-lost from God; therefore it is not a real asking of the question of existence; therefore it is not the death of sinners.

Barth maintains that Brunner's stance extracts a high price:

> (1) That sinful humanity knows God "*in some way*"
> (2) That one is able to give, with the Catholics, a satisfying answer to the question of human responsibility for sin.
> (3) That the least-resolved aspect of the theological method of the Reformers (the problem of the double knowledge of God) may be uncritically continued.

Brunner's response to Barth's letter is marked with the tone of formality which has come upon their correspondence since the argument over eristics at the Bergli.[30] In addition, Brunner's reply is the first in a long sequence of letters whose constant presupposition is that Barth has misunderstood him.

Brunner makes five points. First, "I expressly teach the destruction of the *imago Dei* through sin, but which is not fully eradicated, and of course thereby intend to remain exactly in line with Reformation theology". Second, "I nowhere teach the identity of the *imago Dei* and humanness, but that humanness is contained in the *imago*". In his third point, Brunner makes, for the first time, a conceptual distinction within the image of God:

> Therefore I teach expressly…that the *imago Dei* must be restored precisely where it has been destroyed, but that the *formale* of the God-created person—the *persona quod* in distinction to the *persona quid*, which has its center in the "I-consciousness"—remains preserved, so that we can say: *I* am reconciled, *I* am redeemed…The new creation through grace is not a completely new creation, but precisely a renewal. Otherwise, the awareness of the connection between the old and the new person…would be broken.

Fourth, Brunner argues that Barth's anthropology—based on a destroyed *imago*—is "theology with no significant possibility". Finally, Brunner attempts one last clarification:

> I do not say that the human person *as human* hears God's Word, but that he hears it through the Holy Spirit. But of course, *he* hears it through the Holy Spirit, not the Holy Spirit.

Brunner ends the letter bitterly, clearly upset that Barth has both misunderstood and misrepresented him:

> I am frankly…somewhat surprised what light work you have made of me. We should not dispose of one another like this. Or has it never really occurred to you that there are others…who, in one place or another, might have seen something which you have overlooked? In any case…your lecture mixed-up my entire theological position and frankly perverted it into its opposite; in any case it has shown me that you paid little attention to my position and immediately put it in its place so that your own thinking would not be disturbed in the least. So, naturally a fellowship in work is impossible, for you practice an ethic which is certainly not Biblical: the strong person alone is the mightiest. In the long run, that ethic may not be beneficial to the strongest person.

Brunner's eristics program formalized what Brunner had been saying for several years, that theology only "touches ground" when it is specifically oriented to the questions and struggles of human existence. Barth had seen clearly since 1928 that Gogarten and Bultmann were heading down what he considered to be the dead-end of an anthropological theology. But for Brunner to announce a similar program so boldly prompted Barth to reply publicly to each of the three "pillars" of dialectical theology. To do so, he dusted off an unpublished lecture from 1927, "Theology and Modern Man".[31] He published this lecture with a small but significant addition which attacks all three of his colleagues.

Barth begins by observing that a proper understanding of theology—whose grounding is revelation and faith alone (375–376)— raises three problems for the modern person. First, since the sole criterion of theology is the Word of God, it means that the knowledge of truth is entirely a question of God's free choice to reveal truth; theology thus embarrasses the modern person with its doctrine of predestination (378–380). Second, theology is not a "free science", but is "bound" to the Church; therefore, it poses a challenge to modern thought, which considers itself "free-thinking" (380–382). Third, since theology is a science of faith, the theologian cannot use history, psychology or philosophy as tools for discovering truths which she has not already been given through faith and the Word of God (382–384). This is the third "scandal" theology poses to the modern person, for as a "science of faith" it does not offer any proof for its statements, but demands "pure unsecured obedience, a trust stripped of all guarantees" (384).

Barth then lays out the three modern responses to these three scandals of theology. The first is "brutal atheism", which is the way of "rebellion", a "flight" or "escape" from the proper work of theology (385–388). Atheism is modernity's protest against a science whose sole criterion is a self-attesting, given Truth. A second modern response to the scandal of theology is "domestication, which is the way of 'sentimental Liberalism'" (388–392). This way attempts to secure theology as a "possibility" by "making theology innocuous, domesticating and adapting it...to the best, most proven and surest ways of thinking". Liberalism's motive is to avoid the "bound" aspect of theology so that it can "negotiate" with it (390).

The final response of modernity to the challenge of theology—theology as a science of *faith*—is the way of "control". This is the response of Roman Catholicism, "the most audacious and therefore perhaps the most dangerous" response (392). Barth uses a vivid image to signify the nature of this response as opposed to the other two:

> If one sees a wild and threatening horse galloping straight at you, you could either jump out of the way [atheism] or try to soothe it with friendly words [Liberalism]. Or, if you had enough self-confidence, you could jump on its back and become its rider and master. (393)

This response tries to avoid theology's claim to be a science of "unsecured trust", and seeks to secure theology in a presupposition other than the Word of God. Barth then inserts his addition, laying out (anonymously but clearly) the positions of his colleagues as illustrations of the attempt to control the Word of God:

> Perhaps it might be a negative metaphysics, an apparently very non-Thomistic

metaphysics, not the zenith but the nadir of human knowledge, an ontology of the "hollow space", to whose dimensions faith and theology correspond exactly, and …are clearly indicated [Bultmann]? Perhaps an "eristic" theology, which would have the task of making it clear to the modern person, with paternal wisdom, that he, without recourse to Christian faith, necessarily must become entangled in an evil self-contradiction [Brunner]? Or perhaps a doctrine of history, whose truth would correspond exactly to what the biblical presentation describes as the reality of the relationship of God and humanity [Gogarten]? (394)

These responses seek to build a "supporting leg"—theology becomes not only the science of faith "but also metaphysics, apologetics, anthropology, historical theory, eristics, or whatever one wants to call it". Barth sees these newest attempts at theological control as direct counter-movements to genuine dialectical theology, which stresses the freedom of revelation (395). This third response errs only slightly, but disastrously:

It is more dangerous [than Roman Catholicism] because unbelievably good theology loses its way at one small point: it no longer says that human thinking reckons with the Word of God only through faith. But isn't it precisely on this one little point that everything hinges? Is there any secure place which we can give to theology? Is not theology precisely theology only in the uncertainty of the real science of faith…only as a stranger in the areas of the other sciences, without its own area?…Perhaps this is the fatal question which our generation is asked, whether theologians are in the position to recognize this last and dangerous temptation for what it is. (395–396)

In this article, Barth fired his first public (though veiled) salvo against the developments of his colleagues. It was a defense of *Christian Dogmatics* against Brunner's charge of "theoretical" thinking and Gogarten's criticism of its lack of anthropology.[32] By lumping his colleagues together under the category of "Thomistic Catholicism", it was apparent that Barth was already thinking by the middle of 1930 that the alliance of dialectical theology had reached its end.[33]

In the summer vacation of 1930, Barth and Brunner were able to have another face-to-face conversation. In his follow-up letter to Barth, Brunner indicates he was generally pleased with it: "for once we really heard each other".[34] However, the ensuing appearance of "Theology and Modern Man" prompts Brunner to pursue the conversation.

First, Brunner is completely baffled by the essay's proposition that theology can only proceed from the doctrine of predestination:

A theology constructed out of predestination is an impossibility…Not merely my eristics or Gogarten's anthropology or Bultmann's doctrine of "pre-understanding", but every doctrinal certainty becomes completely out of the question.

He asserts that Barth's position—an actualist predestination—cuts off all relationship between the Word of God and human thinking.

Brunner then tries to show, through an examination of *Christian Dogmatics*, that Barth's theology *also* requires "guarantees" and eristics. Formally, Barth's dogmatic method is "carried out with immense faith in the validity of the logical function of human reason", and recognizes "the suitability of human speech and concepts for pure doctrine". More significantly, Brunner maintains that *Christian Dogmatics* demonstrates a *material* use of eristics:

> The doctrine of the Word of God begins entirely eristically, in that a human gap is uncovered, namely, humanity's not-knowing of God. Is that simply to be *believed*? No, it is demonstrated. It is *shown* that there is not, as far as we are concerned, a knowledge of God; that any alleged knowledge, e.g., Idealism, is only an apparent knowledge; that there can be a knowledge of God only under an entirely different presupposition, namely...revelation.

Brunner argues that Barth is unaware how his use of Anselm points in a direction opposite to his intentions:

> Anselm is a powerful Eristician. Cur *deus homo*: that is entirely and completely an eristic way of asking the question, just as the way he conducts his proof is eristic. Eristics...is the demonstration of the gap which God's revelation or God's grace covers.

Most significantly, Barth (according to Brunner) demonstrates eristic thinking in *Christian Dogmatics* by speaking of "the *conditions* of the *possibility* of grace"[35]: "Whoever says possibility says eristics. Whoever sets up conditions of grace, guarantees it".

Brunner maintains that there are only incidental differences in the way both Barth and Brunner conduct eristics: 1) Barth focuses entirely on formal, cognitive proofs, while Brunner also emphasizes material, existential proofs; 2) Barth is uninterested (*vs.* Brunner) in the different kinds of not-knowing of God; and 3) Barth and Brunner have merely chosen "different fronts" (Barth *vs.* Roman Catholicism, Brunner *vs.* Modernism), "but the procedure is exactly the same".

Brunner concludes that "Theology and Modern Man" is an unhelpful contribution to the debate, since its polemic against a theology seeking "guarantees" is a polemic against all theology, including Barth's. All theologians, *especially* Barth, guarantee their theological work in their confidence in the capability of human logic:

> [Just look at] your vital faith in the power of (theological) logic, with which you trust yourself to examine thoroughly the depths of the Trinity. How solid you must consider the human capacity for thought, that you trust your conclusions

so unconditionally based on a concept of revelation…How does it happen that humanity, which has nothing left of the image of God, has such a phenomenally trustworthy logic?…In reality you trust humanity in its fallen condition no less than I (your proof is not by virtue of a *logica regenitorum*, but is a result of purely natural logic), but you do not want to bring it into relationship with the original possession of a knowledge of God through creation.

Barth responds immediately to Brunner's letter.[36] He completely rejects Brunner's assertion that "Theology and Modern Man" contradicts *Christian Dogmatics*.[37] Barth concludes that he can no longer view their "increasingly visible fundamental differences [as] merely accidental, [which] can be rectified by me through further clarifications". Barth regrets Brunner's theory of "misunderstanding", claiming that it is Brunner who has misunderstood him —his letter "shows that you do not take my earlier work seriously". If he had, Brunner would see that "my earlier work does not run so parallel to yours". Barth feels that Brunner's letter leaves him with only one way to express their differences, "something completely catastrophic":

Accept the fact…that you completely misunderstand not only [*Christian Dogmatics*]…but also my *Romans*, since you have obviously not noticed that since 1920 (not *1930*, but 1920) it has been for me a question of "constructing theology from predestination"…What have I said to you in this lecture that I have not always maintained as my presupposition, and which I have often expressed to you? And which of my "constructions" in all their forms do not spring from the ground of this presupposition, bound to it and conditioned through it, up to the last little proposition? That is true of *Christian Dogmatics* as well.

Barth asserts that they are doing theology differently, and the dividing issue is anthropology:

You have not let it be pointed out to you…that this anthropological background is lacking in me. Thus, my entire work, despite all the manifold similarities, is to be explained differently from yours. Thus, if not from the very beginning, then for a goodly time, you should have made the most fundamental stand against my work.

Barth continues:

Why do you interpret me thus now…as if I indeed work with "guarantees", when you used to be in the habit of reproaching me in other discussions that I lacked such guarantees and that you must, so to speak, supply them with your eristics? …Have you ever heard from me…anything different than that I consider all theology to be nonsense which does not absolutely begin "formally" with obedience ?

Barth ends the letter by asking how to proceed from this point. Barth sees only two possibilities: either Brunner converts Barth to "predestination *and* eristics", or Barth converts Brunner to "a theology which, like a spinning top, supports itself on only one point". Since human understandings are usually more ambiguous than this either/or, Barth is prepared "that we might continue for the rest of our lives with friendly human relationships and with material contiguities". Barth ends the letter poignantly:

> People in the future…will not be completely wrong to always shake their heads a bit regarding our opposition—you in good company, I probably more of a kind of theological crab, with whom it is impossible to deal, one who had once justified such lovely hopes. And…they will rack their brains how things were at that time with the unity and disunity of "dialectical theology".

Thus, in Barth's mind, dialectical theology as a movement had come to an end by Autumn 1930, torn apart over the issues of revelation's relationship to anthropology and reason.[38] It was Brunner's "The Other Task of Theology", in the wake of Barth's "Fate and Idea", which made this conclusion inevitable in Barth's mind. After the disastrous Marburg visit in January 1930, Barth felt he had no choice but to begin to distance himself from his former colleagues ("Theology and Modern Man"). Neither Brunner, Gogarten, nor Bultmann agreed that the differences were as fundamental as Barth perceived them to be.[39] Thus, the "break-up", particularly between Barth and Brunner, dragged on for another six years. But in Barth's perspective, only Thurneysen remained committed to what Barth considered to be his original and persistent insight: the absolute freedom of God in His subjectivity in the Word of God, a reality which creates its own possibility, which is both received *and thought out* only within the realm of Church and faith.

Interlude: Ethics—"Command" or "Orders"? (1927–1932)

Of the many issues causing stress between Barth and Brunner, ethics was a minor one.[40] Its importance in the unraveling of their theological alliance is mostly confined to Brunner's use of "the orders of creation" [*Schöpfungsordnungen*] and their role in the later context of Nazi ideology. Therefore, Barth and Brunner's disagreement over ethics will only be sketched here.[41]

From his first ethical writing[42] through his comprehensive ethical statements in *Church Dogmatics* II/2 and III/4, Barth constructed an ethics of justification—what matters ethically is the action of *God* and our openness (in faith) to receive God's justification of our sinful lives. More specifically, Barth developed a highly actualist "command ethics". For Barth, God's command is concrete and specific (211).[43] To hear God's command is not to hear some general moral law in one's conscience, but to be addressed by a claim which we do not know in advance. If the situation were otherwise, it would mean that determining right and wrong would be up to us (212). On the contrary, Barth argues that the command "encounters us already content-filled, *determined* and *filled*"; therefore "it is a *question* which we must *answer* with our concrete act; not an answer which we ourselves have given, through which we merely repeat or confirm ourselves". However, our "keeping" of this command cannot be our act, because we stand before God as transgressors before a Judge. God's command demands an "Either-Or" response from us, concretely and immediately, and this is precisely what we constantly fail to do (218). Therefore, our "keeping" of the commandments can only be through faith in God's prior justification of our acts; *faith* is keeping the commandments (221–222).

Of special interest to the Barth–Brunner debate is the use Barth makes of the "orders of creation". The concept appears nowhere in Barth except for his 1928 Münster/1930 Bonn ethics lectures.[44] Barth devotes a paragraph (§9) to "Order" in the chapter on "The Command of God the Creator". It is immediately noticeable how uncomfortable Barth is with the concept of order: he protests that employing the concept of "orders of creation" is not building ethics on "natural law" (209); he constantly uses the singular ("order") rather than the plural ("orders"); and his use of "order" is strictly *theological* (213). While Barth endorses the concept of the orders of creation in these lectures, his urge to qualify immediately what he affirms indicates his unease with the concept.[45] Soon after the time he had lightly revised his ethics lectures at Bonn, his rejection became complete. Gogarten and Brunner's increasing reliance upon the "orders of creation", and, more importantly, the increasing voice of Nazism in German politics, put Barth squarely against this concept.

Barth's ethical thinking clearly follows his dogmatic thought. The concern in both is to focus on the *reality* of God's self-revelation in the Word of God rather than on the *possibility* of discerning and making ethical decisions. Barth's ethics are *theo*-logical, and most determinedly non-*anthropo*-logical precisely at the point of the ethical (religious) person. God's freedom to act, the total need for justification of human acts, the hiddenness of the things of faith, the forensic aspect of Christian action—all these indicate the consistency with which Barth is thinking in the years 1927–1930.

Although the fundamental limit on human thought and action indicated by Kantian ethics played a major role in Brunner's "early eristics" ("The Limit of Humanity" to *The Mediator*), it is not until 1928 that Brunner begins to develop a constructive theological ethics. Although he admits being influenced greatly by Barth's "command ethics",[46] Brunner's consistent Kantianism and the increasing impact of Gogarten's employment of the "orders of creation" remain the determinative influences on his ethical position.

Brunner's major ethical writing is his 1932 book *The Divine Impera-tive.*[47] Here we see Brunner gathering together the various influences on his thinking—Kantianism, Ebnerian "personalism", Barth's command ethics, and Gogarten's orders—and attempting to unite them into a coherent ethical program.

The Divine Imperative is divided into three "books", the last two dealing with an exposition of the meaning of "The Command" and "The Orders".[48] The ninety pages of Book I are devoted to an eristic attack on "Natural Mo-rality". The argument is almost an exact duplication in the ethical field of the "Presuppositions" in Part One of *The Mediator*. In Book II, "The Divine Command", Brunner attempts to set forth a radical command ethic:

> The Divine *Command*...can only be perceived by him to whom God Himself speaks His Word, in faith...Hence I cannot know beforehand the content of the Command as I can know that of the Law; I can only receive it afresh each time through the voice of the Spirit. (111)

But for Brunner, the freedom of a command ethic must be balanced by or-der. In Book III, Brunner lays out the place of the "orders of creation" in his ethics. Here, he follows closely what he had written in 1930—the orders of creation embody the command of God the Creator:

> [God] addresses us as the creator, as the one who wills this world, who affirms this world, who maintains it as it is. That is the first fundamental point ...If he wills to maintain it—whatever its condition be—then we must for our part main-tain it. God's will is, thank God, fundamentally conservative. His affirming, main-taining will stands behind reality...[This world] is not a formless matter waiting to be modeled by us...but a world already formed and ordered by God's will. The first question which as ethical subjects we put to the world is therefore not, "What am I to make out of it?" but "How am I to adapt myself?" "What character must my life have, if it is to fit into the order that I find before me?"...The first commandment, the chief commandment, is—Reverence for that which is.[49]

The orders of creation—marriage, family, state—are given by God to pro-vide an ordered framework for God's basic will for humanity, which is community.[50] Thus, for Brunner, the "orders of creation" connect the div-ine command to the actual life of real people, provide fundamental ethical content by providing the framework for community, and give the Church a common base from which it can engage society in meaningful moral dis-cussion.[51]

However, the Christian cannot merely accept the orders as they are, for they are distorted by human sin (and thus are only broken reflections of God's created order) (214–215). Therefore, the second word for the Chris-tian—the command of God the Redeemer—is that "the will of God does not merely tell us to adapt ourselves, to accept, but also to resist, to protest, not to be 'conformed to this world'" (217). Brunner thus structures the relationship between the orders and the commands in a "reformist" manner, what he calls "*critical co-operation*" (272). In fact, his ethics can be best understood by reversing the title of the book—"The Orders and the Command". The orders are the given, they are permanent, they are intended by God. But the orders are "minimalist" in their ethical demands and their ability to support acts of love. Therefore, within the context of the orders, the Christian listens for the divine command, which will direct his action concretely and specifically in a given situation to do the loving thing, which moves the particular order toward the community-producing and community-supporting role God intends it to play.[52]

Thus, in Brunner's ethical writings, we see three strands which put pressure on his relationship with Barth. First, Brunner continues his eristic approach, as he attempts to show how Christian ethics both supplant and fulfill natural ethics. Second, in employing the concept of the orders of creation, Brunner places an emphasis on the doctrine of creation which is independent of christology and revelation in the strict sense.[53] Finally, the whole thrust of Brunner's ethics is an attempt to establish a "point-of-contact" between the ethical message of the Bible and the ethical struggles of the modern person.[54]

The Battle Lines Are Drawn (1931–1932)

The Anselmian Resolution

Barth originally planned to devote a significant part of the 1930 summer semester to a thorough revision *Christian Dogmatics*, in order to purge it of the "existential" or "eristic" elements within it. However, the project got delayed when the topic of his seminar that semester, Anselm's *Proslogion*, began to clarify his thinking about how he could re-state formally what he had been trying to say materially all along. The following summer (1931), Barth published a little book on what he had learned.[55]

Anselm: Fides Quaerens Intellectum is divided into two parts: "The Theological Scheme" and "The Proof of the Existence of God".[56] The first section is important for this book, for in its five chapters Barth examines theology's "necessity", its "possibility", its "conditions", its "manner", and its "aim".

Barth begins with a startling interpretation of Anselm's "proofs" of God. He maintains that while Anselm has a polemical-apologetic aim in mind, this aim is secondary to the primary task of *intelligere*—understanding—whose primary result is "joy" for the believing thinker, and only secondarily a "proof" for non-believers (15). This is because Anselm's slogan—*"fides quaerens intellectum"*—while being a guide to theological activity, is primarily a statement about the nature of faith itself (16).

> What we are speaking of is a spontaneous desire of faith. Fundamentally, the *quaerere intellectum* is really immanent in *fides*...Anselm wants "proof" and "joy" because he wants *intelligere* and he wants *intelligere* because he believes. (16–17)

Thus theology, as the science of faith, must also follow this same inner dynamic to seek understanding (rather than first requiring understanding or proof) (17).

Barth then argues that Anselm sees theology's possibility being founded on the fact that faith itself, from its beginning, is understanding. Barth is attempting to overcome the non-rational view of faith dominant since the eighteenth century (22). In contrast, the Church up until then had understood all subjective *credos* to have "an objective *Credo* of the Church as its unimpeachable point of reference—that is, a number of propositions formulated in human words" (24).

In the third chapter—"The Conditions of Theology"—Barth takes note of the fact that before conducting his proof, Anselm prays for God's enlightenment. For Barth, this is no pious posturing, but rather a fundamental insight into theology's possibility. Barth understands Anselm's placing prayer before theological reflection to mean that God's self-revelation always takes precedence over the human search for understanding:

> Everything depends not only on the fact that God grants him grace to think correctly about him, but also on the fact that God himself comes within his system as the object of his thinking, that he "shows" himself to the thinker and in so doing modifies "correct" thinking to an *intelligere esse in re*. (39)

In the most important chapter of the book—"The Manner of Theology"—Barth attempts to clarify Anselm's epistemology. Here, in a tightly argued section, Barth makes his final break from the "egg-shells of Idealism" and moves to a theological Realism solidly based on the "inalienable subjectivity" of God.[57] For Anselm, *ratio* is not the rationality of the human knowledge of faith (noetic rationality), but rather the rationality of the object which faith knows (ontic rationality) (44–45). Thus, the correct use of the human *ratio* is determined by the *ratio* of its object (46). This means that human knowing cannot be creative or normative, but must "follow" [*nachdenken*] the *ratio* given in the object. Correspondence is established, not through the achievement of the knower, but through the action of Truth itself (who is the master of all noetic and ontic *ratios*), who conforms the noetic *ratio* and the ontic *ratio* to Himself (47).

Barth pushes his argument even further—the *ratio* proper to the object of faith is also *necessary*, that is, the knowledge of God is subordinated to the will of God (49–51). Theology cannot begin by trying to establish what is possible, nor can it construct a system which stands outside its object. Rather, theology can only proceed accordingly: "the noetic *ratio* leads to the discovery of the ontic *ratio* in so far as it follows after it" (53).[58]

Finally, Barth explores "The Aim of Theology (The Proof)". It is difficult not to hear in this chapter a decisive rejection of Brunner's "The Other Task of Theology". Barth's first point is that Anselm's "proof" is really *intelligere*, because all Anselm really does is to explore "How far is what I assume to be true actually true?" (61–62).[59] Therefore, Anselm's theological appeal to unbelievers is free of any uncertainty or anxiety (62). In a key passage for the Barth–Brunner debate, Barth describes Anselm's approach:

> Anselm's Proof works on the assumption that there is a solidarity between the theologian and the worldling which has not come about because the theologian has become one of the crowd, or one voice in a universal debating chamber, but because he is determined to address the worldling as one with whom he has at least this is common—theology. So he is able to promise him instruction on how he could convince himself, given a certain amount of intelligence, of the reasonableness of the Christian faith without having first accepted the truth of the revelation ...Anselm is in no position to serve the world with something other than that with which he himself is served. Not only because he quite honestly has nothing else to offer or because he knows no other proof than the one that convinces him, but also because he knows himself to be responsible to the world and dares not offer it anything less than the best. And for that reason Anselm knows just one question, one language and *one* task of theology.[60] (68–69)

Barth himself was the first one to draw attention to the importance of *Anselm* as he revised *Christian Dogmatics* into *Church Dogmatics* I.[61] What is it about *Anselm* that is decisive for Barth? McCormack argues persuasively that many previous interpretations either over-play or misinterpret the nature of an "Anselmian turn": dialectic is not left behind, analogy does not come to the fore until *Church Dogmatics* I/2 and II/1, and no christological concentration is immediately apparent.[62] Nor, as has been shown, was the Anselm book responsible for Barth's distancing himself from the other dialectical theologians.[63] The importance of *Anselm* is that it marks the resolution of the long process whereby "Barth overcame every last remnant of the attempt to ground, support, or justify theology by means of existential philosophy".[64] Here, Barth found a definitive way to ground the precedence of the actuality of revelation over its possibility.[65] In this book, Barth found historical justification and a way to formulate his rejection of the theologies of his colleagues who were looking for "possibilities" and "certainty" and "contact" for the self-authenticating actuality of God's self-revelation in the Word of God.[66] *Anselm* was not so much a "turning-point" as it was the "the final resolution of the problem of where theology was to find its basis", a resolution for which Barth had been searching since *Romans II*.[67]

"Material Opposition occurring Right down the Line"
The clarification Barth received from Anselm emboldened him to come out publicly against his dialectical colleagues in 1932.[68] This is seen most clearly in Barth's fully revised edition of *Christian Dogmatics*, re-titled *Church Dogmatics* (I/1). In the preface, Barth explains how the new edition is the result of the clarification Barth had gained over the past five years about how to say and how not to say what he had been trying to say all along:

> I now think I have a better understanding of...my own intentions, to the degree that in this second draft I have excluded to the very best of my ability anything that might appear to find for theology a foundation, support, or justification in philosophical existentialism. "The Word or existence?" The first edition gave to acumen, or perhaps stupidity, some ground for putting this question. I may hope that so far as concerns my own intentions the answer to it is now clear. In the former undertaking I can see only a resumption of the line which leads from Schleiermacher by way of Ritschl to Herrmann. And in any conceivable continuation along this line I can see only the plain destruction of Protestant theology and the Protestant Church. (iii)

This is the case because existentialism is ultimately "the exploitation of the *analogia entis*" to which Barth can only "say No at this point", for "I regard the *analogia entis* as the invention of Antichrist".[69]

Barth then engages in his most pointed comments to date about the status of the dialectical theology movement. He unambiguously distances himself from it:

> This book will be the better understood the more it is conceived...as standing on its own, and the less it is conceived as representing a movement, tendency, or school...I certainly cannot think...of those who are commonly associated with me as leaders or adherents of the so-called "dialectical theology" [as a school]. It is only fair to them as well as to me that in its new form, too, this book should not be hailed as the dogmatics of dialectical theology...I only wish I could make things clear to those who would like to see me walking arm in arm with X or Y. (xiv–xv)

For the purposes of this book, the most important part of *Church Dogmatics* is Barth's polemic against Brunner's eristics in §2.1: "The Necessity of Dogmatic Prolegomena". Despite the worthy example of patristic and medieval dogmaticians, Barth argues that in modern times "we are now forbidden to take up the main content of dogmatics without express and expli-

cit discussion of the problem of the way of knowledge" (26). Barth first examines "the customary procedure"—represented by Brunner—which understands the necessity of prolegomena *vis-à-vis* modern unbelief, or due to
the "radicalism of rational thought".[70] It is claimed that this new intellectual
situation demands (if "dogmatics is to be existential theology") that "there
must be recognized and tackled a second task which arises out of the situation" (27). Then, after sketching out Brunner's position on dogmatic prolegomena (eristics and the point-of-contact) as seen in "The Other Task of
Theology", *God and Man*, and "Theology and Church", Barth presents the
case against it. First, there is no *theological* reason to assume that the
modern world-view is any more or less hostile to the Gospel than any other
world-view that has existed throughout the history of the Church (28). Second, the eristic approach to dogmatic prolegomena is wrong because the
struggle between godless human reason and divine revelation is a struggle
which takes place *within* dogmatics itself. The proper question cannot be
"How is human knowledge of revelation possible", but only "What is true
human knowledge of divine revelation?—on the assumption that revelation
itself creates of itself the necessary point-of-contact in man" (29). To focus
prolegomena on an attack on human reason is to "abandon" the sphere of
the Church. Barth quotes "The Other Task of Theology", where Brunner
claims that eristic theology "speaks more *ad hominem*", and comments: "If
there is an emphatic intention of speaking 'to men', not merely the dogmatic attitude but the theological attitude· in general is jeopardized" (29). Barth
states that Brunner's kind of prolegomena leads away from, rather than
towards, the "real work of dogmatics"—Brunner's quite negative attitude to
dogmatics in "The Other Task of Theology" reveals this clearly.

Barth's third point in the case against eristics is his argument that dogmatics is most relevant when it refrains from "self-vindication" and serves
only as "the witness to faith against unbelief" (30). In fact, all apologetics
have always failed, for one of three reasons: 1) they take unbelief so seriously that they cannot take faith with full seriousness; 2) to find the time to
do apologetics implies that all dogmatics is finished, which is a misplaced
confidence; and 3) the task of eristics, once completed, could deceive dogmatics that its statements were now safe and protected (30). Barth concludes:

> Theology is genuinely and effective apologetic and polemical to the extent that
> its proper work, which cannot be done except at the heart of the conflict between
> faith and unbelief, is recognized, empowered and blessed by God as the witness of
> faith, but not to the extent that it adopts particular forms in which it finally be-
> comes only too clear to the opposing partner that it is either deceiving him when
> in proposes to deal with him on the ground of common presuppositions, or that it
> is not quite sure of its own cause in so doing. Either way, there can be no shatter-

ing of the axiom of reason along these lines, but only as theology goes its own way sincerely and with no pretense. Apologetics and polemics can only be an event and not a program. (31)

If eristics is not a proper ground for the necessity of dogmatic prolegomena, what is? Barth responds that the "inner necessity" of prolegomena is not faith *vs.* unbelief, but faith *vs.* itself, i.e., heresy. *This* is theology's struggle (33–34). Protestant dogmatics finds itself before the heresies of Roman Catholicism and Protestant Modernism. It is these heretical forms of Christianity, and not modern unbelief, which force dogmatics to state its formal presuppositions clearly: this is "the inner necessity of dogmatic prolegomena" (35).

Barth could not be more direct in his opposition to Brunner. In the introductory section of his revised dogmatics, he bases his entire dogmatic work on a presupposition specifically at odds with Brunner's eristics. Given the abundant number of apologetic methods even more distant from Barth's own position, his decision to attack Brunner shows right at the beginning of *Church Dogmatics* I/1 that Barth has separated himself from "dialectical theology" and is going his own way.[71] Thus, in the context of this book, *Church Dogmatics* achieves two main things. Positively, Barth, through the help of Anselm, has found a way to speak dogmatically in a manner faithful solely to the subjectivity (and self-given and -controlled objectivity) of God in revelation. Negatively, he shows how his three dialectical colleagues have helped him find this way through their inadequate and ultimately heretical "anthropological" approaches, whether they be "eristic" or "existential" or "theological".

At the end of 1932, Brunner published a second article expressly defining and defending his program of eristics: "The Question of the 'Point-of-Contact' as a Problem for Theology".[72] The essay begins by explaining the importance of the question of the point-of-contact: it is an urgent question because it is the anthropological question, "the question of the relationship between the 'natural person' and the Word of God" (506).[73] Brunner likens the question of the point-of-contact to the task of Bible translation: the early Church did not need to invent new words to convey its new Gospel, but communicated its "wholly new" message by "presupposing" a "pre-understanding" in the "existing religious consciousness", that the meaning of the New Testament's words were "known 'in some way'" (505–508). Brunner presses the analogy of Bible translation by arguing that just as the effective translator must "look in two directions with the same seriousness—to the 'What' and to the 'to Whom'"—so must the preacher and the theologian (508–509).

Brunner then explores the meaning of the point-of-contact in the context of the continuity and discontinuity between the natural person and the new person in Christ. The discontinuity is clear: "The natural knowledge of God is neither real knowledge *of God*, nor real *knowledge* of God…Non-belief is always finally a decisive misunderstanding" (510). However, there are some continuities between the "old" and "new" person. First, both the "old" and "new" person is the same "I": there is an "identity of the subject". Second, God's act is unified: the one act of the Creator- and Redeemer-God establishes a fundamental continuity for the person acted upon. Third, there is continuity between God's free Word and human doctrine. God is free to speak as He wills, and God does this through *human speech*—through God's act, human words witness to him "like iron filings are lined up by a hidden magnet" (513). Thus, because God in his revelation makes contact with human words and thinking (the Incarnation being the ultimate example of God's making contact), we must follow this direction in proclamation.[74]

Brunner next attempts to define precisely the point-of-contact, which he locates on the border between the continuity and discontinuity of the person before and after faith. The question is, what carries over from the "old" to the "new" person? Brunner points to three "carry-overs", three points-of-contact. First, an element of human reason carries over into the new being. This element is the *humanum*, that which defines the formal essence of being human. For Brunner this continuous element of human reason is that human beings are "generally capable of words" (514).[75] The second continuity which carries over from the unbeliever is the negative knowledge (which is "the presupposition of faith") of creaturely finitude, of the "absolutely irrational, accidental givenness of the world…the knowledge that we must die" (515).

Brunner develops the third continuity in more depth, as it was emphasized by the Reformers. Both Luther and Calvin affirmed the natural knowledge of God, "the necessary presupposition for all preaching of the Gospel" (516). While both Reformers denied that the *content* of this natural knowledge was in any way continuous with the revelation of Christ, Brunner praises Luther's "ingenious" solution of the unbeliever's knowledge of the Law: "Humanity knows, naturally, in some way, that its existence is determined and bound through divine law". The Reformers brought together this general knowledge of God and of a moral obligation in the concept of the conscience. The conscience is the necessary presupposition for faith, because here the person comes to understand herself as a sinner, and here faith overcomes her condemnation.

Proclamation which does not make contact with the conscience misses the person; proclamation which doesn't bring the conscience to silence, is not Gospel…This is, in the decisive sense,…the point-of-contact for God's Word. Faith does not oc-

cur other than through this central point of human personal existence, other than
in contact with the natural person's consciousness of guilt, sin, and being lost.
(517)

Thus, the despair of the natural human conscience is the "immanent *possibility*" of faith. However, Brunner immediately points out that the *actuality*
of faith happens only through the work of God's Word and Spirit, that is,
by grace (518).

Having filled out the concept of the point-of-contact, Brunner turns to
anthropology. He argues that his position on the *imago Dei* is perfectly consistent with that of the Reformers, who, even in their most violent defense
of *sola gratia*, never denied that the *imago* contained not only "formal characteristics of humanity" but also "a not-precisely-defined *knowledge of the
Law and of God*"—they never denied "*the grace of creation and preservation*...in order to set the grace of redemption in the correct light" (520–
521). This leads Brunner into a direct discussion with Barth: "Some believe
that these...things must be denied in the interest of the pure doctrine of
grace", indicating Barth as the furthest-going representative of this view
(521, note 12). Brunner sets aside Barth's concerns about a dogmatic focus
on anthropology: 1) God has so created humanity that it is always *formally*
in relation to God, because the human capacity for speech is "response-
ability" before the Word of God (521–522); and 2) "Religion—even if it is
desolate heathenism—is unequivocally a sign of the relatedness of humanity
to God, and at the same time it is the necessary point-of-contact for the true
knowledge of God" (522). Brunner fires off another salvo at Barth in a
footnote:

> If Karl Barth calls this formal and dialectical definition of the point-of-contact
> Thomism, he misses the point in two ways. First it would mean...that all the Re-
> formers were also Thomistic, and that he is the first Protestant. Second, Thomism
> maintains something completely different: the natural knowledge of God is as such
> correct and therefore is merely *completed* through the supernatural. (522–523,
> note 14)

After attempting to steer a middle course between Barth and Bultmann
on the relationship between theological and philosophical anthropology
(525–529), Brunner comes to his concluding points:

> Proclamation in any form is, in the first place, witness to Jesus Christ, an exposi-
> tion of the divine Word of revelation. But the plainest witness to the salvation
> given in Christ is not possible without connection to our ruin, to being lost outside
> of faith. The "You are the one" of direct address...remains an empty phrase it if
> does not "encounter"...the hearer and "affect" him...The disclosure of this *misère
> de l'homme sans dieu* is the nerve of the "homiletic proof", which differentiates

true proclamation as address from mere exegesis. But this "disclosure"—whose success the Holy Spirit alone can bring about...—cannot occur without laying claim to what the natural person knows of himself. To lead the hearer to the place where he knows...the despairing character of his existence—that is the contact; humanly speaking, the success of proclamation is as dependent upon it as it is on "pure doctrine"...The deepest human knowledge perfects itself in the knowledge of faith, in the same way as the knowledge of faith not only presupposes humanity's natural knowledge, but also leads it to that "point" to which it cannot attain on its own. That is what has always happened in every good sermon in all times. (529–530)

Therefore, both preaching and theology must be eristic,

> the clearing away of all ideological, world-view, and metaphysical "excuses" which humanity creates for itself so that it does not have to see how it really is. Eristic theology is a "disclosure" of the true character of existence through the dissolution of these fictions. But this "disclosure" is not possible except through laying claim to that which humanity of itself can know about itself. (531–532)

After a two-year hiatus in the their correspondence, Brunner writes Barth in December 1932 to thank Barth for sending him a copy of *Church Dogmatics* I/1.[76] While praising it as a "powerful structure", Brunner offers three criticisms. First, it confirms that which they both have come to realize, "that we are roughly proceeding in opposite directions". Brunner attributes the difference to Barth's retrograde developments:

> You are heading in the direction on the *theologia perennis*, which rejects the special feature of human questions for every time; you believe that, in the twentieth century, you must also answer the questions of the sixteenth century. I, on the other hand, have turned in the direction of the kind of dogmatics which sees its service as answering the questions asked by the modern person.

Second, Brunner sees their differences exaggerated by the fact that they are writing their respective theologies for different audiences. Barth writes "for the experts, i.e., for pastors". This particularly dismays Brunner, because he still believes that Barth "is far more gifted than all the rest of us at saying a moving word to the world". Finally, Brunner disputes Barth's equation, "theological work = dogmatics":

> Don't you realize that...all theological work [in the early Church] was eristic answers to entirely specific questions, and that this was also the case during the time of the Reformation?...All important theological work has been journalistic in this sense. "For the day". That is the way you spoke early on, and at the time you moved the world...But whereas then you moved from Paul to the questions of our time, now you intentionally pass them by in silence... You are ultimately correct that the questions are always the same. But we don't have the right to ignore the

ultimacy of the special features of the time; otherwise our thinking takes on the character of timeless unreality.

This, Brunner claims, is "where all of our differences have their final ground":

> For me, theological work,…in the end, is nothing other than a particular type of evangelism, namely the battle against pagan thinking…Perhaps (this is still always my hope), when your great work is brought to completion, you will turn yourself again to the work for which you are so specially equipped, and —if God grants it—you will be allowed really to ring the great bell which the whole world can hear.

It is significant that, in this letter, Brunner has mostly gone off the defensive against Barth, and goes on the attack by accusing Barth of becoming scholastic, abstract and elitist.

Barth responds to Brunner after the New Year in a letter which is the definite announcement that, in Barth's view, they are now following fundamentally different theological lines.[77] Barth's disillusionment with Brunner has moved beyond the provoking issue of eristics:

> Your December 13 letter should no longer remain unanswered, although I can only reply with a great, sad shaking of my head. I have read in the meantime your article concerning the point-of-contact…and (for my open evening) the introduction and first part of [*The Divine Imperative*]. Yes, it is as you write: we continue in opposite directions, only for me it has been, for a long time now, a question not only of an opposition of method and style of writing, but even more a material opposition occurring right down the line.

While Barth assures Brunner of continued "good personal encounters and relationships", he can no longer consider Brunner a "theological 'friend'". This leads Barth to formally renounce Brunner as a colleague:

> I can understand as a theological friend only one in whom I have trust that he will not make a pact with the ancient serpent, neither with respect to nature nor with respect to grace. I no longer have this trust in you. You have made this pact on both sides as solemnly as possible…It grieves you to hear that from me. But it has first grieved me to see gradually over the years and now completely clearly that we…want and intend something completely different materially, so that nothing now remains but for us to renounce the fictitious picture that there is a special solidarity in our work…This renunciation is my answer to the point-of-contact…but obviously also to your grounding of ethics…All you need to do is to understand…your letter as radically as possible …in order to get the story of the gulf which divides us. All [its] points are non-debatable for me. At the least, shouldn't the stubbornness with which I say this…make it clear that we are not united *in fundamento*? Here, here at the level of these…points it must be shown

whether we are united in Christology, justification, the Scripture-principle, etc. If we can still be surprised with one another here, how then can it not be that we also intend completely different things in these other doctrines...?...

The hyphen which has bound your name and mine (and mine with Gogarten's) was a fictitious alliance. And it appears to me that everything good and possible which remains of the fellowship between us should include in its background the painful but honest recognition of this state of affairs, precisely in order that it might be good and possible.

Despite this explicit renunciation and specific request that Brunner recognize it as well, Brunner's response one week later shows that, while he considered their impasse serious, he has still "not given up hope of overcoming this opposition".[78] Brunner still believes that it is Barth's misreading of him which contributes to their disagreement—Barth is still guilty of "misunderstandings". Brunner points out two of these. First, Barth mistakes Book I of *The Divine Imperative* for a non-theological grounding of ethics, whereas Brunner intends it as

merely a certain contact with the conversation which others lead concerning ethics, a pre-conversation, in which the Christian ethicist...indicates why he finds their ethics to be disagreeable—thus, a conversation, from the standpoint of Christian ethics, which is a post-legomenon. It is the same misunderstanding as you made in your dogmatics, where you substitute for everything I write about such an engagement the understanding that it is a question of grounding theology from the outside—an idea which I definitely buried in the summer of 1924.[79]

Second, Barth misunderstands Brunner's use of natural theology. In no way is it a "grounding for theology"; rather it is "only a doctrine for sinners, and therefore it is not intended as a usable knowledge of God for the heathen. However, this *theologia naturalis* as such is a point-of-contact for conversation".

Brunner ends with an attempt to find common ground. First, he claims that it is the simple fact that the entire theological tradition stands with Brunner on the issues of the *imago Dei*, natural theology and general revelation. Second, Barth teaches the exact same thing about natural theology as Brunner. He quotes *Church Dogmatics*:

We cannot avoid speaking of a presence and operation of the Holy Spirit which is presupposed in revelation, which is first and general, and which is related to the created existence of man and the world as such. (I/1:472)

Brunner comments: "This is no different than what I mean: that through faith in Christ this 'already beforehand' becomes known, which already *was* beforehand, but was not known. Thomism teaches that this 'beforehand' is knowable by reason, which I, with you, deny".

However, Brunner concludes the letter with the charge that the real issue between them is that Barth is a perversely separatistic man:

> There is truth in the saying: as much unity as is possible in some way. You have always been the strong one; you have perceived yourself to be the mightiest alone. You could accomplish it all by yourself. But also consider what it means for Christian people if you throw off everyone—*everyone*—from yourself, and will have fellowship with no one else who comes to the fore theologically. And what will happen if it comes to the point where you have the theological tradition of the entire Church against you! Do what you must, but we will always ask ourselves whether this separation belongs to the *necessariis*, or to the *dubiis*, where there is *libertas*.

Summary

The years 1929 to 1932 were the decisive ones in the break-down of the theological alliance between Karl Barth and Emil Brunner. The different directions in which they had been moving since 1924 accelerated in this period to the point where they publicly criticized each other, and Barth privately repudiated Brunner.

During these years, Barth attained a way to do dogmatic thinking which expressed his material intention since *Romans II*. In "Fate and Idea", he articulated his understanding of theology's independence from philosophy, thus justifying the "*petitio principii*" in *Christian Dogmatics* of trying to write a dogmatics based solely on revelation. In *Anselm*, Barth found a way to ground the possibility of theology in the prior reality of revelation. Thus, while knowledge of God still remained a miraculous gift of the Holy Spirit received only through faith, this knowledge is a full knowledge, corresponding to the reality of God's own knowledge of himself. Thus, Barth preserved the noetic distance from the side of humanity but overcame it from God's side through the concept of *analogia fidei*.[80] The result of Barth's development was the third (and final) draft of his dogmatics, *Church Dogmatics*.

This line of development by Barth was accelerated by the work of his dialectical colleagues. His questions about Bultmann and Gogarten had been building since 1927. But it was Brunner's "The Other Task of Theology" which angered Barth the most. Despite their uneasy alliance, Brunner was certainly the closest of the three to Barth. To have him proclaim a program of "making contact" with the thoughts and needs of people outside of the revelation in Jesus Christ crystallized for Barth what had bothered him about Brunner, Bultmann, and Gogarten all along—they had never really understood the meaning of Overbeck's radicalism which grasped Barth in 1920, such that they never were able to develop a theology of the Word of God *alone*.[81] These suspicions were confirmed during Barth's visit to Marburg in January 1930, after which, in his mind, the dialectical theology movement had come to an end. It is at this point that Barth began to air his criticisms publicly, though veiled at first. "Theology and Modern Man" castigated the work of his dialectical colleagues as attempts to "control" a theology of revelation under philosophical presuppositions, similar to Roman Catholicism. In *Church Dogmatics* I/1, he took on his colleagues one by one, rejecting Brunner's eristics, Bultmann's existentialism, and Gogarten's anthropology. By January 1933, Barth wrote to Brunner that he had lost "theological trust" in him.

As opposed to Barth, for whom the years 1929–1932 marked the culmination of a decade-long development, these years saw Brunner merely bringing to the fore what he had been thinking and saying since at least 1924. Brunner had been doing eristics since *Mysticism and the Word*. The search for a point-of-contact within the personeity and responsibility of humanity had been fueled by his Ebnerianism and Kantianism for several years. For Brunner, these years thus marked no "turn" or change;[82] rather, he simply pulled all his previous thinking together systematically in one article—"The Other Task of Theology". All his other writings from this period are essentially a re-statement and development of what he announced concisely in 1929. What did change for Brunner in 1929 was that his incompatible theological mix—Kant, Luther, Kierkegaard, Ebner, and Barth — could no longer be held together; what Brunner dropped was his "Barthianism", the radical sense of dialectic and distance.

Brunner's relationship with Barth was more aggravating for him than productive during these years. He was completely taken by surprise by Barth's harsh reaction to "The Other Task of Theology" at their Bergli meeting in the summer of 1929. After all, the article merely stated what he had been doing all along, and *Romans II* (still being re-issued, and still Brunner's favorite work by Barth) was influenced by the same Kierkegaardian anthropological insights. What Brunner saw in Barth during these years was the culmination of the tendency he first noticed during their Gospel-Law debate at Pany in 1924—Barth was becoming more and more objectivist and scholastic in his understanding of revelation, focusing too narrowly on "the Faith" as a set of beliefs rather than on faith as the subjective act of the modern Christian. Brunner entered into a "footnote debate" with Barth, first in *God and Man*, then in *The Divine Imperative*, and most clearly in "The Question of the 'Point-of-Contact'". That the "point-of-contact" became a point of fundamental disagreement between Barth and Brunner should not have been surprising, given their theological approaches from the earliest days of dialectical theology. Brunner had always followed an approach of showing the errors and half-truths of non-Christian thinking: he maintained in both *Experience, Knowledge and Faith* (p. 129) and "The Limits of Humanity" (p. 14) that though religion is unable to cross the divine-human gulf, it is a half-true human attempt towards a true knowledge of God. Barth, for his part, stated clearly in 1922 that there is no way from humanity to the event of faith, but that faith can only be understood as *"God's working* on us (for only he can say to us, in such a way that we will hear it, what *we* can *not* hear)":[83]

> Man is a riddle and nothing else, and his universe, be it ever so vividly seen and felt, is a question…The solution of the riddle, the answer to the question, the satisfaction of our need is the absolutely *new* event whereby the impossible becomes *of itself* possible, *death* becomes life, *eternity* time, and *God* man. There is *no* way which leads to this event; there is *no* faculty in man for apprehending it; for the way and the faculty are themselves new, being the revelation and faith, the knowing and the being known enjoyed by the new man.[84]

Nevertheless, during these years, Brunner did not see any serious threat to his theological alliance with Barth, but rather saw a productive division of labor. In Brunner's mind, both men remained opposed to theology as carried on in Roman Catholicism, Neo-Protestantism, and Pietism, and they both remained committed to a theology of revelation mediated through Luther and Calvin.

The differences between Barth and Brunner illuminated by their writings from 1929–1932 can be expressed by several different contrasts. Barth saw himself as a theologian doing theology in the strictest sense, whereas Brunner saw himself as a theologian in the broadest sense, which necessitated an on-going, in-depth discussion and debate with philosophy. Brunner's theological *loci* centered on anthropological concerns—*imago Dei*, ethics, missionary preaching—whereas Barth's focus was on the doctrine of God—his knowability, predestination, the Trinity, christology. The two theologians can be distinguished with the terms Idealism and Realism, as *Anselm* led Barth towards a theological realism: although God remains "indissolubly Subject", he sovereignly gives himself to be an object to faith (knowledge is determined by the *ratio* of the object who is Subject, and not by the knowing subject). Brunner's Ebnerian-influenced Kantian Idealism emerged in these years from its relative suppression as he sloughed off the Barthian dialectic. Brunner turned again to issues of the psychology of faith: what is it in humanity which allows it to hear the Word of God, and what happens within a person in the event of faith.

At the beginning of 1933, one would have been hard pressed to predict that in less than two years Barth would repudiate Brunner with a vehement and public "No!" Radical changes in German politics and church life were the aggravating factors. However, all that was really surprising about the end of the Barth–Brunner theological alliance in 1934 was how quickly it came and how definitively Barth pronounced it. Anyone who read Barth and Brunner's works closely from 1929–1932 knew their alliance was already coming apart.

NOTES

1. "Fate and Idea in Theology", trans. by George Hunsinger and others, in *The Way of Theology in Karl Barth*, ed. by H. Martin Rumscheidt (Allison Park, PA: Pickwick, 1986), pp. 25–61.
2. "Theology can know about God only to the extent that God makes himself accessible to us, but to that extent theology really does claim to know about God...No step, not even the smallest, can be dared by theology except on the ground that God allows himself to be found before we have ever sought him" (27). "Only one thing keeps [theology] from being doomed to failure: the presupposition of divine miracle" (29).
3. Barth maintains that there should be a sense of community between philosophy and theology, as long as both recognize their limits. The limit of philosophy is the sinfulness of humanity, which means it is unable to reach the Truth (54–55). The limit of theology is that it does not *know*, but can only *believe* that which it can philosophically conceive (55–56). Note also Barth's comment here against natural theology: "Where the synergistic picture holds sway in which 'natural' knowledge of God is agreeably completed by revealed knowledge, what other result can there be than that theology has given itself up as theology—surrendered its character as a theology of revelation and faith?" (55).
4. Gestrich, *Neuzeitliches Denken*, pp. 33–34.
5. Towards the end of his life, Barth repeated similar thoughts about the relation of philosophy and theology in the *Festschrift* for his brother, Heinrich ("Philosophy and Theology", in Rumscheidt, *Way of Theology*, pp. 79–95.
6. "Die andere Aufgabe der Theologie", *ZZ*, 7 (1929), 255–276.
7. Theology's polemical task is "not—as Karl Barth has occasionally expressed himself—...a secondary or tertiary task, which one turns to once the main things are put in order" (258).
8. Jewett (*Brunner's Concept of Revelation*, p. 126) notes astutely that "eristics" for Brunner has the same two-sided meaning as the German word *Auseinandersetzung* (explanation/argument)
9. "The doctrine of the *imago Dei* determines the fate of every theology" (p. 264, note 3).

10. See note 6, pp. 266–267.
11. German: "ansprechbar". Ebner first employed the concept of humanity's "*Ansprechbarkeit*" in *The Word and Spiritual Realities*, in *Schriften* I, p. 87.
12. "If, in his prolegomena…he disputes the right of eristic theology, then we cannot expect good results. And we issue this warning based on the nature of the sermon (just as he does). Apparently, Barth has not (or not clearly) recognized that the sermon has both eristic and dogmatic moments. The sermon proclaims the Word—absolutely!; but it proclaims the Word to *people*. It enters into their hiding-places and fetches them out of them. It illuminates them and their illusions…The sermon that does not do this is a bad sermon, even if it offers 'pure doctrine' a thousand times. Barth himself understands how to really speak to real people. But the danger is great that his principles and attitude will lead him astray…and this means that he will no longer *speak* to the modern person, but *harangue* him. Dogmatic theology will necessarily fall into this danger if it does not have eristic theology beside it" (pp. 274–275).
13. *Contra* Gestrich, *Neuzeitliches Denken*, p. 344
14. Brunner was well aware that *Romans II* (most recently re-issued in 1928, without major changes) also promoted a "negative" natural theology not unlike Brunner's (Torrance, *Karl Barth*, p. 71). See Barth's exegesis of Romans 1.18–2.15, especially pp. 46–48. See also his interpretation of the Gentiles' knowledge of the law, pp. 65–66. See also Attila Szekeres, "Karl Barth und die natürliche Theologie", *EvTh*, 24 (1964), 229–242 (p. 230).
15. Busch, p. 184.
16. *Barth–Brunner*, EB: June 8, 1929 (#71), pp. 174–181.
17. Brunner goes on to argue that *Romans II* has a "genuine eristic character".
18. It should be noted that for Brunner, *theologia naturalis* is not the focus of his theological concern. Rather, it is *one* point in a larger argument about addressing the Gospel to modern people.
19. *Barth–Thurneysen II*, ET: July 3, 1929, p. 669.
20. Ibid., KB: July 9, 1929, p. 672. Barth suggests Karl Hartenstein, the Director of the Basel Mission, whose position and experience would make him a credible critic. Thurneysen writes back that Hartenstein is considering replying to Brunner (though he never did) (ibid., ET: July 24, 1929, p. 674).
21. *Barth–Brunner*, EB: July 9, 1929 (#72), pp. 181–185; KB: July 10, 1929 (#73), pp. 185f.
22. *The Holy Ghost and the Christian Life*, trans. by R. Birch Hoyle (London: Frederick Muller, 1929). This essay is one of the best examples of Barth's "actualism"—the Holy Spirit, and the life it brings, is pure grace, pure gift, and in no way a "possession" of Christians (e.g., pp. 18–20, 23). Although Brunner's name is never mentioned, Barth clearly argues against the direction of Brunner's thinking. There is a clear rejection of using the *imago Dei* to anchor any "given" in humanity (pp. 14–18). There is a strong rejection of an ethics based on "orders of creation" (pp. 21–22) (see above pp. 116–119). Any negative "point-of-contact" in humanity is ex-

pressly denied (pp. 43–46). Most fundamentally, here Barth's "actualism" is seen not as an arbitrary theological method, but as the expression of his intentions since *Romans II*: God is completely sovereign over-against humanity, entirely free in his grace, "inalienably subject" in his revelation. This kind of God can only be known *theologically* through the miracle of faith, and not *philosophically* through the workings of even a faith-enlightened reason.

23. *Barth–Thurneysen II*, September 26, 1929, p. 675.
24. Ibid., KB: January 26, 1930, pp. 700-701.
25. Ibid., ET: February 3, 1930, p. 713.
26. Brunner had recently expressed great anger to Barth over an incident during his 1929 lecture tour to Holland: "Can you deny, when someone asked your opinion [during your 1927 Holland trip], that you said: 'Oh, dear Emil, he always says what I had said three years earlier'? I am convinced that you would no longer say that; but you can understand that such a saying does not strike me as very friendly, in view of its material inaccuracy...I'd rather trudge in my own footsteps than to walk in yours. We have neither the same shoe size nor the same pace" (*Barth–Brunner*, EB: November 6, 1929 (#76), pp. 190f.).
27. Trans. by David Cairns (London: SCM, 1936). See David Cairns, "Introduction", in *God and Man*, pp. 9–37 (pp. 9–15) for chapter summaries.
28. Cairns ("Introduction", pp. 14–15) ably lays out the standard Brunnerian eristic method seen in chapters 1, 2, and 4. For another example of Brunner's eristics from 1930, see "Secularism as a Problem for the Church", *International Review of Missions*, 19 (1930), 495–511.
29. *Barth–Brunner*, KB: June 2, 1930 (#78), pp. 192–196. Barth had moved to the University of Bonn in February, 1930 (see Busch, pp. 188, 198).
30. Ibid., EB: June 12, 1930 (#79), pp. 196-199.
31. "Die Theologie und der heutige Mensch", *ZZ*, 8 (1930), 374–396; Busch, p. 178.
32. Gogarten, "Barths Dogmatik", pp. 70–79.
33. Smart, p. 179. The article immediately following "Theology and Modern Man" in *Heft* 5 of *ZZ*, 8 is Brunner's "Theology and Church" ("Theologie und Kirche", pp. 397–420). In this article, Brunner again takes up the polemical task of theology, though less forcefully than in "The Other Task of Theology" and *God and Man*: dogmatics must combat the error of "continuity philosophy", and theology's "task to the world" should appeal to the *justitia civilis* and the "natural orders of creation" which are not fully destroyed through sin.
34. *Barth–Brunner*, EB: October 20, 1930 (#80), pp. 199–205.
35. *Christian Dogmatics*, §17.
36. *Barth–Brunner*, KB: October 24, 1930 (#81), pp. 205–209.
37. They were, after all, both originally written in 1927
38. Volk, "Christologie", p. 616, and *Gottebenbildlichkeit*, pp. 17–20; Johnson, p. 214; *Contra* McGrath, p. 127.
39. Smart, p. 178. Throughout 1930, Bultmann attempted to arrange a "summit of the

pillars" (Barth, Bultmann, Brunner, Gogarten, Thurneysen) in order to talk through their differences. But Barth successfully resisted Bultmann's efforts (see *Barth–Bultmann*, pp. 49–59).

40. *Contra* Johnson, p. 168. Ethics only became an issue in their correspondence—and a side issue at that—after the publication of Brunner's *The Divine Imperative* at the end of 1932. See *Barth–Brunner*, KB: January 10, 1933 (#83), pp. 213–217 (see above pp. 127-128).

41. For the ample secondary literature on Barth and Brunner's ethics, both individually and comparatively, see: Robert E. Willis, *The Ethics of Karl Barth* (Leiden: Brill, 1971); Eberhard Jüngel, "Gospel and Law", in *Theological Legacy*, pp. 105–126; Nigel Biggar, "Hearing God's Command and Thinking about What's Right", in *Reckoning with Barth*, ed. by Biggar (London: Mowbray, 1988), pp. 101–118; Russell E. Palmer, "Methodological Weaknesses in Barth's Approach to Ethics", *Journal of Religious Thought*, 26 (1969), 70–82; Helmut Gollwitzer, "Zur Einheit von Gesetz und Evangelium" in *Antwort*, pp. 287–309; Gustaf Wingren, "Evangelium und Gesetz", in *Antwort*, pp. 310–322; Reinhold Niebuhr, "The Concept of 'Order of Creation' in Emil Brunner's Social Ethic", in Kegley, pp. 265–271; Paul Ramsey, *Nine Modern Moralists* (London: University Press of America, 1983), pp. 196–208; Niels H. Søe, "The Personal Ethics of Emil Brunner", in Kegley, pp. 247–261; Robin W. Lovin, *Christian Faith and Public Choices* (Philadelphia: Fortress, 1984); René de Visme Williamson, *Politics and Protestant Theology* (Baton Rouge, LA: Louisiana State University Press, 1976), pp. 37–63, 101–137.

42. "The Problem of Ethics Today" (see Chapter 2, note 77).

43. Quotations are from "Das Halten der Gebote", *ZZ*, 5 (1927), 206–227. See also *Ethics*, trans. by Geoffrey W. Bromiley (New York: Seabury, 1981), pp. 63–115 and *CD* II/2:§§37–39.

44. As early as 1923, Barth questioned the role of orders in Christian ethics ("The Problem of Ethics Today", p. 171. In 1929, Barth brings a strong actualism to bear on the concept of orders; see *The Holy Ghost and the Christian Life*, pp. 23–24 (see also his attack on Gogarten's use of the orders, p. 21, note 23).

45. See pp. 215–216 for this back-and-forth, giving-then-taking-away movement. Barth's growing discomfort with his use of the orders of creation is shown in his refusal to publish his Münster lectures (vii).

46. Especially as expressed in Barth's lecture "Keeping the Commandments" (see note 43).

47. Trans. by Olive Wyon (Philadelphia: Westminster, 1947). For Brunner's other ethical writings in this period, see "The Problem of Ethics", in *The Theology of Crisis*; *Von den Ordnungen Gottes* (Bern: Gotthelf-Verlag, 1929); "Justification by Faith and the Problem of Ethics", in *God and Man*, pp. 70–102; and *Das Grundproblem der Ethik* (Zurich: Rascher & Cie. A.-G. , 1931).

48. It is significant, however, that in the four sections of Book II, only the first really deals with the command in itself. The second section deals with the separate issue of

"The New Man" (in which Brunner argues from his Kantian-Ebnerian anthropology —the core of humanity is response-ability). In the last two sections ("The Neighbor", "The Works of Love") the focus begins to shift to the concept of orders. Also see J.M.L. Thomas, "New Protestantism and the ethics of crisis", *Hibbert Journal*, 37 (1938), 14–24 (p. 23).

49. "Justification by Faith and the Problem of Ethics", in *God and Man* (p. 92).

50. See *The Divine Imperative*, pp. 210, 216–219, 293–339.

51. William W. Butler, "A Comparison of the Ethics of Emil Brunner and Dietrich Bonhoeffer with Special Attention to the Orders of Creation and the Mandates" (unpublished doctoral thesis, Emory University, 1970), pp. 143, 404. See also Brunner, *The Christian Doctrine of Creation and Redemption*, trans. by Olive Wyon (Philadelphia: Westminster, 1952), pp. 24–26.

52. Brunner calls this a "dialectical" model of Christian living: "This attitude…is not a compromise, but a paradoxical way of living[; it is] the Pauline principle of living *in* the world without being *of* it…; only as we learn to live in this way can we discover the Divine Command within the 'framework of orders' in which our human life is set" (pp. 338–339). For Brunner's process of ethical decision-making, see p. 204.

53. Douglas J. Schuurman, *Creation, Eschaton, and Ethics* (Bern: Peter Lang, 1991), pp. 14, 69–70, 77. It is not clear why Brunner felt so attracted to the concept of the "orders of creation", a concept that did not appear in his writings until 1930. Clearly, Gogarten's influence is decisive here. However, the dynamics of the Gogarten–Brunner relationship are beyond the scope of this study.

54. For Brunner's continuing development of (and lack of clarity about) his *theologia naturalis*—do natural people know only idols, or is there some real knowledge of the Law?—see p. 555 (note 4) and pp. 618–619 (note 1). For Barth's critique of *The Divine Imperative*, see *CD* III/4/§52.1:19–21.

55. Busch, pp. 205–206.

56. Trans. by Ian W. Robertson (Cleveland: World, 1960). The literature is vast which explores the meaning (and existence!) of Barth's "Anselmian turn". See: Bouillard, pp. 144–148; Torrance, *Karl Barth*, pp. 182–193; Smart, pp. 194–198; Beintker, pp. 183–200; Jüngel, "Barth's Life and Work", pp. 41–43; Rosato, pp. 38–43; Sykes, "The Centre of Theology", pp. 36–38; Manfred Josuttis, *Die Gegenständlichkeit der Offenbarung* (Bonn: H. Bouvier, 1965).

57. *Contra* Beintker, p. 193. In 1929, Brunner comments: "Idealistic strains in Barth's *Romans* are indeed obvious, and doubtless they are more suited to darken than to illuminate biblical thought" ("Rezension von: Friedrich Karl Schumann, «Der Gottesgedanke und der Zerfall der Moderne»", *KfrS*, 85 (1929), 317).

58. I.e., "'to follow a trail' (*e.g.* used of a dog on the scent)" (p. 53, note 1).

59. See *The Göttingen Dogmatics*, pp. 346–347.

60. In answering whether Anselm's approach could have any success, Barth answers Brunner: "Perhaps he was daring to assume that…the doubt, denial and derision of the unbeliever are not really to be takeñ so seriously as the unbeliever himself would

take them…Perhaps for Anselm theology…must move past the listener's tragic *non credo* to our task with a sense of humour, which in this instance is not only permissible but is actually demanded" (pp. 70–71).

61. "How I Changed My Mind, 1928–1938", in *Karl Barth: How I Changed My Mind*, pp. 37–49 (p. 43); "Forward to the Second Edition", in *Anselm*, p. 11: "Most [scholars] have failed to see that in this book on Anselm I am working with the vital key, if not the key, to an understanding of that whole process of thought that has impressed me more and more in my *Church Dogmatics* as the only proper one to theology". One should note McCormack's *caveat* (p. 421), that Barth's understanding of an "Anselmian turning point" was not explicitly stated until *eight years* later. However, it is significant that Barth, untypically, immediately published the first chapter of his book ("Die Notwendigkeit der Theologie bei Anselm von Canterbury", *ZThK*, N.F. 12 (1931), 350–358). Also, note the increase in Anselm references from *Christian Dogmatics* (8) to *Church Dogmatics* I/1 (22).

62. See pp. 434–441; *contra* Beintker, pp. 183, 187–188.

63. *Contra* Christof Gestrich, "Die unbewältigte natürliche Theologie", *ZThK*, 68 (1971), 82–120 (p. 93). While *Anselm* may not have constituted a Barthian "turning-point", it does mark a modification of Barth's radical actualism. An inherent rationality in God which corresponds to a rationality of faith is a more static conception of revelation than Barth had entertained before. See Torrance, *Karl Barth*, pp. 144–147, Frei, p. 51; Josuttis, p. 146.

64. McCormack, p. 438.

65. Beintker, p. 190.

66. It is hard to miss the irony that it is Anselm who is the vehicle for this rejection. One wonders how Barth could bend over backwards to give Anselm's rationalistic proofs of God the most benign understanding imaginable (an interpretation that has little standing amongst Anselm scholars (see Gordon Watson, "Karl Barth and St. Anselm's Theological Programme", *SJT*, 30 (1977), 31–45), whereas he took absolutely no pity on Brunner, interpreting his very slight concession to a *negative, formal* point-of-contact in the most malicious way imaginable.

67. Smart, p. 198. 1931 also saw the publication of Brunner's *The Word and the World*, based on his lecture tour to Great Britain in March 1931 (London: SCM, 1931). These lectures are another example of eristics. Each lecture follows Brunner's now-familiar style: an attack on a modern ideology (reason, history, psychology, science) followed by the fulfillment of this ideology's half-truth by Christianity (God, Jesus Christ, Holy Spirit, the Bible). In a chapter entitled "The Word of the Spirit and Psychology", Brunner again makes the case for a natural, negative point-of-contact in humanity (see p. 79).

68. Barth took on Brunner and the "point-of-contact" (anonymously but clearly) in "Theology and Mission Today" ["Die Theologie und die Mission in der Gegenwart"] *ZZ*, 10 (1932), 189–215 (pp. 197, 214–215). Barth also distanced himself from Brunner by name in the 1932 preface to the English translation of *Romans II*:

"May I...ask my English readers...not to look at me simply through the spectacles of Emil Brunner, not to conform me to his pattern?" (vii).

69. The most obvious evidence of Barth's decisive move away from existentialism is seen in various summary statements. Whereas in *Christian Dogmatics*, the "human contradiction" is brought within the understanding of revelation and the Trinity (summary statements to §§10–14, 17), this "anthropological pole" is excised in the corresponding summary statements in *Church Dogmatics* (see summary statements to §§9–13, 16).

70. Here Barth quotes Brunner in "Theology and Church" (see above, note 33): "In short, it is the problem of reason and revelation" (p. 26).

71. Brunner is not Barth's only target in *CD* I/1. In the next sub-section (§2.2: "The Possibility of Dogmatic Prolegomena"), Barth lumps Bultmann's "pre-understanding" in with Modernism's error of attempting to establish dogmatic knowledge based on an "ontology" of a "self-understanding of human existence which may also at a specific point become the pre-understanding of an existence in the Church or in faith, and therefore the pre-understanding and criterion of theological knowledge" (36–37). Barth also takes on Gogarten in a long excursus at the beginning of §5.1 ("The Question of the Nature of the Word of God"). Here, Barth renounces the "transition" he announced in §5.1 of *Christian Dogmatics* from a "phenomenological" to an "existential methodology"—in the new edition, it is clear that there can be no "kind of grounding of theology in existentialist philosophy" (126). Second, at this point in *Christian Dogmatics* (§§5–7), "an anthropology, albeit a Church anthropology, was ...being advanced as the supposed basis on which we know decisive statements about God's Word" (126–127). In making this move, "I was paying homage to false gods", because "if there is one thing the Word of God certainly is not, it is not a predicate of man, even of the man who receives it" (127). This brings Barth to his attack on Gogarten, for Gogarten had faulted Barth for not developing a "true anthropology" and for speaking of God in isolation from humanity and vice versa (see Gogarten, "Barths Dogmatik", pp. 71–79; see also Gogarten's "Das Problem einer theologischen Anthropologie", *ZZ*, 7 (1929), 493–511).

72. "Die Frage nach dem «Anknüpfungspunkt» als Problem der Theologie" *ZZ*, 10 (1932), 505–532.

73. Brunner immediately adds that anthropology constitutes no independent ground of knowledge: "As everything that we state theologically about creation and sin has its ground and criterion in Jesus Christ alone, *so what we treat here as the question of the point-of-contact also is determined by the word of revelation perceived in faith, and only from there is it understood*" (507).

74. This conclusion—since God has made contact with us in His Word, therefore the preacher must make contact with his words—is not a necessary one. Barth will later exploit this weakness, arguing, rather, that what is common to revelation and preaching is not that both *intend* to make contact, but that in both it is the *Holy Spirit* who makes contact. See below, p. 160.

75. Brunner immediately piles on four more terms to clarify his meaning: *"The ability for words* [Die Fähigkeit zum Wort] *or the capacity for words* [die Wortmächtigkeit], *the speaking and letting oneself be spoken to* [das Sagen- und Sich-Sagenlassenkönnen], *thus the formal personality* [die *formale Personalität*] (*persona-quod*)" (p. 514).

76. *Barth–Brunner*, EB: December 13, 1932 (#82), pp. 210–212.

77. Ibid., KB: January 10, 1933 (#83), pp. 213–217.

78. Ibid., EB: January 16, 1933 (#84), pp. 217–222.

79. The reference is to the time of their Pany meeting (see above, pp. 72–74). But in 1933, as in 1924, Brunner failed to grasp how radically Barth understood the noetic distance between God and humanity.

80. This coincides with Barth's moving beyond Kierkegaard

81. Gestrich, "Unbewältigte natürliche Theologie", p. 93.

82. Bouillard, p. 184.

83. "An Answer to Professor von Harnack's open letter" in *Adolf von Harnack*, ed. by Martin Rumscheidt (London: Collins, 1988), pp. 95–105 (p. 101).

84. "The Word of God and the Task of the Ministry", p. 197.

CHAPTER FIVE

Breaking Up (1933–1935)
The "German-Christians" and Natural Theology

It would be very gratifying...if the quarrel between us could be settled now without material compromise, but simply out of a fellowship of appreciation. It is for many a real scandal.

(Brunner to Barth, February 1934)

It's too late now...This soup finally must be eaten. I wish nothing more than that you had not served it to us!

(Barth to Brunner, October 1934)

Crisis in the German Church (1933–1934)

The Rise of Nazism and the "German-Christian Movement"
The break-up of the dialectical theology movement took place against the background of the rise of Nazism. During the late 1920s, the devastation caused by the Depression in post-war Germany helped the Nazi Party to gain significant influence amid the declining strength of the Weimar Republic.[1] The parliamentary government of the German Reichstag became immobilized as multiple party representation produced unstable coalition governments. In the September 1930 parliamentary elections, the Nazis scored a huge success, surging from 12 seats (in 1928) to 107, making them the second most powerful party by a wide margin. In July 1932, amid further political radicalism and economic instability, the Nazis more than doubled their numbers in the Reichstag—to 230 seats, 97 more than the Social-Democrats (the dominant party since the War). The resulting center-conservative coalition government offered Hitler a position in the Cabinet, but he refused any position but Chancellor. Due to the instability of this government, new elections were called again in November 1932. This time the Nazis suffered defeat, shrinking to 196 seats, but still maintaining a 75 seat

plurality over the Social-Democrats. The confused situation made forming a new government extremely difficult. After several failed alternatives, President Paul von Hindenburg appointed Hitler Chancellor on January 30, 1933. At the very first meeting of the new Cabinet, Hitler called a snap election for March; after the infamous Reichstag fire, he was granted emergency powers and outlawed the Communist Party. In the March election, the Nazis won 288 seats (44%). Supported by the 52 votes of the German National People's Party, on March 23 an "Enabling Act" was pushed through the Reichstag, which granted Hitler legislative and budgetary powers for four years. The Nazis took control of the government and the civil service, and, by July, all other political parties had been banished. Within another year, after Hindenburg's death in August 1934, Hitler proclaimed himself Führer and imperial chancellor—the Nazis had absolute political power.

The political success of the Nazis was accompanied by the rise of a movement of its ideological supporters within the Church—the "Faith-Movement of German Christians".[2] From the turn of the century, theology had become mixed with German nationalism in some quarters. In the 1920s a theologian like Emanuel Hirsch could declare that a faithful preaching of the Gospel in Germany "is possible only in solidarity with the fate and destiny of the German people".[3] Throughout the 1920s and early 1930s, various organizations and movements appeared which gave voice to this and more radical sentiments: de-canonizing the Old Testament, rejecting Paul's "rabbinic" concept of redemption, raising up the concept of "*Volk*" ("people, nation, race"). Respected theologians such as Paul Althaus and Heinrich Bornkamm became associated with such movements. This trend culminated in June 1932, when a party formed within the church which explicitly supported the *Volk*-ideology of Nazism. Originally to be called the "Evangelical National Socialists", Hitler ordered that the name be changed to something more neutral—it became the "Faith Movement of German Christians". The movement soon published its ten "guiding principles" for the reorganization of the German Protestant church, including:

> 7. We see in race, folk, and nation, orders of existence granted and entrusted to us by God. God's law for us is that we look to the preservation of these orders.[4]...
>
> 9. In the mission to the Jews we perceive a grave danger to our nationality. It is an entrance gate for alien blood into our body politic...As long as the Jews possess the right of citizenship and there is thereby the danger of racial camouflage and bastardization, we repudiate a mission to the Jews in Germany. Holy Scripture is also able to speak about a holy wrath and a refusal of love. In particular, marriage between Germans and Jews is to be forbidden.
>
> 10. We want an evangelical Church that is rooted in our nationhood.[5]

The leader of this movement was Pastor Joachim Hossenfelder of Berlin, who had been a Nazi party member since 1929. Almost immediately, the German-Christian movement made itself felt in church elections.

Barth and the German Church Struggle

As early as 1930, Barth began to speak out against the evolving situation in Germany, although he would confine himself primarily to the increasing struggle within the Church against the rise of *Volk*-theology.[6] Of interest to this book is the connection he drew between his stand against the German-Christians and against his former dialectical colleagues.

On March 10, 1933 Barth delivered a lecture in Denmark entitled "The First Commandment as an Axion of Theology".[7] This lecture clearly indicates that the rise of the German-Christian movement sharpened and intensified Barth's previously existing differences with his dialectical colleagues. Barth begins with the assertion that theology's "axiom" is the first commandment (63–67).[8] The first commandment as the axiom of theology means two things. First, underlying this commandment is the event of God's active grace—God liberated the Jews from Egypt before He gave the Law (68). Thus, theology's axiom of grace contrasts with a general concept of "axiom" because it is not timeless or passive (as, for example, are the orders of creation) (69). Second, "no other gods before me" means that theology is forced to choose the narrow way, rather than the broad way of "and-type" theology (71). Barth observes that theology has always complained about the narrowness and isolation that this axiom demands of theology, and has always tried to broaden the theological task by adding some secondary criterion, building a theology of "revelation *and* ..." (72–73). Neo-Protestantism is the classic expression of this complaint, and yet Barth deliberately includes his dialectical colleagues in his indictment: "'New Testament *and* human existence'. 'The commandments *and* the orders of creation'" (73). Barth states that "and-type" theology fails to conform with the axiom of the first commandment because it always allows the second criterion to dominate the criterion of revelation (73–75).[9] Barth then goes after his colleagues:

> *Vis-à-vis* Brunner and Gogarten I have to ask whether "God" is really more than another word for "neighbour"? Is "commandment" more than another word for the orders of creation? Is "justification" more than another word for life in those orders? And *vis-à-vis* Bultmann: Are theology and anthropology really interchangeable concepts?
>
> ...I am really at a loss to interpret differently what I read in Gogarten's book *Ich glaube an den dreieinigen Gott*[10] or in Brunner's ethics about justification. No matter how strenuous the insistence that those orders are to be regarded as the revelation of the sole God, one may well ask whether they would be possible un-

less there were, in fact, rather mighty, domineering and, in their own way, exclusive "other gods" present in those alleged orders of creation. Yet we hear from all sides that is not how it is meant!...Why, then, do they always speak and write those very weighty books as if they did mean it that way? (76)

The decisive question which Barth addresses to all Protestant "and"-theologies is: Are they fundamentally different from Roman Catholicism, from which the Reformers separated themselves because it had "other gods"? (76). While Barth is unwilling to answer the question with a definite No, nonetheless he observes:

> The question of this intra-ecclesial protest (especially today in the complete darening of the theological situation which the last years have brought about, mainly in the staggering statements by Bultmann, Brunner and Gogarten) must be registered with more emphasis than ever before. Many roads lead back to Rome! (77)

Barth concludes by declaring war on natural theology:

> The fight against natural theology, which is unavoidable in view of the first commandment as an axiom of theology, is a fight for right obedience in theology... Theology is right and good when it corresponds to the first commandment and does not oppose it...[Theology today] should take its leave of each and every natural theology and dare, in that narrow isolation, to cling solely to the God who has revealed himself in Jesus Christ. Why? Because that and only that has been commanded of it. Because everything else is arbitrariness which does not lead to, but leads away from, that God. That is the simple meaning of the thesis which is defended here. (77)

The spring and summer of 1933 brought the crisis in the German Church to a head. In March, the German-Christians held their first national convention, during which they demanded the creation of a Reich Church—that the Protestant Church be assimilated into the National Socialist state and adopt their guiding principles. The movement elected Ludwig Müller, a little-known naval chaplain, as its new leader. Within three weeks, Hitler appointed Müller as his adviser and deputy in Church affairs, and gave him the responsibility of creating a Protestant Reich Church. On the same day, the executive committee of the German Evangelical Church Federation voted to draw up a new church order, charging a "committee of three" with this task. The most controversial aspect of this new constitution was the creation of the position of a "Reich Bishop". An election for bishop was held at the end of May, and Dr. Friedrich von Bodelschwingh was elected over Müller on the third ballot. However, his service was short-lived. On June 24, a German-Christian church official fired almost all the elected members of the church's boards in Prussia and replaced them with German-Christians. In a protest widely shared, von Bodelschwingh immediately resigned.

Barth was outraged by this crass political move by the German-Christians. The day of von Bodelschwingh's resignation, Barth issues the pamphlet *Theological Existence Today!*, in which he reviews and criticizes the Church events of the past six months.[11] Writing specifically as a theologian to other theologians and the Church at large, he surprisingly (and famously) begins:

> I must at once make clear that the essence of what I attempt to contribute today bearing on these anxieties and problems cannot be made the theme of a particular manifesto, for the simple reason that...I endeavour to carry on theology, and only theology, now as previously, and as if nothing had happened....I regard the pursuit of theology as the proper attitude to adopt: at any rate it is one befitting Church-politics, and, indirectly, even politics. (9–10)

As a Church theologian, Barth recognizes that the Word of God alone is sufficient, triumphant and needful; therefore what is required now is "theological existence", i.e., that "in the midst of our life...the Word of God may be what it simply is, and only can be to us" (14).

After rejecting the arguments for church reform and for a Reich Bishop (18–46), Barth turns his attention to the German-Christian Movement. Since its aim is to make the Church subordinate to the German state and Nazi ideology, one can only say a complete No to it and all its sympathizers (47–50). While Barth grants that the rise of the German-Christian Movement is anxiety-provoking, nonetheless it cannot be taken too seriously (53–55). What Barth does take seriously is the Church's amazing lack of resistance and its ready accommodation to this movement which, in the end, amounts to the Church's surrender (55–56). The only real issue at stake is "the plain but critical question as to Christian *truth*" (57).

Barth concludes by offering his program: "theological existence today" means to let the Church be the Church. Concretely this means to ignore the enemy and to be the Church in action:

> The *prime* need of our time is for a *spiritual* center of resistance: one that would, for the first time, give a meaning and a content to Church politics. The man who understands this will not "gird himself for any fight", but will put on his programme: "WORK AND PRAY". (76)

> This is not unrealistic impracticality, because where the Church is the Church, she is undefeatable (76–78).[12]

Events proceeded rapidly in the German Church. On June 28, Müller declared a "church state of emergency" and took over (with Hitler's agreement) the administration of the Federation of the Evangelical Church. On July 11 the representatives of the German Churches adopted the new Church constitution, and the elections for new Church officials were swept by the German-Christian candidates.[13] In early September, the Prussian Synod enacted the "Church Law concerning the Legal Status of Ministers and Church Officials" which included the notorious "Aryan paragraph", banning all non-Aryans and those married to non-Aryans from church employment. On September 27, Müller was officially installed as Reich Bishop of the new Protestant Church. Barth, viewing these events as "a public emergency", resigned from his (civil service) office as a theological examiner in his consistory—he considered collaboration with the new Church to be "acquiescence in the rise of heresy".[14]

Brunner writes Barth again in June 1933, just as the German Church struggle is beginning to intensify.[15] He reports that he is working his way through *Church Dogmatics* for the second time and is "pleased (despite the constant contradictions of me in the first part) by the rich instruction which I again and again draw out of it". However, he is especially "saddened" that Barth takes Brunner's ethics "only in the negative sense". He concludes:

> But it will now be wholly good that the greatness of "dialectical theology" breaks apart, so that our foolish wisdom does not conceal the divine foolishness (I Corinthians 1.25). However, one would also like to see a visible sign of the unity of the Church, and it remains painful when people, who stand as near as we do, are seen as opponents by those outside, who see our differences more clearly than what we hold in common.

A month later, during an exchange of letters concerning Barth's leadership role in the Church struggle,[16] Barth comments on the distance in their relationship:

> Perhaps also we will talk about theology while we view Lake Zurich [at the Bergli]. It is truly a sad chapter between us. For I am of the opinion that you have served up an entirely bad devastation with your principal doctrine...But I do not want my answer to your peaceful letter to become disfigured with a newly rude polemics...Come then once to Bergli and bring two lively horses with you. Perhaps on a full day's ride we can clear the battlefield of...a few things.

The two men did have a ride together, and, in Brunner's opinion, had a conversation "like we've never had before".[17] He elaborates:

> I notice that you always have important things to say to me. I had never previously understood so well that you really do not have only some stubbornness against my ethics, but that behind that rests a genuinely biblical concern. My didactic-pedagogical interest misleads me again and again, to listen too much to humanity

instead of to God. What you said to me concerning this listening has made the true sense of your protests as clear to me as lightening.

However, Barth did not find the conversation so positive.

> I did not want to appear to be malicious, and so I repressed something which was on the tip of my tongue: "If you lived in Germany, you would now be with the German-Christians"—because your arguments on both sides of this problem [the Oxford Group Movement][18] irresistibly reminded me precisely of the intent of what the German-Christians propose for us...So (I can certainly say it now without maliciousness) it is obvious to me that, from Zurich's point of view, while maintaining a distance from the German-Christians and not taking up...especially their *crude* errors, nonetheless you maintain their propositions in a more decorous manner.[19]

Barth's stunning verdict about Brunner, along with the events in the Church struggle, bring to a climax the crisis within dialectical theology. At the end of September, Barth tells Georg Merz that he can no longer be involved with *Zwischen den Zeiten*, due to Gogarten's open stance towards the German Christians.[20] For Barth, the point of no return came when Gogarten, in a June 1933 article, expressly accepted the "Stapel dictum": the law of God for German Christians is identical with the law of the German people.[21] In October, the last issue of *Zwischen den Zeiten* appeared, with articles from Barth, Thurneysen, and Merz.[22]

"Abschied" ("Farewell") serves as Barth's official, public separation from Brunner and Gogarten. In the opening pages, Barth offers his interpretation of what went wrong:

> We believed we had in common a few things: to put forth, in opposition to the positive-liberal...theology of Neo-Protestantism...a theology of the Word of God ...But after only a few years of publication, it was no longer a secret to those in the know that, particularly between Gogarten and myself, there was an implicit but not unimportant difference in the programs we presupposed... In addition, I saw Emil Brunner, considered to be a member of our group, becoming occupied with another task both within and outside of our journal. Under this new flag he returned to the flesh-pots of Egypt, seriously *forsaking* what I had understood to be our common starting-point. This new task is the Neo-Protestant—or, as the case may be, Catholic—scheme of "Reason *and* Revelation"...I asked myself, almost despairingly at certain points last winter, if...it [had been] worth our work and struggles of almost twenty years, in which we turned ourselves to the task of the renewal of theological thinking and church proclamation. (536, 538)

Barth then turns to the present. With Gogarten's clear sell-out to the German-Christians, *Zwischen den Zeiten* had become a journal of toleration in a time of crisis (539–540). Barth points with particular horror to *Heft* 4 of

1933, where an article written by Ernst Fuchs (a German-Christian sympathizer) ran back-to-back with Barth's "The First Commandment" (540–541).[23] *Zwischen den Zeiten* had become a journal standing for "the interesting co-existence of the Yes *and* No", when the times called for only an unambiguous No! (541). This prompts Barth to state baldly: "The foundation and continuation of *Zwischen den Zeiten* was a misunderstanding" (541).[24]

Events in the German Church Struggle continued to unfold rapidly. At the end of September, Pastor Martin Niemöller founded a "Pastors' Emergency League" to protest the actions of the Reich Church authorities. In January 1934, a "free synod" of 167 Reformed Churches in Barmen adopted a statement, composed by Barth, which opposed the tide of events.[25] Barth interpreted the declaration himself (in Barmen on January 6) as being not so much an attack on the German-Christians as a statement against the persistent error tempting the Protestant church throughout its history—the temptation to place a second authority alongside God's revelation in Scripture.[26]

The following three months witnessed a series of conferences, synods and assemblies which adopted Barth's (January) Barmen declaration as well as issuing their own declarations, stating that the Reich Church was apostate, that German-Christian theology was heresy, and that the resisters represented the true and legal German Protestant Church.[27] The result of these actions was the formal constitution of a "Confessional Fellowship" in March, temporarily guided by a "Council of Brethren". At the end of April, the Council called a "Free German National Synod" for the end of May in Barmen. Early in May, it appointed a theological commission to prepare a theological declaration for the Synod, naming Barth and two Lutherans to it.[28] The three men met on May 15–16 to work up a draft. During a "three-hour siesta" by the Lutherans, Barth wrote the original draft, which followed the main lines of his January Barmen declaration.[29]

"The Theological Declaration" of Barmen puts forward six statements, each following a strict form: a Scripture quotation, an affirmation, and a rejection. The theses affirm that the claim of Jesus Christ falls upon all aspects of life (including politics (#2)); that the Church is solely Christ's property, and that its order is not changeable due to ideological whim (#3); that Church leadership is service, not power (#4); that the State's divine appointment is limited, not "totalitarian" (#5); and that the mission of the Church is the proclamation of God's Word of free grace, which is not to be used "in the service of any arbitrarily chosen desires, purposes, and plans" (#6). But the most important thesis (in its placement, for Barth, for the German Church struggle, and for the Barth–Brunner debate) is thesis #1:

Jesus Christ, as he is attested for us in Holy Scripture, is the one Word of God which we have to hear and which we have to trust and obey in life and in death.

We reject the false doctrine, as though the Church could and would have to acknowledge as a source of its proclamation, apart from and besides this one Word of God, still other events and powers, figures and truths, as God's revelation.[30]

The Natural Theology Debate (1934)

Nature and Grace

In early 1934, Barth's colleague Ernst Wolf wrote an article for *Theologische Existenz heute* on Martin Luther's view of other religions, including his statements regarding natural theology.[31] That this article was accepted for publication by Barth, "together with what you carried out at the Reformed synod [in Barmen in January] concerning *theologia naturalis*", prompts Brunner to write Barth a "theological letter".[32] Since Brunner can "agree with every statement" in Wolf's article, he feels

hardly touched by your anathema [in "The First Commandment"]; I knew that it was a misunderstanding. If you mean what Luther according Wolf means, then we both mean one and the same thing; I will let it pass whether I expressed it perfectly at first.[33]

Brunner then responds to Barth's rejection of Brunner's alleged theology of "and" in "The First Commandment", calling it "a pure misunderstanding". That Brunner's incorporation of the orders of creation may not have been expressed "dialectically enough" does not mean Brunner's ethics lead to the legitimization of the "historical necessities" of the German-Christians:

I still have expressed too little of the brokenness of these orders. But I have the consolation that it was clear enough so that the German-Christians have declared war on me, and attack me as severely as they ever attacked you.

Brunner's third point concerns Barth's misunderstanding of the point-of-contact. Brunner again refers to Wolf's article, claiming that he also rejects what Wolf rejects—"the Thomistic and Neo-Protestant understanding" of the point-of-contact. Rather, with Luther (according to Wolf), Brunner understands the point-of-contact as "*cognitio legalis*. As you perhaps remember, it has always been for me a matter of this *habent cognitionem legalem*". Brunner also claims that his teaching on the *imago Dei* is completely faithful to Calvin.

Brunner then turns to the state of their "quarrel", writing that "it would be possible for us to come to a real and fundamental understanding with one another on the basis of Wolf's article", because Brunner, too, intends "nothing other than the *sola gratia*, the 'Christ alone', in the sense of the Reformers, especially in Calvin's sense". Brunner maintains that their views are not that far apart, and if Barth would only learn from him as he does from Barth, they both would profit. Their quarrel really should come to an end, Brunner argues, because for many people "it is a real scandal".

Barth replies to Brunner briefly and in a dismissive manner.[34] Barth had sent Brunner's letter to Wolf, and Wolf had given Barth a copy of Wolf's reply to Brunner—Barth now asks to be left out of the middle. Barth writes this letter from Zurich, where he had listened appreciatively to Brunner preach at the Fraumünster Church. But then, up at the Aarau Student Conference,

> I got embroiled in a long conversation with a group of your students...Ah, my dear friend, hearing your reflections in the mouths of these young people, it has become completely clear to me that what exists between us, precisely *in* our whole nearness (which doubtless embarrasses us), is a question of an Either-Or, which one cannot remove by friendly sentiments.

Barth ends by saying that, while he is in Zurich preparing for his Paris lectures, he would be glad to get together to talk some more.[35] But Brunner does not take him up on the offer.

A month and a half later, Brunner writes a short note to Barth, alerting him of the impending publication of his latest monograph, *Nature and Grace: A Contribution to the Discussion with Karl Barth*.[36] Brunner explains the intention behind the pamphlet:

> I ask you to accept this booklet as graciously as possible. I have tried as far as I am able to understand what unites and divides us, and I express our opposition as falling within a Reformation-Biblical co-partnership. And thus my wish for fellowship is as clear as my wish for theological specificity. For that reason, I maintain that your teaching on the *theologia naturalis* is not entirely biblical and is not entirely Reformed. But I know that, despite this, you are united with me that it is important to struggle in our Church and in the world for the value of the biblical message in its Reformation interpretation until the end. I believe in this co-partnership. And the goal of this article is to ask you to show if it is, in fact, as I say it is.[37]

In the opening paragraphs of *Nature and Grace*, Brunner explains that the purpose of the pamphlet is to clarify his position in the wake of "Farewell"—in "the work in which he disowned...all other theologians, Barth's ban struck me also" (15). Brunner is willing to shrug off this broadside. After all, Barth is like a loyal soldier on sentry duty at night, who shoots every one who does not give him the password as he has been commanded, and who therefore from time to time also annihilates a good friend whose password he does not hear or misunderstands in his eagerness. (16)

Brunner intends to demonstrate, positively, that he is in agreement with Barth's main intentions, and negatively, that Barth "draws false conclusions" from his intentions.

Brunner opens by praising Barth for stressing the Reformation's "grace alone" (17–18). He agrees with Barth's thoroughgoing rejection of anything alongside the one divine norm of the word of God. But while Brunner rejects "and"-theology in the sense of "co-ordination", he maintains:

Not even Karl Barth can deny that there is a *problem* concerning Christianity and Culture, Commandment and Ordinances, Reason and Revelation, and that this problem requires thoroughgoing theological treatment. (19)

Brunner then launches into his main argument. He draws together from Barth's writings six conclusions which Barth falsely derives from "grace alone" and "Scripture alone": 1) the image of God is completely obliterated in fallen humanity; 2) there is no general revelation in nature; 3) there is no grace of creation and preservation active in the world; 4) there are no "ordinances of preservation"; 5) there is no "point-of-contact" in humanity for God's saving action; and 6) the new creation is not a perfection of the "old man", but its complete replacement by the "new man" (20–21). Brunner proposes to defend six counter-theses, demonstrating their scriptural and Reformation basis and their "theological and practical significance" (22).

These counter-theses are a summary of the position that Brunner has developed since "The Other Task of Theology". Brunner's first counter-thesis repeats his distinction between a *formal* and *material* image of God in humanity (22–24). His second counter-thesis repeats his argument that God reveals Himself in creation even though sinful humanity cannot recognize it (24–27). Brunner then makes an important distinction between two kinds of natural theology. There is an "objective" natural theology—God's creation reveals God—which Brunner affirms. But there is also a "subjective" natural theology, which maintains that the natural, sinful person is able to recognize this revelation in his own power—this Brunner denies.

Brunner's third counter-thesis is that there exists a preserving grace of God,

that God does not entirely withdraw his grace of creation from the creature in spite of the latter's sin…He provides new means for checking the worst consequences of sin, e.g. the State. (28)

Closely related to this is Brunner's fourth counter-thesis: God provides humanity with orders of creation and preservation (29–31). While these orders are only understood and followed correctly in faith, Brunner maintains that "they are known also to 'natural man' as [orders] that are necessary and somehow holy and are by him respected as such" (31).

Brunner then moves on to re-affirm the "point-of-contact", again defined as the formal *humanum*, the "capacity for words" (*Wortmächtigkeit*) (31–33). Brunner emphasizes that this receptivity is not *material* (humanity is unable in itself to accept God's Word) but purely *formal*: humanity is uniquely able to be addressed. Thus, the

> Word of God does not have to create man's capacity for words…But the Word of God itself creates man's ability to believe the Word of God, i.e. the ability to hear it in *such a way* as is only possible in faith. (32)

Brunner maintains that the point-of-contact is "the necessary, indispensable [presupposition] for divine grace" (33). After presenting his final counter-thesis (the old being is restored, not replaced, 33–34), Brunner concludes this section:

> These theses sum up my *theologia naturalis*, of which Karl Barth is so suspicious. There was a time when—like Karl Barth himself—I did not see the contrast between the Gospel and the natural knowledge of God as clearly as I do at present …But I do not think that I should be prepared to take back anything essential of what I said in the first edition of *The Mediator* concerning the natural knowledge of God. I do not wish to deny that I am still of the opinion that there should be an eristic theology based upon this knowledge. But long before I made use of this concept and raised this problem for discussion I realized that it had nothing to do with the question of the "proof of theology". (34–35)

In the next section, Brunner argues that his position on natural theology is faithful to Calvin (35–45). He also reviews briefly the natural theology of Roman Catholicism and the Enlightenment (which stress natural humanity's ability to know God without revelation), in order to indicate that his position is completely different from these (45–48). Brunner concludes his historical argument by stating that the problem between Brunner and Barth is not Brunner's natural theology (which is faithful to the Reformation) but with Barth's doctrine of revelation. He states that Barth's thinking is too "one-sided", too actualist to make place for the real givenness of revelation (48–49). In contrast, Brunner argues that, while the Spirit must enliven that which is revealed in Scripture and God's works in nature, nonetheless their status as revelation exists before the Spirit's act, like the relationship of "the gramophone record to the sounding music" (49).

The final section of Brunner's article addresses "The Significance of *Theologia Naturalis* for Theology and the Church". Natural theology is crucial for ethics, for only an ethics based on God's orders of creation can "acknowledge divinely appointed objective limits to our freedom and objective guides to the ordering of our society", as opposed to an "invincible individualism" (52). As for dogmatics, Brunner claims that Barth's rejection of natural theology, specifically his polemic against the *analogia entis*, leads to "theological nominalism" (54). In fact, Brunner charges that Barth himself employs the *analogia entis* in a similar manner to Brunner's use of the formal *imago Dei*. Referring to Barth's description of the way in which the Word of God communicates itself to humans,[38] Brunner states:

> This means that the whole Barthian theology rests *de facto* upon the doctrine of the formal *imago Dei*, which he so much dislikes, i.e. upon the doctrine that man …is the only legitimate analogy to God, because he is always a rational being, a subject, a person.…Thus without knowing it and without wishing it, Barth himself argues in favour of *theologia naturalis* and of its fundamental significance in theology…The characteristic of Christian theology…is not the issue *whether* the method of analogy may be used, but *how* this is to be done and *what* analogies are to be employed. (55)

Natural theology is also significant for the work of the Church: the "Church's proclamation must be *comprehensible* else it is useless, however true its contents" (56); Christian education must be concerned with the "How?" as well as the "What?" (58); and natural theology can serve as "an intellectual and conceptual work of preparation" in evangelism to both unbelievers and youth (58–59).

Brunner concludes that Barth's "genius of one-sidedness" may well be his "special mission" (59). But he maintains that even though the last century witnessed the reign of a *false* natural theology, this does not mean the Church can reject *all* natural theology. He ends: "It is the task of our theological generation to find the way back to a true *theologia naturalis*…It is high time to wake up for the opportunity that we have missed" (59–60).

"No!"

On 30 September, Brunner, clearly worried, writes to Barth.[39] This is caused, first, by the fact that "you have yet to acknowledge either my article or my letter [of May 8]"; second, in that "I constantly see people who rely on your theological leadership who completely cannot grasp the point of disagreement between us"; but mostly by

> a detailed report of one of our common students concerning your lecture about your disagreement with my booklet, which…I can judge to be full of what I can only see as a complete misunderstanding of what I want to say.

Brunner takes responsibility for any misunderstanding, due to the fact that he has not always expressed himself clearly. But he is hopeful that these misunderstandings can be cleared up, because "I have constantly measured what I wanted to say against Calvin", and because he feels some misunderstandings have been resolved in his correspondence with Barth's brother, Peter. Brunner points to places in Barth's lecture where he has been misunderstood, specifically concerning the point-of-contact ("I intend to say by it absolutely nothing like what you regard as a 'truism'") and the formal-material distinction in the *imago Dei* ("you shoot...constantly at...a position, which I completely do not represent, but which you read into my words"). Brunner asks for an opportunity to get together one more time:

> I recognize that there is a difference between us; but I see this difference in another place. Therefore, our difference is one of theological schools, but not a Church-difference which requires division...I am not pleading for a different opinion now; I am pleading that your judgment will not be supported by a misunderstanding of my thinking, as I see that it is in all the Barth-students and from the transcript of your lecture. Your lecture makes no sense: you stigmatize a heresy before the whole world under my name, which completely does not exist...It is unfortunate if two theologians such as we battle one another instead of merely seeking clarity with one another...this you cannot deny.

Brunner begs for a meeting in Switzerland. At the meeting, Brunner will also show Barth an upcoming publication[40] which takes on Barth in a few places, "in order to be certain whether at least I correctly understand what I reject of your view. Perhaps there are also many misunderstandings on my side". Brunner's anxiety shines through at the close to the letter:

> See, if there must be a quarrel, then I want to go at it completely confidently. The natural person in me has always loved a quarrel. And I can really say: I'm not afraid. I am certain and completely confident of my position. But it appears to me to be an indefensible luxury if two men, who stand so near to each other as we do, must quarrel before the world.
>
> That we quarrel in our lecture halls...doesn't matter at all...But in front of the world?—No. Today?—No. We are one in *the* matter which must really be fought for today in public opinion. You think your position is the best weapon against the German-Christians, etc.; I think mine is better...But most people, who are neither your nor my students, think about it differently. They think, "This should not matter to both of them. What we understand from them is that they both intend the same thing: one Church, which stands on God's Word alone, and they mean Christ alone, and therefore they think that no peace can be concluded with the German-Christians and the like". Is not this the case? Whoever is finally right, Barth or Brunner—what do the people of the world care about that? You can write calmly against me—that is in order. But not as an enemy, not as against one who stands "on the other side". That should be avoided by all means.

And now forgive this epistle. It should say to you that I, as before, will maintain, despite everything that divides us, our fellowship in the main things, unless you disavow it.

Barth does disavow it, by return post, in a letter which is summed up in its opening line: "It is too late now".[41] Barth says that he has failed to respond because

> from the moment I first read *Nature and Grace*, it was immediately clear to me that I would wait to write personally until I could send it to you with my opposing article, not out of coarseness, but because, of course, I regret the existence of your article in the highest, and I reject its contents most definitely and completely...[42]
>
> I wish you had not written that article! But I must go further: I wish you had not begun the whole campaign which you have led against me since 1929, or at least that you knew exactly what you wanted to say and could and would say it without misunderstanding! But that is a completely idle wish, because now that you must develop your position in this direction I may say..., on the contrary, that your article has created a fact.

This "fact" is *Nature and Grace*'s warm reception by the German-Christians: "You cannot have...the approval of these theologians and be my confederate at the same time". Barth does not accept Brunner's theory of "misunderstanding", his inability to state himself clearly, nor that their disagreement lies elsewhere:

> [Our disagreement] is indebted to your delimitation against me in the matter of *theologia naturalis*, so you can't turn to me with the clarification that you were misunderstood in this matter and that our difference lies in an entirely different area...Even before the noise of all these other voices, nothing else could be concluded from your article other than this: that it contains a *Sic* against which I can only set a completely non-dialectical *Non*.

Barth is particularly annoyed with Brunner's repeated attempts to clarify what he is trying to say:

> All of us, as well as others, have given all our efforts to understand you (it is my impression that we have given this more effort than you have yourself). And it is simply not possible that now (through your recent clearest statements with which one must saddle himself) you come and state that everything is to be understood completely differently!...What in the world did you want, if it wasn't to point out some noteworthy difference over-against me?

As Barth sees it, in the context of the German Church struggle, Brunner has issued a severe challenge to Barth's theological resistance to the German-

Christians, and so Barth must answer it in that vein:

> All the world points to [*Nature and Grace*] and asks me what I have to say. Now I *will* say what I have to say, and that will be a plain No. Although I have for so long kept silent, now I will no longer be impeded...This soup finally must be eaten. I wish nothing more than that you had not served it to us! "I would give anything for him to keep quiet!" one could hear me groan more than once at the Bergli. But now it has happened, and now on both sides everything must be taken up as it lies in the moment.

Barth declines a meeting for the following week due to a family commitment. He ends his letter, "Humanly-speaking as before, with sincere greetings, but theologically-speaking with the deepest imaginable concerns".

Brunner replies by return post in a state of high agitation.[43] He is stupefied by the inability of the "Barthians" to interpret *Nature and Grace* according to its plain meaning. Brunner is also disgusted with Barth's "guilt by association" tactic regarding the reviews of *Nature and Grace*:

> If Herrs Weber, Althaus or Fezer also praise me for my booklet—I didn't know that—that is still no proof to me that my booklet is false or wicked.... What's left of theological scholarship if one makes others' reactions a criterion of truth?

The problem, Brunner states, is Barth's "sectarian spirit",

> that you consider your peculiar doctrine, which goes way beyond anything the Church has ever taught, to be the only legitimate, Christian and Churchly position; that you maintain it in spite of all documentary evidence to the contrary; that you alone teach Reformation doctrine. That is the psychology of the major sects, and it is completely and utterly non-churchly...Since Barth teaches something else, everybody is a heretic who doesn't also teach it his way.

Brunner closes by offering his perspective on their entire relationship.

> This will be the last letter from me for a long time. In the fifteen years since we have occasionally written to each other, you have not written many friendly things. Long before I stood up "against you", you had already written me off. Perhaps you think: "I have always smelled a rat". I would almost like to say, "I am not sorry". But that's not the case. Despite the fact that I see a dangerous doctrinaire in you, I recognize now as before the great things that God has given to you. But I also see (and am troubled by it) that you have become a victim of your own opinions and can no longer see what the Bible teaches.

But Brunner is unable to end the letter. He adds a post-script the next morning before posting the letter.

You have carried out a year-long theological terror. And yet you have been spared, because your hangers-on no longer let even friendly criticism get near to you. Thus, otherwise completely different people were glad if, for once, someone woke you up in some way, who had something to say against you... There are very many righteous ones who have fallen in with you in the Church struggle, but who theologically place themselves on my side, and it is exclusively the Barthians who are annoyed. You obviously have no clue how isolated a theologian you are, not because you represent a peculiar opinion—who doesn't?—but because you identify this peculiar opinion with the *articulus stantis et cadentis ecclesiae*. Thus stands the issue objectively. And outside the Barthian circle—which is almost a magical circle—everybody knows this, whether they are otherwise orthodox, liberal, Calvinist, Lutheran, Pietist or whatever. In this matter, the entire Church stands against: Barthianism.

Brunner had good reason to fear Barth's response to *Nature and Grace*, for Barth disagreed completely with the pamphlet. In "No! Answer to Emil Brunner",[44] Barth immediately sets his vehement rejection of Brunner's article in the context of the German Church struggle:

I can hardly say a clear "No" to Hirsch and his associates, but close my eyes in the case of Brunner, the Calvinist, the Swiss "dialectic theologian". For it seems clear to me that at the decisive point he takes part in the false movement of thought by which the Church today is threatened...The reason why I must resist Brunner so decidedly is that I am thinking of the future theology of compromise, that I regard him as its classical precursor, and that I have heard the applause with which all who are of a like mind have greeted his essay, *Nature and Grace*. His essay is an alarm signal. (67, 69)

Barth's "Angry Introduction" is devoted to a rejection of *Nature and Grace*'s final paragraph, that the task of theology today is "to find the way back to a true *theologia naturalis*". Quite the contrary, Barth finds his sole and continual task to be simply this: "We must learn again to understand revelation as *grace* and grace as *revelation* and therefore turn away from all 'true' or 'false' *theologia naturalis*" (71). These completely different understandings of the theological task indicate that everyone has been "terribly deluded in thinking that we were 'loyal comrades in battle'" (71). In particular, the warm reception given *Nature and Grace* by the "half- or three-quarter 'German Christians'" prompts Barth to separate himself clearly from Brunner (72).

Barth's article follows Brunner's outline in a point-by-point rebuttal (with the exception of an additional section, "Brunner Then and Now"). Barth begins by rejecting Brunner's reconstruction of his position on natural theology. Barth claims these so-called theses imply that he has an interest in natural theology, which he most emphatically does not:

> By "natural theology" I mean every (positive *or* negative) *formulation of a system* which claims to be theological, i.e. to interpret divine revelation, whose *subject*, however, differs fundamentally from the revelation in Jesus Christ, and whose *method* therefore differs equally from the exposition of Holy Scripture. (74–75)

The real difference between himself and Brunner, Barth maintains, is that he has no interest in natural theology as a theological task, whereas Brunner, "even as an adversary of natural theology...would always be addicted to an 'other' task of theology" (77).

Barth then proceeds to criticize Brunner's counter-theses. The decisive question, he proposes, is whether Brunner's opening affirmation of "grace alone" and "Scripture alone" can be sustained in the light of Brunner's natural theology (78). Barth then makes a move which caused some to consider this debate to be a misunderstanding of terms.[45] Barth latches on to Brunner's single usage of the term "capacity for revelation" (*Offenbarungsmächtigkeit*); for the rest of his essay, Barth substitutes this term for Brunner's other key terms ("capacity for words (*Wortmächtigkeit*), "possibility of being addressed" (*Ansprechbarkeit*), etc.).[46] But Barth makes this substitution deliberately, because he sees Brunner's attempt to grant humanity any natural capacity towards God as a denial of humanity's radical dependence on grace:

> [This is] the quintessence of what Brunner wants to teach as "natural theology": there is such a thing as a "capacity for revelation" or "capacity for words" or "receptivity for words" or "possibility of being addressed" which man possesses even apart from revelation...What is the meaning of "sovereign, freely electing grace of God" if without it there is a "capacity for revelation" in man, which is merely supported by grace? What is the meaning of "receptivity for words" if man can do nothing of himself for his salvation, if it is the Holy Spirit that gives him living knowledge of the word of the Cross? (78–79)

Barth first addresses the issue of the *imago Dei*. He grants Brunner's distinction between a formal and material *imago* ("Even as a sinner man is man and not a tortoise"), but asks: How does a person's personality in any way make him suited for revelation?

> The impression given by Brunner's essay has been described roughly like this. If a man had just been saved from drowning by a competent swimmer, would it not be very unsuitable if he proclaimed the fact that he was a man and not a lump of lead as his "capacity for being saved"? Unless he could claim to have helped the man who saved him by a few strokes or the like! (79)

Barth thinks that either the formal/material distinction is irrelevant, or it leads to a human contribution in salvation.[47]

Next, Barth tackles Brunner's position on God's revelation in creation. He latches onto Brunner's vague qualifier "in some way".[48] Barth believes this validates his suspicion of Brunner's formal/material distinction: what the natural person will "somehow" know by herself is either her own projections or the true God. If it is the true God (as Brunner intends), even if this knowledge is darkened by sin, this means there are two kinds of revelation, one with and the other without the Holy Spirit. Barth concludes:

> Has not Brunner added to man's "capacity for revelation", to what we have been assured is purely "formal", something very material: man's practically proven ability to know God, imperfectly it may be, but nevertheless really and therefore surely not without relevance to salvation? Perhaps he can swim a little, after all? (82)

Barth proceeds to contest Brunner's third counter-thesis concerning preserving grace. Barth refuses to recognize any grace which is not specifically related to the grace of Jesus Christ. He accuses Brunner of putting forth a non-biblical, "abstract preserving grace" (84). Barth thinks that Brunner's concept of preserving grace either leads to divine-human cooperation as in Roman Catholicism and Pietism, or to making historical realities divine, which would mean "that the poor 'German Christians' may have been treated most unfairly".

Barth then rebuts Brunner's view of the orders of creation. He argues that outside of faith, the orders are merely products of "instinct and reason" (86). But beyond this problem of knowledge lies a greater difficulty:

> What are we then to think of Brunner's assertion that these ordinances of creation are not only known but also respected and "to some extent realized" by men who do not know the God revealed in Christ? Of what Christian, however faithful, can it be said that he "to some extent realized" the ordinances of God? Is he not "a sinner through and through"? (87)

Barth's polemic reaches its peak over the point-of-contact. He sharpens his original attack upon Brunner's formal/material distinction within the *imago*: either this distinction is pointless (a "man is a man and not a cat") or it is dangerous—it is designed to blur the distinction, giving to humanity a material capacity for God.

> But we have seen that Brunner unfortunately has no intention of stopping at this formal factor. The reason for this is that he departs from the statement that man is "a sinner through and through"...For he has by now also "materially" enriched and adorned man in his relation to God to an amazing extent..."The necessary, indispensable point of contact", which before was defined as the *"formal imago Dei"*, has now, as it were, openly become "what the natural man knows of God,

of the law, and of his own dependence upon God".[49] (89)

Barth sees the point-of-contact as being completely unnecessary, since God is able to "create the conditions" required for an encounter with sinful humanity. He concludes:

> Brunner has been unable to adhere to *sola fide-sola gratia*. He has entered upon the downward path, upon which we find him in *Nature and Grace* more obviously than in any previous pronouncement...I am not wantonly branding him as a heretic, but...this really is how the matter stands. (90)

Finally, Barth comes to Brunner's contention about salvation as restoration *vs.* re-creation. Here, Barth is mostly confused by Brunner. Having seen Brunner's formal/material distinction effectively disappear in theses 2–5, it now re-appears with startling rigidity and banality: "We receive the Holy Spirit, but our personal identity remains. Who would not agree with that?" (91). Barth states that Brunner should re-read the passages where he cites Calvin on "repair", in order to see that there is no mention of humanity's capacity to be repaired:

> This is because the "repair" consists in a *miracle* performed upon man...because his "formal" aptitude for it is the most *uninteresting* and his "material" aptitude the most *impossible* thing in the world. (94)

In the next major section of his critique, Barth seeks to show that Brunner's natural theology is not faithful to Calvin. His main point is that Brunner's exposition of Calvin neglects the historical context. The Reformers drew their battle line against "the very questionable pelagianising formulations of the later Nominalism"; the re-discovery and re-assertion of Thomism had not yet occurred. Thus, it is inappropriate to expect the Reformers to have addressed the modern issue of natural theology with sufficient sharpness (100–101). This historical context is decisive for Barth; in fact, he claims that to be faithful to the Reformers means to re-write them in today's context:

> What Calvin wrote in those first chapters of the *Institutes* has to be written again and this time in such a way that no Przywara and no Althaus can find in it material for their fatal ends. To do this would be to "adhere to the teaching of the Reformation", and would at the same time be worthy of Brunner's own early intentions. (104–105)

Barth concludes:

> Brunner's interpretation of Calvin has one fault which vitiates everything. He

has, with amazing cold blood and consistency, left out the very important brackets within which Calvin always speaks of the natural knowledge of God. They are the expression *si integer stetisset* Adam, which makes it a hypothetical possibility, [and] the reference to Romans i, 20, which makes it a sign of the judgment …By means of leaving all this out, Brunner has brought Calvin over to his side. Also, in detail, the whole process is enough to make one weep. (109)

In the following section—"Brunner Then and Now"—Barth attempts to show that Brunner has stepped onto a slippery slope; his writings show how far he has moved from a limited to a more expansive natural theology. In "The Point-of-Contact", Brunner described humanity's natural knowledge only in the negative sense of knowing God's wrath—the point-of-contact was the sinner's despair. But Barth points out that the point-of-contact is described only *positively* in *Nature and Grace*. He counters that the point-of-contact is "incompatible with the third article of the creed":

The Holy Ghost, who proceeds from the Father and the Son and is therefore revealed and believed to be God, does not stand in need of any point of contact but that which he himself creates. Only retrospectively is it possible to reflect on the way in which he "makes contact" with man, and this retrospect will ever be a retrospect upon a *miracle*. (121)

In the final section of his pamphlet, Barth states his objections to the uses to which Brunner wants to put natural theology in the Church. This section is a wholesale rejection of Brunner's eristic and ethical program. He focuses on Brunner's statement: "The Church also is dependent upon the possibility 'of speaking to man of God at all'".[50] Barth erupts:

Where in the history or teaching of the Bible has Brunner found the slightest support for this sentence with the fatal word "also"?…Does not this sentence betray a theory which thinks that as regards theological and ecclesiastical practice it must find help elsewhere than in the revelation of God—and thinks that it has already found it?…Is that sentence to be understood otherwise than as a statement of human fear, wit and agility, which thinks that it has to improve upon what God has done well and will do well, which is chiefly concerned with *success* and not the command, the promises, and the end?[51] (124–125)

Barth counters that the Church is solely to be concerned about the question of "What?", not "How?": "Has it ever been said and heard to such an extent that we might at least have sufficient time and energy left to turn to an 'other' task of theology?" (125–126). In regard to Brunner's concern for "success", Barth suggests: do not take the non-Christian's unbelief seriously; let the language of preaching be shaped by the text; leave pedagogy alone and teach the Word of God; and build ethics upon God's commands, not "those mythical" orders (127–128).

Barth concludes his tract with the same vehemence with which he began it:

> We are not here at all in order to gather successes. We are commanded to do work that has a reason and foundation. *That* is why there is hope in that work. Natural theology is always the answer to a question which is false if it wishes to be "decisive". That is the question concerning the "How?" of theological and ecclesiastical activity. Hence it has to be rejected *a limine*—right at the outset. Only the theology and the church of the antichrist can profit from it. The Evangelical Church and Evangelical theology would only sicken and die of it.[52] (128)

The Aftermath

In November, Brunner writes to Barth with his formal response to "No!"[53] Brunner confesses that when he first read it, "I had a few heart palpitations".[54] But, again, Brunner thinks that Barth's attack completely missed him:

> The Emil Brunner who you smear there *coram publico* deserves an ample thrashing. A theologian who ventures to say "the human capacity for revelation" is a traitor…But this Emil Brunner exists in the same way as this blasphemous concept of the human capacity for revelation: only in Karl Barth's imagination. Therefore I can…watch with amusement as this guy is thrashed. Oh boy, what kind of a caricature of Emil Brunner you have thrown together there!

In Brunner's view, either he has won the debate, or at the least, Barth has missed with all his punches:

> In what you have to do with me, you really have to do with genuine Calvinism …The only thing I said which is materially false is the sentence at the end, that the *theologia naturalis* is "the task" of our generation. It should be called: an important task. There is indeed a problem of reason and revelation, but under an aspect which is not the central one.

But after this confident beginning, Brunner's tone changes. He upbraids himself for avoiding meeting with Barth in the Spring—he was "intimidated", and "did not want to be inconvenienced by your reactions". If only Brunner had talked with Barth then, "I would not have provoked you to draw such a caricature and thereby to confuse the minds".[55] In Brunner's view, what has changed since 1929 is that Brunner has corrected a weak point in "The Other Task of Theology"—"I have now completely wiped out a hidden synergism in [it]…and have fought my way through entirely to a theology of the *sola gratia*. What you say about it is wrong from A to Z". Brunner signs the letter, "despite everything, still very much allied to you".

Barth responds by return mail.[56] He asks Brunner to finally say exactly what he wants to say in a way that cannot be misunderstood. It is an excuse of which Barth is clearly growing tired. More fundamentally, Barth rejects Brunner's appeal to Calvin:

> If you want to further the debate, get rid of your Calvin-hypothesis, which you cite for vindication way too many times. Instead, show what your authentic intention concerning *theologia naturalis* is, and show how far it is (1) possible and (2) necessary in line with the intentions of Reformation theology (of predestination, justification, *servum arbitrium*, Scripture-principle).[57]

Early in 1935, Brunner issued a second edition of *Nature and Grace*.[58] There were two reasons for its appearance. First, and embarrassingly, in the first edition the references to Calvin's works were completely bungled, so that it was not possible to follow Brunner's argument in the section on "The Reformers' Doctrine and Its Antithesis". The second edition corrected this error. The second reason for a new edition concerned an issue familiar from the Barth–Brunner correspondence:

> It is necessary to protect this unchanged text against misunderstandings through numerous explanatory notes...An answer to Karl Barth is dispensed with. For his surprisingly sharp "No" appears to me to be founded for the most part on misunderstandings, which the explanatory notes should clear away. (v–vi)

Thus, the second edition consisted of a seven-page forward, the text of the first edition, corrected Calvin citations, and sixteen pages of thirty-eight "explanatory notes".

In his forward, Brunner emphasizes that his argument in *Nature and Grace*—humanity's responsibility before God is established in its rejection of general revelation—is the necessary presupposition of justification by grace alone (iii). He maintains that to deal comprehensively with general revelation would only be possible in a book which dealt fully with theological anthropology.[59] The goals of *Nature and Grace* are thus more modest:

> it is only a question of ensuring this biblical doctrine—whose content is...so decisive practically for the Church and theology—and the value it has had for the Church from the first centuries to the present. Dogmatically, the doctrine of general revelation...belongs in the chapter on creation, and it forms a part of the exposition of the first article. Thus it is no "porch" standing outside the creed, but, like all honest theology, it stands within the creed. It is *one* God who reveals Himself in the works of creation, in the law written upon people's consciences, and in Jesus Christ. Therefore it is a *Christian*—not a pagan nor a rational—theology of nature which is at question here. (iv)

Brunner concludes his forward with three points. First, his pamphlet has been misunderstood in two ways: a) "those who have misunderstood in my presentation the fundamental distinction between an objective and subjective *theologia naturalis*", and b) that "despite my exactly repeated definitions", Brunner's use of the term "*theologia naturalis*" led some readers to impute misunderstandings from this term's misuse in history (v). Second, Brunner makes an impassioned statement that reveals his resentment of being lumped together with the German-Christians by Barth:

> I have never had anything to do with German-Christianity, and I have made no se-
> cret of my condemnation of this aberration since its first appearance…If, as it ap-
> pears, individual supporters of this movement took pleasure in my article, it
> means that the fact of the matter is—since many affirm their agreement with me,
> one of their sharpest opponents—that the opposition lies in a completely differ-
> ent place…German-Christianity and related directions have their origin in thought
> about the State, which does not touch upon the problem of natural theology with
> any theological formulations. I have spoken out against German-Christianity at
> many times and for many years in such a way that has yielded the most bitter op-
> position. The Church cannot under any circumstances allow Church-political con-
> siderations…to accuse clear biblical doctrine of heresy, or to push it into the back-
> ground (as has occurred recently in the explanations of certain synods).[60] (vi)

Finally, Brunner likens his struggle in formulating his Christian doctrine of natural revelation to Luther's struggle against Roman Catholicism and the Schwärmers (read: German-Christians) on the one hand as well as against "an ultra-Lutheran antinomian doctrine of *sola gratia*" (read: Barth) on the other (vi–vii).

Brunner's explanatory notes can be gathered together into five groups. First, there is a series of notes which simply cite additional biblical or Ref-ormation texts to support Brunner's argument. Second, in some nine notes Brunner says in different words what he has already said. Another nine notes attempt to clarify terms and expressions, such as "capacity for words", "addressability", "ability for words" and "in some way". A fourth group contains rebuttals to points made in "No!".

The final group of notes centers around the main thrust of the second edition: the absolute distinction between a wholly illegitimate *subjective* natu-ral theology (humanity can know God apart from Christ and Scripture, as found in Roman Catholicism and Neo-Protestantism) *vs.* a very necessary *objective* natural theology (God has objectively revealed Himself in His cre-ation, which humanity has ignored, which makes it responsible for its sin, which is the presupposition of the Gospel).[61] For example, Brunner objects to Barth's changing of "addressability", "ability for words", and "capacity for words" into "capacity for revelation":

I have justly never used the misquoted expression "man's capacity for revelation". That would indeed mean that humanity is "capable of revelation", while my expression states that *the works of God*, since creation, are capable of revealing God. My use of it is objective, but as Barth imputes it to me, it would be used subjectively, "the capacity of humanity for God". (47)

In his final note, Brunner concludes with what is both the closest thing to a retraction but also a renewed pressing of his case. Referring to the fourth-from-last sentence in *Nature and Grace* ("It is the task of our theological generation to find our way back to a true *theologia naturalis*"), Brunner now writes:

This definite article is the most misunderstood thing in my whole article. The entire emphasis lies not on "the", but on "true". The meaning of the entire last paragraph is this: On the one hand, as the history of theology shows, there is a grave danger of deviation at the point where the doctrine of general revelation is dealt with inside of dogmatics itself—directly—and where it comes to have a significant place as the subject matter of proclamation; on the other hand, however, it is dangerous to suppress this doctrine in practice. It is a question of the missionary Church; it is a question of the doctrine of the responsibility of the sinner. The statement can be correctly understood (with the definite article): "It is the task of our theological generation", i.e., "To our generation the task has been given ...". That natural theology is the most important or only task of theology completely misunderstands me, who wrote *The Mediator*. So, let this ominous definite article, in all its forms, be erased. The Christian doctrine of the revelation in creation or the natural revelation of God (which I tentatively called Christian *theologia naturalis*) is obviously only a part (yet because of its missionary-practical significance, an important part) of the task of the reflection concerning the Word of God-become-flesh in Jesus Christ, which is given to us in Scripture alone. (59–60)

After a quick exchange of letters at Christmas time, Brunner re-initiates the correspondence in June 1935, when Barth is again summering at the Bergli.[62] Brunner asks for a meeting with Barth. Though he knows that a "total congruence of our theological and Church outlooks is out of the question", nonetheless he states that "an understanding between us would be for many a joyful event". Brunner is particularly encouraged in light of conversations he has had with Thurneysen about the second edition of *Nature and Grace*. Brunner reflects on the past seven months:

Despite your thundering word against me...I was never really angry with you (after the first effect of the shock had faded); therefore I look forward to another encounter. I think, for our common students' sake and for the Church's sake, we must attempt it.

Barth responds that he is willing to have a conversation, but not if "it is on-

ly a question of resolving a couple of misunderstandings concerning 'bro-
therly strife'".[63] For Barth, the issue is that Brunner has changed since
1929, and this needs to be admitted and examined before meaningful conversation can take place:

> You have thrown a handful of explanatory...remarks at me and the other readers
> [in the second edition], and have not done such things necessary if you disagree
> with a general objection against your entire parade as it has carried itself out for six
> years now. Dear friend, during this time you are responsible for carrying out a
> change over-against the Church 1) in the area of the doctrine of knowledge with
> your *theologia naturalis* and 2) in the area of the doctrine of grace with your pro-
> clamation of the theological relevance of the Oxford Movement.[64] I have taken
> this fact seriously, and I would like to demand that you take it seriously in the
> same way.

Barth states what he fears Brunner is expecting from such a conversation:

> Look:...if the importance of your change should be not entirely clear to you; if it
> is not completely clear to you that I, for my part, cannot surrender one iota of the
> antithesis on this issue, if you think that it only requires a few interpretations and
> re-touching on both sides in order for your and my theological work to hang to-
> gether (like two train cars, in which people evenly distribute themselves, because
> they're all going to the same destination behind the same engine)—if this is what
> you think, then how can we speak meaningfully with one another, alone or before
> witnesses? I will always seek the decision which you always will avoid, and in
> these different intentions we will be at cross purposes with one another even be-
> fore we have opened our mouths...Do you have the intention *either* to convince
> and refute me no matter what the consequences, *or* to be convinced and refuted by
> me no matter what the consequences...? But, oh, dear Emil Brunner, can you and
> do you understand in general the (finally purely formal) concerns that moves me
> to all these questions?

Barth then proposes a discussion, "point by point" of Brunner's latest publication:[65]

> I do not need to state a public "No!" against it...But I must reject it in its entirety,
> in the same definite way as I did *Nature and Grace*, as representative of the un-
> dertaking in which you wish to become entangled.

Brunner writes back, glad for Barth's "readiness for a discussion".[66] He
agrees that "we think completely differently, even concerning the truth of
Jesus Christ", and that "I could...also write a No, for certainly your teaching appears to me to be not a little as misguided as mine is to you". For
Brunner, the ground rules for a constructive conversation must include genuine intellectual openness and prayer. Barth and Brunner did get together.

Brunner writes Barth immediately afterwards with great thanks.[67] Apparently it was a profitable discussion, with points made, essential disagreements voiced, and positions clarified. Brunner admits that Barth scored at least two points against him. First:

> I know that, in reality, not only do my intentions direct my theological thinking, but often simply my preferences do too—and it is clear to me that one must deal rigorously with one's preferences precisely in theological thinking. By nature I would indeed much rather be a philosopher than a theologian. That indeed may well be what to you is suspect about me.

Second, "in what you said you have...materially rattled my theological position. Whether I must give in at one or a few points, I still don't know. But in any case I face my own outlook again with a little critical distance". Brunner sums up his view of their conversation:

> If you reproach me for a return to the positive theology of the nineteenth century, so I would give you something similar in return: above all that you take too importantly the new things that began fifteen years ago. Between the Karl Barth, whose theology only wanted to be "a pinch of spice" and a marginal gloss, and the author of an anticipated eight-volume dogmatics—between the Karl Barth who harnessed Nietzsche and Overbeck to the yoke of Christ, and the author of *Credo*[68]—is an even further distance than from the Brunner of *Mysticism and the Word* to that of *On the Work of the Holy Spirit*.

Barth replies with a postcard, referring to "our memorable visit".[69] He concludes: "A thriving continuation of the forming of our so dialectical relationship will still give us much to think about and to do".

Summary

Several observations can be made about Barth and Brunner's famous "natural theology debate". First, it is clear that "natural theology debate" is a misnomer, for their debate was neither a careful exegesis nor a dogmatic discussion of "natural theology".[70] Rather, the debate was the culmination of Barth and Brunner's disagreement since 1929 (with roots reaching back to 1924) over many issues: the understanding of dialectic and revelation, the relationship of theology and philosophy, the place of anthropology in theology, the task of theology.[71] Thus, the 1934 pamphlets should not be overvalued in assessing the break-up of Barth and Brunner's theological alliance —they merely stated clearly what had been on their minds for at least five years.

A second observation concerns the setting of the natural theology debate

within the context of the German Church struggle. As this book has consistently shown, the lines of thought which were finally expressed in 1934
had been developing in Barth and Brunner certainly since 1929, probably
since 1924/1925, and perhaps as far back as 1920 for Barth and 1922 for
Brunner. That Barth felt required to issue a public and decisive No to Brunner was due to the rise of the German-Christian heresy. However, Barth understood the full range and implications of his disagreement with Brunner
long before the German-Christians appeared on the scene.[72] Barth did not
understand German-Christianity as anything unique; it was simply another
form of the error of Neo-Protestantism with which Brunner constantly
flirted—the desire to correlate God's revelation with a second criterion.
However, the German-Christian context added urgency and decisiveness to
the Barth-Brunner debate. Barth's disagreement with Brunner became extremely pointed and concrete in light of the German-Christian movement's
appeal to natural theology and the orders of creation, whereas for Brunner
these issues remained more abstract questions about the task of theology
and the place of anthropology. It is striking how oblivious Brunner was to
the context into which he hurled *Nature and Grace*.[73] Nonetheless, Barth's
charge (made implicitly in "No!" and explicitly in their correspondence) that
Brunner would have ended up with Gogarten as a German-Christian
sympathizer was both wholly unfair to Brunner and showed that Barth failed
to understand the place of natural theology in Brunner's system. Brunner's
complete rejection of German-Christianity was not an inconsistency in his
thinking, but revealed how limited a place and how specifically intended his
"natural theology" was.

A third observation concerns the weakness of *Nature and Grace* as a
theological argument. The article showed, in a nutshell, that Brunner was
trying to juggle too many conceptual balls, to the end that his thinking was
unclear and contradictory. There was a "dialectic" within Brunner's own
thought—between Kant, Kierkegaard, Ebner, and traditional Calvinism on
the one side, and a radical, actualist Barthian dialectic on the other. This
book has shown that, except for a brief period in 1922–1924, this internal
dialectic was constantly resolved through the suppression of the latter
pole.[74] *Nature and Grace* revealed the impossible synthesis of Brunner's
philosophical-anthropological commitments and Barth's radical "distance":
the over-use of "in some way"; the imprecision about just how much natural humanity knows about God;[75] the failure to understand the crucial difference between his "no legitimate natural knowledge of God" and Barth's
"no natural knowledge of God at all".[76]

Given these problems, why did Brunner hold so tenaciously to natural
theology? First, it indicated his deep commitment to Kantian ethics—the
natural person knows she is claimed by a moral imperative, which is what

makes her responsible and free. Facing the tension between philosophical justice and theological grace, Brunner consistently decided for justice, freedom and responsibility. Second, natural theology reflected Brunner's fundamental eristic (or missionary) concern—the urgency to "make contact" with the way modern unbelievers think.[77] From a *homiletic* which both reaches out to and corrects modern thought, to an *ethics* based on humanity's actually-existing moral orders of community, to a *theology* which always remains existentially in contact with anthropology, Brunner's eristics revealed a theology which was less interested in explaining and re-thinking the biblical-Reformation tradition than in *communicating it effectively* to modern people. The last two chapters have shown how "natural theology" was not, in itself, a fundamental principle for Brunner.[78] Rather, in his increasing polemics with Barth, he was (perhaps too willingly) forced towards natural theology because it provided a way to justify his ethical-anthropological and eristic-existential concerns.[79]

At the same time, "No!" was not Barth's greatest piece of work. For the most part he was able to exploit the ambiguity and weakness of Brunner's argument.[80] Though the historical context made it understandable, Barth's total rejection of natural theology clearly placed him outside of Church tradition as well as the main stream of Scriptural interpretation.[81] Barth rejected Brunner's anthropological arguments simply by refusing to discuss anthropology—it was of no theological "interest".[82] Barth's thinking at this time ruthlessly suppressed the doctrine of creation under the doctrine of reconciliation.[83] But Brunner was incorrect that Barth "misunderstood" him, for, in fact, it was Brunner who had misunderstood Barth since 1924–1925.[84] Barth saw clearly how Brunner stood across a fundamental divide from himself.[85] The natural theology debate—in fact, the entire Barth–Brunner debate—showed how radically Barth proposed to re-think theology from the perspective of a dialectical, actualist, "un-guaranteed" understanding of God and revelation. Given Barth's radical starting-point (announced in *Romans II* and developed dogmatically in *The Göttingen Dogmatics, Christian Dogmatics, Anselm* and *Church Dogmatics*), Barth was correct in seeing Brunner—even Brunner—as standing on the other side.

Nature and Grace was simply the third installment in Brunner's attempt to explain and defend his program of eristics against Barth's objections. And, while "No!" certainly fairly represented Barth's stance against natural theology and his disagreement with Brunner, the vehemence of the "anathema" of "No!" is only understandable as a No against Brunner's "German eulogizers".

NOTES

1. For this chapter's account of Nazism, see: V.R. Berghahn, *Modern Germany*, 2nd edn (Cambridge: Cambridge University Press, 1987), pp. 102–138, 301; *The European World*, ed. by Jerome Blum and others, 2nd edn (Boston: Little, Brown, 1970), pp. 902–903, 936–939; Cochrane, pp. 19–49.

2. For this chapter's account of the German-Christians and the German Church struggle, see: Cochrane, pp. 74–89; Busch, pp. 222–235.

3. Quoted in H. Martin Rumscheidt, "The First Commandment as Axiom for Theology", in *Theology Beyond Christendom*, ed. by John Thompson (Allison Park, PA: Pickwick, 1986), pp. 143–164 (p. 149). See also pp. 149–153.

4. This principle provided the political-Church background for Barth's rejection of Brunner's use of the "order of creation" in his ethics, which was published in this same year.

5. Quoted in Cochrane, pp. 222–223.

6. See "Quousque tandem...?", *ZZ*, 8 (1930), 1–6; "Die Not der Evangelischen Kirche", *ZZ*, 9 (1931), 89–122 (especially p. 115); "Questions Which 'Christianity' Must Face", *Student World*, 25 (1932), 93–100. In the winter semester of 1931/1932, Barth taught a seminar with Erich Przywara on "The Problem of Natural Theology" (J.F. Gerhard Goeters, "Karl Barth in Bonn, 1930–1935", *EvTh*, 47 (1987), 137–150 (p. 142). With Hitler's rise to power in January 1933, Barth suggested that *Zwischen den Zeiten* cease publication so that he could publicly distance himself from Gogarten, who had taken a favorable stand towards several aspects of the German–Christians' position (e.g., the orders of creation, the destiny of history, and the importance of *Volk* and nation (Johnson, p. 241)); see also Gogarten, "Staat und Kirche", *ZZ*, 10 (1932), 390–410). It was decided to continue publishing, but from then on the names of Barth, Gogarten and Thurneysen no longer appeared on the masthead.

7. In Rumscheidt, *Way of Theology*, pp. 63–78.

8. Barth defines an "axiom" as a not provable presupposition upon which a discipline builds and to which it relates all its subsequent statements (63). Jüngel's assertion ("Barth's Theological Beginnings", pp. 93–96), that with this essay Barth moves away from the abstract axiom "God is God" (which is based on a type of natural theology) to the concrete theological axiom of the first commandment, overstates the development in Barth's thinking from 1921 to 1933, especially in light of Barth's thought since 1929.

9. Barth singles out Gogarten and Brunner here, lumping them together with the German-Christians Hirsch and Althaus (pp. 73–74). He also argues that, when the Reformers wandered into natural theology, it was clear that they had "no other gods", as opposed to recent attempts at natural theology (p. 74).

10. Jena: Eugen Diederichs, 1926.

11. Trans. by R. Birch Hoyle (London: Hodder & Stoughton, 1933).

12. See Barth's reflections on this pamphlet six years later ("How I Changed My Mind, 1928–1938", in *Karl Barth: How I Changed My Mind*, p. 46).

13. See Barth's address on the eve of the elections: "Für die Freiheit der Evangeliums", *ThExh*, 2 (1933). Barth argues that "the freedom of the Gospel means...the message that Jesus Christ the Lord...is our only comfort in life and in death...One cannot hear this message without hearing the commandment: Thou shalt have no other gods before me!" (5–6). Practically, the freedom of the Gospel means that the Church can lay no other "books" alongside the Scriptures, it can preach no other "morality" than the Word of God, and it must live its own life in the world (its membership cannot be conditional upon factors of race and blood) (7–8). Barth concludes by seeing in the days' developments the "same old paganism" which has threatened the Church throughout the years—"the Church has simply and entirely forgotten God" (13–14).

14. Quoted in Busch, p. 229.

15. *Barth–Brunner*, EB: June 1, 1933 (#85), pp. 222f. In this letter, Brunner has not heard about Barth's attack on him in "The First Commandment", since the lecture was not published until late summer, 1933. Brunner does not acknowledge it until February 26, 1934 (see above p. 149).

16. Ibid., EB: July 14, 1933 (#86), pp. 224f.; ibid., KB: July 17, 1933 (#87), pp. 226–230.

17. Ibid., EB: Autumn, 1933 (#91), pp. 234–237.

18. See Chapter Six.

19. *Barth–Brunner*, KB: October 22, 1933 (#93), pp. 237–240. Remarkably, Brunner brushes aside this harsh verdict: "As I read your astonishing communication, I was at first, in fact, a little perplexed. Not about the consequences which you have drawn about me—O Karl, your drawing of consequences! You know the Lutheran who could precisely prove that Calvin's God is the devil? I have become cured of being shocked by your drawing of consequences about people" (*Barth–Brunner*, EB: October 27, 1933 (#94), pp. 241–243).

20. Smart, pp. 212–213.

21. Lange, pp. 265–266.

22. "Abschied", *ZZ*, 11 (1933), 536–554. Barth's article is pp. 536–544.

23. Fuchs' article was "Theologie und Metaphysik", pp. 315–326.

24. With the end of *Zwischen den Zeiten*, Barth began to edit frequent "occasional writings" under the title "Theologische Existenz heute" (published by Chr. Kaiser Verlag, Munich).

25. Translated in Rolf Ahlers, *The Barmen Theological Declaration of 1934* (Lewiston, NY: Edwin Mellen, 1986), pp. 124–129. The declaration was Barth's most christologically-centered writing to date, constantly bringing all faith-affirmations up against the criterion of "God's action in Jesus Christ". Its most polemical statements occur in the final section, where it rejects the notion that the Church can on its own responsibility set up a "special office of *Führer*", that the Church can "limit membership and qualification for service in the church to those who belong to a particular

race", and that "the State is the highest or even the "total" form of a historical reality visibly and temporally fashioned, to which the church has to submit and conform with its message and form and into which it has to be incorporate" (p. 14).

26. "Gottes Wille und unsere Wünsche", *ThExh*, 7 (1934), pp. 16–30. In this address Barth declares a firm No to the question, "Is there a 'natural theology' in which God's will and our wishes might be one?" Barth also indicates the historical uniqueness of this No: "This is put to us today much more sharply than it was to Luther and Calvin, and so we cannot find a clear answer to it from them" (p. 25). Barth comes out against the "point-of-contact", connecting it explicitly with the German-Christian heresy (pp. 24–25). Barth states that the doctrine of natural revelation—of "and"—is impossible, because, since we may not ask about the possibility of God's miracle (p. 27).

27. At the beginning of the 1934 winter semester, Barth wrote to the Rector of Bonn University and the Minister of Cultural Affairs that, since he began his lectures with prayer, he considered the required "German salute" to be out of place (Busch, p. 242).

28. Meanwhile, on April 30, Barth had been summoned to the Ministry of Cultural Affairs for an examination of his views, and was immediately put under the status of city arrest in Bonn.

29. Busch, p. 245.

30. Quoted in Cochrane, p. 239. For a detailed study of the text of the Barmen Declaration, see Rolf Ahlers, *Barmen Declaration*. See Barth's reflections on Barmen in *CD* II/1/§26.2: 172–178.

31. "Martin Luther", *ThExh*, 6 (1934). Wolf argues that Luther maintained that, although there is a "natural consciousness" of the existence of God, it always "appears as a mirage of the unsatisfied wishes of humanity, as a material or as a spiritual idol-builder, as *idola*, as *figmenta*..." (9–10). Thus, Wolf maintains, for Luther there is only a natural knowledge of a false "god", but absolutely no knowledge of the true God.

32. *Barth–Brunner*, EB: February 26, 1934 (#96), pp. 244–248. Brunner relates about a dissertation he is currently examining on Calvin's view of natural theology and remarks, "I am nearly terrified how far in this direction Calvin goes, much further in the direction of the 'Catholics' than I would ever dare...I nowhere go beyond the teaching of Calvin; on the contrary, I frequently remain on this side of him, so to speak in your neighborhood".

33. See "Law and Revelation".

34. *Barth–Brunner*, KB: March 13, 1934 (#97), pp. 249f.

35. These lectures were published in *God in Action*, trans. by Elmer G. Homrighausen and Karl J. Ernst (Manhasset, NY: Round Table, 1963), pp. 3–57.

36. *Barth–Brunner*, EB: May 8, 1934 (#98), pp. 250f.; in *Natural Theology*, trans. by Peter Fraenkel (London: Centenary, 1946), pp. 15–64 .

37. Brunner also explains why he passed up Barth's offer to meet when Barth was in

Zurich in March: "You are obviously not completely aware what you wrote to me in your letter [March 13, 1934], or perhaps you are confident...that I have better nerves than I really do. I can, as you once stated in Pany, bear many things, but everything has its limits".

38. *CD* I/1/§5.2:132–143.

39. *Barth–Brunner*, EB: September 30, 1934 (#99), pp. 252–256.

40. *Vom Werk des Heiligen Geistes* (Tübingen: JCB Mohr, 1935).

41. *Barth–Brunner*, KB: October 1, 1934 (#100), pp. 256–261.

42. Barth's immediate reaction can be seen in the notes he scratched in his copy of *Nature and Grace*:

"When B[runner] speaks of God, it becomes and remains dark to my eyes.

He does not know the mystery of God, predestination, freedom, the miracle of grace.

He does not know that the distinction 'formal-material' signifies the resumption of the schema of rationalist orthodoxy.

He does not know how tiresome his struggle against my 'one-sidedness' is...

He has also certainly not understood Calvin.

He makes a caricature of Roman Catholic natural theology so that he can differentiate himself from it.

He has a deadly concept of 'biblical-reformed'.

He has still not fully seen how fundamental our opposition is.

He writes like a school-teacher.

It would have been better if he had not written this article."

(Back insider cover of Barth's copy of *Nature and Grace*, in the Karl Barth Archiv, Basel).

43. *Barth–Brunner*, EB: October 2, 1934 (#101), pp. 261–266.

44. In *Natural Theology*, pp. 65–128.

45. See John Baillie, "Introduction", in *Natural Theology*, pp. 5–12 (pp. 8–9).

46. See *Nature and Grace*, p. 27. The context makes it clear that Brunner is speaking of the capacity of God's works to reveal God, not humanity's capacity to receive God's revelation without the aid of the Holy Spirit.

47. See Joan O'Donovan, "Man in the Image of God", *SJT*, 39 (1986), 433–459). See especially pp. 438, 445–447, 450–453, 458–459 for the problems in Brunner's *imago Dei* formulations.

48. E.g., *Nature and Grace*, pp. 24–25.

49. Gestrich points to this as the heart of the Barth–Brunner debate. For Brunner, modern thinking (specifically existentialism and Ebnerianism) has given certain and obvious information on what humanity is, whereas Barth relies only on how Scripture describes humanity (*Neuzeitliches Denken*, pp. 178–179).

50. *Nature and Grace*, p. 56.

51. Yet, by 1948, Barth could point to his Army contacts with non-churched Swiss soldiers and conclude, "And so I learned anew how a sermon really aimed at a man

must be constructed" ("How I Changed My Mind, 1938–1948", in *Karl Barth: How I Changed My Mind*, pp. 50–60 (p. 53)).

52. For contemporary analyses of the Barth–Brunner natural theology debate, see: Paul Tillich, "Natural and Revealed Religion", *Christendom*, 1 (1935), 159–170 (p. 160); Wilhelm Link, "«Anknüpfung», «Vorverständnis» und die Frage der «Theologischen Anthropologie»", *Theologische Rundschau*, 7 (1935), 205–254; C. Stange, "Natürliche Theologie", *Zeitschrift für systematische Theologie*, 12 (1935), 367–452; E. Reisner, "Zwei Fragen an Karl Barth zum Problem der natürlichen Theologie", *EvTh*, 1 (1934–1935), 396–402.

53. *Barth–Brunner*, EB: November, 1934 (#103), pp. 268–270.

54. Cf. H.H. Brunner, p. 89. Brunner's daughter-in-law comments: "[He] was deeply hurt…It was very difficult for him to talk about it…He didn't feel accepted by Barth, and Barth was not threatened by my father-in-law" (Brunner-Gutekunst interview).

55. See above, p. 152.

56. *Barth–Brunner*, KB: November 12, 1934 (#104), pp. 270–272.

57. Meanwhile, pressure was being put on Barth at Bonn. As a result of his refusal to begin his lectures with the Nazi salute, Barth was suspended from teaching on November 26.

58. Zweite, stark erweiterte Auflage, Tübingen: JCB Mohr, 1935.

59. Brunner attempted such a book in 1937: *Man in Revolt*, trans. by Olive Wyon (Philadelphia: Westminster, 1939).

60. Brunner is referring here to both of the Barmen declarations of 1934, both written by Barth.

61. In particular, Brunner takes on Peter Barth's article, "Das Problem der natürlichen Theologie bei Calvin", *ThExh*, 18 (1935) (see pp. 52–53).

62. *Barth–Brunner*, EB: June 15, 1935 (#107), pp. 276–278. Barth's trial and appeal (for refusing to perform the Nazi salute in his lectures) dragged on until June 1935, and he remained in Bonn until shortly before the final ruling was given. After being dismissed from his professorship, Barth accepted a call from the University of Basel, and went there immediately.

63. Ibid., KB: June 20, 1935 (#108), pp. 279–283.

64. See Chapter Six.

65. *Vom Werk des Heiligen Geistes.*

66. *Barth–Brunner*, EB: June 25, 1935 (#109), pp. 283–285.

67. Ibid., EB: July 1, 1935 (#110), pp. 286–288.

68. In February 1935, Barth delivered a lecture series in Utrecht entitled *Credo*. One can hear Barth continuing the natural theology debate with Brunner (see pp. 11–12, for an explicit rejection of Brunner's point-of-contact).

69. *Barth–Brunner*, KB: August 10, 1935 (#111), p. 288.

70. Claus Westermann, "Karl Barths Nein", *EvTh*, 47 (1987), 386–395 (pp. 389–391) and James Barr ("La Foi Biblique et la Théologie Naturelle", *Études Théologiques et*

Religieuses, 64 (1989), 355–368) point to the superficial exegesis performed by both theologians. However, Barr in particular takes insufficient account of Barth's extensive exegetical argument against natural theology in CD II/1/§26.1:97–126 (see p. 361).

71. T. Koch, "Natur und Gnade", *Kerygma und Dogma*, 16 (1970), 171–187 (p. 172).

72. *Contra* Winzeler, p. 134; *contra* Gestrich, "Unbewältigte natürliche Theologie", p. 82. See Walter Kreck, *Grundentscheidungen in Karl Barths Dogmatik* (Neukirchen-Vluyn: Neukirchener Verlag, 1978), p. 121.

73. Lütz, p. 270; Cochrane, p. 71. This is partly explained by Brunner's different understanding of the threat facing the German Church. For Brunner, this was an *ethical* issue, specifically about the nature of the State, whereas for Barth it was a *theological* issue about the source of revelation. This is confirmed by Brunner's re-claiming of natural law to challenge all forms of political totalitarianism in his 1943 book on social ethics (*Justice and the Social Order*, trans. by Mary Hottinger (London: Harper, 1945). See also the "Translator's Note" in *The Divine Imperative*, p. 13.

74. In fact, Barth's "No!" served to clarify this tension for Brunner: from 1935 on he distinguished himself from Barth's "objectivism" (see *Truth as Encounter,* pp. 41–46, 81–83; *Revelation and Reason*, trans. by Olive Wyon (Philadelphia: Westminster, 1946), pp. 39–40.

75. David Cairns, "The Theology of Brunner", *SJT*, 1 (1948), 294–308 (p. 299).

76. Berkouwer, p. 194. See also Colin Brown, *Karl Barth and the Christian Message* (Downers Grove, IL: IVP, 1966), p. 82.

77. Cairns, "Theology of Brunner", p. 296.

78. *Contra* Stange.

79. That Brunner was "backed into" defending natural theology is confirmed by 1) his continual claim that Barth misunderstood him, and 2) his failure, in *Nature and Grace* or anywhere else for his remaining thirty-two years, to sketch out a constructive natural theology (Brown, p. 87).

80. Brown, p. 81.

81. Robert Crawford, "The Theological Method of Karl Barth", *SJT*, 25 (1972), 320–336 (p. 325).

82. It was not until the publication of *CD* III/2 (1948) that Barth answered Brunner seriously and theologically on the question of anthropology (see especially §44.2:127–132).

83. Berkouwer, pp. 247, 259; Westermann, p. 392. Barth does not deal with creation constructively until 1945 (*CD* III/1).

84. Barth did misunderstand Brunner in that he placed Brunner outside of the Reformation understanding of general revelation and the Law. See Barr, p. 368; John Newton Thomas, "The Place of Natural Theology in the Thought of John Calvin", *Journal of Religious Thought*, 15 (1957–1958), 107–136. Thomas sees a fundamental confusion in Calvin's thought on natural knowledge of God (p. 136).

85. *Contra* Leipold, pp. 289–290.

CHAPTER SIX

The End of a Relationship (1932–1936)
The Oxford Group Movement

Perhaps there will come a time when you will once more have an ear for that which the Groups want—if you understand that we are not blessed through our theology, but only through being-in-Christ. The Groups have brought me closer to this than I have ever been.

(Brunner to Barth, October 1933)

News has constantly reached me of your co-operation with the Group–Movement (which I have always viewed so thoroughly unsympathetically)...from which I see once more that you apparently find yourself in a rapid movement whose Spirit and direction have always been strange to me.

(Barth to Brunner, October 1934)

Chapters Four and Five traced the unraveling and final break-up of the Barth–Brunner theological alliance. Untreated so far, however, is another key point of division between the two theologians from 1932 on—the Oxford Group Movement. This chapter will analyze its effect on the Barth–Brunner partnership, and show how—on both theological and personal levels—it ensured the end of their alliance.

The Oxford Group Movement

The Oxford Group Movement was founded and led by an American, Frank N.D. Buchman (1878–1961).[1] Raised in a pietistic Swiss-German Lutheran family in eastern Pennsylvania and ordained into the Lutheran ministry in 1902, Buchman first served a small parish on the outskirts of Philadelphia. He traveled to England in 1907 and attended the Keswick conference, where he experienced a "profound awakening", which included a call to be an evangelist. In 1909, Buchman became the secretary of the YMCA at Pennsylvania State College. During his six years there, the college experienced a religious revival, as Buchman experimented with several of the evangelistic methods that would later characterize the Oxford Group Movement. After a year of missionary work in India, Korea and Japan, he was appointed to a lectureship in evangelism at Hartford (Connecticut) Seminary. It was during this period that Buchman began an evangelistic ministry on college campuses, most notably at Princeton. His university work progressed rapidly in the early 1920s, ultimately meeting resistance from campus authorities at some schools. During these years, Buchman visited acquaintances in Cambridge and friends at Oxford (mostly Princeton Rhodes scholars). During these visits, he duplicated the evangelistic work he had been doing in the States. Buchman resigned from Hartford Seminary in 1922 in order to devote his full attention to this university ministry, and in 1927 he moved his base of operations to England.

A period of quiet but rapid progress in the 1920s was followed by enormous international success in the early 1930s: teams of Buchman's followers made evangelistic visits to and established groups in Scotland, Holland, Scandinavia, Germany, Switzerland, and South Africa (where, in 1928, a team was first dubbed "The Oxford Group"). Rallies drew thousands of people, and the movement received endorsement by notable people in Church and society.[2] By 1936, the Oxford Group Movement was a worldwide force within Christianity and very much on the minds of the general public, receiving widespread newspaper coverage wherever it went.

The Oxford Group Movement described itself as "A First Century Christian Fellowship".[3] It sought to renew the Church, to evangelize the non-Christian world through personal contacts, and to bring about a "new world order through changed lives". In Buchman's words, "The Oxford Group is a revolution of God-control where God really guides you and your nation".[4]

OGM's methods were intentionally "non-churchy". Friends of OGM members were invited to be guests at a "house-party" (a weekend or week-long conference for about 30–40 people, held in a resort-type setting). During meetings at the house-party, OGM members would give "reports" (testimonies), focusing on the "change" (conversion) they experienced when they put themselves under "God-control" (came to faith), or about remarkable experiences of God's "guidance" in the large and trivial matters of life.[5] While God was clearly mentioned, and evangelical Protestantism was assumed, the OGM people spoke of their commitment to the "Four Absolutes": absolute honesty, absolute purity, absolute unselfishness, and absolute love. Another distinctive practice that was introduced at house-parties was the "Quiet Time" (devotional period): in silence, participants would listen for and write down God's personal "guidance" for the day. After the house-party, those who had experienced a "change" were encouraged to participate in a regular small group meeting with other OGMers for support and accountability in following the Four Absolutes. OGM also conducted large rallies and "Weeks of Witness" in church parishes. But the heart of OGM was Buchman's extraordinary gift for doing pastoral care in personal conversations—many of the key leaders of the movement traced the beginning of their "change" to such an encounter with Buchman.[6]

OGM drew its share of critics. The most common charges included: its intentionally suppressed doctrinal base; its fixation with wealthy and influential people (the "up and outers"); its over-estimation of divine guidance, especially in trivial matters; the exhibitionism of its "reports", including an over-emphasis on sexual expressions of sin; its purely individualistic understanding of sin, especially in its aspirations to usher in a "new world order"; and its ambiguous relationship to the Church. At the same time, many people praised OGM for its ability to reach those outside the walls of the Church, its commitment to evangelism, its vivid sense of the power of the living God, and the real impact it made on the lives of many people—it was, as it billed itself, "Christianity with results".

Of special concern to this book, Buchman paid several visits to Germany in the 1920s.[7] When Hitler rose to power in the 1930s, Buchman attempted to make contacts with the inner Nazi circle.[8] Denied several times in his request to meet Hitler, Buchman met with Heinrich Himmler in September 1934 at a Nazi Party rally in Nuremberg. He was also invited by Professor Karl Fezer of Tübingen and Bishop Heinrich Rendtorff of Mecklenburg to become involved in the German-Christian controversy.[9] This resulted in personal contacts with leading German-Christians, including Reich Bishop Müller; Buchman paid several visits to Müller, including a stay of almost two weeks at his home.

Due to the Nazi restrictions on assembly, OGM was unable to use its evangelistic tactics effectively in Germany. The work progressed mainly through inviting influential Germans to attend house-parties in Oxford. After a second unsuccessful meeting between Buchman and Himmler at the 1936 Olympic Games, OGM's work in Germany dissipated.

OGM also entered Switzerland in the 1930s.[10] The first house-parties were held in 1931 in Geneva and Zurich. Four years later, 250 OGMers arrived in Switzerland to launch a major campaign, an event which received much attention from the Swiss public.[11] The campaign was credited with initiating "a remarkable religious revival".[12]

As Europe moved towards war in the late 1930s, Buchman, capitalizing on the political focus on the question of re-armament, changed the name of his movement to "Moral Re-Armament". Although MRA continued the work of OGM after the war, it never again reached its pre-war impact.

Brunner and the Oxford Group Movement

Emil Brunner first encountered OGM during his 1928 lecture tour of the United States, where he met OGMers at Princeton.[13] Brunner's impression was that OGM was "a new and not especially sympathetic form of a pietistic revival movement of the typically Western type" (268). Two years later, during his lecture tour in Great Britain, he encountered OGM once again. Finally, impressed by a friend's enthusiastic report about the 1931 Geneva house-party, Brunner attended parts of the Zurich house-party that same year.[14] He was especially taken with the "reports":

> One after another reported what Christ, what the Word of the Cross, had done to them, to an attentive audience who no longer listened to Christian sermons... Without pious jargon and yet directly from the Biblical center, the message of sin and the Cross—all of this could not fail to elicit lively questions in me (who had often brooded about the ineffectiveness of the Church sermon). And, in addition, there were the results in my friends' lives. They began really to read the Bible, to pray, and where earlier the Word of Christ had put a dividing wall between us, it now meant now the deepest union. (269–270)

Though his mind was still not made up, Brunner "could not let go of the matter". During the 1932 summer holiday, he attended another house-party in Ermatingen. He was again deeply impressed by the genuineness and effectiveness of OGM in winning a hearing for the Gospel amongst the non-churched "cultural elite". In addition, Brunner was able to have a personal conversation with Buchman there. During the house-party, Brunner experienced a renewal of his own faith.[15]

Brunner quickly became actively involved in OGM, not only as a speaker at house-parties and rallies, but also as a trainer of leaders for OGM's "Bible Study Circles".[16] Since OGM never became as controversial in Switzerland as it was in Great Britain and the United States, and since its work was readily accepted by many Swiss churches, Brunner's involvement was not regarded as peculiar.[17] Brunner's leadership contributed to the development of a "Swiss variant" in OGM: the focus of the group-meetings was much more centered on Bible study than simply on "reports", and there was a greater connection with the Church.[18]

Although Brunner was aware of the problems in OGM,[19] he was deeply attracted to the movement for three major reasons. A personal reason was Brunner's life-long concern for mission and evangelism: "[OGM is the] Church in attack, the missionary and evangelistic Church".[20] Under the impact of OGM, Brunner would begin to refer to his own theology as "missionary theology":

Barth thinks as a churchman for the church; I think rather as a missionary. More and more I come to the view that the church nowadays speaks not chiefly to Christians...[but that] it must speak primarily to "heathen"...The word I shall leave with [the next theological generation] is, "Missionary Theology".[21]

A second, practical reason for Brunner's attraction to OGM was that he viewed the Movement as a breath of fresh air for a Church in need of spiritual renewal and practical re-vitalization.[22] Brunner embraced OGM as an effective means of making the Gospel alive for modern people, a needed example for an institutional European church plagued by dead creedalism.[23] Exactly paralleling his eristic program, Brunner saw OGM as the "other task of the *Church*".[24] Brunner was continually impressed by the effectiveness of OGM's "non-churchy" methods and non-religious paraphrasing of the New Testament message.[25] Brunner also appreciated that OGM, unlike the established Church, valued the ministry of the laity.[26] Finally, he saw the effectiveness of OGM's witness to be directly attributable to the "changed lives" of its members.[27]

The third reason that Brunner was attracted to OGM was theological. As we have seen, from 1927–1932 Brunner explicitly shaped his theology according to 1) the eristic goal and method of "building bridges" and 2) an increased focus on the importance of anthropology. This development was accompanied by Brunner's growing discomfort with Barth's strict dialectic and objectivism. When Brunner encountered OGM in 1932, he was struck with this *practical* example of what he had been moving towards *intellectually*—a movement which took sin and "distance" seriously, but also had a place for a Christian life which was visible and experiential. Thus, OGM hastened Brunner's break away from a Barthian understanding of the third article. Brunner made a definite turn away from Barth's actualist view of the Christian life (which is invisible, only believed) and began to emphasize the doctrine of sanctification and Paul's concept of the "fruit of the Spirit" alongside of justification.[28] Brunner's diagnosis of the contemporary Church was not that it failed to take sin seriously, but that it failed to take the power of God and the reality of the new life seriously.[29] A corresponding change is seen in Brunner's ecclesiology, as he moved from an emphasis on the invisible Church[30] to a position which emphasized the Church's visibility in concrete, personal, small group fellowship.[31] Brunner understood OGM to be practicing true Christian fellowship, the fellowship of the *ekklesia* (the New Testament word for "church"):

Anyone who has learnt the bond of fellowship as it comes into being in the Group —whether he has learnt it in the Group or outside of it—knows for the first time how much was lacking in his previous experience.[32]

Brunner's ecclesiological bias towards non-institutional, evangelism-oriented, lay-led, and fellowship-centered renewal movements remained with him throughout his life.[33]

Brunner understood the rise of dialectical theology and the emergence of OGM as two expressions of the same renewal movement. While dialectical theology focused upon intellectual matters and OGM on pastoral work, both "lead to the same goal, the building up of the true and living Church of Christ".[34] Brunner saw himself to be uniquely positioned to be the mediator between "these two great movements, through which God has already given so much blessing to the Church".[35]

Although Brunner distanced himself from OGM when it became MRA after World War II, he continued to take every opportunity to mention its positive contributions to the Church.[36] Both of his ecclesiological works specifically singled out MRA as an example of a "new structure" (*vs.* the dead structure of Church institutionalism) which preserved the spirit of the New Testament church.[37] In an extraordinary passage from 1955, Brunner credited OGM as being the practical expression towards which all of his major influences pointed:[38]

> The Oxford Group…made me aware, for the first time, of the close connection between spiritual reality and fellowship or communion…The I–thou philosophy gave the philosophical, intellectual explanation or interpretation of this extra-intellectual fact. Now, I could see that and why in the New Testament there is such a close connection, if not identity, between communion or fellowship in Christ and the gift of the Holy Spirit, in the ecclesia. Fellowship was no more a mere ethical attitude but a new reality—the reality of God's Holy Spirit among and in men…
>
> This was, at bottom, the same thing which Soren Kierkegaard meant by the word existential. *You cannot understand the Gospel unless you let yourself be personally engaged, which is the same as being challenged by the Thou which you encounter.* This has become since 1938, the lodestar of my theological thinking, first expressed in the little book [*Truth as Encounter*]…in 1938. It think it was this which, at bottom, Kutter and Ragaz had in mind when they spoke of religious socialism. It certainly is what the two Blumhardts had discovered and experienced as the reality of the Holy Spirit as the element of ecclesia.[39]

Barth vs. Brunner on the Oxford Group Movement

Being pre-occupied with the German Church struggle, Barth did not pay much attention to OGM during 1932–1936. However, from the moment Barth first became aware of OGM (through Thurneysen and Brunner), he took an instant dislike to it, as it went against his understanding of the entire third article of the Creed.

First, and least profoundly, OGM embodied three things to which Barth was never personally sympathetic: a) Barth was a consistent opponent of Pietism;[40] b) he was always suspicious of "movements";[41] and c) he had a European suspicion of "Anglo-Americanism".[42] A second objection Barth held against OGM was based on his conservative understanding of the work of the Church. For Barth, the church is most faithful when it does the most simple thing: Sunday worship centered around sermon and sacraments.[43]

But Barth's greatest objection to OGM was theological. Barth's actualist understanding of revelation, his fundamental insight of the divine-human distance, his material commitments to predestination and justification of the sinner by faith, and his increasingly christological concentration all led him to reject OGM *in toto*. For Barth, the Spirit is always gift and never possession, a gift that remains sovereign even in its self-giving. Barth's ecclesiology focuses on a Church of sinners in fundamental solidarity with those who do not yet believe, a Church which has no achievement in itself but is called to simply and faithfully witness to the Word of God, a witness whose effectiveness is entirely and sovereignly in the hands of the Holy Spirit. The Church and the Christian life are invisible and are seen only in faith, because all that is seen with human eyes remains on *this* side of the "distance" (and is thus sinful). All the actions of the Church and the Christian stand in utter need of divine justification.[44] As early as *Romans II*, one can hear statements which prefigure Barth's stand against OGM.[45] For Barth, the key verse on the Christian life was not OGM's "fruit of the Spirit" (Galatians 5.22–23), but Colossians 3.3—"For you have died, and your life is hidden in Christ with God".[46]

OGM was an important factor in the Barth–Brunner split-up in 1934. Barth saw Brunner's involvement with OGM as an atrocious step, or, more significantly for this book, as a consistent development of Brunner's program of eristics. It was OGM, rather than "No!", which sealed the breakdown of Barth and Brunner's relationship.

OGM first appears in the Barth–Brunner correspondence at the beginning of 1933. Responding to Brunner's comments about *Church Dogmatics* I/1, Barth declares that he no longer has "theological trust" in Brunner, and that their decade-long partnership "was a fictitious alliance".[47] When this letter was treated above in Chapter Four, attention was drawn to Barth's objections to *The Divine Imperative* and "The Question of the 'Point-of-Contact'". However, in this letter Barth clearly links together *three* of Brunner's writings, the third being "Meine Begegnung mit der Oxforder Gruppenbewegung" ("My Encounter with the Oxford Group Movement"): "This renunciation is my answer to the point-of-contact, to the Oxford Group, and obviously also to your grounding of ethics."[48] Barth continued to criticize OGM in a letter of July 17, 1933:[49]

It is a truly sad chapter between us. For I am of the opinion that you have served up an entirely bad devastation, on the one hand with your principal doctrine [natural theology] and, on the other hand, with your crossing over to the O–M.

Barth's opposition to OGM became hardened through a comic-tragic event in October 1933. Brunner felt so positive about his meeting with Barth in September[50] that he invited Barth to attend his OGM small group meeting in Zurich on September 14. But the evening was a "disaster"—apparently, Brunner's friends ganged up on Barth over his critical attitude toward Brunner.[51] Brunner writes Barth to apologize:

I must acknowledge entirely to you: it was a completely impossible and—for me no less truly than for you—painful proceeding...It must have seemed evil to you, as if in some way—without being conscious of it—I wanted to "trap" you...You could not say anything other than No to such a proceeding.[52]

But Brunner ends hopefully:

Perhaps there will come a time when you will once more have an ear for that which the Groups want—if you understand that we are not blessed through our theology, but only through being-in-Christ. The Groups have brought me closer to this than I have ever been.

But Barth had no "ear" for OGM. He responds that the evening had its own "great inner necessity", given how different their theological intentions had become:[53]

You see the possibilities indicated in the "Oxford" direction (apparently this was hidden from you for the past year, but I saw it) which I do not see. Precisely also you see the possibilities on the side of "natural theology" which I do not see. Perhaps it is a question on both sides of a "false tendency" which, in a later stage, you will get rid of. Perhaps not. Or perhaps an enlightenment will yet happen to me, where I will have to revise my position to follow after one or the other side, or perhaps after both. But I do not really believe this will happen. In any case, for the moment it is plain and clear that you intend something—you want what I do not want; you believe what I do not believe. And the other evening has indicated precisely this with great frankness and clarity. Why, then, should we subsequently mourn it?

Barth underlines his point by referring to a recent story in the newspaper of Hossenfelder and Fezer with Buchman in England:

What results for me cannot be disputed—in these German-Christians...Buchman had the appropriate "guidance" and recognized flesh of his own flesh, spirit of his own spirit...Naturally, this is only a symptom, but it is a real symptom of factually existing material connections. And it is indirectly a symptom for my entire unsuitability for the Oxford Movement: I certainly do not belong in a "group" on whose margins Fezer and Hossenfelder can also suddenly appear.[54]

Brunner responds quickly in Buchman's defense:

> While we throw anathemas...he sets off to Berlin, draws to himself the people who he has in his sights, and has them come to London, with the recipe: "Come and see". So, who is right: we, you and I, who on one side stand and curse, or he, who risks to proclaim Christ also to these people, so that they notice that they must cease being who they are, who they were? I...have seen how at a house-party hard-boiled German-Christians [have], with broken hearts and sincere faith, left that Movement. Around here we are accustomed to the fact, from previous experience, that such things happen frequently.[55]

Brunner argues that the simple witness to Christ, a witness done more consistently by OGM, is even more important than theology:

> I come again and again to the conviction that our theological work is indeed something very necessary and good (yours *and* mine!), but that the Church is not renewed through it. The renewal of the Church will just as little happen through theology as the growth of the Church did in the time of the Apostles or afterwards. Both proceed on the much simpler way of "establishing the obedience of faith"...in some way similar to the way it happens in the Groups.
>   Moreover, Frank Buchman is completely indifferent whether one is a German-Christian or whatever. He knows too well *how* relative these Church distinctions are, which we take as so important, because he only values this distinction: whether one really belongs to Christ. That can be the case completely with a German-Christian and completely not be the case with a dialectical theologian, even with a Barthian.[56]

As was seen in the last chapter, Barth linked his public No to Brunner's *Nature and Grace* with an equally firm but private No to another pamphlet by Brunner, written under the influence of OGM: *Vom Werk des Heiligen Geistes* (*On the Work of the Holy Spirit*).[57] In his letter of October 1, 1934 (immediately preceding the publication of "No!"), it is clear that the influence of OGM on Brunner's pneumatology was a significant factor in Barth's decisive rejection of Brunner.[58] After elaborating and defending his reasons for his upcoming public rejection of *Nature and Grace*, Barth warns that their fundamental disagreement on the first article of the Creed is accompanied by a similar opposition over the third article:

> I can swear to you that if you are not completely certain this time to publish your position [*On the Work of the Holy Spirit*], then don't do it. I have a feeling that new and more difficult harm will come to me then: if in your article my position

should be so thought of again, then my rebuttal will also have to make its appearance again. You have really smashed enough dishes already...If you know something new and genuine about the Holy Spirit, then say it to us in a big book, so that there is a better chance that it will be pondered over in a very coherent way, along with the *theologia naturalis*, in a clearer form. It is precisely this coherence which makes me be fundamentally suspicious in advance of what you apparently have in mind to say in your brochure. For your *theologia naturalis*, which I know, is a very wicked business.[59]

On the Work of the Holy Spirit was the focus of Barth and Brunner's discussion during their attempted reconciliation at the Bergli in 1935.[60] Brunner's pamphlet clearly reveals the impact of OGM has made on his pneumatology. In the opening section, Brunner traces the history of powerful out-breaks of the Spirit, which were repeatedly repressed under Church law and theological intellectualism (6–7). Brunner asserts that dialectical theology has similarly stumbled over pneumatology:

> The doctrine of the Holy Spirit has also been an embarrassment to it up to now, or it has attempted to go the way of orthodoxy once more by identifying the Word and Spirit. No wonder! For it is always proved in the doctrine of the Holy Spirit how much the reality of faith stands behind theological reflection. This doctrine will always bring to our awareness our own poverty of Spirit. It is the question whether we stand fast in this judgment, or whether, through an objectivistic falsification of the New Testament witness [read: Barth], we want to hide our nakedness. It is the excellence precisely of this theological theme that it establishes the point-of-contact [*Berührungspunkt*] of divine revelation and the personal experience of faith. (8)

In his pamphlet, Brunner teaches that the Holy Spirit is God becoming present and *experienced*.[61] The doctrine of the Holy Spirit means that God encounters us in such a way that we are "fundamentally changed through this determination, which indeed does not cancel the structure of human being, but orders it completely anew" (10–11). This new order is the (experienced) determination of the Christian life: faith, hope and love (11). The rest of the brochure develops the Christian life and the Holy Spirit in regard to these three determinations.[62] In addition, one sees in this pamphlet how Brunner continued to re-orient his polemics. Whereas before he took on philosophy and subjectivism/mysticism, here he defines himself more and more over-against "theological objectivism" (= Barth). This new polemic stresses the importance of the individual/existential/subjective/ human "I" in the act of faith (14–15, 30–31):

> The Holy Spirit does not confess Jesus as the Christ, as the Lord...The confession is *my* confession. And the Holy Spirit does not know the Lord; for the Holy Spirit has no Lord to recognize. But: that *I myself*, no one other than I, know and

and confess the Lord as my Lord—that happens because *God Himself* says to me that He is my Lord, *in* Christ *through* the Holy Spirit. My subjectness is not "replaced"—that would be mysticism—but Christ gives himself to *me* as the Lord, he makes himself Lord to me myself, he restores me myself, without any grounding other than the certainty that I can confess that he is my Lord.[63] (14–15)

The emphasis of *On the Work of the Holy Spirit* is on the real, visible, experienced *newness* of the life of the Christian and the Church through the renewing work of the Holy Spirit. By comparing Brunner's pamphlet with Barth's "The Holy Spirit and the Christian Life", one can clearly see their disagreements over the third article.

As a result of OGM's 1935 campaign in Switzerland, *The Nation*, a major Swiss news magazine, requested Brunner and Barth to contribute *pro* and *con* articles about OGM. Brunner agreed, but only under the stipulation that each could read the other's article before publication.[64]

Brunner's article does not add much to what he had already written about the Movement.[65] He argues that OGM can only be understood in the context of the spiritual crisis of the day (90% of Western Europeans do not attend church) (1). Brunner thus identifies the starting-point of OGM: "A message which is not verified by astonishing visible results as a divine Word has no chance of being heard today".[66] Brunner sees the positive message of OGM as being

> living biblical Christianity, i.e., there is, truly, the possibility to become different. God re-creates men through Jesus Christ—that is not theory, but a real happening, as in the New Testament. Destroyed human life becomes holy again, destroyed marriages, destroyed relationships between men become good again; men in all callings and standings become so different that one asks them: what has happened to you? (2)

While OGM believes that only God can change people, it recognizes that God uses human instruments (3). Therefore, OGM's goal is to create "life-changers" (through open confession and one-on-one discipleship), in order to change the world. In conclusion, Brunner maintains that OGM is neither works-Christianity nor does it seek to replace the Church (5). He ends:

> The Church suffers most in that it no longer has faith which moves mountains. Where faith becomes living again, there it also moves mountains. We do not only believe it, we also see it: not merely individuals, but also cities and coountries can be re-created through the Spirit of God, today as well as in the time of Zwingli and Calvin…To take this as real, to experience its reality, and to let others take part in this experience—that is the meaning of the Group–Movement.

As Brunner sends off a copy of his typescript to Barth, he begins by expressing his main concern about the whole affair: "Here is my article. I hope that it is such that your answer can be of the type that our *pro* and *contra* will be no scandal for the community".[67] He runs down a list of "amazing results" he could have included in his article, but states that he is addressing OGM theologically. One can clearly hear the "once burned, twice shy" Brunner hoping for the best in this second public exchange of views.

Barth replies within the week, enclosing both Brunner's article and a copy of his own, which is a direct rejoinder to Brunner:

> As you can see, I must speak out against you fundamentally as far as the contents are concerned...At the material point, where my opinion stands opposed to yours, I have let nothing be toned down...You have certainly written your article as a sincere Oxforder, and I have answered with a different sincerity, so that the goal may be reached—to give the readers a picture of both positions. I think it would be best if you let the articles in their entirety go off to *The Nation*. Neither you nor I will change our essential thinking.[68]

Barth's article begins with a bold declaration: "I see between [OGM] and the Church a definite choice, and I must declare myself decisively for the Church, and in no sense for the Groups" (1).[69] Barth levels six charges at OGM. The first is that it presumptuously oversteps its limits. The presumptuous claims of OGM include offering "'a solution of all political and economic questions'" and announcing "that 'great, yes, even colossal life-changing activities' undertaken by certain 'life-changers' are possible, and are already happening" (2).[70] On the contrary, Barth argues:

> We are responsible before God and before men, but we are not responsible *for* God or *for* men. God alone is self-sufficient, and alone suffices for all men. This indicates a limitation of our responsibilities which we must not overstep. He does not honour God who imagines he can deal with God's affairs as with his own. The Group Movement oversteps this limitation deliberately and fundamentally.

Barth's second point is a specific illustration of the first charge: the Church's sole concern for worship is "that it may be performed in due order to the honour of God and the freedom and purity of the faith" (2–3). Thus, the Church "cannot demand of this service that it should be successful, and certainly not that its success should be in 'astonishing and visible results'" (3). If we trust the word of God, we can leave the "success" of our service to God, Barth asserts. If we do not trust God, then, like OGM, we become concerned about the lack of attendance at worship and the ineffectiveness of preaching in reaching people. OGM takes

the attitude of spectators who ask things from the Church which no one is permitted to ask. Therefore the way of the Church and of the Groups cannot be reconciled. (4)

Barth's third critical observation about the Groups is that they use secular criteria for measuring Christian service, relying particularly on large numbers and the social prestige of those changed at house-parties. Conversely, the Church carries out its mission through faithful preaching, teaching and pastoral care, not through "this or that discipline, tactics and method" (4):

[OGM's] creation of this magic land of secular values and standards has nothing to do with prayer, with hope and with the message of the Christian Church, [so] that the Church can only be compromised by the Groups. (5)

Barth's fourth charge against the Group Movement is that its practice of "reports" draws attention to OGMers rather than to Christ. Barth does not deny that these people have experienced a significant changing experience. But by making this the focal point of its message, OGM, in essence, puts forth human mediators (5–6). Barth rejects this method, for

Jesus Christ is the end and the way to the end. The way of the Group is not Jesus Christ, but the ostensibly changed individual. Thus, the Group Movement's method is not a supplement to the Church's message, but a "contradiction". (6)

Barth's fifth point against OGM is that God works out His will in His own, often surprising ways. Therefore, Christians are not "guided" to draw up a "plan or programme" that would predict or detail God's will here and now. God's guidance cannot be confined to neither "life-changing" nor to "a beautiful humanistic and moralistic programme" (7–8).

Barth's final critique is that OGM is a threat to the Church because it is an attempt to secularize the Church. The Church must "guard her secret", that is, recognize that it is God who is at work in her and is responsible for her work: "Therefore she serves without asking for results". OGM's obsession for results is a distorting secularization of the Gospel. Barth finally reaches the "decisive word that must be said against the Oxford Group Movement":

There would be nothing to say against it if it presented itself simply and solely as one of the attempts...to lift the burden of man's guilt and destiny a little by means of moral exhortation and psychological treatment...But what makes it open to criticism is that it wishes to reform Christianity, and this reformation consists in the unveiling of the mystery of the Christian faith, and discrediting the freedom of grace, and the sanctity of the name of God, and in misinterpreting this in every possible way by means of humanistic and moralistic explanations. (9)

Barth concludes:

> A movement like the Group Movement, which is the latest attempt to secularize
> the Church, and which would make it lose its mystery and its spirituality, is not
> able to reform the Church. The Church's answer to the challenge of the Groups
> can only be this: that more than ever she must *be the Church*, and must strive to
> become the Church which God would have her to be.[71] (10)

Brunner writes Barth on Christmas Eve, bitter and hurt, saying there is
nothing he can do but notify *The Nation* of "my renunciation of this project".[72]

> I am concerned not to provoke you once more to an anathema which would be al-
> most more painful than your first one...The first time your curse went against me
> —that I could endure; but this time it goes against the work of Jesus Christ and
> the Holy Spirit, and I do not want to be guilty of that...I would like to avoid dem-
> onstrating once again before the readers of *The Nation*, probably most of whom
> stand far from the Church, the deep disunity of the Church. I am ready to fight the
> matter out with you in front of theologians whenever and wherever you want. But
> *I* cannot be responsible *vis-à-vis* doubting laity.

Brunner makes one last attempt to persuade Barth to refrain from attacking
what Brunner sees as a gracious gift of renewal. After citing the countless
examples of individuals he has seen renewed in their Christian faith through
OGM, Brunner asks:

> Are you really serious that this cannot be the work of the Holy Spirit because it
> happens differently from how it happens in the "Church"? That it is not the work
> of Jesus Christ, although these men learned to believe in him and his redemption,
> as it is not very much believed by our ordinary Church-people; although they call
> upon him daily as their Lord and pray to him to forgive them their sins and to
> purify them from their sins? Is that not Church, simply because it is not
> "Church"? Does this "Church"—organized, paid for and supervised by the state
> ...—have such an unequivocal superiority to be named the Church? Are the thou-
> sand secular means which this Church uses and must use so unequivocally more
> appropriately the proclamation of Christ than the secular means of the Groups?...
> Has the Lord of the Church really given you the commission to maintain that the
> work of the Groups—which in any case *want* nothing other than to make men
> obedient to Christ and to trust in his work for redemption—cannot be the work of
> Christ? Can you be responsible for that?

Barth responds briefly and formally, stating that though he will not publish his article in *The Nation*, he reserves the right to publish it in the future.[73]

The denouement of the OGM debate between Barth and Brunner occurred in June, 1936.[74] Because of OGM's marked impact in Switzerland and the diverse reactions to it, Gottlob Spörri of Zurich University[75] organized a group of pastors who invited Barth, Brunner and Thurneysen to come and present their contrasting positions on OGM at a "colloquium" at Schlößchen Auenstein.[76]

At the colloquium, Brunner read his unpublished article prepared for *The Nation*, and Barth responded with the six theses from his (as yet unpublished) "Church or Group Movement?". Apparently the ensuing discussion did not go well, with Barth being unusually adamant and humorless. The issue boiled down to whether the Church could trust the Holy Spirit to address the Word of God effectively to humanity (Barth), or whether the preacher had to address the Word in an unique way to those listening (Brunner). Again, Brunner felt that he was constantly being misinterpreted, overpowered, and ignored by Barth.[77] During the discussion, Thurneysen kept trying to mediate between Barth and Brunner. At the end, Barth requested a vote—he wanted all the participants to state briefly where they stood on the issue of OGM. Most of the participants believed that, despite some theological objections, OGM was beneficial for the Church; even Thurneysen said he could not reject OGM as a bad thing for the Church. After listening in silence, Barth consented not to write against Brunner or OGM, "but with a threateningly raised finger, he addressed all of us, saying that we now bore the responsibility if spiritual harm happened in the Swiss church".[78]

The harshness of Barth's polemic against Brunner at Schlößchen Auenstein terminated their personal relationship. After 1936, their correspondence dwindled down to simply periodic greetings and brief business messages. Though "No!" sounded the death-knell of their theological alliance, it was Barth's adamant No to OGM which indicated that there was no way forward for their personal relationship.

Summary

The impact of OGM on Brunner and its significant role in the break-up of Barth and Brunner's theological alliance has been consistently overlooked by scholarship.[79] This is due, in part, to the unavailability of the Barth– Brunner correspondence, which clearly shows how Barth viewed Brunner's involvement with OGM as forming a piece with his "orders"-ethics, his eristics, and his natural theology. This omission is also due in part to the embarrassment of Brunner's colleagues and students, who minimized his OGM involvement as a passing phase.[80] This book contributes to the understanding of the deterioration of the Barth–Brunner relationship by bringing to the foreground this overlooked but key factor.

The OGM debate further illuminates the significant differences between Barth and Brunner. Primarily, it extends their explicit disagreement from prolegomena and the first article into the entire range of the third article. Whereas Barth's pneumatology was thoroughly actualist and invisible, Brunner insisted on the visible "fruits" of the Spirit's action in the Christian life.[81] Their differences over the work of the Spirit is clearly summed up by their key Bible verses: "Your life is hidden with Christ in God" (Colossians 3.3) for Barth *vs.* "The only thing that counts is faith working through love" (Galatians 5.6) for Brunner.[82]

Barth lumped Brunner's involvement with OGM together with his position on natural theology because OGM, too, failed to respect the "distance" between God and humanity.[83] Brunner's intellectual flirtation with some kind of general revelation since 1924–1925 and his attempt to build eristic bridges to philosophy was now worked out practically, as OGM made consistent one-to-one correspondences between God and humanity in its views of divine guidance and "changed lives". But OGM's building of bridges to secular society had the same danger as eristics: all bridges are two-way, and thus, Barth asserted, OGM secularized the Church. This can be seen in Barth and Brunner's debate over the visibility or invisibility of the Church. Brunner's effort to see the real Church in the visible fellowship of love was understood by Barth to be a complete abandonment of any kind of *diastasis*, as if a Church of sinful people solely and continually justified by the merciful grace of God could correspond in any way to God's loving action other than through the miraculous intervention of the Holy Spirit.

Part of Brunner's attraction to OGM rested on the one point it held in common with his Kantianism, eristics, ethics, natural theology and anthropology—namely, its focus on sin, guilt and responsibility as the necessary presupposition for faith. OGM's "reports" focused centrally on this consciousness, and gave it the important place Brunner felt it required and deserved. Brunner rejected the charge that OGM preached moralism; rather, it presented a form of the Law and Gospel.[84]

A final insight which the OGM debate provides into the Barth–Brunner relationship is that it helped Brunner to re-focus his theological thinking after the dead-end of the natural theology debate. Brunner never really be-lieved he lost the debate with Barth, and one can see his same arguments be-ing repeated and developed further, especially in *Man in Revolt* (1937), *Revelation and Reason* (1941) and *The Christian Doctrine of God* (1946). However, Brunner shifted his theological focus away from the relationship between theology and philosophy and his eristic attack, and moved it more toward an explication of an "existential" (i.e., experiential) Christian faith. *Truth as Encounter* (1938) was the pivotal book in this change, a work which Brunner himself saw as a key to his theological development.[85] From

1938 on, overcoming the "subject-object opposition in Western thought" became the focus of Brunner's theological program. Correspondingly, his critique of Barth became stereotyped in the charge of "objectivism". Barth was wrong in seeing 1929 as a turn in Brunner's thinking. However, as a result of the debate ensuing from "The Other Task of Theology", and particularly how this debate took shape over the third article and OGM, Brunner's thinking did make a turn in 1934–1936, expressing itself definitively in 1938.

NOTES

1. The major sources for this account of the Oxford Group Movement are: Henry P. Van Dusen, "Apostle to the Twentieth Century", *Atlantic Monthly* (July, 1934), 1–6, and "The Oxford Group Movement", ibid. (August, 1934), 240–252; and Garth Lean, *Frank Buchman* (London: Constable, 1985). See also: Martin Smith and Francis Underhill, *The Group Movement* (London: SPCK, 1934); Walter H. Clark, *The Oxford Group* (New York: Bookman Associates, 1951), pp. 37–56; G.F. Allen, "The Groups in Oxford", in *The Groups in Oxford*, ed. by R.H.S. Crossman (Oxford: Basil Blackwell, 1934), pp. 1–41; Geoffrey Williamson, *Inside Buchmanism* (London: Watts & Co., 1954) and Tom Driberg, *The Mystery of Moral Re-Armament* (London: Secker & Warburg, 1964).
2. For example: J. Ross Stevenson (president of Princeton Theological Seminary), Eric Liddell (Scottish sprinter and missionary), Swiss psychologist Paul Tournier, Carl J. Hambro (president of the Norwegian Parliament), and actress Mae West (Lean, pp. 132, 144, 187, 269–270; G. Williamson, p. 6).
3. Hereafter, the Oxford Group Movement will be referred to as "OGM". However, references to its work after World War II will be to "MRA", as the movement changed its name in 1938 to "Moral Re-Armament".
4. Frank N.D. Buchman, *Remaking the World* (London: Blanford, 1947), p. 46. See also p. 4.
5. For examples of such "reports", see Jack Russell, *For Sinners Only* (London: Hodder and Stoughton, 1932).
6. Buchman himself was a decidedly non-charismatic figure and a modest public speaker.
7. For the work of OGM in Germany, see Lean, pp. 203–214, 233–242, and Driberg, pp. 64–81.
8. "Buchman had put it to his young colleagues that unless they could bring change to such committed people [Nazis], their work was inadequate" (Lean, p. 207). See Bonhoeffer's reaction against OGM, in Eberhard Bethge, *Dietrich Bonhoeffer*, trans. by Eric Mosbacher and others (New York: Harper, 1970), pp. 282–284.

9. For background on Fezer and Rendtorff, see Busch, pp. 242–243; Cochrane, pp. 96, 111–115.
10. This account of OGM in Switzerland comes from Lean, pp. 244–245; H.H. Brunner, pp. 69–78; and Bohren, pp. 158–168.
11. See Barth, "Church or Group Movement?", *The London Quarterly and Holborn Review*, 162 (1937), 1–10 (p. 1).
12. Brunner, "Intellectual Autobiography", p. 10.
13. This account of Brunner's involvement with OGM comes from his article, "Meine Begegnung mit der Oxforder Gruppenbewegung", *KfrS*, 88 (1932) (cited here from *Ein offenes Wort*, I, pp. 268–288).
14. Among the early Swiss OGMers was Brunner's younger sister, Lydi de Trey-Brunner, who later became a full-time MRA worker at its "world training center" in Caux, Switzerland, and who generously supported the movement financially throughout her life. Her daughter and son-in-law also worked for MRA (Brunner-Gutekunst interview).
15. "[A few years later], Brunner described seeing a sandwich-board man advertising a restaurant but looking as if he had not eaten a good meal himself for weeks, and added, 'I have been that sandwich-board man. I was advertising a good meal, but I hadn't eaten the meal myself until I met the Oxford Group'" (Lean, p. 212 (note)).
16. Brunner, pp. 72, 75. In the 1930s, Brunner would write a half-dozen articles specifically on OGM, as well as others on the related topics of fellowship, faith, and church renewal: "Meine Begegnung" (1932); *Um die Erneuerung der Kirche* (Bern: Gotthelf, 1934), containing "Die Kirche als Frage und Aufgabe der Gegenwart" (pp. 5–31) and "Die Gruppenbewegung als Frage an die Kirche" (pp. 32–51); "Gemeinschaft", *Zwinglikalender* (1934) (cited here from *Ein offenes Wort*, I, pp. 326–332); "Was ist and was will die sogenannte Oxford–Gruppe?" *Zwinglikalender* (1935), 48–50; *The Church and the Oxford Group*, trans. by David Cairns (London: Hodder & Stoughton, 1937); "Antwort an Herrn Heinrich Marti", *Neue Wege*, 30 (1936), 70–72; "The Predicament of the Church To-day", in *The Predicament of the Church*, (London: Lutterworth, 1944), pp. 82–99. Brunner's most widely-translated book, *Our Faith* (trans. by John W. Rilling (New York: Scribners, 1954), a theological primer for lay people, was written during this time to support the training and work of the OGM ("Intellectual Autobiography", p. 10).
17. Brunner-Gutekunst interview. However, see David E. Roberts, "Review of four works of Emil Brunner", *Review of Religion*, 2 (1937–1938), 298–314 (p. 309).
18. H.H. Brunner, pp. 74–75.
19. See "Meine Begegnung", pp. 280–286. Brunner singled out guidance, the danger of public testimonies, and OGM's shallow theology. H.H. Brunner (pp. 73–74) adds that he had trouble with the "four absolutes".
20. *The Church and the Oxford Group*, p. 10. "For all missionary and pastoral work the *discovery of the right point of contact* is absolutely decisive. Every missionary and every pastor knows that…The missionary must first of all get himself a hearing"

(ibid., p. 28). See also pp. 28–34. Also, see "Gruppenbewegung als Frage" p. 33; "Meine Begegnung", p. 284; Cairns, "Theology of Brunner", p. 306.

21. "Missionary Theology", p. 817. See also "Intellectual Autobiography", p. 17.

22. "What is the Oxford–Movement? A push, which can and will wake up the sleeping Church in all lands" ("Meine Begegnung", p. 288).

23. *The Church and the Oxford Group*, pp. 25–27, 94–96, 106–108. See also "Gruppenbewegung als Frage", pp. 44–45, 48; "Was ist Oxford–Gruppe?", p. 48; "Antwort an Marti", p. 70.

24. "Kirche als Frage und Aufgabe", pp. 27–31. See also "Gruppenbewegung als Frage", pp. 50–51.

25. See "Antwort an Marti", p. 70; "Gruppenbewegung als Frage", pp. 34–35, 37–38; "Meine Begegnung", p. 285; "Was ist Oxford–Gruppe?", p. 48.

26. See *The Church and the Oxford Group*, pp. 20–24, 38, 62–73; "Meine Begegnung", p. 279.

27. See "Meine Begegnung", pp. 276–277; "Gruppenbewegung als Frage", p. 37; "Antwort an Marti", p. 71; *The Church and the Oxford Group*, pp. 43–44.

28. *The Church and the Oxford Group*, pp. 53–54. See also "Gemeinschaft", p. 331; *The Divine Imperative*, p. 160; Roessler, p. 23.

29. In a clear swipe at Barth, Brunner writes: "In reading certain theological writings of the present one often gets the impression that the most important concern of the Church is to emphasize the invincibility of sin, the opposition to the 'heresy' that in the life of the Christian some real renewal takes place, or that this new element is in any way recognizable" (*The Church and the Oxford Group*, pp. 53–54).

30. Brunner's only significant treatment of ecclesiology before his encounter with OGM is found in *The Divine Imperative*, pp. 523–567. His stress is more on the invisible than the visible Church. See pp. 523, 525–527, 535. However, see pp. 536, 542–543.

31. "Kirche als Frage und Aufgabe", pp. 15–19. See also Wilhelm Stolz, p. 37.

32. *The Church and the Oxford Group*, p. 51, see also pp. 11–12; "Was ist Oxford–Gruppe?" pp. 49–50; "Gruppenbewegung als Frage", p. 46; "Kirche als Frage und Aufgabe", p. 9; "Gemeinschaft", p. 332.

33. See I. John Hesselink, "Emil Brunner: A Centennial Perspective", *Christian Century*, 106 (1989), 1171–1174 (p. 1173)). See also "A Unique Christian Mission", in *Religion and Culture*, ed. by W. Leibrecht (New York: Harper, 1959), pp. 287–290.

34. See *The Church and the Oxford Group*, p. 14; "Was ist Oxford–Gruppe?", p. 50; "Meine Begegnung", p. 284.

35. *The Church and the Oxford Group*, p. 18. See also "Kirche als Frage und Aufgabe", pp. 27–31; "Gruppenbewegung als Frage", pp. 50–51.

36. E.g., see *Justice and Freedom in Society* (Tokyo: Institute of Educational Research and Service, 1955), pp. 358–366.

37. *The Misunderstanding of the Church*, trans. by Harold Knight (London: The Lutterworth Press, 1952), pp. 110–111; *The Christian Doctrine of the Church, Faith, and*

the Consummation, trans. by David Cairns (Philadelphia: Westminster, 1962), pp. 106–116. However, Brunner already had an "anti-institutionalistic" streak to his ecclesiology before his contact with OGM: see *The Divine Imperative*, pp. 523–533, and H.H. Brunner's comments, pp. 247–248.

38. Except Kant.

39. "Spiritual Autobiography", p. 243. See also p. 240: "It was not [Kutter and Blumhardt's] thought, it was the power of the Holy Spirit manifested in their lives and words which attracted so many and which through Kutter impressed us as the reality of God in our midst. *The origin of the so-called dialectical theology is not theological or philosophical thought, but the wondrous reality of the Holy Spirit.*"

40. See *Rev.Theology*, KB: October 5, 1915, p. 33–34; KB: November 20, 1916, pp. 39–41.

41. Busch, p. 124. Barth was suspicious of the Oxford Group Movement, the German-Christian Faith Movement, and the ecumenical movement (see *The Church and the Churches* (Grand Rapids: Eerdmans, 1936), pp. 64–65; "How I Changed My Mind, 1938–1948", pp. 57–58). For Brunner's response to Barth's "anti-movement" bias, see "Gruppenbewegung als Frage", pp. 33–34.

42. See "Questions which 'Christianity' Must Face", p. 94. Barth defines "Americanism" as being "characterized by a naïve egoism combined with brilliant technique and with a primitive but unshakably optimistic morality". See also "Theologie und Mission in Gegenwart", pp. 209–210.

43. "[The Church's] commission consists in witnessing by means of the *preaching of the Gospel* and the *administration of the sacraments*. No third action has a place beside these two, which are in essence one, the *ministerium verbi divini*...Over against this one commission neither pastoral work, nor social service, nor co-operation in the tasks of culture or of politics can claim an independent position and dignity...It is not out of resignation that reserve is enjoined at this point...It is out of *confidence* in the *worth* and relevancy of this command, it is out of the firm *assurance* that by pure proclamation and by the proper administration of the sacraments more is achieved and better results are obtained in the solution of just these pressing problems of life than by the best-intentioned measures for aid, action and enlightenment, that involve our stepping outside of the bounds of this small but mighty domain" (*Credo*, pp. 143–44).

44. For Barth's principle works on ecclesiology and the Christian life, see: *The Christian Life*, trans. by J. Strathearn McNab (London: SCM 1930); "Rechtfertigung und Heiligung", *ZZ*, 5 (1927), 281–309; "Roman Catholicism: a Question to the Protestant Church", in *Th&Ch*, 307–333; "The Holy Ghost and the Christian Life"; "Not der Evangelischen Kirche"; *The Knowledge of God and the Service of God: According to the Teaching of the Reformation*, trans. by J.L.M. Hare and Ian Henderson (London: Hodder and Stoughton, 1938), pp. 113–216; *CD* IV/1/§§62–63, IV/2/§§67–68, IV/3/§§72–73, IV/4/§§74–78.

45. "What behaviour could be more foolish than the behaviour of those newly-converted

men who, after their conversion, leap to embark with confidence upon an adequate moral life? This is, however, to lay grace wholly under suspicion by making it, and human ethical conduct, two separate functions, as though it were possible first to pass under grace and then to proceed to build up a positive ethic" (*Romans* II, p. 430).

46. See *Credo*, pp. 201–202. See also "Roman Catholicism: a Question to the Protestant Church", where one can substitute OGM for Roman Catholicism in almost all Barth's arguments: they both neglect God's lordship and confuse nature and grace, they do not take sin seriously, and they let humanity cooperate in salvation. See also "Theologie und Mission in Gegenwart", where Barth argues against the "baroque spirit" of mission appeals which point to the power of Gospel based on conversions, because these events cannot be directly observed (pp. 206–207).

47. *Barth–Brunner*, KB: January 10, 1933 (#83), pp. 213–217 (see above, pp. 128f.).

48. In Brunner's reply to this decisive letter (*Barth–Brunner*, EB: January 16, 1933 (#84), pp. 220f., see above, pp. 129f.), he first expresses surprise that OGM should be a source of division between them: "My systematic theology has nothing to do with the O–M, but only my pastoral theology and pastoral care...I find its published literature to be as suspect theologically as you do. It is not their message... but it is their pastoral care and their insight into the meaning of the life of fellowship (as Luther says: the *mutua conversatio et consolatio fratrum*, or what he strives for in the German Mass) that interests me in this movement and concerning which, in any case, I have experienced unimpeachable results here in Zurich". He adds significantly, "Eduard [Thurneysen] has completely accepted this Movement with me, and has represented it with me in the fullest fellowship before the Basel pastorate and theological community". Although Brunner overstates Thurneysen's agreement with him about OGM, this is the one instance in the Barth–Brunner relationship where Thurneysen was truly in the middle (see Bohren, pp. 156–162). See Thurneysen's article, "Guidance", *Student World*, 26 (1933), 294–309, especially note 1, p. 302).

49. See above, p. 146.

50. See above, pp. 146f.

51. Bohren, p. 162.

52. *Barth–Brunner*, EB: October, 1933 (#91), pp. 234–237.

53. Ibid., KB: October 22, 1933 (#93), pp. 237–240.

54. Fezer and Hossenfelder attended a commissioning of OGMers by the Bishop of London for a London campaign (see Lean, pp. 210–211).

55. *Barth–Brunner*, EB: October 27, 1933 (#94), pp. 241–243.

56. Actually, Brunner agreed that Buchman's being photographed with Fezer and Hossenfelder was "an awful blunder". Brunner wrote Buchman in December 1933, urging him to stop attempting to "mediate in the German Church struggle", particularly denouncing his association with Hossenfelder (Lean, p. 212). Buchman wrote back to Brunner: "It sounds to me like associating with 'publicans and sinners'...The

Groups in that sense have no reputation, and for myself, I have nothing to lose...I would be proud to have Hossenfelder be in touch with such real Christianity that some day he would say, 'Well, as a young man of thirty-two I made many mistakes, but I have seen a pattern of real Christianity'. It is not a question of this man's past, but of his future" (ibid., pp. 212–213).

57. See above, p. 166.

58. See *Barth–Brunner*, KB: October 1, 1934 (#100), p. 256: "I did not tell you of my presence at the Bergli this past summer, because news constantly reached me there of your co-operation with the Group Movement (which I have always viewed so thoroughly unsympathetically), as well as your article on the Church [*Um die Erneuerung der Kirche*], from which I saw once more that you apparently find yourself in a rapid movement whose Spirit and direction have always been strange to me".

59. In his response to Barth's letter, Brunner writes: "That you find it necessary to treat the 'Oxford Group Movement' disdainfully, which perhaps builds up the Church better than anything else today—when I think about everything that I have *seen* here as the operation of the Spirit of God—it makes me shudder, yes, really shudder" (*Barth–Brunner*, EB: October 2, 1934 (#101), p. 263).

60. See above, pp. 169.

61. "It thus happens that...a Word of God proclaimed to all the world becomes a Word which encounters *me*, and that, in that it *encounters* me, converts me and *recreates* me. How the Word of God moves from a Word to me to a Word *in* me: that is the theme of the doctrine of the Holy Spirit" (8–9).

62. Many of Brunner's characteristic arguments also appear, e.g., guilt as the necessary presupposition of faith (19), salvation as *restitutio* (21), and forays into eristics (25–26).

63. Brunner also makes this point by: stressing equally the *fides qua creditor* alongside the *fides quae creditur*; defining faith as trust *vs.* "mere head-faith"; and keeping the divine-act/human-response paradox intact (30, 42–47).

64. *Barth–Brunner*, KB: December 23, 1935 (#114), p. 293.

65. "Was ist and was will die sogenannte Oxford–Gruppenbewegung?", unpublished article, Emil Brunner-Stiftung, Zurich.

66. "The miracle of changed lives is the 'sign' which the Lord of the Church gives his ambassadors as he orders them to march out in the world to proclaim. Just as a bank-cashier tests the gold coin, the world tests by such signs the genuineness of Christian proclamation....For just as [modern people] hunger after the reality of God, they are bored with the mere words about God" (pp. 1–2).

67. *Barth–Brunner*, EB: December 16, 1935 (#112), pp. 288–291.

68. Ibid., KB: December 22, 1935 (#113), pp. 291–293.

69. "Church or Group Movement?" (see note 11).

70. Interior quotation marks refer to Brunner's unpublished article.

71. For Barth's other references to MRA, see *CD*: III/4/§53.2:78 and §55.3:506–507;

IV/2/§66.4: 582–583.

72. *Barth–Brunner*, EB: December 24, 1935 (#115), pp. 294–297.

73. Ibid., KB: January 4, 1936 (#116), p. 298. Barth published his article the following June in *Evangelische Theologie* at the request of the editor (p. 1, note 11). For a rebuttal to Barth's article by an English OGMer, see: B.H. Streeter, "Professor Barth and the Oxford Group", *The London Quarterly and Holborn Review*, Sixth Series, 6 (April, 1937), 145–149.

74. This entire account is taken from Bohren, pp. 163–168.

75. Professor of Romance Languages at the University of Zurich, one of Brunner's closest friends, and active in OGM.

76. Thurneysen experienced such anxiety about another Barth–Brunner confrontation that, on his first night at the retreat, he dreamt that Barth, Brunner and himself were walking on the *Hochbrücke* in St.Gallen-Bruggen, when Barth suddenly seized Brunner and started to throw him over the side. Thurneysen woke up screaming "In the name of God, what are you doing?" However, Thurneysen's screams did not awaken Barth, who was sleeping in the next bed—and also dreaming. Barth dreamt that he was skipping stones on the shore of a lake when Brunner approached and tried to rip the last stone out of Barth's hand. Barth fought him off and was able to throw the last stone (Wolfgang Schildmann, *Was sind das für Zeichen? Karl Barths Träume im Kontext von Leben und Lehre* (Munich: Chr. Kaiser, 1991). Schildmann analyses the Barth–Brunner relationship as a sibling rivalry: Barth, being an oldest son, was threatened and needed to re-establish his dominance; Brunner, the only son with four sisters, needed to re-assert his masculinity, and thus challenged male authority. For Schildmann, Barth's dream refers to the hurling of his "No's" against Brunner—he had already thrown one stone ("No!"), and was free (despite Brunner's efforts) to throw another one (against OGM).

77. Thurneysen rebuked Barth afterwards: "You did not have to treat Brunner like that. You eviscerated him like a butcher with a slaughtered animal" (quoted in Bohren, p. 165). Although he agreed with Barth's position, Thurneysen felt Barth was being too adamant on an issue which was not comparable to the German Church struggle (ibid., p. 166).

78. Quoted in Bohren, p. 165.

79. See, for example, Gestrich, *Neuzeitliches Denken*, pp. 345–346.

80. E.g., Theodore A. Gill, "Emil Brunner as Teacher and Preacher", in Kegley, pp. 305–321 (pp. 317–319). Those who did not shy away from Brunner's embrace of OGM were those who were sympathetic themselves, e.g. David Cairns.

81. See G.J. Sirks, "The Cinderella of Theology", *Harvard Theological Review*, 50 (1957), 77–89 (pp. 78, 79)); Smail, p. 94.

82. Brunner would continue to criticize Barth's view of sanctification (e.g., see *The Christian Doctrine of the Church*, note 1, p. 340. For Barth on the Christian life, see Eberhard Busch, "Karl Barth's understanding of the church a witness", *Saint Luke's Journal of Theology*, 33 (1989–1990), 87–101 (pp. 97–98)).

83. See Rosato, pp. 43, 48, 70, 148–149.
84. "*Illustrated exposition of God's challenge* and sinful failure to meet it—that is the first stage of the Group way" (*The Church and the Oxford Group*, p. 41).
85. "Intellectual Autobiography", p. 12. See also Cairns, "Theology of Brunner", p. 303; Roessler, p. 29; Volk, "Christologie", note 2, p. 654; W. Stolz, p. 4; Reidar Hague, "Truth as Encounter", trans. by I. John Hesselink, in Kegley, pp. 133–154.

CHAPTER SEVEN

Reflections

Naturally I have been considering, too, the question how it really was, and how it came to be, between him and me...From my standpoint the fact was that God not only led him and me on very different paths, but in his unfathomable goodness and wisdom willed us already to be very different people—so different that properly there could be no question at all of strife or suffering between us. And yet we did strive and suffer on both sides. And if I am right he suffered more at my hands than I did at his.

(Barth to Brunner's widow, April 1966)

Further Interaction

The Auenstein meeting in 1936 effectively marked the end of Barth and Brunner's theological relationship.[1] This is evidenced most clearly in their correspondence—it becomes less frequent and briefer, focusing on topics distant from their past disagreements. However, Barth and Brunner continued to debate each other as a side-line in their respective theological developments.

The Remains of the "Natural Theology Debate"
Although the 1934 articles comprised the heart of Barth and Brunner's debate over "natural theology", the debate continued on—indirectly and less vehemently—for the next fourteen years. In a series of appendices in *Man in Revolt*, Brunner repeated and clarified the argument he had been making since "The Other Task of Theology" (499–541).[2] For his part, Barth developed his position in "No!" more positively in his 1937–1938 Gifford Lectures.[3] Barth argues that, from the Reformed perspective, there really is no such thing as a natural knowledge of God (5). Reformed doctrine begins with the fact that the knowledge of God is the gift of God in His revelation in Jesus Christ, received only through the act of the Holy Spirit through faith (13–24). Thus, to know God is to obey God by believing in Jesus

Christ (102–109).

Barth offered his definitive thoughts on natural theology in *Church Dog-matics* II/1, Chapter V ("The Knowledge of God"): the knowledge of God is actual in the Church, bound to the Word of God (§25.1); God is known in faith as he makes himself faith's object, based on who he is as subject (§25.2:31–38); God remains a mystery even in his revelation (38–43); the triune God is known through God alone (43–62). Barth argues that the knowability of God rests solely on God's readiness to be known, which is his grace encroaching upon humanity in revelation (§26.1: 63–85). After devoting fifty pages to exploring why natural theology has been so persis-tent in the church (including a direct but anonymous rebuttal of Brunner, pp. 88–97), Barth maintains that the vitality of natural theology in the Church rests on humanity's resistance to grace in Jesus Christ (§26.2). He concludes by arguing that God's hiddenness means both humanity's real ig-norance (in its own capacity) and real knowledge (through the miracle of revelation and faith)(§27.1), and that God creates an "analogy of faith"—a partial but true correspondence between our words and his revelation—which grounds our knowledge of God in Jesus Christ (§27.2).[4] In *Revela-tion and Reason* (77–80), Brunner responded to Barth's argument, main-taining that Barth at first accepts his position of an objective natural theolo-gy, only subsequently to confuse the *principium cognoscendi* and the *prin-cipium essendi*. In addition, in the first ten chapters of the prolegomena to his dogmatics, Brunner constantly warns against an objectivistic theology which damages the personal character of faith (read: "Barth").[5] Brunner still defends "theology as eristics" and argues for the "journalistic" meaning of theology.[6]

Brunner took up the natural theology debate one last time in a review of *Church Dogmatics* III/2.[7] Brunner thinks he sees a "new Barth", pointing out seven points of anthropological agreement between them (125).[8] Brun-ner claims that, in light of all of the changes Barth has made since 1934, an-thropology is no longer a dividing point between them (despite Barth's going "too far" in his "determinism").

Other Debates

In 1948, a public debate between Barth and Brunner broke out for a second time. In the Spring of that year, Barth visited some Reformed churches in Hungary, publishing a report about his visit when he returned.[9] Brunner was distressed to read of Barth's advice of neutrality to churches living under Communist rule, and so he addressed a open letter to Barth.[10] The prob-lem, according to Brunner, is Barth's inconsistency: while he spoke an un-conditional No to Nazism, Barth fails to see that Communism is simply an-other expression of the same thing—totalitarianism.[11] Barth responded with a "general statement" and two questions.[12] The general statement is that the Church is not called to "vindicate its faith" or "give an explanation...eternally with various 'isms' and systems, but with historical realities as seen in the light of the Word of God and of faith" (114). "Therefore, the church never thinks, speaks or acts 'on principle'. Rather, it judges spiritually and by individual cases". Barth's first question—whether it was necessary for the Church to speak out against Nazism—is answered affirmatively, because the Church was spiritually tempted by Nazism (114–155). But Barth answers his second question—whether a similar situation exists in 1948—negatively, because no one is tempted by Communism, since everyone sees its evils clearly (115–117). Barth concludes that, in any political situation, "everything depends on whether the Church, not bound to abstract principles but to its living Lord, will seek and find its own way and also learn to choose freely the time for speech and the time for silence...without thereby becoming confused by any law other than that of the gospel" (118).

Barth and Brunner's final direct theological exchange came in *Church Dogmatics* IV/2/§67.1,4 (1955),[13] where Barth delivers a christological critique of the pneumatological ecclesiology which Brunner had developed in *The Misunderstanding of the Church* (1951).

Final Exchanges
Barth and Brunner met face to face for the last time in 1960, through the prompting of a common student.[14] Although this meeting was in no way a theological reconciliation, it was a time for putting personal animosities and hurts behind.[15] Barth made an effort toward theological reconciliation in an address the following year:

> One should never bind oneself to the things which one says in confrontation...
> The same is true with my sharp No against E. Brunner in 1934...Later I brought
> *theologia naturalis* back in via christology. Today my criticism would run: One
> must say it differently, specifically, christologically.[16]

Brunner, on the other hand, attacked Barth for his "one-sided objectivism" again in his enlarged second edition to *Truth as Encounter*.[17] Barth was angered enough to write Brunner's son (a former student of his), appealing for his help in restraining his father, and even proposing another get-together.[18]

The end of the Barth–Brunner relationship came right before Brunner's death, as Barth hurried off a letter to Brunner's pastor upon hearing of Brunner's critical condition:

> If I were more active after my two-year illness I would take the next train to
> press Emil Brunner's hand again.

If he is still alive and it is possible, tell him I commend him to *our* God. And tell him the time when I thought I should say No to him is long since past, and we all live only by the fact that a great and merciful God speaks his gracious Yes to all of us.[19]

Two weeks later, after Brunner's death, Barth wrote Brunner's widow:

Naturally I have been considering, too, the question how it really was, and how it came to be, between him and me…From my standpoint the fact was that God not only led him and me on very different paths, but in his unfathomable goodness and wisdom willed us already to be very different people—so different that properly there could be no question at all of strife or suffering between us. And yet we did strive and suffer on both sides. And if I am right he suffered more at my hands than I did at his.[20]

Key Factors in the Barth–Brunner Debate

In analyzing the break-up of the theological alliance between Karl Barth and Emil Brunner, there are several factors which stand out as being particularly important. Among these are personal characteristics, material commitments, and theological method. With regard to the latter, issues concerning the use of dialectic, the task of theology, the relationship between theology, philosophy, and anthropology, and the appropriation of the Reformers and Kierkegaard are central.

Personal Characteristics
It is indisputable that the personality differences between Barth and Brunner contributed to the break-up of their theological alliance. These men had different personal and theological temperaments.[21] Barth consistently showed himself to be a radical, all-or-nothing, either/or kind of person; he tended to embrace "one-sided" positions. There has never been another theologian in the history of the Church who has been severe enough with himself to completely re-write his first two major works! Part of Barth's theological greatness stems from his uncompromising personality. And yet he himself sadly remarked on the "centrifugal" effect he had on friends.[22] Barth was by nature a polemicist rather than one for dialogue.[23]

Brunner, on the other hand, was by nature a mediating personality and theologian.[24] His eristics were an expression of this, as Brunner reached out to the good in secular thinking in order to make a contact for the Gospel. Brunner was a "both/and" kind of person, a bridge-builder. It has been observed that, uniquely among the dialectical theologians, "Brunner's thought is closely related to or can at least readily be connected with that of all the others".[25] Given these contrasting personalities, it is not surprising that Barth always found Brunner to be compromising, while Brunner always felt Barth went "too far".[26]

A second personal factor which contributed to Barth and Brunner's break-up was that there was an "older brother-younger brother" dynamic to their relationship.[27] There was always in Barth something which did not respect Brunner as a full colleague, and there was always a bit of a chip on Brunner's shoulder regarding Barth's pre-eminence. Through the years, Brunner reacted both graciously and jealously to Barth's greater reputation.[28] For his part, Barth, near the end of his life, wrote this devastating comment about Brunner in a letter to Friedrich Schmid, concerning Schmid's book[29]:

> In your Part II it struck me for the first time that I might have done better thirty years ago to direct my frontal attack against Gogarten instead of the much weaker Brunner, whom you surprisingly (but rightly) disregarded.[30]

Brunner's son concludes: "When all is said and done, Emil Brunner's activities were of little importance for [Barth's] own activities".[31]

In the end, the decisive personal difference was that Barth was simply a superior intellect and theologian to Brunner. Barth was one of the few geniuses in twentieth century theology, whose creativity and complexity have proven to be consistently rewarding.[32] He was a theologian whose "imaginative construal" empowered him to do theology in endlessly surprising and profound ways.[33] On the other hand, while Brunner was constantly praised for the clarity of his expression, many commentators note a certain shallowness, an inability to think things through, and a predictable consistency.[34] While Barth remains at the forefront of theological discussion, Brunner has been universally demoted to the second rank of twentieth century theologians.[35] In their battle of wits, Brunner was the weaker man.[36]

Material Commitments

In addition to personal characteristics, Barth and Brunner saw their alliance crumble due to differing material emphases. For the purpose of this book, four contrasts are significant.

First, Barth and Brunner emphasized different poles of the divine-human action. For Barth, who took "God is God" in its most radical sense, the doctrines of election and predestination were the touchstones of theology.[37] Barth took the *sola* slogans of the Reformation seriously and thought them through radically.[38] On the other hand, Brunner's non-negotiable beliefs were human freedom and responsibility.[39] One sees this issue arising between them early in the correspondence, and it is one of the clearest differences in the natural theology debate from 1929–1935. For Barth, theology returned again and again to the grace of God, while for Brunner, theology always returned to human sin. In Brunner's thinking, the great disturbance in life—the "crisis"—was the fact of human sin; for Barth, the crisis was the disturbance caused by the grace of God.[40] For Barth, the key decision was the one made by God in the eternal election of humanity in Jesus Christ; for Brunner, the key decision was the responsible decision of the individual for faith.

Underlying this first material contrast is a second one: their different understanding of the act of faith and the place of God's judgment. For Brunner, to believe meant to trust with one's whole heart, to become existentially committed, to cast oneself on God's mercy in a definite life-act. Not only is this act of faith all-consuming, it is also decisive, for God's judgment lies in the future. Unless one comes to faith in Jesus Christ, one faces eternal condemnation. For Barth, faith was knowledge, acknowledgment, learning about reality as it really is in view of God's act in Jesus Christ. And "the way reality really is" is that all people have already been saved, and are already saved, in Jesus Christ's vicarious and effective act of atonement— God's judgment lies in the past. Though Barth denied he was a universalist (which would bind God's freedom), it is clear that he had the confident hope that God's grace is far greater than we can imagine.[41]

This very basic soteriological difference fueled Barth and Brunner's debate, beginning with their disagreement over the law and gospel in 1924. Brunner's eristics and anthropology developed from his conviction of the importance of moral responsibility, the decisiveness of the act of faith, and the threat of God's judgment. Conversely, Barth rejected Brunner's "other task" because he did not take unbelievers' unbelief "too seriously", since they were already saved *de jure* and *de facto*—faith simply makes one aware of what God has already done sufficiently on our part.

Third, not only did Barth and Brunner emphasize different poles of the divine-human action, they also understood God's action in the world differently. For Brunner, the eyes of faith enabled one to see the hand of God at work—in creation, in "changed lives". God is invisible, but God makes himself visible to the eyes of faith. For Barth, God is invisible, even to faith. Anything visible to which the Church can point—order in creation, fruit of the Spirit, fellowship in the Church, knowledge of God—is all ambivalent and relative. God's action is entirely free, and thus cannot be contained or explained or verified by any human phenomenon.[42]

Finally, Barth and Brunner understood the relationship between Church and world differently. Barth saw a fundamental solidarity between the Church and world—they stand together under the crisis of God's judgment, they stand in equal distance from the knowledge of God, and they stand in equal need of God's constant grace and justification. Thus, there is no sense of "us *vs.* them" in Barth—theology's task is to focus exclusively on putting the Church's own house in order, leaving the world to the care of God.[43] However, for Brunner, there is a fundamental difference between the Church and the world. The Church has a secure standpoint from which it can eristically engage the world and challenge its unbelief.[44] Barth rejected the self-righteousness implied in Brunner's "missionary" stance—this was the "paternalism" of eristics which Barth so disliked.[45]

Theological Method

The use of dialectic. The single most important factor in understanding Barth and Brunner's theological alliance and its collapse is their different understandings of the concept of "dialectic". The method of dialectic acknowledges that humanity cannot speak directly of God, even the self-revealing God, who remains concealed even in His self-revelation. Thus, dialectic is both the theologian's humble act of obedience as well as an all-out assault on the smug confidence of Neo-Protestantism.

However, from the very beginning, Barth and Brunner understood theological dialectic differently (see Chapter Two). When Barth's 1916 "turn" was radicalized in 1920 under the influence of Overbeck and Kierkegaard, he began to take the fundamental ontological and noetic gap between God and humanity in its most radical sense. All theology can do is point out its own inadequacy through the use of paradoxical and dialectical statements, which point toward God, but in no way capture him.[46] There is, therefore, no human possibility of theology—it is only possible as the Church's thoughtful obedience of faith, "following after" the revelation as witnessed to in Scripture, and always standing in need of God's justifying grace.[47] There is no way to justify theology to reason—it begins within the circle of faith and can only proceed from there. The "crisis" of Barth's theology is that which is brought upon the Church, the believer and the theologian— they must recognize their total need for grace in order to respond in words, acts and thoughts to the act of God in Jesus Christ.[48]

Brunner's Idealist background made it difficult for him to accept such a radically discontinuous understanding of dialectic. This can be seen most clearly in the Obstalden meeting referred to in Brunner's letter of September 2, 1920.[49] Barth's "dialectical watch-dog" was too indiscriminate for Brunner, who preferred a "critical (i.e., Kantian) watch-dog". At this point, a parting of the ways seemed likely. But, after reading *Romans II*, Brunner appeared to adopt Barth's radical dialectic. However, as has been argued, this was simply a temporary appropriation by Brunner—although up through *The Mediator* he could make very "Barthian" statements, in fact Brunner had simply pasted Barthian dialectic onto his other fundamental commitments (Kantian critical Idealism, Kierkegaardian existentialism, Ebnerian personalism, and a traditional understanding of the Reformers). Since the radicalism of the Barthian dialectic did not lend itself to assimila-tion, as early as 1924–1925 (and certainly by 1929) Brunner began to slough it off, allowing his other commitments to come to the fore. Stefan Scheld's contrast is quite helpful: Barth practiced dialectical theology, while Brunner, spurred on by his discovery of Ebner, developed a *dialogical* theology.[50]

The contrast between Barth and Brunner's understanding of dialectic can be stated in many ways. For Barth, dialectic had to do with God in himself and in his revelation (God is wholly Other, He is always the sovereign Subject); for Brunner, dialectic had to do with the Christian life (natural and special revelation, command and orders, law and gospel). For Barth, *discontinuity* was always stressed: there is a fundamental ontological *and* noetic distance between God and humanity, revelation and faith are miracles, new life is re-creation, revelation says something entirely new, "religion" is opposed to God, even the justified sinner always stands at an incomparable distance from God. For Brunner, *continuity* was the underlying theme: humanity is created in a fundamental relation to God (*imago Dei*),[51] natural knowledge points beyond its limits, new life is restoration, revelation confirms and corrects what we know in part and for which we have striven blindly, all religions contain elements of truth, the Holy Spirit is experienced and visible in the life in the believer. Brunner's whole argument erected around the "point-of-contact" was motivated by the presupposition of continuity.[52]

An important distinction is necessary here. The whole shape of Brunner's eristic argument from *Mysticism and the Word* on was to attack the fundamental error of "identity-continuity philosophy".[53] Brunner attacked the denial of the *ontological* distinction between God and humanity—both Barth and Brunner were completely united as Kutter's disciples in maintaining "God is God." However, Brunner's understanding of the *noetic* distance between God and humanity was more complex, and this was where he and Barth parted company. For Brunner, there is no natural knowledge of *God*. However, there is a natural knowledge of "limit", which is experienced as moral failure or existential despair, and which points humanity beyond itself towards the solution to the question to life (thus, a *via negativa*).[54] A noetic distance is maintained, but it is presupposed that humanity, on its own, understands its need and lack.[55] For the believer, through faith and revelation, there is no longer any noetic distance, as God has revealed himself effectively and savingly.[56]

Other contrasts illuminate the distinctions in Barth and Brunner's understanding of dialectic. For Barth, that which revelation communicates is completely and utterly new, for it is God Himself coming to sinful human-ity—revelation is *defined exclusively* through the second article; for Brun-ner, that which revelation communicates is new, but as fulfillment, perfec-tion, completion of what is already known by the natural person "in some way"—revelation is *determined* by the second article, but it *presupposes* the first article. For Barth, dialectic is *radical*: since both the world *and the Church's* knowledge of God stands in judgment, the Church's concern is the *Church's* faltering obedience. For Brunner, dialectic is *critical*: since the Church is aware of the world's false knowledge of God, theology involves attacking the world's ignorance; the concern is Church *vs.* world. For Barth, dialectic means that the Church's thinking must leap within a circular way of thought—its presupposition is that revelation has happened, and its task is to think through its interrelations and implications; for Brunner, dialectic means that once the possibility of revelation has been established through a point-of-contact (humanity's sense of lack, its addressability, its response-ability), it then can be shown that knowledge of God can only come through God's act of revelation. For Barth, dialectic means actualism —God is the uniquely sovereign subject of his revelation, and therefore faith, knowledge, and obedience are never our possession, but given ever-anew by God;[57] for Brunner, there is a real givenness—in creation, in the structure of humanity, and in the experiences of the Christian life.[58]

Another way of contrasting Barth and Brunner's use of dialectic is to look at what they risked—for Barth, it was monism, for Brunner it was dualism. Brunner's dialectic was always in danger of dissipating its energy into flatness, synthesis, or dualism. In his ethics, Brunner's intended con-structive dialectical tension between God's command and the orders of cre-ation is constantly flattened out into a *status quo* ethics of creation, with a little pinch of "reform" from following the demand of love within the framework of the "orders". In Brunner's eristic schema, the dialectic is one of thesis/antithesis (Idealism/naturalism, philosophy's half-truths/half-er-rors, humanity's *imago*/Fall) which is too easily resolved in a synthesis of the Gospel. Sometimes Brunner's dialectic breaks apart into simple dualism: his understanding of the dialectic of the Law and Gospel leaves one with an angry God in His "alien work" and a gracious God in His "proper work". One can substitute "tension" or "balance" for dialectic in most of Brunner's writings with no change of meaning. This is certainly a legitimate linguistic use of word "dialectic", but it completely misses the connotation which Barth gave to the word.

On the other hand, Barth always fought the tendency to collapse dialectic into a christological monism.[59] Barth's emphasis on the inalienable subjec-tivity of God in his revelation led him, in the *Church Dogmatics*, to place the dialectical tension solely within the history and person of Jesus Christ (electing God/rejected person; God's readiness for humanity/humanity's readiness of God; the Lord as Servant/the Servant as Lord; revealed in His hiddenness/hidden in His revealing).[60] Barth resolved his dialectic "up" into God's being and history (christology), while Brunner tended to resolve his "down" into humanity's faith and life experience (general/special revelation, command/orders, law/gospel). If Brunner collapsed the dialectic into a precedence of creation (that which is given) over redemption (reform), Barth tended to lose track of the middle ground of "now" between the poles of what was accomplished in Christ in eternity past and its unveiling at the Consummation. In the end, what fueled Barth's monistic tendency was the conviction that *God's* subjectivity must always be safeguarded against the threat of "anthropology masquerading as theology", while Brunner's dualism was fed when his unshakable theological presupposition (God is sovereign) ran up against his fundamental material commitment—the subjectivity of the person-in-decision.

Dogmatics vs. philosophy. Another note which runs throughout the history of the Barth–Brunner relationship is their different understandings of theology as dogmatics *vs.* philosophy. When Barth and Brunner embarked on the development of constructive theology at the beginning of their academic careers, they moved in two entirely different directions (see Chapter Three).

For Barth, theological thinking is dogmatic thinking because theology is not a free science, but a thinking bound to the sphere of the Church. Specifically, theology starts from the dogma, which is the Church's formulation of its understanding of the Word of God proclaimed to it through the Scriptures and which it must proclaim to the world. Theology as dogmatics certainly uses philosophy as a necessary tool of human expression, but it is an *incidental* tool employed solely for clearer reflection on theology's object. Since revelation and faith are both miraculous acts whose subject is God, it is impossible to explain them or understand them from any human point of view.[61] Since the object of theology is the living sovereign Lord, there is no standing-place for theology as it follows after the Word of God in its thinking; theology has no exterior supports, no guarantees. Since theology is only possible within the sphere of faith, one cannot be a theologian *cum* philosopher, which would require that one could somehow stand outside of faith in order to contrast it with other ways of thinking.[62] For Barth, theology operates in a sphere independent of philosophy, and thus needs no philosophical justification. The theologian can never start with the question of what is possible philosophically, but only with what is actual theologically. Philosophy is a tool which helps explain this actuality to human thought, but it can neither establish nor control this actuality.[63]

Brunner did not dispute Barth's view that the foundation of theology is dogmatics, and Brunner readily conceded Barth's great dogmatic skills. However, Brunner was also interested in the philosophical expression of theology. He pursued theology philosophically due to the discipline philosophy places upon thought—this is the Kantian "soberness" to which he constantly referred. Since theology is human thinking, the question is not *whether* theology thinks philosophically, but rather, *with what kind* of philosophy.[64] In addition, Brunner sees the use of philosophy as necessary in order to engage the modern person— philosophy is simply an entry-point to theology.[65] Thus, Brunner always pursues his philosophical interests, both out of personal preference and as a "division of labor" with Barth the dogmatician.

Brunner's concession after his meeting with Barth in the summer of 1935 reveals this aspect of their disagreement: "By nature I would indeed much rather be a philosopher than a theologian. That indeed may well be what to you is suspect about me".[66] This is at the heart of the on-going conflict between Barth and Brunner. Brunner's fundamental and consistent commitment to Kantianism decisively influenced his theological development, as it was philosophical issues, rather than dogmatic ones, which continually engaged his attention.[67] It is revealing that Barth's first book was a theological commentary on a biblical epistle whereas Brunner's was an attack upon the philosophical assumptions of Schleiermacher.

This issue of dogmatic *vs.* philosophical theology is indicative of the nuanced yet substantial differences in the way Barth and Brunner understood revelation. For Barth, the fundamental presupposition of faith and theology is that revelation has happened, happens and will happen: "God speaks". It is completely moot and improper to inquire whether or under what conditions revelation can happen; the only proper *theological* question is "to what extent" revelation has happened and what are its implications. Thus, Barth starts with the *actuality* of revelation, and discovers its *possibility* within this presupposed actuality. Anselm enabled Barth to declare that theology has a self-authenticating epistemology and needs no grounding independent of revelation. On the other hand, one of the major impulses driving Brunner in his eristics and the natural theology debate was his desire to ground the *possibility* of revelation. While he sought this grounding within the action of revelation (attested by Scripture), nonetheless he maintained there were certain conditions (created by God) which were necessary in order for revelation to be possible—humanity's ability to speak, its addressability, its "formal" image of God, its response-ability. If God had not created this "formal structure" of humanity, then it would not be possible for God to reveal himself to humanity.

This dogmatic *vs.* philosophical difference is also seen in the way the two theologians used tradition. Brunner's major historical conversation partners were the ancient Greek philosophers, the New Testament, the Reformers, and the leaders of theological and philosophical thought in the eighteenth and nineteenth centuries. The contrast to Barth is sharp: Barth's use of tradition was dogmatic, thus his primary conversation was within the Church.[68] A second point makes the contrast even clearer. Although Brunner spent more time in conversation with non-Christian (or Neo-Protestant) philosophers, he engaged them to defeat them, not to learn from them. In contrast, at times Barth really listened and learned from modern philosophy (e.g., Overbeck, Feuerbach). This points to a hidden reason why Barth rejected Brunner's eristics: Barth thought that Brunner neither understood nor was able to refute difficult philosophical questions.[69]

The task of theology. When Brunner explicitly announced a second task of theology in 1929, it revealed an already existing disagreement in Barth and Brunner's understandings of theology's aims (see Chapter Four).

From his first dogmatics at Göttingen, Barth was clear about what he was trying to accomplish as a theologian. He was a dogmatician, a theologian whose service is to reflect critically on the Church's proclamation, being guided by the Church's dogmas and creeds in order to correct the speaking of the Church according to the one measure of Scripture, in order that the Church would speak faithfully about the center of Scripture, Jesus Christ. While Barth struggled throughout the 1920s and early 1930s to find the best way to accomplish this task, the task itself was decided upon very early: "Barth's belief was that the theme of theology must be Jesus Christ, its source should be the Bible, and its locus the Church".[70] This, Barth believed, was the only way theology could be a theology of revelation—bound to "following the path" of the Word of God in its three forms. To be concerned with anything else than this one Word of God would cause theology to become a *non sequitur*: a theology of revelation "and" something else. Thus, Barth was always suspicious of any kind of apologetics in theology, since it compromised the self-authenticating revelation with other criteria.[71] Theology, as a "thinking-after" the Word of God, is free from anxiety and uncertainty,[72] because the effectiveness of theology is left to the power of the Word of God, not to the persuasiveness of the theologian or preacher.[73] Faithfulness to the subject matter, not effectiveness in "results", is the charge given to theology and preaching, since God is in control of the event of revelation.[74]

While Brunner granted this perennial dogmatic task of theology, he believed that in the modern situation another task of theology had a place and, in fact, was the more urgent task to be done. He called this task "eristics"— engaging in a conversation with modern, unbelieving people (outside *and inside* the Church).[75]

Brunner's eristics can be easily contrasted to Barth's dogmatics. It is focused on proclamation's destination rather than on its subject matter. It is concerned with bringing people to the moment of decision, rather than drawing Church proclamation closer to doctrinal truth. It is a missionary task focused on the unique secularity of modern people as opposed to a Church task of the constant, ever-renewed reflection of the Church.[76] Whereas Barth's dogmatic definition of theology presupposes a doctrine of revelation (the unity of the Word of God in its three forms, its self-authenticating nature and independent effectiveness), the presupposition of Brunner's eristics is the unique antagonism of modernism. Certainly, sinful humanity is always resistant morally to the Gospel; but Brunner argued that ever since the Enlightenment, secular human thinking itself had become opposed to the Christian understanding of God, humanity and life. The Holy Spirit is always required to break the rebellion of the sinful person to bring her to faithful obedience. But, in the modern context, before this divine action can take place, theology must build a bridge across the *intellectual/conceptual* gap between modernity and Christianity's presuppositions about reality.[77] This is theology as evangelistic preaching, the success of which hinges on finding an effective and exploitable "point-of-contact"—a place where the Good News can make its entrance into the thinking of the unbeliever, to begin the process of conversion.[78]

In essence, Brunner's eristics was a modernization of revivalism. In the revival pattern, the preacher spends considerable time upon the "bad news" (sin, judgment, hell), bringing people (on the "sinners' bench") to a "conviction of sin", in order that they would turn to Christ in faith. Brunner found the logic of this evangelistic strategy impeccable, but its form had to be completely revised since modern people rejected the concepts of sin, judgment and hell. Therefore, Brunner updated it: the eristician (an intellectual) reasons (not preaches) with modern people about the weakness of their world-view by appealing to their feelings of existential despair and moral failure, in order that they would examine Christianity as an alternative and valid explanation of reality.[79] This "updated revivalism" is precisely what appealed to Brunner in the Oxford Group Movement.

In Brunner's mind, Barth's equation (theology = dogmatics) was unnecessarily restrictive. In Barth's view, Brunner's position (theology = provocative proclamation to intellectuals) did not respect the proper limits of theology as a Church science.

Theology vs. anthropology. The combination of "The Other Task of Theology" and the January 1930 visit to Marburg convinced Barth that his dialectical colleagues were continuing to do theology as anthropology (see Chapter Four). In Brunner's case, Barth's concerns about his increased focus on anthropological concerns (*imago Dei, humanum*, etc.) culminated in the natural theology debate (see Chapter Five). In a very different but re-lated way, Brunner's involvement with the Oxford Group Movement gave Barth further evidence of Brunner's fundamentally anthropological con-cerns (Chapter Six). Thus, another key factor in the Barth–Brunner debate is Barth's continuing focus on the doctrine of God (*theo*-logy) *vs.* Brunner's ever-increasing interest in the meaning of the Gospel for human existence (*anthropo*-logy). Put succinctly, Barth always strove to get it right in his statements about God, whereas Brunner always sought to state correctly the relationship between God and humanity.

Brunner's anthropological concerns were clearly not a throw-back to Neo-Protestantism, to "speaking about God by speaking of humanity in a loud voice". Nonetheless, for Brunner "the cardinal point of my theology [is] the doctrine of man".[80] As an eristic theologian, Brunner focused on the "hinge" doctrine of anthropology: "Knowledge of Man is the common theme and the common concern both of secular and Christian (theological) wisdom".[81] Brunner's discovery of Ebner's "dialogical" thought-scheme encouraged him in this anthropological direction.[82] All of Brunner's works in the decisive period of 1929–1937 focused on the place where the Gospel "makes contact" with the need and questions of humanity, because Brun-ner's main theological problem was the relation between *The Word of God and Modern Man*.[83] Theology's task is a conversation with unbelieving hu-manity ("The Other Task of Theology"); where, precisely, is the *entrée* for the Gospel in humanity? ("The Question of the 'Point-of-Contact'"); the "changed person" is the result of the Gospel (the Oxford Group Move-ment).[84] It is revealing that Brunner conceded to Barth that "my didactic-pedagogic interest misleads me again and again to listen too much to hu-manity instead of to God".[85]

Brunner's interest in anthropology also had to do with his interest in the Christian life—thus, his stress on "encounter", fellowship, "faith active in love". It was Brunner's concern for the Christian believer that led to his re-jection of Barth's theological development as "objectivism".[86]

Barth, on the other hand, was constantly careful to give anthropology a very secondary role in theology. Once he had "turned" from Neo-Protes-tantism—anthropology masquerading as theology—he never wanted to al-low himself to be tempted down that slippery slope again. From Barth's "No!" to culture and religion in *Romans II*, through his negative evaluation of the first question of the Heidelberg Catechism in 1921,[87] to his early sus-picions about Bultmann's existentialism,[88] through "Theology and Modern Man" and *Church Dogmatics* I/1, Barth found anthropology to be the great temptation for theology. As a dogmatic theologian focusing on theology's subject matter, Barth believed theology's first question is always about the nature and being and activity of *God*—and since this is an exhaustive question, anthropology as a "second" question can be deferred almost indefinitely.[89] Since, for Barth, the knowledge of God preceded human self-understanding, theology must keep its focus on its proper object.[90] This is done without concern for theology's anthropological "relevance", for God is not a predicate of human needs.[91] For Barth, the first word in theology was God and grace; there *is* a second word (humanity and faith), but Barth always emphasized the first word first, putting the second word in its proper place by not giving it much attention.[92]

This "theology-anthropology" contrast runs throughout the Barth–Brunner conflict. It is seen in their different understandings of dialectic: Barth stressed it as an ontological reality about God (the wholly Other), while Brunner emphasized it as a soteriological reality about humanity (it is fallen and "in contradiction"). It is seen in their anthropologies: both developed "theological anthropologies" based on the knowledge of humanity given in revelation, but Brunner stressed the creation of humanity (true humanity is the restored image of God,) whereas Barth emphasized the vicarious humanity of Jesus Christ, who Himself is the true human being.[93] It can be seen in their different appropriation of the Reformation: for Brunner, its fundamental message was justification by faith (*sola fidei*, faith being understood as personal trust), for Barth it was election (*soli Deo gloria*). Finally, it is seen in the natural theology debate, where Brunner went to shaky extremes to maintain his bottom line (humanity is responsible) just as Barth went out on a limb to defend his ultimate cause (grace alone).

The use of the Reformers. Another methodological contrast between Barth and Brunner is the way they each used the Reformers. It is fair to use a phrase such as "Neo-Reformationist" to describe Brunner. Throughout his works, especially when he was pressed, Brunner appealed to the authority of the Reformers to vindicate his teaching. In fact, Brunner saw himself as simply updating the message of the Reformation for modern people, de-emphasizing some doctrines, such as predestination, and re-stating others, such as sin and general revelation, in order to help the message of the Reformers span the three hundred year time- and culture-gap.

Barth, too, saw Luther and Calvin as his main authorities, but he cannot be called a "Neo-Reformationist". Rather, Barth took what he found faithful in the Reformers and developed it radically.[94] Specifically, Barth saw the brilliance of the Reformers to reside in their *sola*-slogans,[95] and he thought them through to their ultimate extreme—grace alone (he flirted with universalism), faith alone (understood epistemologically[96]), Scripture alone (interpreted theologically), and Christ alone (a universal vicariousness of

Jesus Christ, i.e., justification *and* sanctification are Christ's work, Christ has already accomplished salvation for all *de facto*, etc.).

This different use of the Reformers helps to explain two of Barth and Brunner's debates. One of the reasons that Barth was dissatisfied with *Mysticism and the Word* was that Brunner failed to see that "the case of Schleiermacher is a slap in the face that resounds back into the sixteenth century in part".[97] In addition, their different appropriation of the Reformation partly explains why Barth and Brunner talked past each other in the natural theology debate. Barth wearied of Brunner's citations of Calvin, since Brunner missed "the intentions of Reformation theology".[98] Brunner, for his part, was highly suspicious of Barth's claim that, in order to "adhere to the teaching of the Reformation" it was necessary to re-write "what Calvin wrote in those first chapters of the *Institutes*".[99] Brunner was constantly exasperated by Barth's historical argument because he assumed that Barth was using the Reformers in the same way as himself—i.e., in a "Neo-Reformationist" manner—rather than Barth's free and radical manner.

The appropriation of Kierkegaard. All of these contrasts in Barth and Brunner's theological method are illustrated in their different appropriation of Kierkegaard. Both Barth and Brunner saw in Kierkegaard a way to attack the bourgeois, neutrally-scientific, philosophy-of-religion style of Neo-Protestantism, for Kierkegaard understood that God was not an object to be studied, but the living and judging God. Barth paid special homage to Kierkegaard in *Romans II* and *Christian Dogmatics*. Brunner's reliance on Kierkegaard has been noted, especially in his 1924–1925 essays. But by the time Brunner published a lecture on Kierkegaard in 1930,[100] it had become clear that Kierkegaard was becoming a point of division, rather than a point of unity, between Barth and Brunner.[101] Disturbed by Barth's increasing "objectivism" (as witnessed in *Christian Dogmatics* and "Theology and Modern Man"), Brunner's article sought to re-assert the *subjectivity* of Christianity—the "existential" subjectivity of the Christian's personal faith.[102]

Barth's early reliance upon Kierkegaard is seen throughout his works and lectures.[103] Barth found in Kierkegaard ammunition with which to fight the necessary early battles against historicism and Idealism.[104] But as early as 1925, Barth had second thoughts about Kierkegaard, which arose both from his strong turn toward Trinitarian, constructive, dogmatic theology in Göttingen, as well as the way his fellow dialectical theologians were lifting up the subjective emphases of Kierkegaard.[105] For Barth, the fundamental issue was not to emphasize human subjectivity, but "the divine subjectivity in revelation."[106] Although, in 1927, Barth still included Kierkegaard in his theological "hall of fame",[107] by 1928 he was voicing concerns in his ethics lectures.[108] With the shift of emphasis seen in *Anselm* to the God-given and God-controlled objectivity of faith's knowledge (and faith itself as acknowledgment), Barth turned away from Kierkegaard.[109] It is most revealing that in his Bonn 1932–1933 lectures on *Protestant Theology in the Nineteenth Century*, Barth did not treat Kierkegaard at all.[110]

There are at least three ways in which Barth and Brunner drew differently from Kierkegaard. First, Brunner was always appreciative of Kierkegaard's stress on the subjective reality of personal faith, faith as existence.[111] Brunner adopted Kierkegaard's whole "existential psychology" of faith: the awareness of need, guilt and despair; the need for decision and the "leap"; the whole progressive scheme of moving from aesthetic to ethical to religious stages.[112] In contrast, Barth drew upon Kierkegaard's stress on the *divine* subjectivity, that God is free over the Church and religion, and that theology can only speak paradoxically of God. Second, Brunner adopted Kierkegaard as the "Father of eristics".[113] From *The Philosophy of Religion* through "The Other Task of Theology" and beyond, Brunner saw Kierkegaard as the inspiration for his theological task.[114] On the contrary, the Kierkegaardian attack appropriated by Barth was his prophetic critique of the Church. Finally, Barth understood Kierkegaard's paradox as pointing primarily to the discontinuity between God and humanity, while Brunner responded more enthusiastically to the Kierkegaardian dialectic within human existence.[115]

One need only read Barth's "The Word of God and the Task of the Ministry" (1922) to hear the same issues Brunner would press in "The Other Task of Theology"—humanity has an existential question (in fact, humanity *is* the question) to which the Gospel responds.[116] Brunner never wavered in the importance he placed on Kierkegaard's understanding of the Gospel and the modern person, for it provided an understanding of humanity which opened a "point-of-contact" for the Gospel.[117] At the same time, one can trace Barth's theological development by the progressively smaller role "Kierkegaardian existentialism" played, from its explicit affirmation in *Romans II*, to its smaller niche in *Christian Dogmatics*, to its explicit rejection in *Church Dogmatics* I/1.

Conclusion

Karl Barth and Emil Brunner were brought together in the second decade of this century through a common affirmation of the Blumhardt–Kutter insight of the "Godness of God" and a corresponding rejection of Neo-Protestantism, as well as a common friendship with Eduard Thurneysen. When Barth radicalized his theology under the influence of Overbeck and Kierkegaard,

Brunner initially balked, due to his Idealist commitments, and a parting of the ways seemed likely.[118] However, the combined influence of *Romans II* and Ebner's "I–Thou" philosophy enabled Brunner to break away from Neo-Kantianism and to join forces again with Barth.[119] But, from 1924 on, Barth and Brunner headed in separate directions—Barth towards dogmatic theology, seeking to base theology on the actuality of revelation alone, and Brunner towards philosophical theology, seeking to establish bridges between a theology of revelation and contemporary philosophies in order to confront the latter with the truth of the Gospel.[120] When both theologians reached definitive expressions of their programs in 1929–1930, the depth of their differences became apparent.[121] From 1929 on, every new writing emphasized these differences—from natural theology, to ethics, to prolegomena, to ecclesiology, to pneumatology, to anthropology; their alliance had become, a best, a distant one.[122] The crisis in the German Church in 1933–1934[123] and the success of the Oxford Group Movement in Switzerland in 1932–1936[124] sharpened their differences beyond Barth's capacity for toleration—Barth could only say "No!" to Brunner. The permanence of their theological break-up from 1936 to the end of their lives underlined the fundamental disagreement that lay under the surface of their relationship from the start.

It is the thesis of this book that Barth and Brunner represent fundamentally different ways of doing theology. This thesis is maintained despite the fact that, viewed within the context of the history of theology, it would be difficult to find any theologian closer to Barth than Brunner, or closer to Brunner than Barth. Nonetheless, they are separated by a decisive gulf, revealing how differently theology can be done given a common commitment to revelation, the Reformation, the authority of Scripture, and Kutter's "God is God".

The inner tension of their relationship is particularly illuminated in the two external crises which engulfed them in 1929–1934. The first crisis was the break-up of the dialectical theology group. It does not require hindsight to understand why Barth and Bultmann, and Barth and Gogarten, went different ways. But the dissolution of the Barth–Brunner alliance shows how radically and fundamentally Barth took his task of building a theology based on the actuality and sovereignty of revelation alone—even Brunner's dabbling in "strategic apologetics" was considered to be completely unacceptable. The second crisis was the struggle in the German Church against Nazi ideology. Again, it is no surprise that Barth and Althaus ended up on different sides. But that Barth would anathematize his closest theological colleague (next to Thurneysen) over an article which was only marginally related to this struggle shows again how radically Barth understood his approach to constructing a theology of revelation.

Brunner's relationship with Barth pushed Brunner back towards his Kantian leanings. Once he moved beyond his rejection of Neo-Protestantism and Pietism, Brunner realized, through his arguments with Barth, that he wanted to maintain a noetic relatedness between God and humanity, and a Christian faith which is existential and experiential.[125] Barth's relationship with Brunner (with his modest concessions to philosophy and anthropology) clarified his desire to construct "a theology which, like a spinning top, supports itself on only one point".[126] In the end, the break-up of the Barth–Brunner relationship tells us less about Brunner's theology than it does about Barth's. For what separated Brunner from Barth is what separates Barth from *every theologian*—he built his theology on a radically christocentric, strongly actualist, thorough-going radicalizing of the Reformation *solas*. Though the gulf is narrowest between Barth and Brunner, this is the gulf which completely surrounds Barth in the history of theology.

This examination of the Barth–Brunner relationship indicates that continuity, rather than "stages" or "turns", is more helpful in understanding both Barth and Brunner's individual theological development.

Up until 1922, Brunner's concerns (epistemology) and influences (Kant, Natorp, Kutter) remained constant.[127] *Romans II*, however, forced Brunner to re-evaluate his theological program. The immediate result was both negative (freeing himself from Neo-Kantianism) and positive (adopting the Barthian dialectic). However, the positive turn was only temporary—only "The Limits of Humanity" can be understood as a thoroughly "dialectical" work. The reason for this is twofold. First, Brunner's Kantianism never allowed him to genuinely take on board Barth's radical dialectic. Second, Brunner's sloughing off of Neo-Kantianism was immediately followed by his appropriation of Ebner's correlating "I–Thou" philosophy. The superficial nature of this 1922 "turn" is already visible in his 1923–1925 lectures, as well as in the direction of his thinking in *The Philosophy of Religion* and *The Mediator* (Part I).[128] Brunner experienced no "turn" in 1929 with "The Other Task of Theology"; there was an increased focus on anthropology and creation, but these *loci* were developed precisely along the same lines as before.[129] What changed in 1929 was Barth's sudden staunch opposition— Barth's complete rejection of Brunner's eristics, anthropology and ethics crystallized Brunner's doubts about Barth's actualist dialectic. This conflict with Barth's "objectivism", and the increasing importance of Kierkegaard and Ebner, as well as the pneumatological insights of the Oxford Group Movement, led Brunner into a "dialogical" kind of theology. What remained constant for Brunner was the influence of Kant (moral responsibility, the centrality of sin), Ebner (the divine-human continuity in human response-ability),[130] Kierkegaard (existential subjectivity), and a traditional understanding of the Reformers. In addition, from his first writings in the 1920s to his final publications, Brunner was always an "eristic" theologian.[131]

Similarly, it is argued here that continuity is more important than "turns" in understanding Barth's theological development. Barth experienced one fundamental turn—the 1916 turn back to the Bible and the embrace of Kutter and the Blumhardts' *theo*-centric theology. This new intention was radicalized, but not re-directed, through the influence of Kierkegaard and Overbeck. From this point on, Barth's fundamental intentions—God as wholly Other, a "from above" method, revelation as miraculous grace, the rejection of anthropological determinations, God's sovereignty—remained the same.[132] What changed for Barth was the way he expressed this conviction: eschatology and dialectic (*Romans II*), the Trinity as God's inalienable subjectivity (*The Göttingen Dogmatics*), Christo-vicariousness ("The Holy Spirit and the Christian Life"), election ("Theology and Modern Man"), and "faith seeking understanding" (*Anselm, Church Dogmatics*). After 1936,[133] Barth expressed this conviction christocentrically, which gave a determinative and gracious shape to his stress on God's freedom.[134]

Thus, the Barth–Brunner relationship reveals that Barth's basic conviction (God is God) and his basic methodology (dialectic) remained constant. There was no "Anselmian turn". Rather, Barth continually searched for ways to express his fundamental conviction more and more clearly.

A final way to understand the end of the Barth–Brunner theological alliance is to view both men in relation to Schleiermacher. On one level, Brunner "disposed of" Schleiermacher too readily, while Barth continued to struggle with him. However, a deeper look shows exactly the opposite. Barth's whole theology is a constant and radical No to the nineteenth century in all its forms. By early 1930, he concluded that all of his dialectical colleagues still stood on the nineteenth-century side of the great divide, for they were still seeking some beginning or possibility for theology in anthropology and philosophy. The Barth–Brunner debate clearly reveals how radically Barth believed this—if even Brunner was on the wrong side of this gulf,[135] then Barth saw himself standing completely alone over-against the nineteenth century.

Barth's suspicions about Brunner's program of eristics have their grounds here.[136] In effect, Brunner said that nineteenth century theology did not take the wrong approach, for eristics also starts with the world's questions and concerns. But while Neo-Protestantism attempted to respond in terms of the world's thinking, seeking a synthesis between the world and the Gospel, Brunner answered from the Gospel. Thus, Brunner can be understood as trying to re-claim and reform the method of Neo-Protestantism —he "made contact" with the presuppositions of natural thought "within the limits of revelation". Barth considered this method was bankrupt in any conceivable form, because, by definition, it starts outside the bounds of revelation. One must start with the *Gospel's* questions in order to hear the Gospel's *answer.*[137] For Karl Barth, the only place for theology to build was upon revelation—alone.

NOTES

1. After World War II, Barth and Brunner only met face to face three times: in 1948 at the World Council of Churches Assembly in Amsterdam; in 1953 at the Zurich airport (when Barth came to wish Brunner farewell on his move to Japan), and in 1960 (see above, p. 203) (I. John Hesselink, "Karl Barth and Emil Brunner: A Tangled Tale with a Happy Ending", in *How Karl Barth Changed My Mind*, ed. by Donald K. McKim (Grand Rapids: Eerdmans, 1986), pp. 131–142 (p. 135)).

2. See also Brunner, "Banalität oder Irrlehre?", *KfrS*, 96 (1940), 260–265.

3. *The Knowledge and Service of God: According to the Teaching of the Reformation,* trans. by J.L.M. Hare and Ian Henderson (London: Hodder and Stoughton, 1938).

4. On the question whether Barth ultimately moderated his complete opposition to natural theology, based on statements in *CD* IV/3/§69.2:110–165, see Hermann Fischer, "Natürliche Theologie im Wandel", *ZThK*, 80 (1983), 85–102; von Balthasar, pp. 147–150; Hinrich Stoevesandt, "Was heißt 'theologische Existenz'", *EvTh*, 44 (1984), 147–177 (p. 151); Hans Küng, "Karl Barth and the postmodern paradigm", *Princeton Seminary Bulletin*, n.s. 9 (1988), 8–31 (pp. 14, 27).

5. *The Christian Doctrine of God*, trans. by Olive Wyon (London: Lutterworth, 1949), pp. 6–13, 60–66. See also "Intellectual Autobiography", p. 16.

6. *The Christian Doctrine of God*, pp. 67–72, 78–85, 98–103.

7. "The New Barth", trans. by John C. Campbell, *SJT*, 4 (1951), 123–35.

8. For scholars who agree that Barth's anthropology moved remarkably close to Brunner's, see: Volk, "Christologie", p. 640; Roessler, pp. 102–103; von Balthasar, pp. 163–166; Dieter Becker, *Karl Barth und Martin Buber* (Göttingen: Vandenhoeck & Ruprecht, 1986), p. 11.

9. This report was re-issued, along with several of Barth's addresses in Hungary, in "The Christian Community in the Midst of Political Change", in *Against the Stream*, ed. by Roland Gregor Smith, trans. by E.M. Delacour and Stanley Goodman (London: SCM, 1954), pp. 51–124.

10. "An Open Letter to Karl Barth", in *Against the Stream*, pp. 106–113.

11. See especially p. 113. For Brunner's strong anti-Communism, see also "Missionary Theology", p. 817; *Justice and the Social Order*, pp. 176–180, 202–207. See also: Gill, p. 318; H.H. Brunner, pp. 133–134.

12. "Karl Barth's Reply", in *Against the Stream*, pp. 113–118.

13. Pp. 614–615, 616, 640, 679–686.
14. See Hesselink, "Tangled Tale", pp. 135–137.
15. Ibid., p. 139. But, see Busch, p. 449.
16. Quoted in Fischer, p. 86. See also Kreck, pp. 108–109.
17. Pp. 41–46.
18. *Karl Barth: Letters, 1961–1968*, trans. by Geoffrey W. Bromiley from the 2nd German edn (1978) (Grand Rapids: Eerdmans, 1981), pp. 140–141.
19. Ibid., p. 202. Note 3 (p. 203) states that Barth's letter contained the last words Brunner heard before he slipped into a coma.
20. Ibid., pp. 203–204.
21. "They were different men; they had different structures" (Brunner-Gutekunst interview). Bouillard (p. 175) calls it a clash between the "spirit of fire" (Barth) and the "spirit of water" (Brunner). Barth suggested they were as different as an elephant and a whale (Hesselink, "Tangled Tale", p. 134).
22. "How I Changed My Mind, 1928–1938", p. 41
23. Rosato, p. 185; Berkouwer, p. 166; Lehmann, p. 351.
24. Thurneysen once told Brunner that he possessed a gift which Barth lacked: the ability "to work together with those different from you" (Bohren, pp. 157–158).
25. Pauck, p. 34. See also: J.M.L. Thomas, p. 20; Kegley, "Special Introduction", in Kegley, pp. xi–xiv (p. xi); Gestrich, *Neuzeitliches Denken*, p. 344; and Brunner ("Reply to Interpretation", p. 328).
26. Brown, p. 84.
27. See Schildmann. See also Brunner's defensiveness about standing in Barth's shadow ("Intellectual Autobiography", pp. 8, 9, 11–12).
28. For Brunner's graciousness towards Barth, see Gill, pp. 319–320; George S. Hendry, "Appraisal of Brunner's Theology", *Theology Today*, 19 (1963), 523–31 (p. 531); Hesselink, "Tangled Tale", p. 133. For Brunner's jealousy of Barth, see H.H. Brunner, pp. 136–137; Hesselink, ibid., p. 132.
29. *Verkündigung und Dogmatik in der Theologie Karl Barths* (Munich, 1964).
30. *Letters, 1961–1968*, p. 170.
31. H.H. Brunner, p. 136.
32. See Clifford Green, "Karl Barth's Life and Theology", in *Karl Barth*, ed. by Green (London: Collins, 1989), pp. 11–45 (p. 12); Torrance, "Introduction", pp. 9–10
33. The term is from David H. Kelsey, *The Uses of Scripture in Recent Theology* (Philadelphia: Fortress, 1975).
34. See Lütz, p. 267; Hesselink, "Centennial Perspective", p. 1172; Hendry, "Appraisal of Brunner", p. 523; J.M.L. Thomas, p. 14.
35. One needs only to look through *Dissertation Abstracts International* to note the sudden drop-off in studies on Brunner following the publication of *The Christian Doctrine of the Church* (1960). Brunner himself was aware of his lessening influence at the end of his life (J. Robert Nelson, "Emil Brunner—Teacher Unsurpassed", *Theology Today*, 19 (1963), 532–535 (p. 486)). See also Hesselink, "Centennial Perspec-

tive", pp. 1171, 1174.

36. Other personal dynamics exacerbating the Barth–Brunner relationship include Barth's directness (or tactlessness) coupled with Brunner's sensitivity (or touchiness) (see above, p. 35 and p. 135 [note 26]), and Barth's constant annoyance with Brunner's "school teacher-like" manner (see above, p. 78 and p. 173 [note 42]). H.H. Brunner (pp. 135–138) also notes the role of regional differences (Basel *vs.* Zurich), and that Brunner never understood Barth's personal and theological sense of irony.

37. "Theology and Modern Man". See also Berkouwer, pp. 89, 194; Von Balthasar, pp. 155–156, 181; Colm O'Grady, *The Church in Catholic Theology* (Washington: Corpus Books, 1969), pp. 31–33, 42; Herbert H. Hartwell, *The Theology of Karl Barth* (Philadelphia: Westminster, 1964), pp. 105–112; Paul Jersild, "Natural Theology and the Doctrine of God in Albert Ritschl and Karl Barth", *Lutheran Quarterly*, 14 (1962), 239–257 (pp. 250–251).

38. O'Grady, pp. 8, 19.

39. See *Nature and Grace* (2nd edn), p. 59. See Daniel D. Williams, "Brunner and Barth on philosophy", *Journal of Religion*, 27 (1947), 241–254 (p. 247). See Brunner's weak doctrine of election in *The Christian Doctrine of God*, pp. 303–320.

40. Gestrich, *Neuzeitliches Denken*, p. 52.

41. See *CD* II/2:§§32–35, especially §35.1:305–325, §35.3:417–423, §35.4:475–477, and Brunner's rebuttal in *The Christian Doctrine of God*, pp. 346–352.

42. Von Balthasar, pp. 162, 272–277. See also Hunsinger, *How to Read Karl Barth*, pp. 38, 119–120.

43. See Busch, "Church as Witness", p. 88; Y.C. Furuya, "Apologetic or Kerygmatic Theology?", *Theology Today*, 16 (1960), 471–80 (p. 479); "How I Changed My Mind, 1938–1948", p. 96.

44. Williams, pp. 249–250.

45. "Theology and Modern Man", p. 394.

46. Von Balthasar, pp. 232–234.

47. Modifying Barth's vivid metaphor from "Theology and Modern Man" (p. 393): God's revelation is a wild, galloping horse—wild, powerful, and solely in charge of where it is going. Barth's concept of dialectic radically respects revelation's sovereign freedom, its inability to be controlled; therefore, the theologian's task is to "follow after" the horse by clinging for dear life to the horse's tail.

48. Sonderegger, p. 81; see also Green, p. 23.

49. See above, pp. 30–31.

50. Scheld, p. 98.

51. Cf. Hunsinger, *How to Read Karl Barth*, pp. 30–31.

52. Attila Szekeres, *De Structuur van Emil Brunners Theologie* (Utrecht: H.J. Smits, 1952), p. 97.

53. J.C. Bixler, "Emil Brunner as a Representative of the Theology of Crisis", *Journal of Religion*, 9 (1929), 446–459 (p. 452).

54. "This 'An-die-Grenze-Kommen' [arriving at the limit] is an essential condition for the possibility of faith" (George A. Schrader, "Brunner's Conception of Philosophy", in Kegley, pp. 111–129 (p. 115)). See also Roberts, p. 300.

55. Williams (p. 253) asks: "Can the mind 'point' to God without having some real knowledge of him? It is difficult to see that such a distinction can be maintained".

56. Ibid., pp. 249–250.

57. Ibid., p. 254. See *CD* II/1/§26.2:161, §28.1:263, §29:335–350; Wendebourg, p. 242.

58. The issue of actualism can be seen throughout the Barth–Brunner debate: *Re*: knowledge of God—for Barth humanity *is* not in the image of God, but God maintains relationship to it (it relies totally on grace); for Brunner, humanity *is* in the image of God, and thus knows something (it is response-able). *Re*: ethics—for Barth God gives his command ever anew; for Brunner, God has given his will in the order of the structures of life. *Re*: OGM—for Barth, the Church and the Christian do not *have* anything, there is no continuity between them and God, but only a relationship established ever anew unilaterally from God's side by grace; for Brunner, God has *given* the Church and the Christian new life, which is visible in "changed lives" and the fellowship of love.

59. See Berkouwer, p. 253.

60. See David F. Ford, "Conclusion" in Sykes, *Karl Barth*, pp. 194–201 (p. 194).

61. Tillich, "Dialectic Theology", p. 108.

62. Williams, p. 252.

63. See Barth's praise of Herrmann's doctrine of "autopistia" in "The Principles of Dogmatics according to Wilhelm Herrmann", in *Th&Ch*, pp. 238–271 (pp. 258–261). See also Hunsinger, *How to Read Karl Barth*, p. 33; Hugh Vernon White, "Brunner's Missionary Theology", in Kegley, pp. 55–71 (p. 55); Paul Matheny, *Dogmatics and Ethics* (Bern: Peter Lang, 1990), pp. 33–35.

64. See *The Christian Doctrine of God*, p. 76. See also Cairns, "Theology of Brunner", p. 305; Schrader, pp. 113, 127–128; Williams, p. 254.

65. Jewett, *Brunner's Concept of Revelation*, p. 173; Salakka, pp. 186–188; Gestrich, "Unbewältigte natürliche Theologie", note 51, pp. 97–98.

66. *Barth–Brunner*, EB: July 1, 1935 (#110), pp. 286–288.

67. Brunner's lasting concern—from his doctoral dissertation to *Experience, Knowledge & Faith*, from "The Limits of Humanity" and "Revelation as the Ground and Subject Matter of Theology" to the natural theology debate, from *Truth as Encounter* to *Revelation and Reason*—was epistemology. See "Reply to Interpretation", p. 336. See also: *Barth–Brunner*, KB: March 13, 1925 (#47), pp. 114–118; Schrader, pp. 118–119, 125–126; Volken, p. 8.

68. Not only is the Church the *locus* of his conversation, Barth covers the entire gamut of the theological tradition: Old and New Testaments, the Fathers, the medieval Scholastics, the Reformers, the Protestant Scholastics, the Neo-Protestants as well as the modern "positive" theologians.

69. Furuya (pp. 476–477) notes that, despite Brunner's efforts, most Japanese non-

Christians found him to be doing bad philosophy in a self-complacent manner

70. Crawford, p. 320.
71. "Concluding Unscientific Postscript", pp. 267–268. Barth's suspicions of apologetics extends back to *Romans II*, pp. 363–346. See also *Ethics*, pp. 21–22; Hunsinger, *How to Read Karl Barth*, p. 52.
72. *Anselm*, p. 62.
73. *Romans II*, p. 35.
74. See "Die Kirche Jesu Christi", *ThExh*, 5 (1933), pp. 3–4.
75. See "Spiritual Autobiography", p. 242. Brunner's 1947–1948 Gifford Lectures (*Christianity and Civilisation*, 2 vols (London: Nisbet, 1948–1949)) are another example of Brunner's eristics. Ironically, Brunner himself noted the problem with this approach in *The Divine Imperative*: "When the Church tries to be modern she always arrives too late, and the world—rightly—is only amused by her 'modernity'" (p. 566).
76. See for example, Brunner's article, "The Present-Day Task of Theology", *Religion in Life*, 8 (1939), 176–186.
77. "Spiritual Autobiography", pp. 241–242, 244; "The Present Day Task of Theology", pp. 179, 186; "Missionary Theology", p. 816. See also H.V. White, p. 67. Williams, however, argues that Brunner's conceptual engagement is quite shallow (pp. 242, 250). He also brilliantly draws upon a Kierkegaardian parable to illustrate Barth's rejection of Brunner's "bridge-building" eristics: "Imagine a fortress, absolutely impregnable, provisioned for an eternity. Then there comes a new commandment. He conceives that it might be a good idea to build bridges over the moats—so as to be able to attack the besiegers. *Charmant*. He transforms the fortress into a country estate—and naturally the enemy takes it. So it is with Christianity. They changed the method—and naturally the world conquered" (p. 252, cited from Walter Lowrie, *Kierkegaard* (London: Oxford University Press, 1938), p. 536).
78. "The Present Day Task of Theology", p. 177; "Missionary Theology", p. 818. See also: Gill, p. 317; Maud Keister Jensen, "The Missionary Motif in the Theology of Emil Brunner and its relation to specific doctrines" (unpublished doctoral thesis, Drew University, 1978), pp. 65–66; Roessler, p. 51; Leipold, pp. 288–289; Peter Vogelsanger, "Brunner as Apologist", in Kegley, pp. 289–301.
79. Thus, for Brunner: 1) modern times experience the despair of nihilistic philosophy —the answer is revelation (eristics); 2) modern life is crippled by individualism—the answer is the orders of creation as the basic forms of community (ethics); 3) modern life experiences alienation—the answer is fellowship (OGM).
80. "Reply to Interpretation", p. 331. Leipold (pp. 160–161) sees Gogarten as a decisive influence on Brunner at this point.
81. *The Christian Doctrine of Creation and* Redemption, p. 46. Many scholars point to *Man in Revolt* as Brunner's best book, e.g. Cairns, "Theology of Brunner", p. 302; Humphrey, p. 164.
82. Johnson, p. 167.

83. Trans. by David Cairns (London: Epworth, 1965). See also "Missionary Theology", p. 816; Brunner, *Eternal Hope*, translated by Harold Knight (London: Lutterworth), p. 213; Szekeres, *Structuur van Brunners Theologie*, pp. 97–98.

84. Leipold (pp. 159–160) argues correctly that the "point-of-contact" was the culmination of this stream in Brunner's thought, rather than (as Barth charged) a later innovation. Anthropology itself is the "point-of-contact" (p. 151).

85. *Barth–Brunner*, EB: October, 1933 (#91), pp. 234–237.

86. Roessler, pp. 67–68. Paul Schempp criticizes Barth at this point in a manner very similar to Brunner (pp. 194–195).

87. *Rev.Theology*, KB: November 18, 1921, p. 77.

88. Ibid., KB: February 15, 1925, p. 206.

89. See Frei, pp. 43–44; Lehmann, p. 339.

90. Matheny, p. 43.

91. George Hunsinger, "Beyond literalism and expressivism", *Modern Theology*, 3 (1987), 209–223 (p. 219).

92. This is what Brunner saw as Barth's "one-sidedness"—for Brunner, theology cannot say the first word without also saying the second word, or it becomes "speculative", "intellectualistic", or "objectivistic".

93. *CD* III/2/§44.

94. Thomas C. Oden speaks of Barth's "revolution through tradition" (*The Promise of Barth* (Philadelphia: Lippincott, 1969), p. 22).

95. Barth broke with the Reformers when they failed to follow their own insights (e.g., Church and State, general revelation, Law and Gospel, double predestination).

96. I.e., in contrast to natural knowledge (not in contrast to "works").

97. *Rev.Theology*, KB: March 4, 1924, p. 175.

98. *Barth–Brunner*, KB: November 12, 1934 (#104), pp. 270–272.

99. "No!", pp. 104–105.

100. "Die Botschaft Søren Kierkegaard", *Neue Schweizer Rundschau* 23:2 (1930). Cited here from *Ein offenes Wort*, I, pp. 209–226. Brunner states that Kierkegaard's central message is "subjectivity is truth", which sums up his double struggle against aestheticism and against the Church (p. 213). Since his philosophy of existence argues that true human existence is being-in-passion and being-in-decision, Kierkegaard scolds the Church for its flight from subjectivity into the objectivity of churchliness and orthodoxy (p. 221). Instead, Kierkegaard attempted to regain faith as personal existence—a passionate, decision-making existence (pp. 222–223).

101. See Jüngel, "Von Dialektik zur Analogie", pp. 175–178.

102. "Truth as encounter" is Brunner's ultimate way of expressing this concern. See H.H. Brunner, pp. 91, 96–97. See also Brunner's "Christlicher Existentialismus" (*Kirchliche Zeitfragen*, 39 (1956), also in *Ein offenes Wort*, II, pp. 318–334).

103. *Romans II*, pp. 4, 10, 494–498; "The Problem of Ethics Today", p. 176; "The Need and Promise of Christian Preaching", p. 98–99; *The Göttingen Dogmatics*, pp. 77, 137–138, 143, 178.

104. Cornelius van der Kooi, *Anfängliche Theologie* (Munich: Chr. Kaiser, 1987), p. 192.
105. *Rev.Theology*, KB: February 15, 1925, p. 206.
106. McCormack, p. 238.
107. *Christian Dogmatics*, p. 4.
108. *Ethics*, pp. 8, 17.
109. "Because I cannot regard subjectivity as being the truth, after a brief encounter I have had to move away from Kierkegaard again" (quoted in Busch, p. 173). See also *CD* I/1:xiii, §1.3:20, §2.2:36–37.
110. For later criticisms of Kierkegaard, see *CD* III/2/§43.2:21; IV/1/§58.4:150, §63.1:741. In the last years of his life, Barth would publish two short essays explaining his move away from Kierkegaard. In "A Thank You and a Bow", (trans. by Eric Mosbacher, in *Fragments Grave and Gay*, ed. by H. Martin Rumscheidt (London: Collins, 1971), pp. 95–101), Barth maintains that he remained faithful to Kierkegaard's main intention: the radical suspicion of theology's persistent temptations to "make the scriptural message innocuous" by blurring the infinite qualitative distinction and playing down the absolute claims of the Gospel (p. 98). However, Kierkegaard's voice became more and more muted in Barth's writings because of three questionable tendencies: 1) Kierkegaard's *negations* too easily became a law, hiding the Gospel of God's free grace; 2) he was too individualistic; and 3) he laid the groundwork for a new anthropocentric system which was simply a continuation of Schleiermacher's turning theology into anthropology (pp. 99–100). While Kierkegaard was good seasoning, the theological "food" that Barth had to discover beyond Kierkegaard was that "primarily, the Gospel is the glad news of God's 'yes' to man" (p. 101). See also "Kierkegaard and the Theologians" in *Fragments Grave and Gay*, pp. 102–104. See also Colin Gunton, "Karl Barth and the Western Intellectual Tradition", in Thompson, pp. 285–301 (pp. 295–297).
111. "There is no such thing as 'theological existence'; there is only theological *thinking* and *believing* existence" (*The Christian Doctrine of God*, p. 84). See also *Eternal Hope*, pp. 215–216; *The Christian Doctrine of the Church*, pp. 212–213.
112. For Brunner, these stages translated as speculative Idealism, to Kantianism, to Christianity.
113. See "Spiritual Autobiography", p. 241. Hermann Diem maintains that this is a fundamental misunderstanding of Kierkegaard ("Zur Psychologie der Kierkegaard-Renaissance", *ZZ*, 10 (1932), 216–248 (pp. 223–224)). See also Cochrane, p. 69; Schrader, pp. 112–113.
114. *Philosophy of Religion*, p. 51; "Missionary Theology", p. 817.
115. Jüngel, "Von Dialektik zur Analogie", pp. 142–143. A single quote from Kierkegaard indicates how both Barth and Brunner drew faithfully, if one-sidedly, from him: "The Christian cause is in need of no *defense*, it is not served by any *defense*—it is *aggressive*; to defend it is of all misrepresentations the most inexcusable, it is *unconscious crafty treachery*. Christianity is aggressive; in Christendom, as a matter of course, it attacks from behind" (*Christian Discourses, etc.*, trans. by Walter Lowrie

(Oxford: Oxford University Press, 1940), p. 168).

116. However, see Barth's comments against a *via negativa* in "The Problem of Ethics Today", p. 140.

117. "Reply to Interpretation", p. 329.

118. See the August 1920 Obstalden visit. Compare "Unsettled Questions for Theology Today" with *Experience, Knowledge and Faith.*

119. See *Barth–Brunner*, EB: January 5, 1922 (#32), pp. 68–72; "The Limits of Humanity".

120. See the 1924 Pany visit. Compare *The Göttingen Dogmatics* with "Revelation and Law", *Christian Dogmatics* with *Philosophy of Religion* and *The Mediator* (Part I). See also *Man in Revolt*, pp. 514–515.

121. See the 1929 Bergli meeting. Compare "Fate and Idea" and "Theology and Modern Man" with "The Other Task of Theology" and *God and Man.*

122. *Barth–Brunner*, EB: December 13, 1932 (#82), pp. 210–212; KB: January 2, 1933 (#83), pp. 213–217; EB: January 16, 1933 (#84), pp. 217–222.

123. See the October 1933 Zurich meeting. Compare "The First Commandment" and "No!" with *Nature and Grace.*

124. See the 1936 Auenstein conference. Compare "Church of Group Movement?" with *The Church and the Oxford Group.*

125. Ebner was the conceptual key for Brunner, because "dialogue" staked out a ground between continuity and discontinuity.

126. *Barth–Brunner*, KB: October 24, 1930 (#81), p. 209.

127. Traditional views of Brunner's development identify three periods, e.g. pre-critical (1914–1920); dialectical (1921–1928), eristic (1929–1937) (Salakka, Scheld).

128. The years 1923–1927 should be understood as years when Brunner let dialectic control his *expression*, but not his *thinking.*

129. *Contra* Roessler, pp. 32–33.

130. Before Ebner's *The Word of God and Spiritual Realities* (1921), Neo-Kantianism's concepts of *Ursprung* [origin] and *Geist* [spirit] supplied this continuity.

131. *Contra* Scheld, p. 220.

132. "How I Changed My Mind, 1928–1938", p. 37. Thus: revelation is always God's act, always a miracle, always new, always controlled by God, both hiding and revealing God. Thus: justification and sanctification are acts of God on behalf of humanity, not experiences human beings possess. Thus: God acts "on behalf of us" rather than "in us". Thus: ethics consist of God's command alone, for if humanity is the ethical decision-maker, God is not Lord of the ethical event. Thus: Church and the Christian life are not static possessions, and they only become visible by God's sovereign action.

133. "Gottes Gnadenwahl", *ThExh*, 47 (1936).

134. "The Being of God as the One Who Loves in Freedom" (*CD* II/1/§28).

135. *Barth–Brunner*, EB: July 1, 1935 (#110), pp. 286–288.

136. Cf. Gestrich, *Neuzeitliches Denken*, p. 39.

137. Rolf Ahlers, *The Community of Freedom* (Bern: Peter Lang, 1989), pp. 58–59.

BIBLIOGRAPHY

Works by Karl Barth

Correspondence

Karl Barth: Letters, 1961–1968, trans. by Geoffrey W. Bromiley from the 2nd German edn (1978) (Grand Rapids: Eerdmans, 1981).

Karl Barth: Offene Briefe, 1945–1968, ed. by Diether Koch (Zurich: Theologischer Verlag, 1984).

With Emil Brunner, *Karl Barth–Emil Brunner Briefwechsel, 1916–1966*, ed. by Eberhard Busch (Zurich: Theologischer Verlag, 2000).

With Rudolf Bultmann, *Karl Barth–Rudolf Bultmann: Letters, 1922–1966*, trans. by Geoffrey W. Bromiley (Grand Rapids: Eerdmans, 1981).

With Eduard Thurneysen, *Karl Barth–Eduard Thurneysen Briefwechsel*, ed. by Eduard Thurneysen, 2 vols (Zuirch: Theologischer Verlag, 1973, 1974).

With Eduard Thurneysen, *Revolutionary Theology in the Making*, trans. by James D. Smart (Richmond: John Knox, 1964).

Collections

Against the Stream, ed. by Roland Gregor Smith, trans. by E.M. Delacour and Stanley Goodman (London: SCM, 1954).

Fragments Grave and Gay, ed. by H. Martin Rumscheidt (London: Collins, 1971).

The Humanity of God, trans. by Thomas Weiser and others (Atlanta: John Knox Press, 1960).

Karl Barth: How I Changed My Mind, ed. by John Godsey (Richmond: John Knox, 1966).

Theology and Church (London: SCM, 1962).

Vorträge und kleinere Arbeiten, 1922–1925, ed. by Holger Finze (Zurich: Theologischer Verlag, 1990).

The Word of God and the Word of Man, trans. by Douglas Horton (London: Hodder and Stoughton, 1928).

With Emil Brunner, *Natural Theology*, trans. by Peter Fraenkel (London: Centenary Press, 1946).

Rumscheidt, H. Martin, ed., *The Way of Theology in Karl Barth*, trans. by George Hunsinger and others (Allison Park, PA: Pickwick, 1986).

Individual Works

"Abschied", *Zwischen den Zeiten*, 11 (1933), 536–544.

"An Answer to Professor von Harnack's open letter" in Rumscheidt, *Adolf von Harnack*, pp. 95–105.

Anselm: Fides Quaerens Intellectum, trans. by Ian W. Robertson (Cleveland: World, 1960).

"Autobiographical Sketches of Karl Barth from the faculty albums…at Münster and Bonn", in *Karl Barth–Rudolf Bultmann: Letters*, pp. 151–158.

"Biblical Questions, Insights and Vistas", in *The Word of God and the Word of Man*, pp. 51–96.

"Brunners Schleiermacherbuch", *Zwischen den Zeiten*, VIII (1924), 49–64.

Credo, no translator given (New York: Scribners, 1962).

"The Christian Community in the Midst of Political Change", in *Against the Stream*, pp. 51–124.

The Christian Life: Church Dogmatics IV,4, trans. by Geoffrey W. Bromiley (Grand Rapids: Eerdmans, 1981).

The Christian Life, trans. by J. Strathearn McNab (London: SCM 1930).

"The Christian's Place in Society", in *The Word of God and the Word of Man*, pp. 272–327 (p. 282).

Die christliche Dogmatik im Entwurf, Erster Band: Die Lehre vom Worte Gottes, Prolegomena zur christlichen Dogmatik, ed. by Gerhard Sauter (Zurich: Theologischer Verlag, 1982).

The Church and the Churches (Grand Rapids: Eerdmans, 1936).

Church Dogmatics, ed. by G.W. Bromiley and T.F. Torrance (Edinburgh: T&T Clark).
Volume I: *The Doctrine of the Word of God*
    I/1: 2nd ed, trans. by G.W. Bromiley, 1975.
    I/2: trans. by G.T. Thomson and Harold Knight, 1956.
Volume II: *The Doctrine of God*
    II/1: trans. by T.H.L. Parker and others, 1957.
    II/2: trans. by T.H.L. Parker and others, 1957.
Volume III: *The Doctrine of Creation*
    III/1: trans. by J.W. Edwards and others, 1958.
    III/2: trans. by Harold Knight and others, 1960.
    III/4: trans. by A.T. Mackay and others, 1961.
Volume IV: *The Doctrine of Reconciliation*
    IV/1: trans. by G.W. Bromiley, 1956.
    IV/2: trans. by G.W. Bromiley, 1958.
    IV/3: trans. by G.W. Bromiley, first half 1961, second half 1962.
    IV/4 (*Fragment*): trans. by G.W. Bromiley, 1969.

"Church or Group Movement?", *The London Quarterly and Holborn Review*, 162 (1937), 1–10.

"Concluding Unscientific Postscript on Schleiermacher", in *The Theology of Schleiermacher*, pp. 261–279.

"Das Eine Notwendige", *Die XX. Christliche Studenten-Konferenz* (Aarau, 1916) (Bern: Franke, 1916), pp. 5–15.

The Epistle to the Romans, trans. by Edwyn C. Hoskyns, 6th edn (London: Oxford University Press, 1933).

Ethics, trans. by Geoffrey W. Bromiley (New York: Seabury, 1981).

"Evangelical Theology in the 19th Century", trans. by Thomas Wieser, in *The Humanity of God*, pp. 11–33.

"Fate and Idea in Theology", in *The Way of Theology in Karl Barth*, ed. by Rumscheidt, pp. 25–61.

"The First Commandment as an Axiom of Theology", in *The Way of Theology in Karl Barth*, ed. by Rumscheidt, pp. 63–78.

"Foreword", in Heppe, *Reformed Dogmatics*, pp. v–vii.

"Für die Freiheit der Evangeliums", *Theologische Existenz heute*, 2 (1933).

God in Action, trans. by Elmer G. Homrighausen and Karl J. Ernst (Manhasset, NY: Round Table, 1963), pp. 3–57.

"Gospel and Law", in *God, Grace and Gospel*, trans. by James Strathearn McNab, Scottish Journal of Theology Occasional Papers, 8 (Edinburgh: Oliver and Boyd, 1959), pp. 3–27.

"Gottes Gnadenwahl", *Theologische Existenz heute*, 47 (1936).

"Gottes Wille und unsere Wünsche", *Theologische Existenz heute*, 7 (1934).

The Göttingen Dogmatics, trans. by Geoffrey W. Bromiley, 2 vols (Grand Rapids: Eerdmans, 1991–).

"Das Halten der Gebote", *Zwischen den Zeiten*, 5 (1927), 206–227.

The Holy Ghost and the Christian Life, trans. by R. Birch Hoyle (London: Frederick Muller, 1929).

"How I Changed My Mind, 1928–1938", in *Karl Barth: How I Changed My Mind*, pp. 37–49.

"How I Changed My Mind, 1938–1948", in *Karl Barth: How I Changed My Mind*, pp. 50–60.

"The Humanity of God", in *The Humanity of God*, pp. 37–65.

"Introduction", in *Revolutionary Theology in the Making*, pp. 65–73.

"Karl Barth's Reply", in *Against the Stream*, pp. 113–118.

"Kierkegaard and the Theologians", in *Fragments Grave and Gay*, pp. 102–104.

"Die Kirche Jesu Christi", *Theologische Existenz heute*, 5 (1933).

The Knowledge of God and the Service of God: According to the Teaching of the Reformation, trans. by J.L.M. Hare and Ian Henderson (London: Hodder and Stoughton, 1938).

"Menschenwort und Gotteswort in der christlichen Predigt", *Zwischen den Zeiten*, 3 (1925), 119–140.

"The Need and Promise of Christian Preaching", in *The Word of God and the Word of Man*, pp. 97–135.

"No! Answer to Emil Brunner", in *Natural Theology*, pp. 65–128.

"Die Not der Evangelischen Kirche", *Zwischen den Zeiten*, 9 (1931), 89–122.

"Die Notwendigkeit der Theologie bei Anselm von Canterbury", *Zeitschrift für Theologie und Kirche*, N.F. 12 (1931), 350–358.

"Der Pfarrer, der es den Leuten recht macht", *Christliche Welt*, 30 (1916), 262–267.

"Philosophy and Theology", in *The Way of Theology in Karl Barth*, ed. by Rumscheidt, pp. 79–95.

"The Principles of Dogmatics according to Wilhelm Herrmann", in *Theology and Church*, pp. 238–271.

"The Problem of Ethics Today", in *The Word of God and the Word of Man*, pp. 136–182.

Protestant Theology in the Nineteenth Century, trans. by Brian Cozens and others, (London: SCM Press, 1959).

"Questions Which 'Christianity' Must Face", *Student World*, 25 (1932), 93–100.

"Quousque tandem...?", *Zwischen den Zeiten*, 8 (1930), 1–6.

"Rechtfertigung und Heiligung", *Zwischen den Zeiten*, 5 (1927), 281–309.

"The Righteousness of God", in *The Word of God and the Word of Man*, pp. 9–27.

"Roman Catholicism: a Question to the Protestant Church", in *Theology and Church*, 307–333.

Der Römerbrief, ed. by Hermann Schmidt, 1st edn (Zurich: Theologischer Verlag, 1985).

"Schleiermacher", in *Theology and Church*, pp. 159–199.

"Schleiermacher's *Celebration of Christmas*", in *Theology and Church*, pp. 136–158.

"The Strange New World of the Bible", in *The Word of God and the Word of Man*, pp. 28–50.

"A Thank You and a Bow", trans. by Eric Mosbacher, in *Fragments Grave and Gay*, pp. 95–101.

"Theological Declaration of Barmen", in Ahlers, *The Barmen Theological Declaration of 1934*, pp. 124–129.

Theological Existence Today!, trans. by R. Birch Hoyle (London: Hodder & Stoughton, 1933).

"Die Theologie und der heutige Mensch", *Zwischen den Zeiten*, 8 (1930), 374–396.

"Die Theologie und die Mission in der Gegenwart", *Zwischen den Zeiten*, 10 (1932), 189–215.

The Theology of Schleiermacher, trans. by Geoffrey W. Bromiley (Grand Rapids: Eerdmans, 1982).

"Unsettled Questions for Theology Today", in *Theology and Church*, pp. 55–73.

"The Word of God and the Task of the Ministry", in *The Word of God and the Word of Man*, pp. 183–217.

With Eduard Thurneysen, *Suchet Gott, so werdet ihr leben!* (Bern: G.A. Bäschlin, 1917).

Works by Emil Brunner

Collections
Ein offenes Wort: Vorträge und Aufsätze, 1917–1962, ed. by Rudolf Wehrli, 2 vols (Zurich: Theologischer Verlag, 1981).

Individual Works
"Die andere Aufgabe der Theologie", *Zwischen den Zeiten*, 7 (1929), 255–276.

"Antwort an Herrn Heinrich Marti", *Neue Wege*, 30 (1936), 70–72.

"Banalität oder Irrlehre? Zum Problem der Anthropologie und des Anknüpfungspunkt", *Kirchenblatt für die reformierte Schweiz*, 96 (1940), 260–265.

"Die Botschaft Søren Kierkegaard", in *Ein offenes Wort*, I, pp. 209–226.

The Christian Doctrine of Creation and Redemption, trans. by Olive Wyon (Philadelphia: Westminster, 1952).

The Christian Doctrine of God, trans. by Olive Wyon (London: Lutterworth, 1949).

The Christian Doctrine of the Church, Faith, and the Consummation, trans. by David Cairns (Philadelphia: Westminster, 1962).

Christianity and Civilisation, 2 vols (London: Nisbet, 1948–1949).

"Christlicher Existentialismus", in *Ein offenes Wort*, II, pp. 318–334.

The Church and the Oxford Group, trans. by David Cairns (London: Hodder & Stoughton, 1937).

"Comments by Brunner", in Hesselink, I. John, "Encounter in Japan: Emil Brunner—An Interpretation", *Reformed Review*, 9 (1956), 12–33 (pp. 32–33).

The Divine Imperative, trans. by Olive Wyon (Philadelphia: Westminster, 1947).

"Das Elend der Theologie", *Kirchenblatt für die reformierte Schweiz*, 35 (1920), 197–199, 201–203.

"The Epistle to the Romans by Karl Barth: An Up-to-Date, Unmodern Paraphrase", in *The Beginnings of Dialectical Theology*, ed. by Robinson, pp. 63–71.

Erlebnis, Erkenntnis und Glaube, 2nd rev. edn (Tübingen: J.C.B. Mohr, 1923).

Eternal Hope, translated by Harold Knight (London: Lutterworth, 1954).

"Die Frage nach dem «Anknüpfungspunkt» als Problem der Theologie", *Zwischen den Zeiten*, 10 (1932), 505–532.

"Geist", *Gemeindeblatt für die reformierten Kirchgemeinden des Kantons Glarus*, 3:6 (1916).

"Gemeinschaft", in *Ein offenes Wort*, I, pp. 326–332.

"Gesetz und Offenbarung: Eine theologische Grundlegung", *Theologische Blätter*, 4 (1925), 53–58.

"Gnosis und Glaube", in *Philosophie und Offenbarung* (Tübingen: J.C.B. Mohr, 1925), pp. 29–48.

God and Man, trans. by David Cairns (London: SCM, 1936).

"Die Grenzen der Humanität", in *Ein offenes Wort*, I, pp. 76–97.

Das Grundproblem der Ethik (Zurich: Rascher & Cie. A.-G., 1931).

"Das Grundproblem der Philosophie bei Kant und Kierkegaard", *Zwischen den Zeiten*, VI (1924), 31–46.

"Grundsätzliches zum Kapitel 'Die Jungen Theologen'", *Kirchenblatt für die reformierte Schweiz*, 31 (1916), 57–59.

"Die Gruppenbewegung als Frage an die Kirche", in *Um die Erneuerung der Kirche* (Bern: Gotthelf, 1934), pp. 32–51.

"Intellectual Autobiography of Emil Brunner", trans. by Keith Chamberlain, in *The Theology of Emil Brunner*, ed. by Kegley, pp. 3–20.

"Ist die sogenannte kritische Theologie wirklich kritische?" *Kirchenblatt für die reformierte Schweiz*, 36 (1921), 101–102, 105–106.

Justice and Freedom in Society (Tokyo: Institute of Educational Research and Service, 1955).

Justice and the Social Order, trans. by Mary Hottinger (London: Harper, 1945).

"Die Kirche als Frage und Aufgabe der Gegenwart", in *Um die Erneuerung der Kirche* (Bern: Gotthelf, 1934), pp. 5–31.

"Konservativ oder Radical?", *Neue Wege*, 12:2 (1918).

"Die Krisis der Religion", *Kirchenblatt für die reformierte Schweiz*, 37 (1922), 65–66.

Man in Revolt, trans. by Olive Wyon (Philadelphia: Westminster, 1939).

The Mediator, trans. by Olive Wyon from the 2nd (unaltered) edn (London: Lutterworth,

1934).

"Meine Begegnung mit der Oxforder Gruppenbewegung", in *Ein offenes Wort*, I, pp. 268–288.

The Misunderstanding of the Church, trans. by Harold Knight (London: The Lutterworth Press, 1952).

Die Mystik und das Wort (Tübingen: J.C.B. Mohr, 1924; 2nd edn, 1928).

Natur und Gnade, 2nd edn (Tübingen: JCB Mohr, 1935).

"Nature and Grace", (1st edn), in Natural Theology, pp. 15–64.

"The New Barth", trans. by John C. Campbell, *Scottish Journal of Theology*, 4 (1951), 123–35

"Die Offenbarung als Grund und Gegenstand der Theologie", in *Ein offenes Wort*, I, pp. 98–122.

"An Open Letter to Karl Barth", in *Against the Stream*, pp. 106–113.

Our Faith, trans. by John W. Rilling (New York: Scribners, 1954).

The Philosophy of Religion From the Standpoint of Protestant Theology, trans. by A.J.D. Farrer and Bertram Lee Woolf (New York: Scribners, 1937).

"The Predicament of the Church To-day", in *The Predicament of the Church*, (London: Lutterworth, 1944), pp. 82–99.

"The Present-Day Task of Theology", *Religion in Life*, 8 (1939), 176–186.

Reformation und Romantik (Munich: Chr. Kaiser, 1925).

"Reply to Interpretation and Criticism", trans. by Marle Hoyle Schroeder, in *The Theology of Emil Brunner*, ed. by Kegley, pp. 325–352.

Revelation and Reason, trans. by Olive Wyon (Philadelphia: Westminster, 1946).

"Rezension von: Friedrich Karl Schumann, «Der Gottesgedanke und der Zerfall der Moderne»", *Kirchenblatt für die reformierte Schweiz*, 85 (1929), 317.

"Secularism as a Problem for the Church", *International Review of Missions*, 19 (1930), 495–511.

"A Spiritual Autobiography", *Japan Christian Quarterly*, 21 (1955), 238–244.

Das Symbolische in der religiösen Erkenntnis, (Tübingen: J.C.B. Mohr, 1914).

"Theologie und Kirche", *Zwischen den Zeiten*, 8 (1930), 397–420.

The Theology of Crisis (New York: Scribners, 1929).

"Toward a Missionary Theology (How I Changed My Mind)", *Christian Century*, 66 (1949), 816–818.

Truth as Encounter: A New Edition, trans. by Amandus W. Loos and David Cairns (London: SCM, 1964).

"A Unique Christian Mission: The Mukyokai ('Non-Church') Movement in Japan", in *Religion and Culture: Essays in Honor of Paul Tillich*, ed. by W. Leibrecht (New York: Harper, 1959), pp. 287–290.

Von den Ordnungen Gottes (Bern: Gotthelf-Verlag, 1929).

"Was ist und was will die sogenannte Oxford-Gruppe?" *Zwinglikalender* (1935), 48–50.

"Was ist und was will die sogenannte Oxford-Gruppenbewegung?", unpublished article, Emil Brunner-Stiftung, Zurich.

Vom Werk des Heiligen Geistes (Tübingen: J.C.B. Mohr, 1935).

The Word and the World (London: SCM, 1931).

The Word of God and Modern Man, trans. by David Cairns (London: Epworth, 1965)

"Der Zorn Gottes und die Versöhnung durch Christus", *Zwischen den Zeiten*, 5 (1927), 93–115.

Works by Others

Ahlers, Rolf, *The Barmen Theological Declaration of 1934: The Archeology of a Confessional Text* (Lewiston, NY: Edwin Mellen, 1986).

_____, *The Community of Freedom: Barth and Presuppositionless Theology* (Bern: Peter Lang, 1989).

Allen, Diogenes, *Philosophy for Understanding Theology* (Atlanta: John Knox, 1985).

Allen, Edgar L., *Creation and Grace: A guide to the thought of Emil Brunner* (New York: The Philosophical Library, 1951).

Allen, G.F., "The Groups in Oxford", in *The Groups in Oxford*, ed. by R.H.S. Crossman (Oxford: Basil Blackwell, 1934), pp. 1–41.

Baillie, John, "Introduction", in *Natural Theology* (London: Centenary, 1946) , pp. 5–12.

Barr, James, "La Foi Biblique et la Théologie Naturelle", *Études Théologiques et Religieuses*, 64 (1989), 355–368.

Barth, Peter, "Das Problem der natürlichen Theologie bei Calvin", *Theologische Existenz heute*, 18 (1935).

Beck, Lewis White, "Neo-Kantianism", in *The Encyclopedia of Philosophy*, ed. by Paul Edwards, 8 vols (London: Collier-Macmillan, 1967), V, pp. 468–473.

Becker, Dieter, *Karl Barth und Martin Buber: Denker in dialogischer Nachbarschaft?* (Göttingen: Vandenhoeck & Ruprecht, 1986).

Beintker, Michael, *Die Dialektik in der "dialektischen Theologie" Karl Barths*, Beiträge zur evangelischen Theologie, 101 (Munich: Chr. Kaiser Verlag, 1987).

Berghahn, V.R., *Modern Germany: Society, economy and politics in the twentieth century*, 2nd edn (Cambridge: Cambridge University Press, 1987).

Berkouwer, G.C., *The Triumph of Grace in the Theology of Karl Barth*, trans. by Harry R. Boer (Grand Rapids: Eerdmans, 1954).

Bethge, Eberhard, *Dietrich Bonhoeffer*, trans. by Eric Mosbacher and others (New York: Harper, 1970).

Biggar, Nigel, "Hearing God's Command and Thinking about What's Right: With and Beyond Barth", in *Reckoning with Barth: Essays in Commemoration of the Centenary of Karl Barth's Birth*, ed. by Biggar (London: Mowbray, 1988), pp. 101–118.

Bixler, J.C., "Emil Brunner as a Representative of the Theology of Crisis", *Journal of Re-*

ligion, 9 (1929), 446–459.

Blum, Jerome, and others, eds., *The European World: A History*, 2nd edn (Boston: Little, Brown, 1970).

Bohlin, Torsten, "Luther, Kierkegaard und die dialektische Theologie", übersetzt von Anne Marie Sundwall-Honer, *Zeitschrift für Theologie und Kirche*, N.F. 7 (1926), 163–198, 268–279.

Bohren, Rudolf, *Prophetie und Seelsorge: Eduard Thurneysen* (Vluyn: Neukirchener Verlag, 1982).

Bonhoeffer, Dietrich, "Die Geschichte der systematischen Theologie des 20. Jahrhunderts", in *Gesammelte Schriften*, ed. by Eberhard Bethge, 6 vols (Munich: Chr. Kaiser, 1958–1974), V, pp. 181–227.

Bouillard, Henri, *Karl Barth: Genèse et Évolution de la théologie dialectique* (Aubier: Éditions Montaigne, 1957).

Bromiley, Geoffrey W., "The Abiding Significance of Karl Barth", in *Theology Beyond Christendom*, ed. by Thompson pp. 331–350.

Brown, Colin, *Karl Barth and the Christian Message* (Downers Grove, IL: IVP, 1966).

Brunner, Hans Heinrich, *Mein Vater und Sein Ältester*, (Zurich: Theologischer Verlag, 1986).

Brunner-Gutekunst, Lilo, Interview with John W. Hart, January 13, 1992, Erlenbach, Switzerland.

Brunner-Gutekunst, Lilo, Letter to John W. Hart, January 10, 1993.

Buber, Martin, *I and Thou*, 2nd edn, trans. by Roland Gregor Smith (New York: Collier-Macmillan, 1958).

Buchman, Frank N.D., *Remaking the World* (London: Blanford, 1947).

Busch, Eberhard, "Dialectical Theology: Karl Barth's Reveille", trans. by H. Martin Rumscheidt, *Canadian Journal of Theology*, 16 (1970), 165–74.

_____, *Karl Barth: His Life from Letters and Autobiographical Texts*, trans. by John Bowden from the 2nd rev edn (London: SCM, 1976).

_____, "Karl Barth's understanding of the church a witness", *Saint Luke's Journal of Theology*, 33 (1989–1990), 87–101.

Butler, William W., "A Comparison of the Ethics of Emil Brunner and Dietrich Bonhoeffer with Special Attention to the Orders of Creation and the Mandates" (unpublished doctoral thesis, Emory University, 1970).

Cairns, David, "Introduction", in Brunner, *God and Man*, pp. 9–37.

_____, "The Theology of Brunner", *Scottish Journal of Theology*, 1 (1948), 294–308.

Campo, Mariano, "Natorp", trans. by Robert M. Connolly, in *The Encyclopedia of Philosophy*, ed. by Paul Edwards, 8 vols (London: Collier-Macmillan, 1967), V, pp. 445–448.

Clark, Walter H., *The Oxford Group: Its History and Significance* (New York: Bookman Associates, 1951).

Cochrane, Arthur C., *The Church's Confession under Hitler* (Philadelphia: Westminster, 1962).

Collins, Alice, "Barth's relationship to Schleiermacher: A Re-assessment", *Studies in Religion*, 17 (1988), 213–224.

Copleston, Frederick, *A History of Philosophy*, 9 vols (London: Burns, Oates & Washbourne, 1946–1975).

Crawford, Robert, "The Theological Method of Karl Barth", *Scottish Journal of Theology*, 25 (1972), 320–336.

Crimmann, Ralph P., *Karl Barths frühe Publikationen und ihre Rezeption*, Basler und Berner Studien zur historischen und systematischen Theologie, 45 (Bern: Peter Lang, 1981).

Davison, James E., "Can God Speak a Word to Man?: Barth's Critique of Schleiermacher's Theology", *Scottish Journal of Theology*, 37 (1984), 189–211.

Diem, Hermann, "Zur Psychologie der Kierkegaard-Renaissance", *Zwischen den Zeiten*, 10 (1932), 216–248.

Driberg, Tom, *The Mystery of Moral Re-Armament: A Study of Frank Buchman and His Movement* (London: Secker & Warburg, 1964).

Duke, James O., and Robert F. Streetman, eds., *Barth and Schleiermacher: Beyond the Impasse?* (Philadelphia: Fortress, 1988).

Ebner, Ferdinand, *Das Wort und die geistigen Realitäten*, in *Schriften*, ed. by Franz Seyr, 3 vols (Munich: Kösel, 1963–1965), I, pp. 75–342.

Fischer, Hermann, "Natürliche Theologie im Wandel", *Zeitschrift für Theologie und Kirche*, 80 (1983), 85–102.

Fisher, Simon, *Revelatory Positivism? Barth's Earliest Theology and the Marburg School*, Oxford Theological Monographs (Oxford: Oxford University Press, 1988).

Ford, David F., "Conclusion: Assessing Barth", in *Karl Barth: Studies in His Theological Method*, ed. by Sykes, pp. 194–201.

Fraser, David Allen, "Foundations for Christian Social Ethics: Karl Barth's Christological Anthropology and the Social Sciences" (unpublished doctoral thesis, Vanderbuilt University, 1986).

Frei, Hans, "Niebuhr's Theological Background", in *Faith and Ethics: The Theology of H. Richard Niebuhr*, ed. by Paul Ramsey (New York: Harper and Row, 1957), pp. 9–64.

Fuchs, Ernst, "Theologie und Metaphysik", *Zwischen den Zeiten*, 11 (1933), 315–326.

Furuya,Y.C., "Apologetic or Kerygmatic Theology?", *Theology Today*, 16 (1960), 471–80.

Gestrich, Christof, *Neuzeitliches Denken and die Spaltung der dialektischen Theologie: Zur Frage der natürlichen Theologie*, Beiträge zur historischen Theologie, 52 (Tübingen: J.C.B. Mohr, 1977).

_____, "Die unbewältigte natürliche Theologie", *Zeitschrift für Theologie und Kirche*, 68 (1971), 82–120.

Gill, Theodore A., "Emil Brunner as Teacher and Preacher", in *The Theology of Emil Brunner*, ed. by Kegley, pp. 305–321.

Godsey, John D., "Barth's Life Until 1928", in *Karl Barth: How I Changed My Mind*, pp. 17–33.

Goeters, J.F. Gerhard, "Karl Barth in Bonn, 1930–1935", *Evangelische Theologie*, 47 (1987), 137–150.

Gogarten, Friedrich, *Glaube und Wirklichkeit* (Jena: Eugen Diederichs, 1928).

_____, *Ich glaube an den dreieinigen Gott* (Jena: Eugen Diederichs, 1926).

_____, "Karl Barths Dogmatik", *Theologische Rundschau*, N.F. 1 (1929), 60–80.

_____, "Die Krisis unserer Kultur", *Christliche Welt*, 34 (1920), 770–777, 786–791.

_____, "Das Problem einer theologischen Anthropologie", *Zwischen den Zeiten*, 7 (1929), 493–511.

_____, *Die religiöse Entscheidung* (Jena: Eugen Diederichs, 1921).

_____, "Staat und Kirche", *Zwischen den Zeiten*, 10 (1932), 390–410.

Gollwitzer, Helmut, "Zur Einheit von Gesetz und Evangelium", in *Antwort,* ed. by Wolf and others, pp. 287–309.

Graby, James K., "The Significance of Friedrich Schleiermacher in the Development of the Theology of Emil Brunner, with Special Attention to the Early Period (1914–1929)" (unpublished doctoral thesis, Drew University, 1966).

Grass, Hans, "Karl Barth und Marburg", in *Aus Theologie und Kirche* (Marburg: N.G. Elwert, 1988), pp. 212–221.

Green, Clifford, "Karl Barth's Life and Theology", in *Karl Barth: Theologian of Freedom*, ed. by Green (London: Collins, 1989), pp. 11–45.

Gunton, Colin, "Karl Barth and the Western Intellectual Tradition", in *Theology Beyond Christendom*, ed. by Thompson, pp. 285–301.

Hamer, Jerome, *Karl Barth*, trans. by Dominic M. Maruca (Westminster, MD: Newman, 1962).

Hartwell, Herbert H., *The Theology of Karl Barth: An Introduction* (Philadelphia: Westminster, 1964).

Hauge, Reidar, "Truth as Encounter", trans. by I. John Hesselink, in *The Theology of Emil Brunner*, ed. by Kegley, pp. 133–154.

Heideman, E.P., *The Relation of Revelation and Reason in E. Brunner and H. Bavinck* (Assen, Netherlands: Koninklijke Van Gorcum, 1959).

Hendry, George S., "Appraisal of Brunner's Theology", *Theology Today*, 19 (1963), 523–31.

_____, "The Transcendental Method in the Theology of Karl Barth", *Scottish Journal of Theology*, 37 (1984), 213–227.

Heppe, Heinrich, *Reformed Dogmatics*, trans. by G.T. Thomson (Grand Rapids: Baker, 1978).

Heron, Alasdair I.C., "Barth, Schleiermacher and the Task of Dogmatics", in *Theology Beyond Christendom*, ed. by Thompson, pp. 267–283.

Hesselink, I. John, "Emil Brunner: A Centennial Perspective", *Christian Century*, 106 (1989), 1171–1174.

_____, "Karl Barth and Emil Brunner: A Tangled Tale with a Happy Ending (or, The Story of a Relationship)", in *How Karl Barth Changed My Mind*, ed. by Donald K. McKim (Grand Rapids: Eerdmans, 1986), pp. 131–142.

Humphrey, J. Edward, *Emil Brunner* (Waco, TX: Word, 1976).

Hunsinger, George, "Beyond literalism and expressivism", *Modern Theology*, 3 (1987), 209–223.

_____, *How to Read Karl Barth: The Shape of His Theology* (Oxford: Oxford University Press, 1991).

Jensen, Maud Keister, "The Missionary Motif in the Theology of Emil Brunner and its relation to specific doctrines" (unpublished doctoral thesis, Drew University, 1978).

Jenson, Robert W., "Karl Barth", in *The Modern Theologians*, ed. by David F. Ford, 2 vols (Oxford: Blackwell, 1989), I, pp. 23–49.

Jersild, Paul, "Natural Theology and the Doctrine of God in Albert Ritschl and Karl Barth", *Lutheran Quarterly*, 14 (1962), 239–257.

Jewett, Paul K., "Ebnerian Personalism and its influence on Emil Brunner's Theology", *Westminster Theological Journal*, 14 (1951–1952), 113–147.

_____, *Emil Brunner's Concept of Revelation* (London: James Clarke, 1954).

Johnson, Wendell G., "Soteriology as a function of epistemology in the thought of Emil

Brunner" (unpublished doctoral thesis, Rice University, 1989).

Josuttis, Manfred, *Die Gegenständlichkeit der Offenbarung: Karl Barths Anselm-Buch und die Denkform seiner Theologie* (Bonn: H. Bouvier, 1965).

Jüngel, Eberhard, *Karl Barth: A Theological Legacy*, trans. by Garrett E. Paul (Philadelphia: Westminster, 1986): "Barth's Life and Work", pp. 22–52; "Gospel and Law", pp. 105–126; "Barth's Theological Beginnings", pp. 53–104.

_____, "Von der Dialektik zur Analogie: Die Schule Kierkegaards und der Einspruch Petersons", in *Barth-Studien* (Zurich-Cologne: Benziger Verlag, 1982), 127–179.

Kegley, Charles W., "Special Introduction", in *The Theology of Emil Brunner*, ed. by Kegley, pp. xi–xiv.

Kegley, Charles W., ed., *The Theology of Emil Brunner* (New York: Macmillan, 1962).

Kelsey, David H., *The Uses of Scripture in Recent Theology* (Philadelphia: Fortress, 1975).

Kierkegaard, Søren, *Christian Discourses, etc.*, trans. by Walter Lowrie (Oxford: Oxford University Press, 1940).

_____, *Fear and Trembling and Sickness unto Death*, trans. by Walter Lowrie, 2nd edn (Princeton: Princeton University Press, 1954).

Koch, T., "Natur und Gnade: Zur neuren Diskussion", *Kerygma und Dogma*, 16 (1970), 171–187.

Konrad, Johanna, "Zum Problem der philosophischen Grundlegung bei Emil Brunner", *Zeitschrift für Theologie und Kirche*, N.F. 12 (1931), 192–216.

Kreck, Walter, *Grundentscheidungen in Karl Barths Dogmatik* (Neukirchen-Vluyn: Neukirchener Verlag, 1978).

Küng, Hans, "Karl Barth and the postmodern paradigm", *Princeton Seminary Bulletin*, n.s. 9 (1988), 8–31.

Kutter, Hermann, *Das Unmittelbare* (Berlin, 1902).

Lange, Peter, *Konkrete Theologie? Karl Barth und Friedrich Gogarten «Zwischen den Zeiten» (1922–1933)* (Zurich: Theologischer Verlag, 1972).

Lean, Garth, *Frank Buchman: A Life* (London: Constable, 1985).

Lehmann, Paul L., "The Changing Course of a Corrective Theology", *Theology Today*, 13 (1956), 332–357.

Leipold, Heinrich, *Missionarische Theologie: Emil Brunners theologischen Anthropologie* (Göttingen: Vandenhoeck & Ruprecht, 1974).

Link, Wilhelm, "«Anknüpfung», «Vorverständnis» und die Frage der «Theologischen Anthropologie»", *Theologische Rundschau*, 7 (1935), 205–254.

Livingston, James C., *Modern Christian Thought: From the Enlightenment to Vatican II* (New York: Macmillan, 1971).

Lovin, Robin W., *Christian Faith and Public Choices: the Social Ethics of Barth, Brunner and Bonhoeffer* (Philadelphia: Fortress, 1984).

Lowe, W., "Barth as Critic of Dualism: Re-Reading the Römerbrief", *Scottish Journal of Theology*, 41 (1988), 377–395.

Lütz, Dietmar, *Homo Viator: Karl Barths Ringen mit Schleiermacher* (Zurich: Theologischer Verlag, 1988).

MacKintosh, H.R., "The Swiss Group", *Expository Times*, 36 (1924), 73–75.

Marquardt, Friedrich-Wilhelm, *Theologie und Sozialismus: Das Beispiel Karl Barths* (Munich: Chr. Kaiser Verlag, 1972).

_____, "Vom gepredigten Jesus zum gelehrten Christus", *Evangelische Theologie*, 46 (1986), 315–325.

Matheny, Paul, *Dogmatics and Ethics: The Theological Realism and Ethics of Karl Barth's Church Dogmatics* (Bern: Peter Lang, 1990).

McConnachie, John, "The Barthian School: 3. Friedrich Gogarten", *Expository Times*, 43 (1932), pp. 391–395, 461–466.

McCormack, Bruce L., *Karl Barth's Critically Realistic Dialectical Theology: Its Genesis and Development, 1909–1036* (Oxford: Clarendon Press, 1995).

McGrath, Alistair E., *The Making of Modern German Christology* (Oxford: Basil Blackwell, 1986).

Meland, Bernard E., "The Thought of Emil Brunner—an Evaluation", *Journal of Bible and Religion*, 16 (1948), 165–168.

Mielke, Robert H.E., "The Doctrine of the Imago Dei in the Theology of Emil Brunner" (unpublished doctoral thesis, Drew University, 1951).

Migliore, Daniel L., "Karl Barth's First Lectures in Dogmatics: Instruction in the Christian Religion", in *The Göttingen Dogmatics*, pp. xv–lxii.

Müller, Hans Michael, "Credo, ut intelligam", *Theologische Blätter*, 7 (1928), 167–176.

Murray, Noland P., "Personalism in the Ethical Theory of Emil Brunner" (unpublished doctoral thesis, Duke University, 1963).

Nelson, J. Robert, "Emil Brunner—Teacher Unsurpassed", *Theology Today*, 19 (1963), 532–535.

Neubauer, Ernst, "Die Theologie der 'Krisis' und des 'Wortes': Ihre allgemeinsen Voraussetzungen und Prinzipien", *Zeitschrift für Theologie und Kirche*, N.F. 7 (1926), 1–36.

Neuser, W.H., *Karl Barth in Münster, 1925–1930*, Theologische Studien, 130 (Zurich: Theologischer Verlag, 1985).

Niebuhr, Reinhold, "The Concept of 'Order of Creation' in Emil Brunner's Social Ethic", in *The Theology of Emil Brunner*, ed. by Kegley, pp. 265–271.

Nygren, Anders, "Emil Brunner's Doctrine of God", in *The Theology of Emil Brunner*, ed. by Kegley, pp. 177–186.

O'Donovan, Joan E., "Man in the Image of God: The Disagreement between Barth and Brunner Reconsidered", *Scottish Journal of Theology*, 39 (1986), 433–459.

O'Grady, Colm, *The Church in Catholic Theology: Dialogue with Karl Barth* (Washington: Corpus Books, 1969).

Oden, Thomas C., *The Promise of Barth: The Ethics of Freedom* (Philadelphia: Lippincott, 1969).

Overbeck, Franz, *Christentum und Kultur*, ed. by Carl Albrecht Bernoulli (Basel: Benno Schwabe, 1919).

Palmer, Russell W., "Methodological Weaknesses in Barth's Approach to Ethics", *Jour-

nal of Religious Thought, 26 (1969), 70–82.

Pauck, Wilhelm, "The Church-Historical Setting of Brunner's Theology", in *The Theology of Emil Brunner*, ed. by Kegley, pp. 25–38.

Ramsey, Paul, *Nine Modern Moralists* (London: University Press of America, 1983).

Reisner, E., "Zwei Fragen an Karl Barth zum Problem der natürlichen Theologie", *Evangelische Theologie*, 1 (1934–1935), 396–402.

Reymond, Robert L., *Brunner's Dialectical Encounter* (Philadelphia: Presbyterian and Reformed, 1967).

Roberts, David E., "Review of four works of Emil Brunner", *Review of Religion*, 2 (1937–1938), 298–314.

Robinson, James M., ed., *The Beginnings of Dialectical Theology*, trans. by Keith Crim and others (Richmond, VA: John Knox, 1968).

_____, "Introduction", in *The Beginnings of Dialectical Theology*, ed. by Robinson, pp.9–30.

Roessler, R., *Person und Glaube: Der Personalismus des Gottesbezeihung bei Emil Brunner*, Forschungen zur Geschichte und Lehre des Protestantismus, 10th series, 30 (Munich: Chr. Kaiser, 1965).

Rosato, Philip J., *The Spirit as Lord: The Pneumatology of Karl Barth* (Edinburgh: T&T Clark, 1981).

Rumscheidt, H. Martin, "The First Commandment as Axiom for Theology", in *Theology Beyond Christendom*, ed. by Thompson, pp. 143–164.

_____, *Revelation and Theology: An Analysis of the Barth–Harnack Correspondence of 1923* (Cambridge: Cambridge University Press 1972).

Ruschke, Werner M., *Entstehung und Ausführung der Diastasen-theologie in Karl Barths zweiten Römerbrief* (Neukirchen-Vluyn: Neukirchener Verlag, 1987).

Russell, Jack, *For Sinners Only* (London: Hodder and Stoughton, 1932).

Salakka, Yrjö, *Person und Offenbarung in der Theologie Emil Brunners*, Schriften der Luther-Agricola-Gesellschaft, 12 (Helsinki, 1960).

Scheld, Stefan, *Die Christologie Emil Brunners* (Wiesbaden: Franz Steiner Verlag, 1981).

Schempp, Paul, "Marginal Glosses on Barthianism", in *The Beginnings of Dialectical Theology*, ed. by Robinson, pp. 191–199.

Schildmann, Wolfgang, *Was sind das für Zeichen? Karl Barths Träume im Kontext von Leben und Lehre* (Munich: Chr. Kaiser, 1991).

Schrader, George A., "Brunner's Conception of Philosophy", in *The Theology of Emil Brunner*, ed. by Kegley, pp. 111–129.

Schuurman, Douglas J., *Creation, Eschaton, and Ethics: The Ethical Significance of the Creation-Eschaton Relation in Moltmann and Brunner* (Bern: Peter Lang, 1991).

Sirks, G.J., "The Cinderella of Theology: The Doctrine of the Holy Spirit", *Harvard Theological Review*, 50 (1957), 77–89.

Smail, Thomas A., "The Doctrine of the Holy Spirit", in *Theology Beyond Christendom*, ed. by Thompson, pp. 87–110.

Smart, James D., *The Divided Mind of Modern Theology: Karl Barth and Rudolf Bultmann, 1908–1933* (Philadelphia: Westminster, 1967).

Smith, Martin, and Francis Underhill, *The Group Movement* (London: SPCK, 1934).

Søe, Niels H., "The Personal Ethics of Emil Brunner", in *The Theology of Emil Brunner*, ed. by Kegley, pp. 247–261.

Sonderegger, Katherine, "On Style in Karl Barth", *Scottish Journal of Theology*, 45 (1992), 65–83.

Spieckermann, Ingrid, *Gotteserkenntnis: Ein Beitrag zur Grundfrage der neuen Theologie Karl Barths*, Beiträge zur evangelischen Theologie, 97 (Munich: Chr. Kaiser, 1985).

Stange, C., "Natürliche Theologie: Zur Krisis der dialektischer Theologie", *Zeitschrift für systematische Theologie*, 12 (1935), 367–452.

Steinmann, Theophil, "Zur Auseinandersetzung mit Gogarten, Brunner und Barth", *Zeitschrift für Theologie und Kirche*, N.F. 10 (1929), 220– 237, 452–70.

Stephan, Horst, "Der Neue Kampf um Schleiermacher", *Zeitschrift für Theologie und Kirche*, N.F. VI (1925), 159–215

Stoevesandt, Hinrich, "Was heißt 'theologische Existenz': Über Absicht und Bedeutung von Karl Barths Schrift 'Theologische Existenz heute'", *Evangelische Theologie*, 44 (1984), 147–177.

Stolz, Heinrich, *Christentum und Wissenschaft in Schleiermachers Glaubenslehre*, 2nd edn (Leipzig, 1911).

Stolz, Wilhelm, *Theologisch-dialektischer Personalismus und kirchliche Einheit: Apologetische-kritische Studie zu Emil Brunners Lehre von der Kirche im Lichte der Thomastischen Theologie* (Freiburg: Universitätsverlag, 1953).

Streeter, B.H., "Professor Barth and the Oxford Group", *The London Quarterly and Holborn Review*, Sixth Series, 6 (April, 1937), 145–149.

Sykes, S.W., "Barth on the Centre of Theology", in *Karl Barth: Studies in His Theological Method*, ed. by S.W. Sykes (Oxford: Clarendon, 1979), pp. 17–54.

Szekeres, Attila, "Karl Barth und die natürliche Theologie", *Evangelische Theologie*, 24 (1964), 229–242.

_____, *De Structuur van Emil Brunners Theologie* (Utrecht: H.J. Smits, 1952).

Thiel, John H., "Barth's Early Interpretation of Schleiermacher", in *Barth and Schleiermacher: Beyond the Impasse?*, ed. by Duke and Streetman, pp. 11–22.

Thomas, J.M.L., "New Protestantism and the ethics of crisis", *Hibbert Journal*, 37 (1938), 14–24.

Thomas, John Newton, "The Place of Natural Theology in the Thought of John Calvin", *Journal of Religious Thought*, 15 (1957–1958), 107–136.

Thompson, John, ed., *Theology Beyond Christendom* (Allison Park, PA: Pickwick, 1986).

Thurneysen, Eduard, "Introduction", in *Revolutionary Theology in the Making*, pp. 11–25.

_____, "Guidance", *Student World*, 26 (1933), 294–309.

Tice, Terrence N., "Interviews with Karl Barth and Reflections on His Interpretations of Schleiermacher", in *Barth and Schleiermacher: Beyond the Impasse?*, ed. by Duke and Streetman, pp. 43–62.

Tillich, Paul, "Natural and Revealed Religion", *Christendom*, 1 (1935), 159–170.

_____, "What is wrong with the 'Dialectic Theology'?", in *Paul Tillich: Theologian of the Boundaries*, ed. by Mark Kline Taylor (London: Collins, 1987), pp. 104–115.

Torrance, Thomas F., "Introduction", in *Theology and Church*, pp. 7–54.

_____, *Karl Barth: An Introduction to His Early Theology, 1910–1931* (London: SCM, 1962).

van der Kooi, Cornelius, *Anfängliche Theologie: Der Denkweg des jungen Karl Barth*, Beiträge zur evangelische Theologie, 103 (Munich: Chr. Kaiser, 1987).

van Dusen, Henry P., "Apostle to the Twentieth Century: F.N.D. Buchman", *Atlantic Monthly*, 154 (July, 1934), 1–24.

_____, "The Oxford Group Movement", *Atlantic Monthly*, 154 (August, 1934), 240–252.

Vogelsanger, Peter, "Brunner as Apologist", in *The Theology of Emil Brunner*, ed. by Kegley, pp. 289–301.

Volk, Hermann, "Die Christologie bei Karl Barth und Emil Brunner", in *Das Konzil von Chalkedon: Geschichte und Gegenwart*, ed. by Aloys Grillmeier and Heinrich Bacht, 3 vols (Würzburg: Echter-Verlag, 1954), III, 613–673.

_____, *Emil Brunners Lehre von der ursprünglichen Gottebenbildlichkeit des Menschen* (Emsdetten: Verlagsanstalt Heinr. & J. Lechte, 1939).

Volken, Lorenz, *Der Glaube bei Emil Brunner*, Studia Friburgensia, N.F. 1 (Freiburg: Paulusverlag, 1947).

von Balthasar, Hans Urs, *The Theology of Karl Barth*, trans. by John Drury (New York: Holt, Rinehart and Winston, 1971).

Warnock, Mary, *Existentialism* (Oxford: Oxford University Press, 1970).

Watson, Gordon, "Karl Barth and St. Anselm's Theological Programme", *Scottish Journal of Theology*, 30 (1977), 31–45.

Weber, J.C., "Feuerbach, Barth and Theological Method", *Journal of Religion*, 46 (1966), 24–36.

Wendebourg, Ernst-Wilhelm, *Die Christusgemeinde und ihr Herr: Eine kritische Studie zur Ekklesiologie Karl Barths* (Berlin: Lutherisches Verlaghaus, 1967).

Westermann, Claus, "Karl Barths Nein: Eine Kontroversie um die theologia naturalis, Emil Brunner–Karl Barth (1934)", *Evangelische Theologie*, 47 (1987), 386–395.

White, Graham, "Karl Barth's Theological Realism", *Neue Zeitschrift für systematische Theologie und Philosophie*, 26 (1984), 54–70.

White, Hugh Vernon, "Brunner's Missionary Theology", in *The Theology of Emil Brunner*, ed. by Kegley, pp. 55–71.

Williams, Daniel D., "Brunner and Barth on philosophy", *Journal of Religion*, 27 (1947), 241–254.

Williamson, Geoffrey, *Inside Buchmanism* (London: Watts & Co., 1954).

Williamson, René de Visme, *Politics and Protestant Theology* (Baton Rouge, LA: Louisiana State University Press, 1976).

Willis, Robert E., *The Ethics of Karl Barth* (Leiden: Brill, 1971).

Wingren, Gustaf, "Evangelium und Gesetz", in *Antwort*, ed. by Wolf and others, pp. 310–322.

Winzeler, Peter, *Widerstehende Theologie: Karl Barth, 1920–1935* (Stuttgart: Alektor Verlag, 1982).

Wolf, Ernst, "Martin Luther", *Theologische Existenz heute*, 6 (1934).

Wolf, Ernst, and others, eds., *Antwort* (Zollikon-Zurich: Evangelischer Verlag, 1956).

INDEX